Next Generation
Application Integration

Addison-Wesley Information Technology Series
Capers Jones and David S. Linthicum, Consulting Editors

The information technology (IT) industry is in the public eye now more than ever before because of a number of major issues in which software technology and national policies are closely related. As the use of software expands, there is a continuing need for business and software professionals to stay current with the state of the art in software methodologies and technologies. The goal of the **Addison-Wesley Information Technology Series** is to cover any and all topics that affect the IT community. These books illustrate and explore how information technology can be aligned with business practices to achieve business goals and support business imperatives. Addison-Wesley has created this innovative series to empower you with the benefits of the industry experts' experience.

For more information point your browser to www.awprofessional.com/itseries

Sid Adelman, Larissa Terpeluk Moss, *Data Warehouse Project Management.* ISBN: 0-201-61635-1

Sid Adelman et al., *Impossible Data Warehouse Situations: Solutions from the Experts.* ISBN: 0-201-76033-9

Wayne Applehans, Alden Globe, and Greg Laugero, *Managing Knowledge: A Practical Web-Based Approach.* ISBN: 0-201-43315-X

David Leon Clark, *Enterprise Security: The Manager's Defense Guide.* ISBN: 0-201-71972-X

Frank P. Coyle, *XML, Web Services, and the Data Revolution.* ISBN: 0-201-77641-3

Kevin Dick, *XML, Second Edition: A Manager's Guide.* ISBN: 0-201-77006-7

Jill Dyché, *e-Data: Turning Data into Information with Data Warehousing.* ISBN: 0-201-65780-5

Jill Dyché, *The CRM Handbook: A Business Guide to Customer Relationship Management.* ISBN: 0-201-73062-6

Patricia L. Ferdinandi, *A Requirements Pattern: Succeeding in the Internet Economy.* ISBN: 0-201-73826-0

David Garmus and David Herron, *Function Point Analysis: Measurement Practices for Successful Software Projects.* ISBN: 0-201-69944-3

John Harney, *Application Service Providers (ASPs): A Manager's Guide.* ISBN: 0-201-72659-9

International Function Point Users Group, *IT Measurement: Practical Advice from the Experts.* ISBN: 0-201-74158-X

Capers Jones, *Software Assessments, Benchmarks, and Best Practices.* ISBN: 0-201-48542-7

Ravi Kalakota and Marcia Robinson, *e-Business 2.0: Roadmap for Success.* ISBN: 0-201-72165-1

Ravi Kalakota and Marcia Robinson, *Services Blueprint: Roadmap for Execution.* ISBN: 0-321-15039-2

Greg Laugero and Alden Globe, *Enterprise Content Services: Connecting Information and Profitability.* ISBN: 0-201-73016-2

David S. Linthicum, *B2B Application Integration: e-Business-Enable Your Enterprise.* ISBN: 0-201-70936-8

David S. Linthicum, *Enterprise Application Integration.* ISBN: 0-201-61583-5

David S. Linthicum, *Next Generation Application Integration: From Simple Information to Web Services.* ISBN: 0-201-84456-7

Sergio Lozinsky, *Enterprise-Wide Software Solutions: Integration Strategies and Practices.* ISBN: 0-201-30971-8

Anne Thomas Manes, *Web Services: A Manager's Guide.* ISBN: 0-321-18577-3

Larissa T. Moss and Shaku Atre, *Business Intelligence Roadmap: The Complete Project Lifecycle for Decision-Support Applications.* ISBN: 0-201-78420-3

Bud Porter-Roth, *Request for Proposal: A Guide to Effective RFP Development.* ISBN: 0-201-77575-1

Ronald G. Ross, *Principles of the Business Rule Approach.* ISBN: 0-201-78893-4

Dan Sullivan, *Proven Portals: Best Practices for Planning, Designing, and Developing Enterprise Portals.* ISBN: 0-321-12520-7

Karl E. Wiegers, *Peer Reviews in Software: A Practical Guide.* ISBN: 0-201-73485-0

Ralph R. Young, *Effective Requirements Practices.* ISBN: 0-201-70912-0

Bill Zoellick, *CyberRegs: A Business Guide to Web Property, Privacy, and Patents.* ISBN: 0-201-72230-5

Next Generation Application Integration

From Simple Information to Web Services

David S. Linthicum

✦✦ Addison-Wesley

Boston • San Francisco • New York • Toronto • Montreal
London • Munich • Paris • Madrid
Capetown • Sydney • Tokyo • Singapore • Mexico City

Many of the designations used by manufacturers and sellers to distinguish their products are claimed as trademarks. Where those designations appear in this book, and Addison-Wesley was aware of a trademark claim, the designations have been printed in initial capital letters or in all capitals.

The author and publisher have taken care in the preparation of this book, but make no expressed or implied warranty of any kind and assume no responsibility for errors or omissions. No liability is assumed for incidental or consequential damages in connection with or arising out of the use of the information or programs contained herein.

The publisher offers discounts on this book when ordered in quantity for bulk purchases and special sales. For more information, please contact:

>U.S. Corporate and Government Sales
>(800) 382-3419
>corpsales@pearsontechgroup.com

For sales outside of the U.S., please contact:

>International Sales
>international@pearsoned.com

Visit Addison-Wesley on the Web: www.awprofessional.com

Library of Congress Cataloging-in-Publication Data

Linthicum, David S., 1962–
    Next generation application integration : from simple information to
    Web services / David S. Linthicum
        p.   cm.
    Includes bibliographical references and index.
    ISBN 0-201-84456-7 (pbk. : alk. paper)
    1. Application software—Development.   2. Business enterprise—Data
processing.   3. Web services.   I. Title.
    QA76.76.A65 L58 2003
    005.2'76—dc21   2003010186

For information on obtaining permission for use of material from this work, please submit a written request to:

>Pearson Education, Inc.
>Rights and Contracts Department
>One Lake Street
>Upper Saddle River, NJ 07458

ISBN 0-201-84456-7
Text printed on recycled paper
3 4 5 6 7 8 9 10 11 12—CRS—0807060504
Third printing, October 2004

Contents

PART II Application Integration Technology

CHAPTER 6 MIDDLEWARE BASICS   115

CHAPTER 7   MIDDLEWARE TYPES AND APPLICATION
             INTEGRATION: WHAT WORKS WHERE?   137

CHAPTER 10   **ADAPTERS AND THE J2EE CONNECTOR ARCHITECTURE   217**

PART III   Application Integration Standards

CHAPTER 11   **XML, XSLT, AND APPLICATION INTEGRATION   235**

CHAPTER 15   SOAP, WSDL, AND UDDI, OH MY . . . WEB SERVICES FOUNDATIONS AND APPLICATION INTEGRATION   311

CHAPTER 16   OTHER STANDARDS   325

PART IV Advanced Topics

CHAPTER 19   LEVERAGING ONTOLOGIES AND APPLICATION INTEGRATION   393

CHAPTER 20   APPLICATION INTEGRATION MANIFESTO   405

APPENDIX C **KNOWLEDGE-ORIENTED MIDDLEWARE 461**

Preface

In the last several years, application integration, at least the notion of it, has worked its way into most information technology departments. This has been driven by a number of emerging developments, including the need to expose information found in existing systems to the Web, the need to participate in electronic marketplaces, the need to integrate their supply chain, and most importantly, the need for their existing enterprise systems to finally share information and common processes.

By now we know that application integration is important; there is not much need for me to restate that here. What is not as well understood is the amount of planning and coordination that needs to occur in order to pull off application integration today, Enterprise Application Integration (EAI) or business-to-business (B2B); this, despite the availability of some pretty good technology that can make short work of joining systems together.

Moreover, while many are interested in application integration, few have taken the time to read books such as this, or the books I've written in the past, to better understand both the limitations and the opportunities. More often than not, application integration architects are driven more by the hype around the emerging standards and technology and less by their business needs and technology requirements. The end result is many failed projects, more due to lack of knowledge than lack of technology.

In essence, application integration is less about J2EE versus .NET, and more about understanding the requirements and future growth of the problem domain, a not-so-sexy activity that is all too often left on the side of the road, choosing, instead, "management by magazine."

Indeed, application integration is more of an all-encompassing concept, consisting of, but not limited to, metadata, business logic, interfaces, performance management, business processes, workflow, information processing, database integrity, standards strategies, vertical subsystems, accountability, application design, and middleware technology. Application integration is a strategic activity and a technology set that can enable an organization to run much more efficiently and, in most instances, provide a significant competitive advantage.

Why a New Book?

If you've been following my writings for the last several years you'll know that this is my third book on application integration, and perhaps the most significant. We need a new book for a few reasons:

First, the arrival of a new *service-oriented* middleware technology standard, Web services. As we move further into the world of application integration, we're finding that service-based approaches make sense for many problem domains. I've stated that in previous books. Now with the advent of a new service-based approach, Web services, we have another opportunity to put that into perspective. I'll talk about Web services and how they relate to application integration, even though this is not a book about Web services, just the proper application of Web services in the application integration problem domain.

Second, there is a need to take application integration to the next level. My first book on application integration, *Enterprise Application Integration* (the first of its kind), covered the basic concepts of allowing two or more business systems to share processes and data. That book was written for the rank beginner because EAI, at least the notion and buzzword, was new. The next book, *B2B Application Integration: e-Business-Enable Your Enterprise,* really extended the concepts put forth in the first book to the interenterprise problem domain. That book reused many of the same approaches and technologies, but required knowledge of old and new B2B standards and technologies including XML, EDI, RosettaNet, BizTalk, and ebXML.

This book is all about looking at advanced application integration concepts, approaches, and technologies, with many topics typically not covered in the previous books (or any other books, for that matter). I'll be looking at how to approach very complex and challenging application integration problem domains, and leverage forward-looking concepts and technology, including how to understand your problem domain, determine your requirements, create a logical application integration architecture, and most importantly, back the correct grouping of application integration technologies into your solution to create an infrastructure that is strategic to the success of your organization.

Target Audience

This book is written with the technical manager and enterprise architect in mind, those who live on the front lines of technology every day and have to make key technology decisions that can make or break their businesses. This does not mean, however, that developers and IT executives won't benefit from this information, especially when it comes to understanding application integration in context of their day-to-day activities.

What This Book Is; What This Book Is Not

At its essence this is an information technology strategy book with some detailed technology discussion—just enough technology content to support the notions put forth. This book takes an important topic, application integration, to the next level by suggesting certain ways to view the problem that may not have been understood in the past.

This means I'll focus on higher-level approaches and solutions, rather than spend a lot of time describing the technologies. There are plenty of other books that do that. For example, I talk about the Java Message System (JMS) in terms of the general ideas behind this important standard; you can obtain more details about its use in an application integration solution set by reading the 200-page standard found at www.javasoft.com, or other books specifically on JMS. The same can be said about .NET, J2EE, ebXML, and other technologies I'll discuss in this book.

Indeed, I will cover the enabling technologies by focusing on their value in solving the application integration problem. For most of you, further research into these technologies or standards won't be required; there will be enough information here. However, those of you looking for implementation-level details will have to take a deeper dive using further research outside the scope of this book.

Organization

This book follows a clear structure that will make your reading experience more valuable.

There are four parts:

- Part I: Types of Application Integration
- Part II: Application Integration Technology
- Part III: Application Integration Standards
- Part IV: Advanced Topics

In *Part I* I focus on the types of application integration approaches you'll find in your problem domain—in other words, general approaches to sharing information, processes, and application services between any number of applications. It's important that you read this section because it sets up concepts for the rest of the book. Also, if you've read my previous books you'll see how my thinking is morphing after building and implementing a lot of application integration technology.

In *Part II* I talk about application integration technology including middleware, and specifically application integration middleware such as integration servers and application servers. Once again, I will discuss the technology in terms of their uses within the world of application integration. Even if you're a middleware god, you might want to read this section anyway, as it will be a good review.

In *Part III* I talk about application integration standards. If you've been in this world at all you'll know that standards are the way people are looking to approach this problem, rather than vendor solutions. In this section I'll talk about these issues, as well as describe the standards that are relevant to application integration.

In *Part IV* I talk about how you need to approach your own application integration problem domain, including procedures, methodologies, and techniques that you can employ to improve your chance of success. Moreover, I'll address advanced application integration topics, including the advent of vertically oriented application integration technology as well as the advanced use of metadata.

Other Stuff

From time to time, I'll include a few sidebar-type bits of content, embedded in the text. We'll call these "tidbits," and they look like this:

Application Servers and Application Integration

Application servers, while providing good application development environments, may not be so good at application integration.

There are also the appendixes. There you'll find some useful reference information supporting the core content of the book. While in many cases people skip the appendixes, I urge you to read through what's there.

So, as you move on to Chapter 1, relax. It will be a painless process, perhaps fun. See you at the end.

Acknowledgments

As always there are lots of people to thank. First, Mary O'Brien and Brenda Mulligan at Addison-Wesley Professional, whose good work and patience made this book possible. I would also like to thank Yvelisse Buenaventura and Holli Klein, my assistants, for doing much of the heavy lifting to get this book out. I'm grateful to Karen Freschi for the good graphics work. Finally, I would like to thank the technology team at Mercator who created an atmosphere of innovation, and the executive team that supported this book.

## CHAPTER ONE

Approaching Application Integration

This chapter sets the stage for application integration concepts and introduces ways to view application integration solution patterns. The reader should focus on the concepts rather than the details. More technical details will come later in the book.

Application integration is a strategic approach to binding many information systems together, at both the service and information levels, supporting their ability to exchange information and leverage processes in real time. While this sounds like a pure technology play, the resulting information and process flow between internal and external systems provides enterprises with a clear strategic business advantage: the ability to do business in real time, in an event-driven atmosphere, and with reduced latency (see the tidbit on page 2). The business value of this is apparent.

Application integration can take many forms, including internal application integration—Enterprise Application Integration (EAI)—or external application integration—Business-to-Business Application Integration (B2B). While each form has its own set of eccentricities, once you dig into the technology, you'll find that both inter- and intracompany integration solutions share many common patterns. For example, there almost always has to be transformation technology present to account for the difference in application semantics, routing technology

1

to ensure that the information goes to the correct destinations, and rules process-ing to define integration behavior. However, there is much more to application integration.

Keep in mind that the application integration concept is nothing new. We've been dealing with mechanisms to connect applications together since we've had more than two business systems and a network to run between them. What is new is understanding the need for application integration solutions to support strate-gic business initiatives going forward, such as participating in electronic markets, supply chain enablement, Web visibility, Customer Relationship Management (CRM), and the real need to get all internal systems exchanging information and services. Indeed, as time marches on, we see the need to view application integra-tion as a true paradigm, something that requires a great deal of business definition and architectural planning. Moreover, the application of new technology, such as integration brokers, to solve this problem brings more opportunity.

So, how do innovative enterprises leverage application integration? It's really a matter of understanding the need first, then the requirements, and finally how to solve the problem for their domain. Make no mistake: This is a difficult and com-plex process, but one you can handle when armed with the right information.

Moving to Real-Time Business Integration: An Example

Few examples illuminate the difference between the conventional (non-integrated) method of doing business and an integrated business more clearly than the purchase of a new car. Currently, a customer walks into an automobile dealership and orders a car. That order is then placed with the auto manufacturer. The manufacturer, in turn, orders the parts and creates the car, while the suppliers order raw materials to create the parts. Paper purchase orders are sent to the suppliers, who ship the materials and send paper invoices to request payment. Only then, when all the parts are received from the suppliers, can the car be manufac-tured and sent to the dealer—resulting in even more paper.

This process typically takes months, not weeks. It should only take days.

We need to think more comprehensively about how we capture and react to events. We need to recognize that all components of the inte-grated enterprise, or extended enterprise, affect the supply chain itself.

For example, when a customer walks into our car dealership and orders a car, or when the customer orders a car via the Internet, that action is, in and of itself, a business event that is captured. Our system must react to this event by performing several tasks instantaneously: logging the event, processing the rules bound to such an event, and moving information to other interested systems or humans.

The event must be logged so that it won't be forgotten should there be a failure as it is being processed. We need to process rules bound to the event, such as price limits and credit requirements. The internal (e.g., inventory) systems and external (supplier) systems must be informed of the event. Finally, the information created by this event, in this example, customer and car configuration information, must move forward to the appropriate systems. Typically, this should be a second, subprocess.

What is of note here is that all relevant systems are notified of the event and are supplied with all appropriate information, in real time, so that they can, in turn, instantly react to the event. In our car purchase example above, the sales event captured by our manufacturer's system generates an instant requirement for parts to create the car. In turn, this information triggers a cascading series of additional events within systems owned by the suppliers, events such as notifying a supplier of the raw materials required to build the parts. A single, primary event could thus trigger as many as several hundred other events, which, in turn, could trigger several thousand more events. It is exactly this chain reaction of events—events that serve a business need—that we hope to create.

Remember, this real-time application integration scenario is an instantaneous process. Within seconds of the initial order, the suppliers are processing requests for the raw materials, the factory floor is scheduling workers, and the logistic group is assigning resources in order to ship a car to a particular dealer. There may be hundreds of systems involved with the sale, creation, and movement of this car, all exchanging event information simultaneously. Of equal relevance is that all systems participating in the event will be notified instantly should there be any change along the supply chain. That is, if demand changes (e.g., if car sales are down) or if there is a parts shortage. Instantaneous notification is a two-way street, from orders to suppliers, from suppliers to orders.

Simply put, application integration is a complex problem. The simple reality is that most application integration projects exist just at the entry level. We have yet to see the real-time coupling of thousands of applications. This should not necessarily be discouraging. As with any complex problem, once it is broken down to its component parts, the solution becomes simply the aggregation of a number of solution sets. In this case, it's a combination of a variety of approaches and several types of technology. This seems to fly in the face of those who want to oversimplify the concept of application integration, thinking that a simple standard, such as XML, or a particular technology, such as application servers, holds the answers to all of their problems. Unfortunately, it's just not that simple.

The world of application integration is no different from the larger world of technology—it is advancing and changing rapidly. Ironically, as the technology changes, so does the problem it is designed to solve. The application integration problem is morphing from the very simple to the very complex, even as it moves from a departmental problem to an enterprise-wide problem, and, ultimately, to a trading community problem. Consequently, few companies have been able to get ahead of the "application integration curve." Without a complete solution, they remain short of discovering the full potential and benefits of application integration.

We are seeing that, as the problem grows, so do the potential benefits of the solution. The technology continues to respond to a perceived need. In this context, our pursuit of application integration is like chasing the tail of a growing beast. For now, that "beast" has remained ahead of us. A great deal of work remains ahead of us. But rest assured, a solution will be found and the once-unimaginable benefits of application integration will become an everyday reality.

As I've suggested above, as the problem domains become more complex, the application integration solution set evolves to address that growing complexity. No sooner is a "traditional" application integration problem solved (such as application-to-application and database-to-database integration), than the developed application integration expertise and technology is applied to more complex, but more rewarding, business issues.

Moving from Information-Oriented to Service-Oriented Application Integration

A clear trend is the movement away from information-oriented to service-based integration. Information-oriented integration provides an inexpensive mechanism to integrate applications because, in most instances, there is no need to change the applications.

While information-oriented integration provides a functional solution for many application integration problem domains, it is the integration of both application services and application methods that generally provides more value in the long run. That is the underlying theme of this book.

For example, a trading community looking to automate the processing of ordering raw materials may find that simply sharing information (order goes out, and confirmation comes in) is just fine to solve their integration problem. However, in another trading community, there may be a need to access remote services, such as the calculation of duty for intercountry trades. Again, you have to leverage the right approach for the business problem you are looking to solve.

Service-based application integration is not a new approach. We've been looking for mechanisms to bind applications together at the service level for years, including frameworks, transactions, and distributed objects—all in wide use today. However, the new notion of Web services, such as Microsoft's .NET strategy, is picking up steam as we attempt to identify a new mechanism that's better able to leverage the power of the Internet to provide access to remote application services through a well-defined interface and directory service: Universal Description, Discovery and Integration (UDDI).

The uses for this type of integration are endless, including the creation of composite applications, or applications that aggregate the processes and information of many applications. For example, using this paradigm, application developers simply need to create the interface and add the application services by binding the interface to as many Internet-connected application services as are required.

The downside, at least with service-based integration, is that this makes it necessary to change the source and target applications or, worse in a number of instances, to create a new application (a composite application). This has the effect of adding cost to the application integration project and is the reason many choose to stay at the information level.

Still, the upside of this approach is that it is consistent with the "baby step" approach most enterprises find comfortable when implementing solutions to integration problems. Service-based solutions tend to be created in a series of small, lower-risk steps. This type of implementation can be successful from the department to the enterprise to the trading community, but never the other way around—from the trading community to the department.

Application Integration Approaches

As we've come to appreciate, application integration is a combination of problems. Each organization and trading community has its own set of integration issues that must be addressed. Because of this, it is next to impossible to find a single technological solution set that can be applied universally. Therefore, each application integration solution will generally require different approaches. At this time, and in the foreseeable future, one-stop shopping is simply not an application integration reality.

Although approaches to application integration vary considerably, it is possible to create some general categories, which include

- Information-oriented
- Business process integration-oriented
- Service-oriented
- Portal-oriented

Information-Oriented

Technologists who promote the information-oriented approach to application integration argue that integration should occur between the databases (or proprietary APIs that produce information, such as BAPI)—that is, databases or information-producing APIs should be viewed as the primary points of integration (see Figure 1.1). Within Information-Oriented Application Integration (IOAI), there are many approaches. Information-oriented solutions can be grouped into three categories: data replication, data federation, and interface processing.

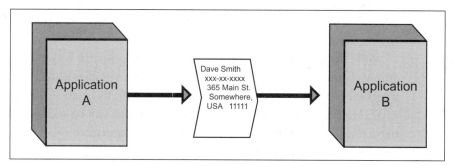

Figure 1.1   Information-Oriented Application Integration deals with the simple exchange of information between two or more systems.

Data Replication

Data replication is simply moving data between two or more databases. These databases can come from the same vendor, or from many vendors (see Figure 1.2). They can even be databases that employ different models. The fundamental requirement of database replication is that it accounts for the differences between database models and database schemas by providing the infrastructure to exchange data. Solutions that provide for such infrastructures are plentiful and inexpensive.

Many database-oriented middleware solutions currently on the market provide database replication services, as well. Replication services are accomplished by placing a layer of software between two or more databases. On one side, the data is extracted from the source database or databases, and on the other side, the data is placed in the target database or databases. Many of these solutions provide transformation services, as well—the ability to adjust the schemas and the content so they make sense to the target database.

The advantages of database replication are simplicity and low cost. Database replication is easy to implement, and the technology is cheap to purchase and install. Unfortunately, these advantages are quickly lost if methods need to be bound to the data, or if methods are shared along with the data. If these requirements exist, service-based solutions must be considered.

Data Federation

Database federation is the integration of multiple databases and database models into a single, unified view of the databases (see Figure 1.3). Put another way,

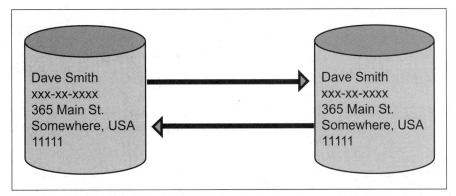

Figure 1.2 **Database replication is the simple exchange of information between databases.**

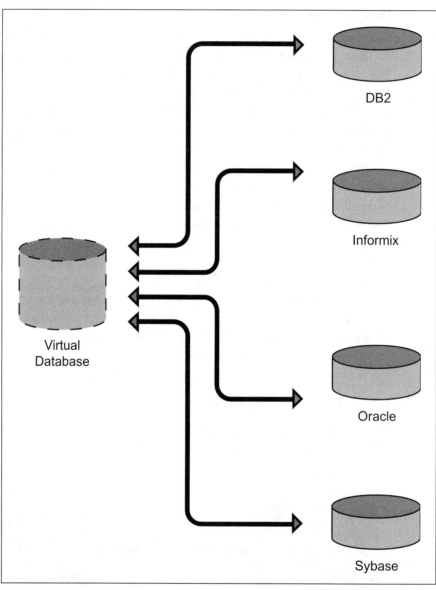

Figure 1.3   Data federation allows many databases to appear as a single database.

database federations are virtual enterprise databases that are comprised of many real, physical databases. While database federation has been around for some time, the solution set has been perfected only recently.

Database federation software places a layer of software (middleware) between the physical distributed databases and the applications that view the data. This layer connects to the back-end databases using available interfaces and maps the physical databases to a virtual database model that exists only in the software. The application uses this virtual database to access the required information. The database federation handles the collection and distribution of the data, as needed, to the physical databases.

The advantage of using this software is that it can bind many different data types into a unified model that supports information exchange.

Database federation allows access to any connected database in the enterprise through a single, well-defined interface. This is the most elegant solution to the data-oriented application integration problem. Unlike replication, this solution does not require changes to the source or target applications. Still, changes do have to be made at the application-oriented level to support federated database software. This is due to the fact that different interfaces are being used to access a different database model (the virtual database).

Interface Processing

Interface processing solutions use well-defined application interfaces to focus on the integration of both packaged and custom applications (see Figure 1.4). Currently, interest in integrating popular Enterprise Resource Planning (ERP) applications (e.g., SAP, PeopleSoft, and Oracle) has made this the most exciting application integration sector.

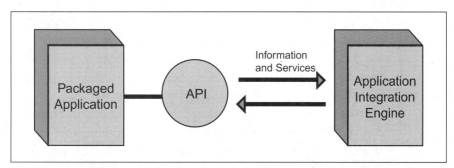

Figure 1.4   Interface processing externalizes information out of packaged applications through a well-defined API.

Integration brokers support application interface processing solutions by providing adapters to connect to as many custom or packaged applications as possible, externalizing information out of those applications through their open or, more often than not, proprietary interfaces. They also connect to technology solutions that include middleware and screen scrapers as points of integration.

The efficient integration of many different types of applications defines the primary advantage of using application integration-oriented products. In just days, it is possible to connect a SAP R/3 application to an Oracle application, with the application interface processing solution accounting for differences between schema, content, and application semantics by translating on the fly the information moving between the systems.

The downside to using application interface-oriented products is that there is little regard for business logic and methods within the source or target systems—logic and methods that may be relevant to a particular integration effort. In such a case, service-based solutions probably make the better choice. Ultimately, application interface processing technology will learn to share methods as well as information, perhaps by joining forces with service-based approaches.

Business Process Integration-Oriented

Simply put, business process integration-oriented products layer a set of easily defined and centrally managed processes on top of existing sets of processes contained within a set of enterprise applications (see Figure 1.5).

Packaged Application Interfaces: Information versus Services

While packaged application interfaces are primarily information oriented, there are a few that provide access to application services as well. These are hybrids. The best example of this is Business Application Programming Interfaces (BAPI) from SAP, but a few others also exist.

These interfaces allow you to invoke remote application services, such as processing a credit check or calculating shipping costs—processes that are more service than information oriented.

Packaged application interfaces, as you'll discover in Chapter 2, provide very different approaches to access both information and services. There are no standards for packaged application integration, even though the J2EE Connector Architect (JCA) is attempting to set some.

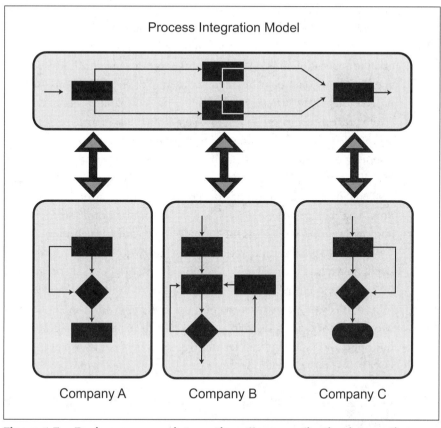

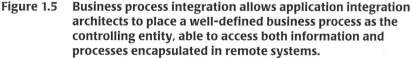

Figure 1.5   Business process integration allows application integration architects to place a well-defined business process as the controlling entity, able to access both information and processes encapsulated in remote systems.

Business process integration (BPI) is the science and mechanism of managing the movement of data, and the invocation of processes in the correct and proper order to support the management and execution of common processes that exist in and between applications. Business Process Integration-Oriented Application Integration (BPIOAI) provides another layer of easily defined and centrally managed processes that exist on top of an existing set of processes and data contained within a set of applications.

The goal is to bring together relevant processes found in an enterprise or trading community to obtain the maximum amount of value, while supporting the flow of information and control logic between these processes. These products view the middleware, or the "plumbing," as a commodity and provide easy-to-use visual interfaces for binding these processes together.

In reality, business process integration is another layer of value resting upon existing application integration solutions, solutions that include integration servers, application servers, distributed objects, and other middleware layers. Business process integration offers a mechanism to bind disparate processes together and to create process-to-process solutions that automate tasks once performed manually.

However, by diminishing the importance of the plumbing, it is too easy to lose sight of the larger picture. In reality, no single application integration vendor has solved the plumbing issues. Ultimately, the solution to these issues will be delivered by a combination of business process integration and middleware vendors. That being the case, it is clear that the binding of middleware and process automation tools represents the future of application integration.

Business process integration is a strategy, as much as technology, which strengthens your organization's ability to interact with disparate applications by integrating entire business processes, both within and between enterprises. Indeed, business process integration delivers application integration by dealing with several organizations using various metadata, platforms, and processes. Thus, business process integration technology must be flexible, providing a translation layer between the source and target systems, and the business process integration engine.

There are many differences between more traditional application integration and business process integration.

- A single instance of business process integration typically spans many instances of traditional application integration.
- Application integration typically means the exchange of information between two or more systems without visibility into internal processes.
- Business process integration leads with a process model and moves information between applications in support of that model.
- Application integration is typically a tactical solution, motivated by the requirement for two or more applications to communicate.
- Business process integration is strategic, leveraging business rules to determine how systems should interact and better leverage the business value from each system through a common abstract business model.

BPIOAI views middleware, or the plumbing, as a commodity, with the ability to leverage both message-oriented and transactional middleware as points of integration into any number of source or target systems. In fact, most integration servers and application servers are beginning to offer business process integration tools that support their middleware technology. Indeed, business process integration generally provides easy-to-use visual interfaces for binding these processes together and, along the way, creates visual BPIOAI.

While some may question the relevance of Business Process Integration-Oriented Application Integration, and even of application integration itself, I would argue that BPIOAI is the ultimate destination of application integration (acknowledging that we still have a long way to go to perfect the middleware). Despite current shortcomings, many application integration vendors are aggressively promoting BPIOAI as a vital component of their application integration technology package. In doing so, their strategy is clear—they are anxious to join the world of high-end, BPIOAI modeling tools. They hope that their application integration-enabled middleware, such as integration servers and application servers, will accomplish just that.

BPIOAI is best defined as applying appropriate rules, in an agreed-upon logical sequence, in order to pass information between participating systems, as well as visualize and share application-level processes, including the creation of a common abstract process that spans both internal and external systems. This definition holds true regardless of whether the business processes are automated or not. For example, processing an insurance claim and delivering a car to a customer are business events that can be automated with BPIOAI.

To this end, there are three main services that business process integration provides: the visualization of processes contained within all trading partner systems, interface abstraction, and the real-time measurement of business process performance.

By visualizing enterprise and cross-enterprise processes contained within trading partners, business managers are able to become involved in enterprise integration. The use of graphics and diagrams provides a powerful tool for communication and consensus building. Moreover, this approach provides a business-oriented view of the integration scenarios, with real-time integration with the enabling middleware or points of integration. This provides business analysts with the ability to make changes to the process model, implement it within the trading community, and typically not involve the respective IT departments.

Interface abstraction refers to the mapping of the business process integration model to physical system interfaces and the abstraction of both connectivity and system integration solutions from the business analyst. Business process

BPI by Example

There are three companies that participate in a trading community: Companies A, B, and C. Company A produces parts for skateboards, while Company B assembles and tests the skateboards, and finally, Company C sells the skateboards. Each has its own set of processes that are native to the respective company and its internal systems: a production system, an assembly system, and a sales system, respectively. Until now, automated integration has been nonexistent, and mail and fax serve communication needs between companies.

In order to integrate these applications, the trading community has decided to implement BPIOAI, defining a common process model that spans all companies and internal systems. This process model defines a sequence and logical order of events from the realization of consumer demand, the purchase of raw materials, the creation of the parts, the assembly of parts into a product, the testing of the product, and finally, the sale of the product to the ultimate consumer. This common model integrates with local systems by having visibility into their internal application processes, if possible, or perhaps through more primitive layers such as the database or application interface. What's important is that the common process model is able to produce events that are understood by the systems participating in the process, as well as react to events that the applications communicate back to the business process integration engine.

The use of a common process model that spans multiple companies for application integration provides many advantages, including:

- The ability to create a common, agreed-upon process between companies automating the integration of all information systems to react to business events such as increased consumer demand, material shortages, and quality problems in real time.
- The ability to monitor all aspects of the business and trading community to determine the current state of the process in real time.
- The ability to redefine the process at any given time in support of the business, and thus makes the process more efficient.
- The ability to hide the complexities of the local applications from the business users and to have the business user work with a common set of business semantics.

integration exists at the uppermost level in the application integration middleware stack. Those who use business process integration tools are able to view the world at a logical business level and are not limited by physical integration flows, interfaces, or adapters. What's more, the middleware mechanisms employed are

---

Walking Through a Process

Although each business process integration tool and project may take a slightly different approach, the internal process of interacting with the physical systems typically consists of the following set of events:

1. The source system that exists inside of a company posts an event to the business process integration engine; for example, a skateboard is sold.

2. The event is transformed, if required, so the event adheres to a standard set of business semantics and information processing mechanisms (synchronous versus asynchronous). This is going to be engine dependent, but there always has to be a common set of process semantics and information processing mechanisms defined at the engine level so the analyst can make sense of a business process that spans many types of applications, platforms, and databases.

3. The business process integration engine reacts to the event, once transformed, invoking other processes in other systems to support the execution of the common process model. For example, if a skateboard is sold, then send an order to the skateboard assembler, posting an event from the process engine to the assembler's target system (typically over the Internet).

4. Based on receiving that event, the local system reacts as per its internal processes and posts an event back to the process engines (say, when the skateboard is assembled).

5. The common process model sequences the master process, sending and receiving other events in support of the common process model. This is an ongoing activity, with information moving up to the process engine from the local systems, transformed if required, and down from the process engine to the local systems in support of the execution of the process model.

---

also abstracted and are not a concern of the business process analyst, as long as the common process model is interacting correctly with all source and target systems that exist within all companies.

Another way to view the process of creating a business process integration model is defining the hierarchy of processes within the trading community. This means that smaller subprocesses can be linked at the lower tier of integration or are native to the source or target systems. Building up from the lower-level processes to the higher-level processes, you may link the subprocesses into higher-level processes within the domain of the trading community.

The measurement of business process performance provides the business process integration with the ability to analyze a business in real time. By leveraging tight integration with the process model and the middleware, business analysts are able to gather business statistics in real time from the trading community; for example, the performance of a supplier in shipping goods to the plant, and the plant's ability to turn those raw materials into product.

Moreover, business process integration enables the technology user to track and direct each instance of a business process; for example, processing individual orders or medical insurance claims through a life cycle that may consume seconds, minutes, hours, days, or weeks. Finally, we need to measure and maintain contextual information for the duration of a process instance that spans many individual activities.

Indeed, the goal of BPIOAI, and of application integration in general, is to automate the data movement and process flow so that another layer of BPIOAI will exist over and above the processes encapsulated in existing systems. In other words, BPIOAI completes application integration, allowing the integration of systems, not only by sharing information readily, but also by managing the sharing of that information with easy-to-use tools.

In general, business process integration logic addresses only process flow and integration. It is not a traditional programming logic, such as processing a user interface, updating a database, or executing a transaction. Indeed, in most BPIOAI scenarios, the process logic is separated from the application logic. It functions solely to coordinate, or manage, the information flow between many source and target applications that exist within organizations.

Service-Oriented

Service-Oriented Application Integration (SOAI) allows applications to share common business logic or methods. This is accomplished either by defining methods that can be shared, and therefore integrated, or by providing the infrastructure for such method sharing such as Web services (see Figure 1.6). Methods may be shared either by being hosted on a central server, by accessing them interapplication (e.g., distributed objects), or through standard Web services mechanisms, such as .NET.

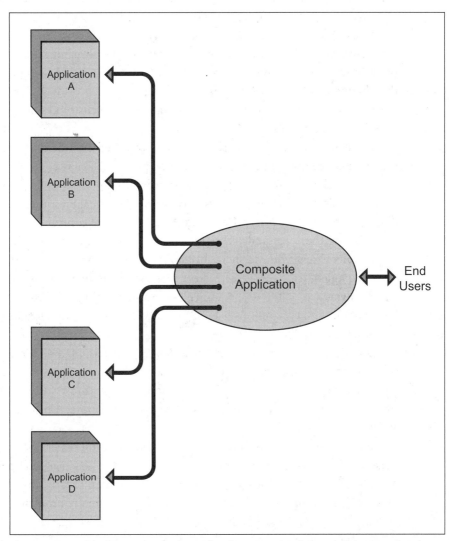

Figure 1.6   Service-Oriented Application Integration provides mechanisms to create composite applications, leveraging services found in many remote systems.

Attempts to share common processes have a long history, one that began more than ten years ago with the multitiered client/server—a set of shared services on a common server that provided the enterprise with the infrastructure for reuse and, now, for integration—and the distributed object movement. "Reusability" is a valuable objective. A common set of methods among enterprise applications invites reusability and, as a result, significantly reduces the need for redundant methods and/or applications.

While most methods exist for single-organization use, we are learning that there are times when it makes sense to share between organizations. In a new twist on the longstanding practice of reusability, we are now hoping to expand this sharing beyond intraenterprise—to trading partners, as well; for example, sharing a common logic to process credit requests from customers or to calculate shipping costs using a set of Web services.

Unfortunately, absolute reuse has yet to be achieved on the enterprise level. It is an even more distant goal between trading partners. The reasons for this failure are primarily political. They range from internal politics to the inability to select a consistent technology set. In most cases, the actual limit on reuse results directly from a lack of enterprise architecture and central control.

Utilizing the tools and techniques of application integration gives us the opportunity to learn how to share common methods. More than that, these tools and techniques create the infrastructure that can make such sharing a reality. By taking advantage of this opportunity, we are integrating applications so that information can be shared, even as we provide the infrastructure for the reuse of business logic.

Sounds great, doesn't it? The downside might give you pause, however. This "great-sounding" application integration solution also confronts us with the most invasive level of application integration, thus the most costly. This is no small matter if you're considering Web services, distributed objects, or transactional frameworks.

While IOAI generally does not require changes to either the source or target applications, SOAI requires that most, if not all, enterprise applications be changed in order to take advantage of the paradigm. Clearly, this downside makes SOAI a tough sell. However, it is applicable in many problem domains. You just need to make sure you leverage SOAI only when you need it.

Changing applications is a very expensive proposition. In addition to changing application logic, there is the need to test, integrate, and redeploy the application within the enterprise—a process that often causes costs to spiral upward. This seems to be the case, no matter if you're approaching SOAI with older technologies such as Common Object Request Broker Architecture (CORBA), or new technologies such as .NET, the latest service-based architecture to come down the road.

Before embracing the invasiveness and expense of SOAI, enterprises must clearly understand both its opportunities and its risks. Only then can its value be evaluated objectively. The opportunity to share application services that are common to many applications—and therefore making it possible to integrate those applications—represents a tremendous benefit. However, that benefit comes with the very real risk that the expense of implementing SOAI will outpace its value.

Portal-Oriented

Portal-Oriented Application Integration (POAI) allows us to view a multitude of systems—both internal enterprise systems and external trading community systems—through a single-user interface or application. POAI benefits us by avoiding the back-end integration problem altogether; it adapts the user interface of each system to a common user interface (aggregated user interface)—most often a Web browser (see Figure 1.7). As a result, it integrates all participating systems through the browser, although the applications are not directly integrated within or between the enterprises.

While the other types of application integration are focused on the real-time exchange of information (or adherence to a common process model) between systems and companies, POAI is concerned with externalizing information out of a multitude of enterprise systems to a single application and interface. That's clearly an approach that goes against the notions of the other types of application integration, which are more real-time- and event-driven-oriented, and the inclusion in this book of POAI was somewhat of a judgment call.

However, application integration, while typically referring to the automated movement of information or the binding of processes between two or more applications, without the assistance of an end user, can clearly also occur at the user interface. Indeed, most examples of B2B information exchange today are also examples of POAI, with digital exchanges leading the way. Therefore, it's different, but it still belongs within the discussion of application integration.

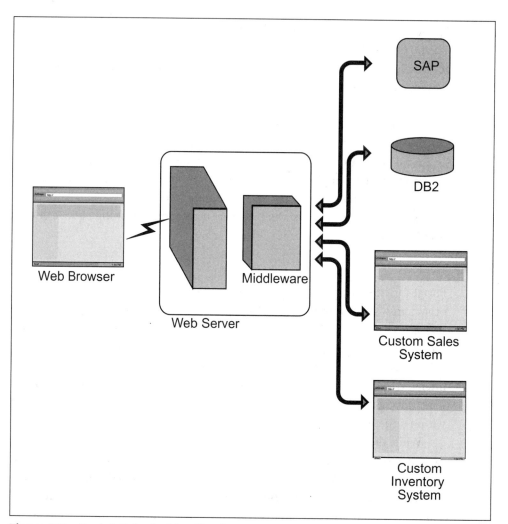

Figure 1.7   Portal-Oriented Application Integration.

Application Integration: Clearly the Future

Enter application integration—along with an opportunity to finally integrate all of these disparate systems with a minimum impact on the applications and the way an enterprise does business. Application integration provides a clear competitive advantage for most industries, an advantage that includes the ability to do business at light speed, along with the ability to satisfy customer demand in record time (by using automated processes instead of paper, faxes, and humans).

We are truly moving forward into a digital economy, where business runs within and between computers, where everything is automated, and where customers expect no less than instantaneous access to information.

What's important in meeting this goal is not just the application of technology to bind applications together, or externalize information to outside parties, but also the way in which you do it. Application integration is of little use if it's not quickly deployed, if it's not correct in operation, and if it's not able to adjust quickly as business needs change. This being the case, the way in which you approach your problem domain, the architecture you employ, and the technology you leverage has everything to do with the value of your application integration project going forward. Remember, application integration, if done right, is the strategic application of technology to provide an enterprise with the infrastructure required to handle most business events electronically, and in real time. In the end, that's what makes all the difference.

## PART I

Types of
Application Integration

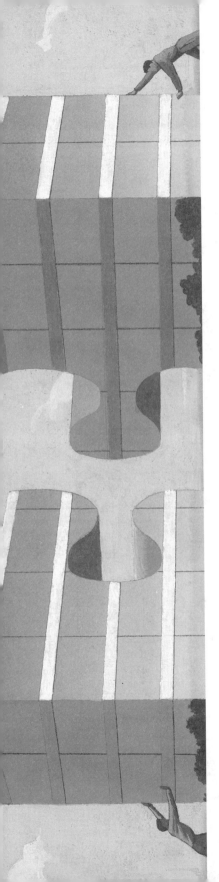

## CHAPTER TWO

Information-Oriented Application Integration

In this chapter we'll focus on the notion of moving information between two or more systems. This is the primary function of application integration. Although this seems to be a straightforward theory, you may want to watch out for some new concepts here including transformation, routing, and data analysis. Those topics will appear again later in the book.

Most application integration projects will leverage Information-Oriented Application Integration (IOAI). Indeed, IOAI is the ground floor of application integration, providing a simple mechanism to exchange information between two or more systems. This does not mean, as we covered in Chapter 1, that you can't mix IOAI with the other approaches to application integration, including service, portal, and business process integration. In fact, most application integration problem domains will eventually leverage all types. As we'll cover in later chapters, Service-, Portal-, and Business Process-Oriented Application Integrations are more invasive and thus more expensive, but in some cases, they are more valuable to the business as well.

Getting that out of the way, IOAI allows information to move between source and target systems. The data could come from a database, an API (e.g., SAP's BAPI), or perhaps an imbedded device. What's important to understand is that we're dealing with simple information, and not with processes or application services. The information-oriented approach to application integration professes that integration occurs between the systems by exchanging simple information (see Figure 2.1). We've been doing application integration this way for more than 30 years.

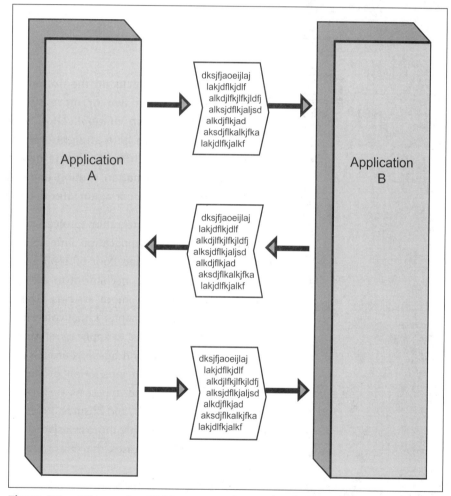

Figure 2.1   **When using IOAI we are only moving information between the source and target systems; we are not addressing the notion of encapsulated processes or application services. However, that does not mean that IOAI is the only way to address application integration in this domain.**

IOAI offers certain advantages.

- First, we're dealing with simple information, so we usually don't have to change source and target systems. Most applications, certainly databases, already know how to produce and consume simple information.
- Second, we don't need to manage complex issues such as state, logic, and sequence because there is no notion of behavior.
- Finally, this approach is easy to understand and in wide use.

In many cases, the information-oriented approach is the correct solution. Using service or business process integration to integrate systems is contraindicated for many problem domains when looking at the business problems they are trying to solve. In fact, you'll find that service and business process integration approaches to application integration are overapplied.

Accessing information within databases and applications is a relatively easy task, accomplished with few—if any—significant changes to the application logic or database structure. This is a tremendous asset because altering applications is not possible in many problem domains, such as supply chains, where you are likely dealing with systems that are beyond your direct control.

However, the straightforward appearance of IOAI should not create the impression that it is simple. It is not. Migrating data from one system to another sounds straightforward and reasonable enough, but in order for IOAI to actually work, architects and developers need to understand all integrated systems in detail. We'll cover how to do this later in the chapter.

Application semantics make this problem even more complex. Typically, application semantics in one system are not compatible with other systems—the semantics are so different that the two systems just can't understand each other. For example, sales accounting practices might be different, as well as invoice numbers and customer sales data. Thus, IOAI is not just about moving information between data stores, but also managing the differences in schema and content.

Coupling versus Cohesion

In looking at the applications and databases that make up the application integration problem domain, you should always consider an integration alternative that, generally, comes down to one of two choices—coupling or cohesion. This concept extends to Chapter 4.

Coupling, in the context of application integration, is the binding of applications together in such a way that they are dependent on each other, sharing the same methods, interfaces, and perhaps data.

At first glance, coupling may seem like the perfect idea. However, you should not lose sight of what it really requires—the tight binding of one application domain to the next. As a consequence of this requirement, all coupled applications and databases will have to be extensively changed to couple them. Further, as events and circumstances evolve over time, any change to any source or target system demands a corresponding change to the coupled systems as well. Coupling creates one application and database out of many, with each tightly dependent upon the other. Service-Oriented Application Integration (SOAI) clearly leverages coupling in binding applications together.

Because coupling requires changes to source and target systems, it may not fit with most application integration problem domains, where the participating systems are not under central control.

In contrast to coupling, *cohesion* is the "act or state of sticking together" or "the logical agreement." Cohesively integrated applications and databases are independent from one another. Changes to any source or target system should not affect the others directly. In this scenario, information can be shared between databases and applications without worrying about changes to the applications or databases, leveraging some type of loosely coupled middleware layer to move information between applications, and make adjustments for differences in application semantics.

You need to consider the tradeoffs. Cohesion provides the greatest flexibility as the application integration solution moves into the future. Systems can be added to, changed, or removed from a cohesive application integration solution without typically requiring changes to any of the other systems in the problem domain. Integration brokers provide the technology infrastructure of most cohesive application integration solutions. They are able to account for the differences between systems, accommodating differences in application semantics within a middle-tier process.

Despite cohesion's flexibility, if common business processes are to be reused, then a coupled approach provides more value. Distributed objects, transaction processing (TP) monitors, application servers, and, of course, Web services provide a good technology solution for a coupled application integration solution. We'll cover that in Chapter 4.

It's Just Data

IOAI's simplicity and speed-to-market advantages are the consequences of a business logic that rarely has to be altered (a cohesive rather than coupled approach). It frees the enterprise from having to endure seemingly endless testing cycles, or the risk and expense of implementing newer versions of applications. Indeed, most users and applications will remain blissfully ignorant of the fact that data is being shared at the back end, because application behavior rarely changes.

The advent of application integration-specific technology, such as integration brokers, application integration management layers, and simple data movement engines, enables the enterprise to move data from one place to another—from anywhere to anywhere—without altering the target application source. What's more, this can now be done in real time, with automated mechanisms for transformation and routing.

Although the technology for moving data between two or more applications is familiar and well tested in real applications, this familiarity does not exempt the architect or developer from understanding the data that is being moved, or from understanding the flow and business rules that must be applied to that data.

IOAI by Example

Just as a picture is worth a thousand words, it is likely that understanding IOAI is sometimes made easier by "painting a picture," that is, examining a particular application integration problem. For example, let us say that a copper wiring manufacturing company would like to hook up to the inventory control system that exists at its raw material goods supplier: a client/server system using PowerBuilder and Oracle at the manufacturing site, and an Enterprise Resource Planning (ERP) system using an Informix relational database at the supplier site. Because the data movement requirements are light to moderate, and changing the proprietary ERP application to bind its logic with the inventory control system is not an option (the supplier won't allow it), the company would like to solve this application integration problem using IOAI and the Internet.

(continued)

IOAI by Example (*continued*)

First, in order to move data from the Oracle database to Informix, the application integration architect and developer need to understand the metadata for each database so they can select the data that will move from one database to the next. In our example, let us assume that only sales data must move from one database to the other. So, when a sale is recorded in the inventory system (creating an event), the new information is copied over to the supplier's ERP system to ensure that the correct amount of raw materials will be available to create the amount of copper wire recorded in the sale.

Second, the architect and developer must determine the frequency of the data movement. In our example, let us determine that real time is a requirement for this problem domain. The event to be captured must also be defined in order to signal when the data needs to be copied, such as a specific increment of time (e.g., every 5 seconds) or when a state changes (e.g., an update to a table occurs).

Once these two determinations are made, the architect and developer must choose the method for moving the data. As we have come to understand, there are many technologies and techniques for moving the data from one database to the next, including database replication software, integration brokers, and custom-built utilities. There are advantages and disadvantages to each, advantages and disadvantages that will become apparent later in this book. In our example, we'll choose to go with a database replication and integration solution—a piece of software that runs between the databases that can extract information from one database, say the Informix database, reformat it (changing content and schema) if needed, and update the Oracle database (see Figure 2.2).

While ours is a one-to-one scenario, one-to-many works in the same way, as does many-to-many (albeit with more splitting, combining, and reformatting).

With the middle-tier database replication software in place, the information is extracted, reformatted, and updated from the Oracle database to the Informix database, and then back again. The information is replicated between the two databases when an update occurs at either end of the corresponding sales table.

Using this simple approach, the data moves between the databases at the data level. The application logic is completely bypassed. There are no changes to the application logic at the source, or, as in this case, the target systems. Clearly, this approach provides an effective application integration solution whenever an application cannot be changed, which, as we've noted many times, is generally the case with application integration problem domains.

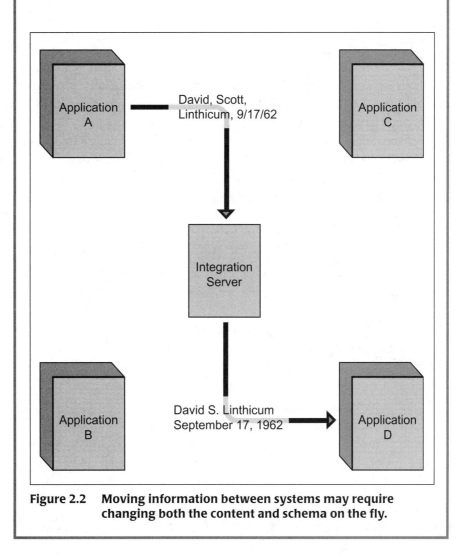

Figure 2.2 **Moving information between systems may require changing both the content and schema on the fly.**

IOAI makes sense for more complex problem domains as well, domains such as moving data between traditional mainframe, file-oriented databases and more modern, relational databases; relational databases to object databases; multi-dimensional databases to mainframe databases; or any combination of these. As in other domains, database replication and translation software and message brokers provide the best solutions. They are able to tie all source and target databases together cohesively, without requiring changes to the connected databases or application logic.

IOAI: The Gory Details

When leveraging IOAI, we need to focus on the information. We assume that the systems participating in the application integration problem domain can both produce and consume information. What's more, we assume that we can understand the structure and content of information coming from a source system or systems, account for the differences in a schema and content transformation layer, and publish that information, using the appropriate structure and content in the target system or systems. We can do this one-to-one, one-to-many, or many-to-many.

Moreover, we may mix and match integration types, as we stated above; thus, you may find that while ten systems participate in the application integration domain using IOAI, three may leverage application services and all ten may be integrated using business process integration. What's more, we may externalize information from all integrated systems to a Web site using portals (see Figure 2.3). Clearly, in many instances, the application integration problem domains are complex, requiring many types of integration approaches.

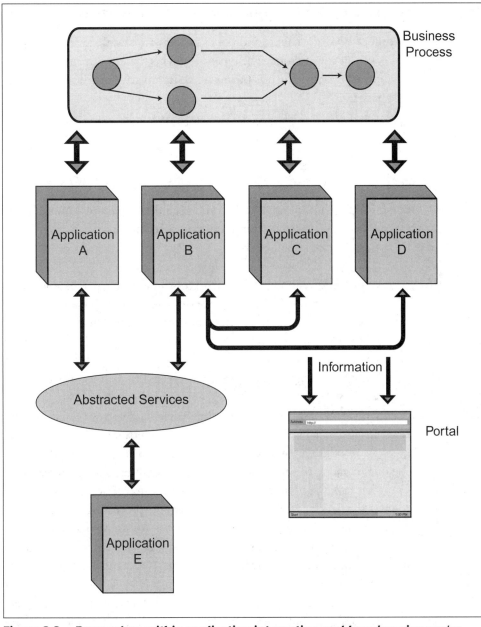

Figure 2.3 Remember, within application integration problem domains you're going to mix and match integration approaches.

Information Producers and Consumers: Common Patterns

In the world of IOAI the source and target systems are always entities that produce and consume information. The types of systems that produce and consume information vary greatly. For our purposes, we can place them into one of the following patterns:

- Database
- Application
- User interface
- Embedded device

Within IOAI, it's important that you understand each pattern, how each pattern behaves, and advantages and limitations of each pattern type.

Database

The most popular information producer and consumer by far, databases are natural points of integration because they were designed to produce and consume data, and thus provide the best interface into source and target applications exchanging information. We interact with databases using whatever database interface makes the most sense, typically native Structured Query Language (SQL), or perhaps through a Call-Level Interface (CLI) such as Java Database Connectivity (JDBC).

When requesting information from the source database, we typically send the request using a language that the database can understand, such as SQL. The database then responds with a result set; just the information requested. This could be one or many records, and the information returns to the integration server, or other calling program. The source database either accepts the request and produces the data, or works through an exception-processing scenario.

When sending information to a target database we simply request that we update the database, once again using a language the database can understand, and send the information in the proper format. The target database either accepts or rejects the updates (see Figure 2.4).

While all databases basically function in the same way, there are some differences in the databases out there. You have many different models that are employed, including relational, object, XML, file-oriented, and hierarchical, as well as the languages they use and the formats they produce. There are many books on database technology, so it does not make sense for us to go into detail

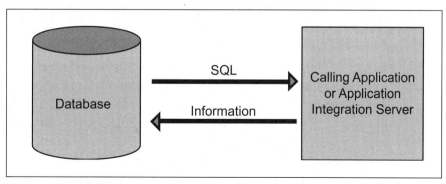

Figure 2.4   Databases produce and consume information through interfaces they provide.

here. In many application integration domains, adapters may account for the differences in the database technologies and how requests and updates execute, or you may have to account for the differences using custom code.

The upside of using the database as a point of integration is that the interfaces are almost always well defined and tested, and there are many different types of result sets you can request. That's what they do. The downside is that the information produced is typically not bound to business entities. Thus, while you may get all of the information to create a purchase order, you have to figure out how the information in the result set pertains to the purchase order (and even calculate some fields). In contrast, application interfaces usually produce data bound to business entities, such as invoices, sales orders, or purchase orders.

Application

Application interfaces are much more complex than databases due to the simple fact that applications all take a different approach to how they consume and produce information (if they do it at all). Therefore, the interfaces that exist from application to application don't share common patterns or standards; thus, you need to address each packaged application individually, perhaps programmatically or through adapters provided by application integration vendors.

It's also worth noting up front that while application interfaces provide access to encapsulated information, a producer of information if you will, they also provide access to encapsulated application services. In this book we talk about application interfaces in the context of IOAI, but application interfaces are clearly a part of application service-based access as well.

Application interfaces are interfaces that developers expose from packaged or custom applications to gain access to various levels or services of those applications. Some interfaces are limited in scope, while others are "feature rich." Some interfaces allow access to business processes only; some allow access directly to the data. Some allow access to both.

Packaged application vendors (e.g., SAP) and developers (e.g., the guy who wrote your accounting system) expose these interfaces to provide access to the business processes and data encapsulated within their applications without requiring other developers to invoke the user interface or to go directly to the database. The use of such interfaces creates a benefit for application integration by allowing external applications to access the information found in these applications without making any changes to the packages or to applications themselves (see Figure 2.5). Exposing these interfaces also provides a mechanism to allow encapsulated information to be shared. For example, if SAP data is required from Excel, SAP exposes the interfaces that allow you to invoke a business process and/or gather common data.

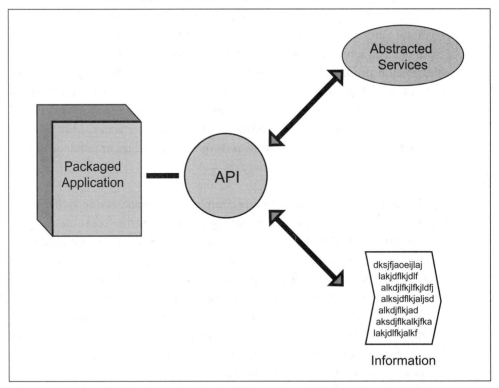

Figure 2.5   Application interfaces provide access to information as well as encapsulated processes.

In addition to the potential complexities of application interfaces and their dynamic nature, this difference in approach distinguishes application interface application integration from other types of application integration. The range, in terms of the number and quality of features different application interfaces provide, makes it nearly impossible to know what to anticipate when invoking a particular application interface. This is certainly true of packaged applications, which are "all over the board."

However, recently we've moved quickly toward standard application interfaces such as J2EE Connectivity Architecture (JCA), and even Web services. While this is a step in the right direction, there is much work to be done before all applications have exposed their internals using a standards-based API. What's more, many may find that the standards themselves are limiting, and thus they will have to mature more to be effective. For example, the first generation of the JCA specification only defined information moving in one direction. We'll talk much more about JCA and Web services later in this book.

Interface by Example

Let us say we are attempting to integrate an ERP system that was just configured and installed at the site of our supplier and our long-running, custom COBOL system. Both systems exist on their own processor at their respective sites, connected by the Internet.

In our example, we are fortunate that the ERP vendor understood and anticipated the need to integrate business processes and data with the outside world. The vendor provided an API that works within C++, C, and Java environments, with the libraries that drive the API being downloadable from the company's Web site.

For example, from a C application with the appropriate existing API libraries, the function GetInvoiceInformation("12345") would produce

```
<BOM>
John Smith
222 Main Street
Smalltown, VA 88888
Invoice Number: 12345
001        Red Bricks      1000      .50      500.00
<EOM>
```

(continued)

Interface by Example (*continued*)

The information returned from the API call is generated by invoking an API and passing in an invoice number as an argument. For processing, this information would have to be placed within the application program in an array, or in another memory location. From this point, the information may be placed within a middleware layer—such as an integration broker—or within XML, for transmission to other systems. Note that the database itself was never accessed. Further, the data is already bound to a business entity—namely an invoice.

Using this same interface, we can also get at customer information:

```
GetCustomerInformation("cust_no")
```

Or inventory information:

```
QuantityAvailable("product_no").
```

Our example might not be so straightforward in COBOL. Here, the developer and application architect who built the application failed to build in an API to access encapsulated business processes. Therefore, the application must be redesigned and rebuilt to expose an API so that the processes of the application may be bound with the processes of the remote ERP application.

The generally high cost of development and testing makes building interfaces into existing applications an unattractive option. However, let's assume in our current example that the application interface is the best solution. Once we've gone ahead and built an interface into the COBOL application, our next move is simple—select the right middleware to bind to the ERP API within the supplier and the custom API locally. The middleware then allows the application integration subsystem to extract business information (e.g., credit information) from one and place it in another. Middleware that will work in this scenario might include integration servers, message queuing (MQ) middleware, and application servers.

Packaged applications (most often present in a typical application integration problem domain) are only now beginning to open their interfaces to grant outside access and, consequently, integration. While each application determines exactly what these interfaces should be and what services they will provide, there is an evolving "consensus" to provide access at the business model, data, and object levels.

As we have come to appreciate in the world of custom applications, anything is possible. Access to the source code allows us to define a particular interface, or to open the application with standard interfaces such as CORBA, Component Object Model (COM), JCA, or Web services. For example, rather than accessing the user interface (scraping screens) to get to an existing COBOL application residing on a mainframe, we can build an API for that application simply by exposing its services through an API. In most cases, this will require mapping the business processes—once accessible only through screens and menus—directly to the API.

If the world were a perfect place, all the features and functions provided by packaged applications would also be accessible through their "well-defined" APIs. Sadly, the world is not a perfect place, and the reality is a bit more sobering. Nearly every packaged application provides some interfaces but, as we have emphasized above, they are uneven in their scope and quality. While some provide open interfaces based on open interface standards such as Java APIs (e.g., J2EE Connection Architecture), many others provide more proprietary APIs that are useful only in a limited set of programming languages (e.g., COBOL, Java, C, and C++). Most disturbing of all is the harsh reality that too many packaged applications fail to offer so much as a solitary interface. When confronted with these applications, there is no opportunity for an application or middleware layer to access services cleanly. As a result, the business processes and data contained within the application remain "off limits." In these situations, half the anticipated expense of moving forward must be dedicated to more traditional mechanisms, such as leveraging scraping screens, or database application integration.

Packaged applications are natural stovepipes. This reality not only places them squarely within the problem domain of most application integration projects, but it also makes them the most challenging applications to integrate. You may find yourself needing to access the information in these stovepipes and needing to share the business logic locked up within them with others in your organization or trading community.

SAP, PeopleSoft, Oracle, and Siebel have come to dominate the many packaged applications on the market today because they have recognized, and responded to, the need to share information. This is a tremendous advantage over their competitors. However, before availing yourself of this advantage, you must remember that, over the years, hundreds of packaged applications have likely entered your enterprise. The sad reality is that many of these packaged applications no longer enjoy the support of their vendors or, perhaps more likely, their vendors have gone out of business. Because the number of these older, packaged applications in your application integration problem domain could easily be in the hundreds, you will be confronted with special challenges for application integration. Most of these applications will provide some points of integration, while others will not.

Packaged applications come in all shapes and sizes. Most large packaged applications that exist within the enterprise are "business critical." SAP, for example, provides modules for accounting, inventory, human resources, manufacturing, and other vital functions. PeopleSoft and Baan provide many of the same types of services and modules.

Vendors such as Lawson Software, J.D. Edwards, and others—some with less than a dozen installations—offer packaged applications. For example, Scopus, a call-center management application, is limited to highly selected and specialized applications. Siebel, a sales-force automation package, is designed to allow sales organizations to function more effectively.

User Interface

Leveraging the user interface as a point of information integration is a process known as "screen scraping," or accessing screen information through a programmatic mechanism. Middleware drives a user interface (e.g., 3270 user interface) in order to access information. Simply put, many application integration projects will have no other choice but to leverage user interfaces to access application data and processes. Sometimes access to underlying databases and application interfaces does not exist.

There really isn't much to user interface access. It is just one of many techniques and technologies that can be used to access, or place, information in an application. The technology has been around for a number of years. As a consequence, there is very little risk involved in using it. There are, however, problems that need to be overcome. A user interface was never designed to serve up data, but it is now being used for precisely that purpose. It should go without saying that the data-gathering performance of user screens leaves a lot to be desired. In addition, this type of solution can't scale, so it is unable to handle more than a few screen interfaces at any given time. Finally, if the application integration architect and developer do not set up these mechanisms carefully, they may prove unstable. Controller and server bouncing are common problems.

There are, of course, a number of tricks for sidestepping these limitations, but they bring additional risk to the project. Still, with so many closed and proprietary applications out there, the application integration architect has little choice. The name of the game is accessing information—by any means possible. Ultimately, going directly to the user interface to get at the data is like many other types of technology—not necessarily pretty, but it gets the job done.

For the reasons noted previously, user interface-level application integration should be the "last-ditch effort" for accessing information that resides in source systems. It should be turned to only when there is no well-defined application interface, such as those provided by many ERP applications, or when it doesn't make sense to leverage the database. Having said that, we can also state that user interface-level application integration needn't be avoided. In most cases, it will prove to be successful in extracting information from existing applications and as a mechanism to invoke application logic.

Using the User Interface

An existing mainframe application created using DB2 and COBOL needs to share processes and data with a custom distributed object system running on Linux and with PeopleSoft running on NT. The mainframe application is older and does not have an application interface, nor do the skills exist within the company to create one.

Instead of creating an application interface, or moving information between databases, the application integration architect opts to leverage the user interface. Using this approach, the application integration architect is able to extract both application data and business information from the COBOL/DB2 system exposed by the user interface. The application integration architect may leverage this approach, perhaps to save money and lower the risk of the application integration project, or due to the simple fact that this may be the only solution when considering the state of the technology (the most popular reason).

(continued)

Using the User Interface (*continued*)

The process of extracting information using the user interface is really a matter of defining how to get to the appropriate screens, locating the correct information on the screens, reading the information from the screens, and, finally, processing the information. You're creating an automated program that simulates an actual user, navigating through screens, emulating keystrokes, and reading screens into memory. Once in memory, the information is parsed, reformatted, and transported to any number of middleware layers, where it's ultimately sent to the target system, for example, the PeopleSoft system. You also need to check for errors and be able to handle and recover from the inevitable problems such as system and network failures.

You need to consider the business case. In this instance it may not make good business sense to create a new interface into the older mainframe-based system, and it may not make sense to integrate the applications at the database level (e.g., if we need to extract calculated information versus just raw data). By creating a new interface, the existing mainframe system will typically have to undergo a small to medium rearchitecture effort, redevelopment to add the application interface, and redeployment and testing of the application before it's placed into production. This is a long and drawn-out process, and perhaps it's not needed, considering what we can do these days with user-level application integration. Is it the best solution? It's another tradeoff.

As in other levels of application integration, the architect or the developer has the responsibility to understand the application, the application architecture, and the database information in great detail. At the user-level interface, this may prove difficult. Remember, the decision to leverage user interface-level application integration was made specifically to bypass the restrictions of closed proprietary systems, or because it just makes good business sense not to augment an existing system to create an interface, or because other application integration levels are not applicable.

In spite of the difficulty, this information is necessary for two reasons: one, the need to understand all the information that an application is producing, and two, to understand how all the data and methods residing within an application relate to all the data and methods existing within the enterprise. In short, it is necessary to know how the application data and methods fit within the enterprise metadata model and the enterprise object models, and map the source system into this logical and physical layer. Using the user interface as a point of integration does not free us from this requirement.

In order to implement user interface-level application integration, it is necessary to understand the application. This requires understanding the underlying data storage schema, much of the application logic, and, most important, how the information is presented to the user interface. In order to understand how the data elements are represented on the screen, it is necessary to understand how they exist within the application. Unlike other interface levels, information presented to a user interface may not map back to a database. Most of the data elements on the screen, such as calculated fields (e.g., an order total), are created by the application logic and do not come directly from the database.

This being the case, it is evident that an understanding of the application logic is also desirable. This requires reading the documentation so that the mechanisms of the application—as well as the logic—can be understood. Unfortunately, as in other contexts, the applications are not always well documented. If this proves to be the case, the source code itself will have to be read. Ultimately, regardless of how it is achieved, the goal is to be able to trace all data that appears on the screen to the application logic and database schema information.

Reaching this goal will often require "breaking the data out" from its representation on the screen, a task accomplished with simple mathematical formulas. There are times when it will be necessary to break out six separate data elements from a single number presented on the user interface. This, in and of itself, is a strong statement that the application integration architect or developer needs to understand the application logic in detail. There are many cases of user interface application integration projects where a failure to understand the application has led to a misreading of the user interfaces and, consequently, erroneous data being fed into target applications.

Embedded Device

Finally, you may find that, in some cases, information comes from embedded devices, such as temperature sensors, call-counting machines, or perhaps wireless devices. Dealing with embedded devices is similar to dealing with applications; the interfaces are typically API based and proprietary, although some standards are beginning to emerge.

A common pattern when dealing with embedded devices as source or target systems is the fact that information must flow freely from the device because

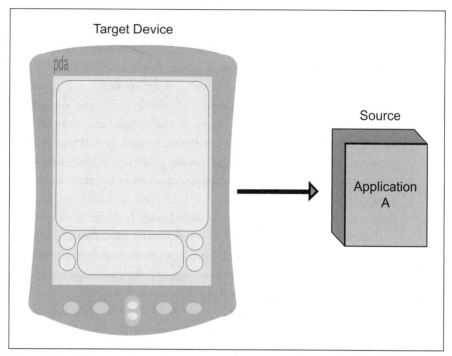

Figure 2.6   When using embedded devices, you may not be able to queue up information. Use it or lose it.

most devices can't store information (as can true applications). Thus, when you request information you're typically obtaining the information at that time, not information that's in a queue (see Figure 2.6).

Approaching Information Integration

So, now that we know what information-based application integration is, the larger question is, How do we approach our problem domain? Although there are many different ways to address information integration within an application integration solution set, I've found the best way is to follow these steps:

1. Identify the data.
2. Catalog the data.
3. Build the enterprise metadata model (which will be used as a master guide for integrating the various information stores that exist within the enterprise).

In short, implementing an application integration solution demands more than the movement of data between databases and/or applications. A successful solution requires that the enterprise also define both how that information flows through it and how it does business.

Identify the Data

Unfortunately, there are no shortcuts to identifying data within an enterprise. All too often, information about the data, both business and technical, is scattered throughout the enterprise and of a quality that ranges from "somewhat useful" to "you've got to be kidding me!"

The first step in identifying and locating information about the data is to create a list of candidate systems. This list will make it possible to determine which databases exist in support of those candidate systems. The next step requires the determination of who owns the databases, where they are physically located, relevant design information, and such basic information as brand, model, and revisions of the database technology.

Any technology that can reverse-engineer existing physical and logical database schemas will prove helpful in identifying data within the problem domains. However, while the schema and database model may give insight into the structure of the database or databases, they cannot determine how that information is used within the context of the application.

The Data Dictionary

Detailed information can be culled by examining the data dictionaries (if they exist) linked to the data stores being analyzed. Such an examination may illuminate such important information as

- The reason for the existence of particular data elements
- Ownership
- Format
- Security parameters
- The role within both the logical and physical data structure

While the concept of the data dictionary is fairly constant from database to database, the dictionaries themselves may vary widely in form and content. Some contain more information than others. Some are open. Most are proprietary. Some don't even exist—which is often the case with less sophisticated software.

Integrity Issues

When analyzing databases for IOAI, integrity issues constantly crop up. In order to address these, it is important to understand the rules and regulations that were applied to the construction of the database. For example, will the application allow the update of customer information in a customer table without first updating demographics information in the demographics table?

Most middleware fails to take into account the structure or rules built into the databases being connected. As a result, there exists the very real threat of damage to the integrity of target databases. While some databases do come with built-in integrity controls, such as stored procedures or triggers, most rely on the application logic to handle integrity issues on behalf of the database. Unfortunately, the faith implicit in this reliance is not always well placed. Indeed, all too often it is painfully naive.

The lack of integrity controls at the data level (or, in the case of existing integrity controls, bypassing the application logic to access the database directly) could result in profound problems. Application integration architects and developers need to approach this danger cautiously, making sure not to compromise the database's integrity in their zeal to achieve integration. Perhaps this is where a decision to use another application integration level as a primary point of integration might be considered.

Data Latency

Data latency—the characteristic of the data that defines how current the information needs to be—is another property of the data that needs to be determined for the purposes of application integration. Such information will allow application integration architects to determine when the information should be copied, or moved, to another enterprise system, and how fast.

While an argument can be made to support a number of different categories of data latency, for the purpose of application integration within the enterprise, there are really only three:

1. Real time
2. Near time
3. One time

Real-time data is precisely what it sounds like—information that is placed in the database as it occurs, with little or no latency. Monitoring stock price information through a real-time feed from Wall Street is an example of real-time data. Real-time data is updated as it enters the database, and that information is available immediately to anyone, or any application, that requires it for processing.

While zero-latency real time is clearly the goal of application integration, achieving it represents a huge challenge. In order to achieve zero latency, application integration implementation requires constant returns to the database, application, or other resource to retrieve new and/or updated information. In the context of real-time updates, database performance must also be considered— while one process updates the database as quickly as possible, another process must be simultaneously extracting the updated information.

The successful implementation of zero latency presents architects and developers with the opportunity to create such innovative solutions as service-level application integration, where business processes are integrated within the application integration solution. In many cases, SOAI makes better sense than IOAI solutions, because it allows data and common business processes to be shared at

---

Application Integration Brings Real-Time Data to the Data Warehouse

Unlike application integration, which can support real-time data movement, data warehousing provides adequate business information without up-to-the-minute access of information. In many cases, the data is weeks, even months, old, and the data mart or data warehouse is updated through antiquated batch, extract-aggregate-and-load, processes.

Application integration, and the technology that comes with it, allows data warehouse architects and developers to move information— no matter where it comes from or where it is going—as quickly as they want to move it. As a result, it is not unheard of to have all participating databases in an application integration solution receiving new data constantly, thus providing more value to those using the source and target systems—including those who use them as a data warehouse or data mart. Therefore, the rise of application integration will also lead to the rise of real-time data warehouse solutions, with many users able to leverage up-to-the-minute information to make better business decisions.

the same time. The downside to SOAI is that it is also the most expensive to implement. We'll find out more about that in the next few chapters.

Near-time data refers to information that is updated at set intervals rather than instantaneously. Stock quotes posted on the Web are a good example of near-time data. They are typically delayed 20 minutes or more, because the Web sites distributing the quotes are generally unable to process real-time data. Near-time data can be thought of as "good-enough" latency data. In other words, data only as timely as needed.

Although near-time data is not updated constantly, it still faces many of the same challenges as real-time data, including overcoming performance and management issues.

One-time data is typically updated only once. Customer addresses or account numbers are examples of one-time information. Within the context of application integration, the intervals of data copy, or data movement, do not require the kind of aggressiveness needed to accomplish real-time or near-time data exchange.

The notion of data typing goes well beyond the classification of the data as real-time, near-time, or one-time. It is really a complex process of determining the properties of the data, including updates and edit increments, as well as the behavior of the data over time. What do the applications use the particular data for? How often do they use it? What happens with the data over time? These are questions that must be addressed in order to create the most effective application integration solution.

Data Structure

Another identifying component of data is data structure. How information is structured, including the properties of the data elements existing within that structure, can be gleaned from a knowledge of the data format. Likewise, length, data type (character or numeric), name of the data element, and type of information stored (binary, text, spatial, etc.) are additional characteristics of the data that may be determined by its format.

Resolution of data structure conflicts must be accomplished within such application integration technologies as integration brokers and/or application servers. Different structures and schemas existing within the enterprise must be transformed as information is moved from one system to another. The need to resolve these conflicts in structure and schema makes knowing the structure of the data at both the source and target systems vital.

Our discussion of integration broker technology in Chapter 9 will deal with how such brokers are able to adapt to differences in data formats found in different databases that exist within the enterprise. For now, it is enough to note that message brokers are able to transform a message or database schema from one format to another so that it makes sense, both contextually and semantically, to the application receiving the information (see Figure 2.7). Often, this needs to be accomplished without changing the source or target applications, or the database schemas. Integration broker technology allows two or more systems with different data formats to communicate successfully.

Catalog the Data

Once the logical and physical characteristics of the databases to be integrated are understood, it is time to do the "grunge" work—data cataloging. In the world of application integration, data cataloging is the process of gathering metadata and other data throughout the problem domain. Once accomplished, it is possible to create an enterprise-wide catalog of all data elements that may exist within the enterprise. The resulting catalog then becomes the basis of understanding needed to create the enterprise metadata model—the foundation of IOAI.

For most medium to large enterprises, the creation of this data catalog is a massive undertaking. In essence, it demands the creation of the "mother of all data dictionaries," a data dictionary that includes not only the traditional data dictionary information, but also all the information that is of interest to application integration—system information, security information, ownership, connected processes, communication mechanisms, and integrity issues—along with traditional metadata such as format, name of attribute, and description.

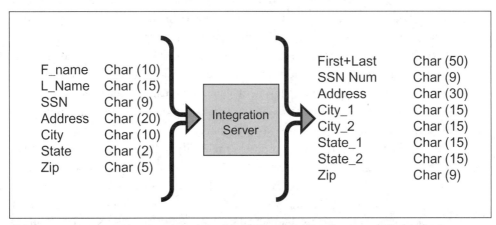

Figure 2.7   Integration servers are able to transform schemas and content, accounting for the differences in application semantics and database structure between applications and databases.

While there is no standard for cataloging data within application integration projects, the guiding principle stands clear: the more information, the better. The catalog will become both the repository for the application integration engine to be built and the foundation to discover new business flows. It will also become a way to automate existing business flows within the enterprise.

It is an understatement to suggest that this catalog will be huge. Most enterprises and trading communities will find tens of thousands of data elements to identify and catalog, even after reducing redundancies among some of the data elements. In addition to being huge, the data catalog will be a dynamic structure. In a very real sense, it will never be complete. A person, or persons, will have to be assigned to maintain the data catalog over time, ensuring that the information in the catalog remains correct and timely, and that the architects and developers have access to the catalog in order to create the application integration solution.

Logical Model

Just as with traditional database design methods, the enterprise metadata model used for IOAI can be broken into two components: the logical and the physical. And, just as with the former, the same techniques apply to the latter. Creating the logical model is the process of creating an architecture for all data stores that are independent of a physical database model, development tool, or particular DBMS (e.g., Oracle, Sybase, or Informix).

A logical model is a sound approach to an application integration project in that it will allow architects and developers to make objective IOAI decisions, moving from high-level requirements to implementation details. The logical data model is an integrated view of business data throughout the application domain, or data pertinent to the application integration solution under construction. The primary difference between using a logical data model for application integration versus traditional database development is the information source. While traditional development, generally speaking, defines new databases based on business requirements, a logical data model arising from an application integration project is based on existing databases.

At the heart of the logical model is the Entity Relationship Diagram (ERD). An ERD is a graphical representation of data entities, attributes, and relationships between entities (see Figure 2.8) for all databases existing in the enterprise.

Computer-Aided Software Engineering (CASE) technology is but one of the many tools to automate the logical database modeling process. Not only do these tools provide an easy way to create logical database models, they can also build

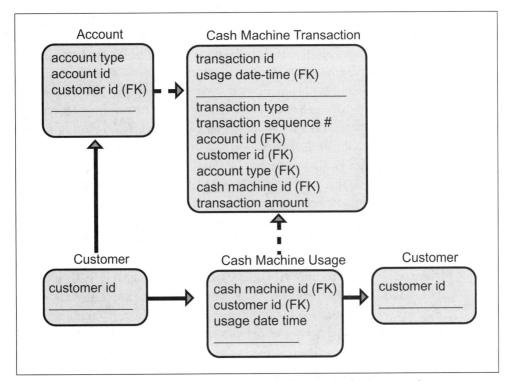

**Figure 2.8   Entity Relationship Diagram depicting the logical enterprise
information model.**

logical database models into physical database models. In addition, they create
the physical schema on the target database(s) through standard middleware.

Building the Enterprise Metadata Model

Once all the information about all the data in the enterprise is contained in the
data catalog, it is time to focus on the enterprise metadata model. The difference
between the two is sometimes subtle. It is best to think of the data catalog as the
list of potential solutions to your application integration problem and to think of
the metadata model as the IOAI solution. The metadata model defines not only
all the data structures existing in the enterprise, but also how those data structures will interact within the application integration solution domain.

Once constructed, the enterprise metadata model is the enterprise's database
repository of sorts: the master directory for the application integration solution.
In many cases, the repository will be hooked on to the integration broker and

used as a reference point for locating not only the data, but also the rules and logic that apply to that data. However, the repository is more than simply the storage of metadata information. It is the heart of the ultimate application integration solution, containing both data and business model information.

A metadata repository built with the processes outlined in this chapter will not only solve the IOAI problem, it will also provide the basis for other types of application integration, as well. We'll discuss more about this in the next several chapters. As in the world of client/server and data warehousing, the process builds up from the data to the application (and from the application to the interface, if necessary). This "hierarchical" flow identifies IOAI as the foundation for the larger application integration solution.

Physical Model

The myriad of database types in any given enterprise minimizes the importance of the physical enterprise model because, with so many database types, the physical model will rarely be used. The reason is clear—there is simply no clear way to create a physical model that maps down to object-oriented, multidimensional, hierarchy, flat-file, and relational databases, all at the same time. However, if those databases are to be integrated, some common physical representation must be selected. Only then can the model be transformed as required.

Our discussion of the physical model is only for those times when it is possible to map the logical to the physical. That is, those times when an enterprise uses a homogeneous database approach, usually all relational. The input for the physical model is both the logical model and the data catalog. When accessing this information, consider the data dictionary, business rules, and other user processing requirements.

Normalizing the Problem Domain

Before the logical—and sometimes physical—database is completed, it is desirable to normalize the model. This is a process of decomposing complex data structures into simple relations using a series of dependency rules. Normalization means reducing the amount of redundant data that will exist in the database or, in the case of application integration, in the enterprise. It is a good idea to do this in both the logical and physical database design, or the application integration redesign.

When considered within the context of application integration, the normalization process is very complex and risky. Because there can be no control over most of the databases that are being integrated, normalizing the logical enterprise metadata model often results in a new version of the model that has no chance of being implemented physically. This result violates an essential credo of application integration: Whenever possible, it is best to leave the applications and databases alone. Changes to databases inevitably translate into expense and risk. Furthermore, most enterprises employ a chaotic mosaic of database technology, making it technically unfeasible to accomplish such changes without rehosting the data. This is almost always completely out of the question.

However, the issue remains: Are changes to be made to source and target databases, or not? Generally, it is wise to normalize the logical enterprise metadata model to discover areas within the enterprise that may benefit from changes in their data structures. Changes to databases may allow the enterprise to reduce the amount of redundant data and thus increase the reliability of the integrated data. Remember, the notion of IOAI is to perceive all the information within the enterprise as a single source of information and, in turn, to make that huge amount of enterprise information as efficient as possible through processes such as normalization.

Working with Information-Oriented Application Integration

The difficulty with IOAI is the large scope of integrating various databases within the enterprise. Your initial goal might be to solve all the integration woes of your enterprise or trading community at the same time by integrating all databases that need to communicate. However, given the complexity of the task, it is often better to move forward in a clear, paced manner. Attempting to accomplish the entire process at once is a massive undertaking and, for most trading communities and enterprises, too much change to accommodate at one time.

You, your enterprise, and your trading community should consider taking "baby steps" toward the goal of IOAI—and application integration in general. A smart strategy would be to first integrate two or three databases, allow them to become successful, and then move forward to bigger problem domains. This strategy would ease the burden on the application integration architects, who are shouldering a huge workload, by pushing forward a new concept of application integration. It also eases the burden on users who have to test the systems and work through problems as they become apparent.

## CHAPTER THREE

Business Process Integration-Oriented Application Integration

Pay close attention to this chapter. This is the future of application integration. As the technology moves forward, we will not control the integration of applications through the exchange of information or the binding of processes, but through the modeling and execution of a business process model that binds processes and information within many systems, intra- or intercompany.

This is a key concept for the future of the technology and also controls how we deal with information movement and the invocation of local and remote application services. They all roll up into a BPIOAI model that controls the application integration domain, inside and outside the company.

Also, take careful note of BPI-centric standards such as RosettaNet and ebXML. We'll cover those topics later in this book.

From Chapter 2, we now know that IOAI is the science of exchanging information between many applications so that they benefit one another within an enterprise or trading community. IOAI is more traditional and occurs at the data level by simply exchanging information between systems, inter- or intracompany. Typically, this means defining information flows at the physical level, not taking into account abstract business concepts such as business processes (inter- or intracompany) that are becoming critical for application integration. Incorporating business concepts into information flow definitions is the purpose of this chapter.

Until now, what was missing from the application integration mix was the notion of Business Process Integration-Oriented Application Integration (BPIOAI). BPIOAI is the ability to define a common business process model that addresses the sequence, hierarchy, events, execution logic, and information movement between systems residing in the same organization (application integration) and systems residing in multiple organizations (B2B). Indeed, the idea of BPIOAI is to provide a single logical model that spans many applications and data stores, providing the notion of a common business process that controls how systems and humans interact to fulfill a unique business requirement.

Please note that this is a complimentary form of application integration to both IOAPI and Service-Oriented Application Integration (SOAI)—(even Portal-Oriented Application Integration in some instances). BPIOAI provides a control mechanism of sorts that defines and executes the movement of information and the invocation of processes that span many systems. The goal is to abstract both the encapsulated application services and application information into a single controlling business process model (see Figure 3.1).

BPIOAI may be applied to any number of business events including:

- Processing a customer request.
- Manufacturing an automobile.
- Delivering a product to a customer.
- Processing a financial transaction.

The notion is simple. Place a layer of control logic on top of the integration technology that allows the control logic to bind the systems into a single unified multistep business process that can carry out the unique functions of the business process. It must do so in the correct order, with the proper information, control sequences, state maintenance, durability, and the ability to handle exceptions.

BPIOAI is a strategy as much as a technology. It strengthens your organization's ability to interact with any number of systems—inside or outside the organization—by integrating entire business processes both within and between enterprises. Indeed, BPIOAI delivers application integration by dealing with several organizations and internal systems, using various metadata, platforms, and processes. BPIOAI even deals with people and other non-IT-related entities that may participate in a process. Thus, BPIOAI technology must be flexible, providing

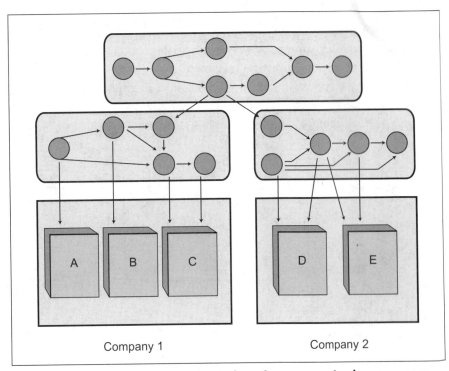

Company 1   Company 2

Figure 3.1   BPIOAI introduces the notion of a common business process model that controls the movement of information and the invocation of application services across many different systems, both inter- and intracompany.

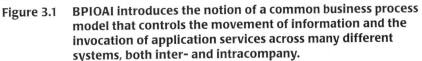

BPIOAI Technology: A Deeper Dive

BPIOAI technology is typically made up of a:

- *Graphic modeling tool,* where the business model is created and behavior defined.
- *Business process engine* that controls the execution of the multistep business process and maintains state and the interactions with the middleware, which in turn, interacts with any number of source or target systems.
- *Business process monitoring interface* that allows end users to monitor and control the execution of a business process in real time and optimize where needed.

(continued)

BPIOAI Technology: A Deeper Dive (*continued*)

- *Business process engine interface* that allows other applications to access the business process engine.
- *Integration technology* or application integration middleware (such as an integration server or application server) that connects the source and target systems to the BPIOIA technology (see Figure 3.2).

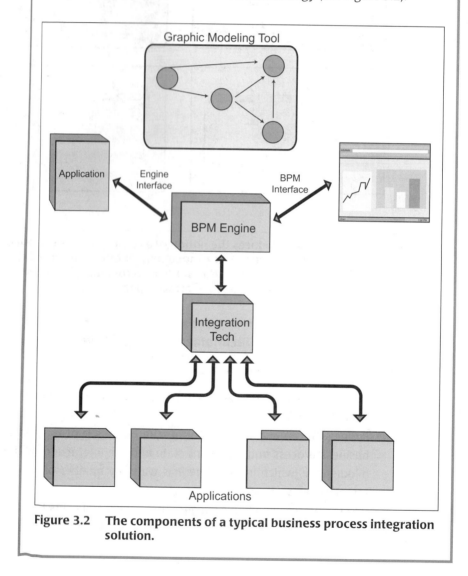

Figure 3.2   The components of a typical business process integration solution.

a translation layer between the source and target systems and the process integration engine. Moreover, BPIOAI technology needs to work with several types of technologies and interface patterns.

BPIOAI Defined

So, what does BPIOAI bring to the application integration table? It's really another complete layer on the stack, over and above more traditional application integration approaches, including IOAI and SOAI (see Figure 3.3). These differences include the following:

- A single instance of BPIOAI typically spans many instances of traditional application integration, including IOAI and SOAI.
- Application integration typically means the exchange of information between two or more systems without visibility into internal processes. BPIOAI defines a master application that has visibility into many encapsulated application services and application information.
- BPIOAI leads with a process model, moves information between applications, and invokes internal application services in support of that model.

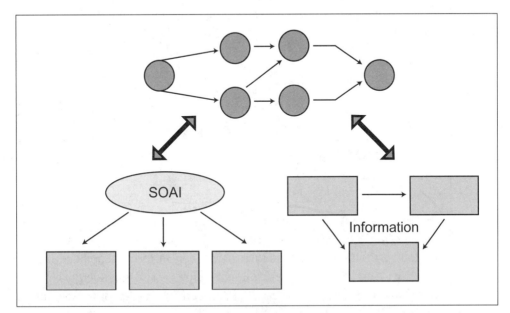

Figure 3.3   BPIOAI provides another layer of control over IOAI and SOAI.

- BPIOAI is independent of the source and target applications. Changes can be made to the processes without having to change the source or target systems.
- Application integration is typically a tactical solution, motivated by the requirement for two or more applications to communicate. BPIOAI is strategic, leveraging business rules to determine how systems should interact and better leverage the business value from each system through a common abstract business model.

BPIOAI by Example

So, it's not clear to you yet? You need to walk through a simple example? No problem. Say you're building a model plane, and you have three main processes:

- First, the process of cutting the parts.
- Second, the process of assembling the parts.
- Finally, finishing the plane (painting and attaching the decals).

These are the higher-level processes; of course, many processes will be contained inside these processes.

In the terms of BPIOAI we can define the three main processes as:

- "Cut Parts."
- "Assemble Parts."
- "Finish Plane."

And we have to build these processes on top of three source and target systems:

1. Inventory (SAP)
2. Sales (Custom Build)
3. Manufacturing (Oracle)

Using the assumptions above we could define "Cut Parts" as a process that is kicked off by a sales event from the Sales system that's posted to the Manufacturing system. We can in turn decompose that "Cut Parts" process down to additional subprocesses if needed (we are not going to do that here). After the parts are cut we let Manufacturing

(continued)

know that the process is complete and it in turn kicks off the process to assemble the parts. Once that is complete, we return information back again to the Manufacturing system, and it kicks off the finishing processing. Once that occurs, the Inventory system is updated with the information on the completed product, and the Sales system is updated with the fact that the product is complete and is ready for shipping.

The key idea here is that the higher-level processes, the meta application in a sense, is driving the processes here, coordinating the exchange of information between the source and target system and abstracting the encapsulated processes up to a higher-level set of processes in support of this business event.

Although this is very simplistic example, it's nonetheless a good depiction of the higher-level activities and concepts of process integration.

Thus, BPIOAI is the science and mechanism of managing the movement of data and the invocation of application services in the correct and proper order to support the management and execution of common processes that exist in and between organizations and internal applications (see Figure 3.4). BPIOAI provides another layer of easily defined and centrally managed processes that exist on top of an existing set of processes, application services, and data within any set of applications.

The goal of our discussion is to define a mechanism to bind relevant processes that exist between internal and external systems in order to support the flow of information and logic between them, thus maximizing their mutual value. Moreover, we're looking to define a common, agreed-upon process that exists between many organizations and has visibility into any number of integrated systems, as well as being visible to any system that needs to leverage the common process model.

BPIOAI views middleware (e.g., integration servers and application servers), or the "plumbing," as a commodity with the ability to leverage both message-oriented and transactional middleware as points of integration into any number of source or target systems. In fact, most integration brokers and application servers are beginning to offer BPIOAI tools that support their middleware technology.

BPIOAI is the ultimate destination of application integration. Despite current shortcomings, many application integration vendors are aggressively promoting

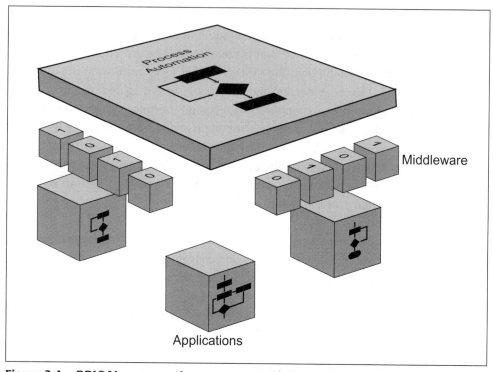

Figure 3.4   BPIOAI manages the movement of information and the sharing of common process models between trading partners and internal systems, using business-oriented semantics, control logic, exception handling, and the ability to monitor the processes in real time.

BPIOAI as a vital component of their application integration technology package. In doing so, their strategy is clear—they are eager to join the world of high-end BPIOAI modeling tools. They hope that their application integration-enabled middleware, such as integration brokers and application servers, will accomplish just that.

The good news is that most business processes are already automated. The bad news is that they tend to be loosely coupled and exist on different systems. For example, adding a customer to a packaged accounting application may establish the customer in that system, but it may still be necessary to use another system (a different system that may exist within a trading partner) to perform a credit check on that customer, and still another system to process an invoice (see Figure 3.5). You needn't possess exceptional insight to recognize the potential for disaster that exists in this scenario. Not only do these disparate systems need to

Understanding the Semantics

As we move into the world of BPIOAI, we are finding that the names for particular types of technologies and approaches can be somewhat confusing. As we mentioned earlier in this chapter, no standard definitions exist for these concepts, so perhaps it's time we created them.

- *Business Process Modeling (BPM)* provides tools and approaches for the graphical design and simulation of business processes. Typically, these tools are not hooked up to existing enterprise processes, but work as pure modeling tools.
- *Business Process Automation (BPA)* tools and approaches provide mechanisms for the automation of business processes without end-user interaction at execution time. Most application integration tools provide this type of subsystem.
- *Workflow* tools allow for the automation of business processes with end-user interaction at execution time. These categories of technology and approaches are typically document oriented, moving document information between human decision makers.
- *BPIOAI* is an aggregation of business process modeling, business process automation, and workflow. This approach implements and manages transactions and real-time business processes that span multiple applications, providing a layer to create common processes that span many processes in integrated systems.

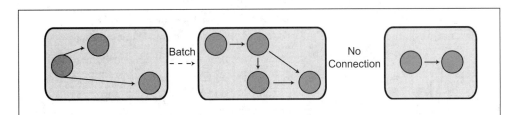

Figure 3.5   **Although many automated processes exist within most trading communities, they tend to be loosely coupled or not coupled at all.**

share information, but also they need to share that information in an orderly and efficient manner.

Indeed, the goal of BPIOAI, and of application integration in general, is to automate data movement and process flow so that another layer of BPIOAI will exist over and above the processes encapsulated in existing systems. In other words, BPIOAI completes application integration, allowing the integration of systems not only by sharing information readily, but also by managing the sharing of that information with easy-to-use tools.

Drilling Down on BPIOAI?

BPIOAI is best defined as applying appropriate rules in an agreed-upon, logical, multistep sequence in order to pass information between participating systems and to visualize and share application services, including the creation of a common abstract process that spans both internal and external systems. This definition holds true whether the business processes are automated or not.

BPIOAI may be best defined through an example. Companies A, B, and C participate in a trading community. Company A produces parts for skateboards, while Company B assembles and tests the skateboards, and finally, Company C sells the skateboards. Each has its own native set of processes and its own internal systems: a production system, an assembly system, and a sales system. Until now, automated integration has been nonexistent, and mail and fax provide communication between the companies.

In order to integrate these applications, the trading community has decided to implement BPIOAI by defining a common process model that spans all companies and internal systems. This process model defines a sequence and logical order of events from the realization of consumer demand, the purchase of raw materials, the creation of the parts, the assembly of parts into a product, the testing of the product, and finally, the sale of the product to the ultimate consumer (see Figure 3.6).

This common model integrates with local systems by having visibility into their internal application processes, if possible, or perhaps through more primitive layers, such as the database or application interface. What's important is that the common process model can produce events that are understood by the systems participating in the process, as well as react to events that the applications communicate back to the BPIOAI engine. This model must also account for exceptions that come up and handle them accordingly. Moreover, this model must maintain state, perhaps over a long period of time: days, weeks, and months.

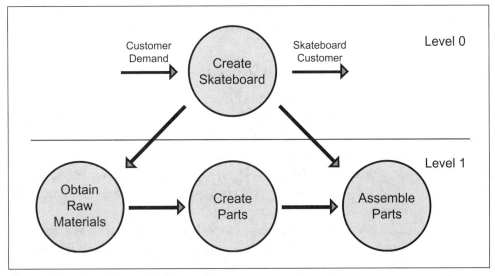

Figure 3.6   Creating a skateboard.

The use of a common process model that spans multiple systems and companies for application integration provides many advantages, including:

- *Modeling*, or the ability to create a common agreed-upon process between computer systems, automating the integration of all information systems to react in real time to business events such as increased consumer demand, material shortages, and quality problems
- *Monitoring*, or the ability to analyze all aspects of the business and enterprise or trading community to determine the current state of the process in real time
- *Optimization*, or the ability to redefine the process at any given time in support of the business and thus make the process more efficient
- *Abstraction*, or the ability to hide the complexities of the local applications from the business users and have the business users work with a common set of business semantics

By visualizing enterprise and cross-enterprise processes within internal and external systems, business managers can become involved in enterprise integration. The use of graphics and diagrams provides a powerful tool for communication and consensus building. Moreover, this approach provides a business-oriented view of the integration scenarios that illustrates real-time integration with the

---

Types of Processes

There are three types of processes to visualize enterprise and cross-enterprise processes: internal, shared, and specialized processes.

- *Internal processes* exist at the intracompany level, allowing the business user to define common processes that span only systems that are within the enterprise and not visible to the trading partners or to community-wide processes. For example, the process of hiring an employee may span several systems within the enterprise but should not be visible to processes that span an enterprise or trading community or other organizations.
- *Shared processes* exist between companies and consist of a set of agreed-upon procedures for exchanging information and automating business processes within a community.
- *Specialized processes* are created for a special requirement, such as collaboration on a common product development effort that only exists between two companies and has a limited life span.

---

enabling middleware or points of integration. This visualization enables business analysts to make changes to the process model, implement it within the enterprise or trading community, and, typically, not involve the respective IT departments.

Interface abstraction refers to the mapping of the BPIOAI model to physical system interfaces and the abstraction of both connectivity and system integration solutions from the business analyst. BPIOAI exists at the uppermost level in the application integration middleware stack. Those who use BPIOAI tools can view the world at a logical business level and are not limited by physical integration flows, interfaces, or adapters. What's more, the middleware mechanisms employed are also abstracted and are not a concern of the business process analyst, as long as the common process model is interacting correctly with all source and target systems that exist within all companies.

Although each BPIOAI tool and project may take a slightly different approach, the internal process of interacting with the physical systems typically consists of the following set of events.

1. The source system that exists inside a company posts an event to the BPIOAI engine—for example, a skateboard is sold.

2. The event is transformed, if required, so it adheres to a standard set of business semantics and information processing mechanisms (synchronous versus asynchronous). This will be engine dependent, but a common set of process semantics and information processing mechanisms must always be defined at the engine level so the analyst can make sense of a business process that spans many types of applications, platforms, and databases.

3. The BPIOAI engine reacts to the event, once transformed, invoking other processes in other systems to support execution of the common B2B process model. For example, if a skateboard is sold, it then sends an order to the skateboard assembler, posting an event from the process engine to the assembler's target system, typically over the Internet.

4. Based on receipt of that event, the local system reacts in accordance with its internal processes and posts an event back to the process engine (say, when the skateboard is assembled).

5. The common process model sequences the master process, sending and receiving other events in support of the common B2B process model. This is an ongoing activity, with information moving up to the process engine from the local systems, transformed if required, and moving down from the process engine to the local systems in support of the execution of the process model (see Figure 3.7).

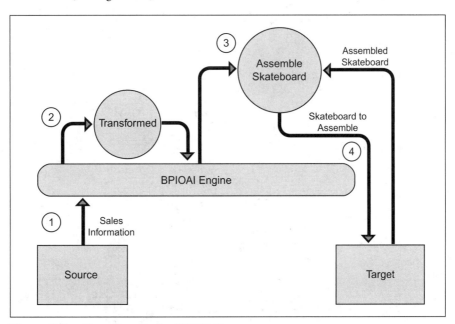

Figure 3.7   Steps in a typical BPIOAI process.

Another way to view and execute the process is by defining the hierarchy of processes within the business process model. This means that smaller sub-processes can be linked at the lower tier of integration or are native to the source or target systems. This is called nesting (see Figure 3.8). Building up from the lower-level processes to the higher-level processes, you may link the subprocesses into higher-level processes within the domain of the enterprise or trading community. You may also decompose from the higher-level processes to the lower-level processes.

The measurement of business process performance enables BPIOAI to analyze a business in real time (see Figure 3.9). By leveraging tight integration with the process model and the middleware, business analysts can gather business statistics in real time from the enterprise or trading community—for example, the performance of a supplier in shipping goods to the plant and the plant's ability to turn those raw materials into products.

Moreover, BPIOAI enables the technology user to track and direct each instance of a business process—for example, processing individual orders or medical insurance claims through a life cycle that may consume seconds, minutes, hours, days, or weeks. Finally, we need to measure and maintain contextual information for the duration of a process instance that spans many individual activities.

In general, BPIOAI logic addresses only process flow and integration. It is not traditional programming logic, such as user interface processing, database

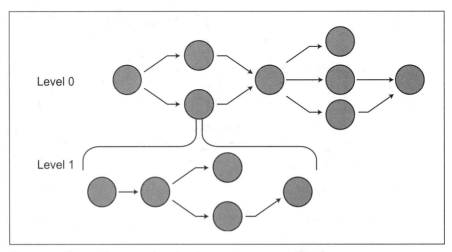

Figure 3.8   Nesting within a business process model.

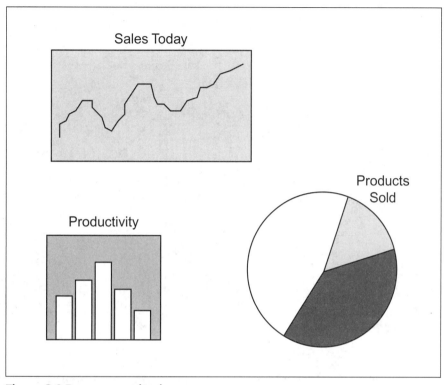

Figure 3.9 Process monitoring.

updates, or the execution of transactions. Indeed, in most BPIOAI scenarios, the process logic is separated from the application logic. It functions solely to coordinate, or manage, the information flow or invocation of application services between many source and target applications that exist within organizations (see Figure 3.10).

Such a system operates on three levels of technology (see Figure 3.11). At the uppermost layer is the BPIOAI level. Here, the BPIOAI modeling tools and engines exist, and the application service of information movement is defined.

At the next level—the transformation, routing, and rules-processing layer—information movement and formatting occur. Usually, this layer is an integration broker or perhaps a B2B exchange server, but it could also be transaction-oriented middleware and even Web services. The only requirement here is that we employ middleware technology or interfaces that can work with the BPIOAI

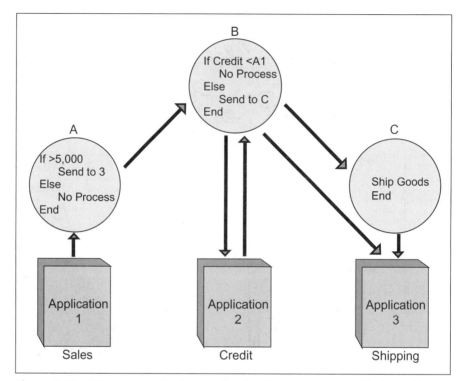

Figure 3.10   **The process logic coordinates the movement of information, and the invocation of application services between many connected applications or data stores.**

engine. Typically, the BPIOAI engine interfaces with these various sets of enabling technology through adapters or APIs. The adapters or APIs abstract the native interfaces and/or middleware for the BPIOAI engine, allowing the BPIOAI analyst to deal with all systems using a common set of process and business semantics.

The bottom layer is occupied by the messaging system, which is responsible for moving information between all connected applications. Although application servers and other enterprise middleware function here, this layer is generally dominated by message-oriented middleware or servers that use standards-based messaging such as XML or EDI.

This schema graphically demonstrates that the most primitive layers reside at the bottom, while the more sophisticated layers reside at the top. Information ascends through the layers from the source system where it is processed, and descends to the target system where it is delivered.

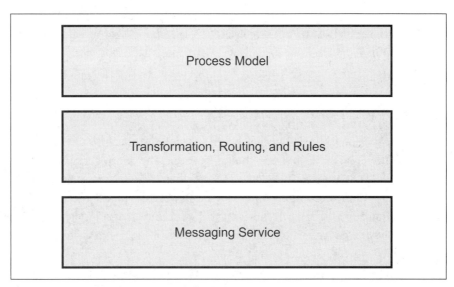

Figure 3.11   The three layers of BPIOAI.

BPIOAI Standards

Although they are covered later in this book, it's helpful to take a quick look at some standards that provide common mechanisms and semantics for BPIOAI.

RosettaNet. A process-oriented standard created for the technology industry that defines a set of high-level business process flows called Partner Interface Processes (PIPs), which are exchanged and managed between trading partners.

ebXML. Electronic Business Extensible Markup Language (ebXML) is a joint venture between the United Nations Body for Trade Facilitation and Electronic Business and the Organization for the Advancement of Structured Information Standards (OASIS), which are developing a framework for using XML to exchange business data with visibility into common processes.

BPML. The Business Process Modeling Language (BPML) is a meta-language for the modeling of business processes, just as XML is a meta-language for the modeling of business data. BPML provides an abstracted execution model for collaborative and transactional business processes based on the concept of a transactional finite-state machine.

Over the years, many existing business processes have been automated with fair success. But as we have seen with the application integration problem, the problem of how these systems will share information between companies has not received the same attention.

Implementing BPIOAI

Integration of business applications into a BPIOAI solution requires the removal of flow dependency from the application. The routing feature found in most BPIOAI solutions allows relevant information to be extracted from any source application, target application, or data store. It also allows the invocation of application services. The advantage of this solution is that only the model itself needs to be altered when a change in process flow or logic is required. There is no need to change the applications that are part of the process model. In addition, this approach allows you to reuse any source or target system from model to model.

Here, as in almost every other context, appearances are sometimes deceiving. Implementing BPIOAI solutions may very well appear to be relatively straightforward. It isn't. In many respects, it is similar in function to traditional business process re-engineering (BPR) solutions. The primary difference is a layer of automation underneath the model.

You should consider the following issues when implementing a BPIOAI solution:

- Business processes that exist within your enterprise or trading partner must be documented. You must understand all processes and data within the source and target enterprise systems of each trading partner. This is a requirement of every type of application integration solution.
- The missing processes required to tie existing processes together must be defined. You must understand not only how each process works, but also how each must leverage the other to create a more efficient set of processes.
- The processes using BPIOAI technology to tie these processes together must be executed.

Tools and Approaches

As with every type of application integration, a particular set of technologies and tools is available to approach the problem. A BPIOAI modeling tool provides the user with the technology to depict the integration graphically (see Figure 3.12).

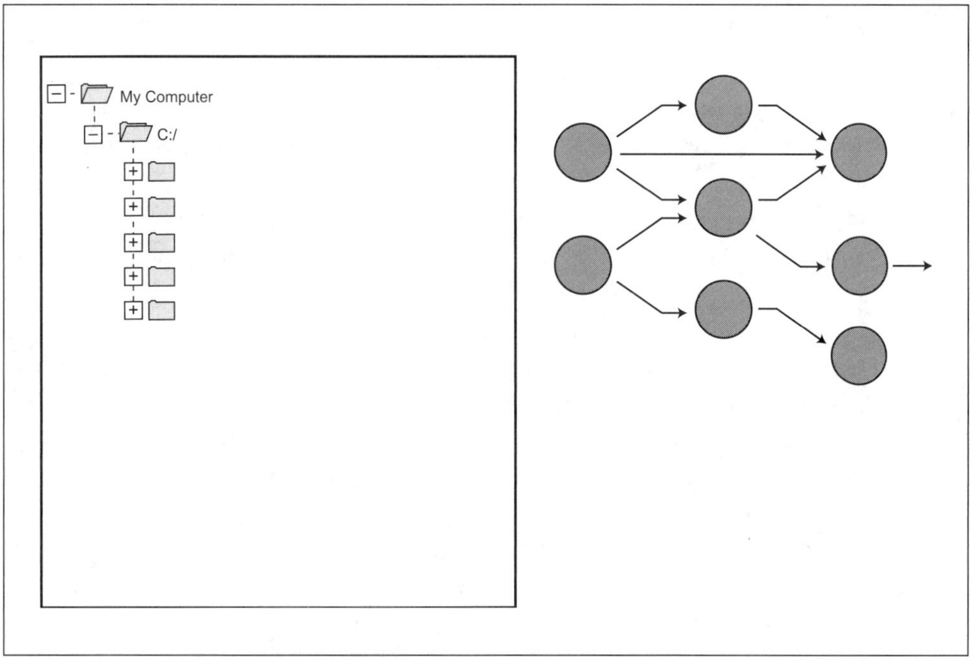

Figure 3.12   BPIOAI-modeling tool.

The components of a BPIOAI model are

- The common process model
- Real entities, such as companies, organizations, or people
- The source and target systems

Although it should be self-evident that every process-modeling tool takes a slightly different approach, each generally models the preceding components. The process-modeling tool binds the components together to create the final solution by modeling

- The processes, either automated or manual
- The sequence of the processes and applicable logic
- The human resources involved in the processes, if any of the activities can take place at the same time
- Visibility into all local processes through events
- Visibility into all data stores through events

Process Modeling

Creating the model using the BPIOAI modeling tool generally means drawing a diagram that depicts the processes, resources (systems and people), logic, the movement of information, and the sharing of application services between the systems. If the process becomes too complex, subprocesses might have to be defined and even reused from model to model. For example, a credit check may be a complex subprocess that is included within many separate processes.

Drawing a process using a BPIOAI modeling tool is simply a matter of selecting items (e.g., resources, processes, and data) from a palette and pasting them on a diagram. Once the diagram is in place, all that remains to be done is to define the process's connections and sequence.

Using this model, we can further define the BPIOAI logic, or the process logic, that is being layered on top of the existing process logic.

Each BPIOAI tool approaches this generic description of activities in very different ways. As time goes on, de facto approaches will emerge and each tool will function in a consistent manner according to a commonly accepted approach.

Middleware Interfaces

A BPIOAI tool is just that—a tool. Without the proper connections to the source or target systems within the enterprise or trading community, the process model that is created using such tools cannot execute a new model. In order to make those connections, we need to employ traditional application integration-enabled middleware such as integration brokers, application servers, and other middleware solutions.

Middleware vendors are seeking ways to incorporate sophisticated BPIOAI within their products, either by building their own product or by licensing a tool from a BPIOAI tool vendor. At the same time, BPIOAI tool vendors are building or licensing the middleware.

BPIOAI and Application Integration

BPIOAI is now a part of most application integration solutions. Once we understand how to connect any data and process point to any other data and process point, workflow will be the way the movement, or flow, of information is managed intra- or interenterprise.

Most application integration middleware vendors are shipping BPIOAI modeling tools to augment their existing middleware solutions. This is a step in the right direction. You may also purchase BPI tools that don't have canned interfaces to source or target systems, but rather require you to create the interfaces. Still, most client organizations will want to pick and choose from the best-of-the-breed solutions. In other words, they will want to mix and match middleware, adapters, and BPIOAI modeling tools. This is not possible today. However, once the industry responds with standard interfaces, definitions, and workflow engines, mixing and matching will be easily accomplished, and the ultimate solution to any particular problem domain will be well within reach.

The customization of BPIOAI models for particular vertical industries is another direction under development. For example, we can create models that define best practices in BPIOAI and integration within any set of banking systems because information moves in very similar ways within all banks (see Figure 3.13). Although sharable vertical-market process models are still a few years away, the potential benefit is plain.

The question remains: How will the next-generation BPIOAI tools and technology add value to a typical enterprise or trading community? As businesses rapidly evolve over time, the need for flexible information movement and integrated infrastructures increases, moving from the information to the process

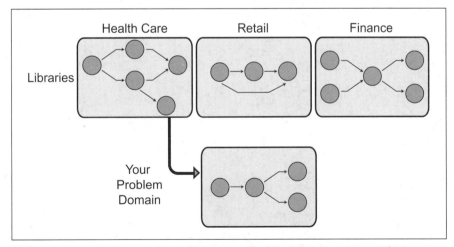

Figure 3.13   BPIOAI models will eventually be shared across vertical industries.

level. Although state-of-the-art application integration solutions (such as integration brokers) provide flexible solutions today, a tremendous amount of work still remains to be done to bind systems together at the back end. Every time things change, similar "plumbing" work must be repeated. BPIOAI will provide the ultimate in flexibility because you, the user, will no longer have to address these issues of plumbing. Most of the complexity will be abstracted for you. This notion will define application integration as the technology moves forward.

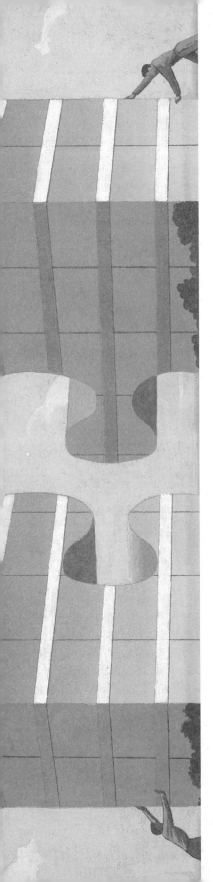

## CHAPTER FOUR

Service-Oriented Application Integration

This chapter describes the next dimension in application integration: the joining of applications together through the exchange of simple information and the linking of application services.

This approach is nothing new; we have been doing this for years through custom coding, or through standards such as distributed objects. However, with the advent of Web services we now have another tool in the shed that will get us to SOAI . . . hopefully, with more success.

You should focus on the concepts more than the mechanisms while reading this chapter. We'll talk more about the mechanisms later in the book. Also, keep in mind that this approach to application integration is more invasive, thus more costly. Therefore, you have to justify its use.

By now we know that application integration is innate to almost all e-Business system development. Applications can no longer exist as standalone entities. Instead they must share information with other information systems, inside and outside corporations. Indeed, organizations have been moving closer to a well-integrated enterprise and (in some instances) supply chain that provides most information systems with access to real-time information from other applications when needed. This Information-Oriented Application Integration (IOAI) is the most popular way of doing application integration today.

However, as real-time information exchange (IOAI) between systems improves, the trend is to view application integration at a higher level of abstraction, or through business processes. This approach allows those exchanging information between various applications to view the information flow in the context of a business model, or business processes that define business logic, sequence, subprocesses, and hierarchies of processes. This ability to control application integration through abstract business process automation abstractions—that also account for lower-level mechanisms such as transformation and intelligent routing—can be called BPIOAI (see Chapter 3).

While IOAI and BPIOAI provide a functional solution for many application integration problem domains, it is the integration of both application services that generally provides more value in the long run, albeit at a cost.

Organizations have been looking for mechanisms to bind applications together at the service level for years. Some successful mechanisms include frameworks, transactions, and distributed objects, which are all in wide use today. However, the notion of Web services, such as Microsoft's .NET strategy, not to mention strategies from IBM, BEA, HP and Sun, is gaining steam. The goal is to identify a new mechanism that can better leverage the power of the Internet to provide access to remote application services through a well-defined interface and directory services. The proper use of Web services in the context of application integration is the future of application integration. Therefore, much of the remainder of this book will concentrate on this aspect of implementation, as well as review competing standards and technologies.

The Basics

Service-Oriented Application Integration (SOAI) allows enterprises to share common application services as well as information. Enterprises accomplish this sharing either by defining application services they can share, and therefore integrate, or by providing the infrastructure for such application service sharing. Application services can be shared either by hosting them on a central server or by accessing them interapplication (e.g., through distributed objects or Web services).

Attempts to share common processes have a long history, one that began more than ten years ago with multitier client/server—a set of shared services on a common server that provided the enterprise with the infrastructure for reuse and now provides for integration—and the distributed object movement. "Reusability" is a valuable objective. A common set of application services among enterprise applications invites reusability and, as a result, significantly reduces the need for redundant application services and/or applications.

Although most application services exist for single-organization use, at times it makes sense to share between organizations. In a new twist on the long-standing practice of reusability, we now hope to expand this sharing beyond intra-enterprise to external enterprises as well—for example, sharing common logic to process customers' credit requests or to calculate shipping costs. This is the notion of Web services, the ability to access remote application services through a well-defined interface (Web Services Description Language, or WSDL), directory (Universal Description, Discovery and Integration, or UDDI), and transport protocol (Simple Object Access Protocol, or SOAP).

Unfortunately, we have yet to achieve absolute reuse on the enterprise level. It is a more distant goal between enterprises. The reasons for this failure are primarily political. They range from internal politics to the inability to select a consistent technology set. In most cases, the actual limit on reuse results directly from a lack of enterprise architecture and central control. With Web services in the picture we now have another opportunity to create an infrastructure that facilitates the sharing of application services as well as information. However, there is a long way between "we're able to do this" and "we've done it." Indeed, it is an evolution in thinking as well as the implementation of technology.

What Is an Application Service?

Good question. Here's a better question: How does an application service differ from information integration?

When using an application service, we leverage a remote method or behavior versus simply extracting or publishing information to a remote system. Moreover, we typically abstract this remote service into another application known as a composite application (see Figure 4.1).

A good example of an application service is a risk analysis process, which runs within an enterprise to calculate the risk of a financial transaction. This remote application service is of little use by itself, but when abstracted into a larger application—for example, a trading system—then that remote application service has additional value.

Note that we leverage the behavior of this remote service more than the information it produces or consumes. If you're a programmer,

(continued)

What Is an Application Service? (*continued*)

you can view application services as subroutines or methods; something you invoke to make something happen.

The basic notion of SOAI is to leverage these remote services using some controlled infrastructure that allows applications to invoke remote application services as if they were local to the application. The result (or goal) is a composite application made up of many local and remote application services. Think about the possibilities.

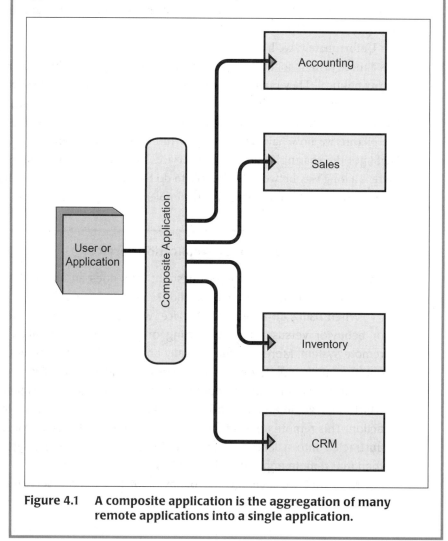

Figure 4.1   A composite application is the aggregation of many remote applications into a single application.

Application integration gives us the tools and techniques to learn how to share common application services. More than that, these tools and techniques create the infrastructure that can make such sharing a reality. By taking advantage of this opportunity, we can integrate applications to share information, even as we provide the infrastructure for the reuse of business logic.

Although IOAI generally does not require changes to source or target applications, SOAI does require changes to most—if not all—enterprise and B2B applications in order to take advantage of the paradigm. This downside makes the service-oriented approach a tough sell between enterprises. Web services promise to change this, putting everyone on the same technology standards, so to speak, but there are still some changes that inevitably have to occur within source and target systems in support of Web services. In other words, most systems that we desire to leverage using SOAI are existing systems, built prior to the arrival of Web services (or other SOAI technology, for that matter). Those systems will have to be changed or rebuilt from scratch.

As noted in Chapter 1, changing applications is a very expensive proposition. In addition to changing application logic, we need to test, integrate, and redeploy the application within the enterprise—a process that often causes costs to spiral upward (see Figure 4.2).

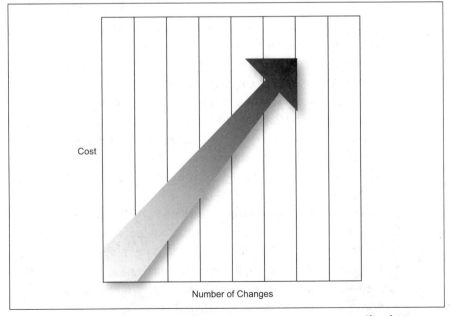

Cost

Number of Changes

**Figure 4.2   As the number of changes to source or target applications
increases, so do the costs.**

When to Leverage SOAI

By now, some of you may be a bit confused about SOAI and its use when establishing B2B connections between two or more organizations. Although many businesses are looking to exchange information with enterprises, and even to participate in shared processes, few are looking to create applications that share application services with systems not under their control.

However, in some instances, SOAI is a good fit.

- When two or more companies need to share common program logic, such as the calculation of shipping costs from a common supplier, which constantly changes.
- When two or more companies want to share the development costs and the value of a common application.
- When the problem domain is small and specialized, and is able to collaborate on a common application that all companies share.

A clear example of the potential benefit of SOAI is the simple binding of two or more applications in order to integrate both business processes and data. Let us assume that two applications exist within a given enterprise. One application is C++ based and runs on a Linux machine. The other is an NT-based client/server application written in Java on the front end, with Sybase serving as the back-end database.

Confronted with these independent applications, the application integration architect seeks to create a composite application using SOAI techniques and technology. To accomplish this, the applications need to be tightly coupled so that common business logic can be shared and the business logic of both applications can be exposed to other applications for future use.

Unlike other application integration levels, at the service level, the architect has no option but to rebuild the applications to support SOAI. The architect has only two choices in determining how to accomplish this. One, she can move much of the business logic to a shared server, such as an application server. Two, she can rebuild each application using an application service-sharing mechanism, such as distributed object technology, to create a tightly coupled application that allows easy cross-accessing of application services.

If the architect decides the second choice is the most attractive, she will have to "wrap" the application logic encapsulated inside both applications. To accomplish this, she will use a distributed object technology (CORBA, COM+, or perhaps Web services) that provides a common mechanism to share application services remotely. This will require rewriting the applications and then testing them. Fortunately, this task is not as daunting as it might appear. Tools exist for each environment to wrap each application, re-creating the applications as truly distributed systems able to share both application services and data.

Even with such tools, the process is laborious. For example, if both applications need to add a common customer to their systems, they may invoke different application services; for example:

```
Add_Cust();
```

on the Linux/C++ system and:

```
AddNewCustomer();
```

on the NT/Java system.

By using a distributed object standard or a custom programming solution, the architect could expose each application service. As a result, she could bind the application services, or invoke one or the other. Once the application services are bound, the applications move to a coupled state where application services and data are easily shared within both domains, thus solving the application integration problem.

Before embracing the invasiveness and expense of SOAI, enterprises must clearly understand both its opportunities and its risks. Only then can they objectively evaluate its value. The opportunity to share business logic that is common to many applications—therefore making it possible to integrate those applications—represents a tremendous benefit. However, that benefit comes with the very real risk that the expense of implementing SOAI will outpace its value.

Enter Web Services

Despite the usual drawbacks of emerging technology, Web services—at least the notion of Web services—is an interesting technology for the world of inter- and intracompany application integration. Web services hold the promise of moving beyond the simple exchange of information—the dominating mechanism for application integration today—to the concept of accessing application services that are encapsulated within old and new applications. This means organizations can not only move information from application to application, they can also create composite applications, leveraging any number of back-end application services found in any number of applications, local or remote. This is the idea behind SOAI.

Key to this concept is figuring out how Web services fit into the existing application integration technology and approaches. For example, when is the use of Web services appropriate and how is cost-effectiveness determined? Keep in mind that implementing Web services is bound to be an invasive process, and

---

Web Services by Example

So, now that we know what Web services are, how do we use them in practice? Say we have a very good application that we build to calculate tariffs on goods coming into the United States, and we would like to allow others outside of our company to access this service using Web services (perhaps for a fee).

To accomplish this we must do the following:

First, change the application so it knows how to expose itself as a Web service; for example, it is able to respond to a SOAP request.

Second, create and send the WSDL to those applications that would like to invoke this service (perhaps send the WSDL to UDDI for more of a global reach).

Finally, the client applications should be able to invoke the server application and execute the service as if it was local to the calling applications—functionally equivalent to an RPC.

After this infrastructure is set up the tariff application service is exposed to the calling applications and accessible as if it were local to the application.

thus more expensive than enabling systems for simple information exchange. We'll cover some of the basics here, and then explore more about Web services later in this book, including specific standards and technologies.

Web Services Exposed

The uses for application services-type of integration are endless, including creation of composite applications, or applications that aggregate the processes/services and information of many applications. For example, using this paradigm, application developers simply need to create the interface, then add the application services by binding the interface to as many Internet-connected application services as required.

Indeed, Web services promise to deliver additional value to application integration, including a standard application service for publishing and subscribing to software services, local and remote. Applications locate the services using UDDI and determine the interface definition using Web Services Description Language (see the following tidbit.)

Think of Web services as application services exposed by a company or software program that are both discoverable and accessible by other programs or organizations that are in need of a particular service, such as purchasing a product, reserving a flight, or calculating tariffs. These are discrete business services that have value to many organizations.

The downside, as we alluded to above, with serviced-based integration is that this makes it necessary to change the source and target applications or worse, in a number of instances, to create a new application (a composite application). This adds cost to the application integration project and is the reason that many choose to stay at the IOAI level going forward. Indeed, most problem domains only require IOAI.

Still, the upside of this approach is that it is consistent with the "baby step" approach most enterprises find comfortable when implementing solutions to integration problems. Service-based solutions (e.g., Web services) tend to be created in a series of small, lower-risk steps.

WSDL

Web Services Description Language provides a standard approach for Web services providers and those who use the services, or a standard agreement between users and services on interfaces. WSDL provides an automated mechanism to generate proxies for Web services using a standard language. This standard is analogous to Interface Definition Languages (IDLs) found in both COM and CORBA. In other words, it's a simple, standard contract between client and server.

WSDL defines an XML grammar to describe network services as a collection of communication endpoints that can exchange information. The WSDL services definition serves as a recipe to automate the way applications communicate.

Within the world of WSDL, services are a collection of network endpoints, also known as ports, and the abstract definition of endpoint. This mechanism provides for the reuse of abstract definitions, or messages. Messages are abstract descriptions of information flowing from application to application, and messages are separated from the data format bindings. Port types, another WSDL entity, are abstract connections of an operation, which is an abstract description of an action that is supported by the service. Bindings are a concrete protocol and data format specification for an instance of a port type.

Where's the Fit?

So, if Web services are coming, and application integration needs this mechanism to add even more value to the enterprise or trading community, how do Web services fit with "traditional" approaches to application integration? The answer has many parts, including:

- Requirement patterns.
- Solution patterns.
- Changing enabling technology.

The fact of the matter is that many inter- and intraenterprise problem domains don't need service-level access to applications; information exchange is good enough, if not desirable. Moreover, most organizations don't have application integration strategies. These organizations need to get their own houses under control first, determine their integration requirements, create a plan, and then select the correct approach to application integration and matching technology. Simply jumping to Web services without understanding the business requirements could be disastrous or, worse, could cause the organization to miss strategic opportunities.

Organizations that require Web services have a need to access both information and application services that exist in local and remote information systems. Typically, these problem domains have the following characteristics:

- There are redundant application services that exist at two or more systems.
- There is a need to create a new application that satisfies a business need, but is also able to leverage aggregated application services from remote systems.
- The information residing within the source or target system is of significantly less value when decoupled from the services.

When applying Web services technology to solve application integration problems, there are patterns or architectures to consider, as well. These are

- Event-driven
- Composite
- Autonomous-distributed

It's also correct to consider these solution patterns as an evolution of the Web services integration technology over time, as well as options.

Event-driven Web services solutions refer to those architectures that deal more with information movement than application service aggregation (see Figure 4.3). Data moves from system to system in support of a particular business transaction, but there is also a requirement to access application services. For example, moving order information from system to system and company to company to support the purchase of a car, or employing a common Web service to calculate logistics information, sharable by all source and target systems. This is a hybrid architecture that mixes both Web services and traditional application integration technology, such as integration servers.

Composite-application solutions refer to architectures that require many application services to aggregate into a single instance of an application (see Figure 4.4). Organizations have been dealing with this paradigm for years as component-oriented programming, where many predefined application compo-

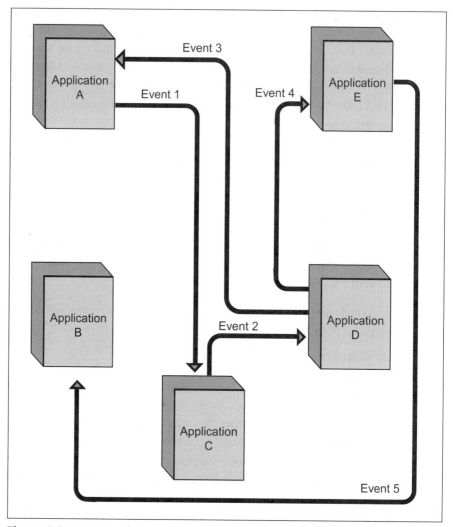

Figure 4.3   Event-driven solution.

nents combine to create a single application. However, within the notion of Web services, the application components reside on a remote computer, and the Web services are accessed as pieces of an application. For instance, the master application that monitors shipments invokes a series of Web services (running on remote computers) that provide application services for logistics processes, least-cost routing, billing, and so on. Going forward, this will be the most popular architecture for Web services, because it's closest to the concept.

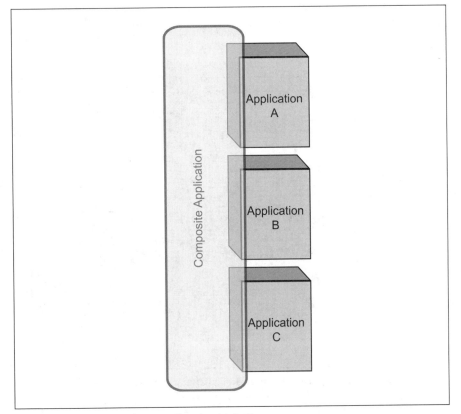

Figure 4.4   Composite-application solution.

Autonomous-distributed solutions refer to those architectures where the Web services are so tightly coupled that they appear as a single application (see Figure 4.5). This is the final destination for Web services, binding many applications together, inter- and intracompany, into a single, unified whole. However, the proliferation of this architecture is years away.

Finally, the enabling technology is morphing to accommodate Web services. In addition to development tools that support the creation of Web services-enabled applications, "traditional" application integration products are moving to Web services through the addition of several new features. These include the creation of new adapters that provide service-level (as well as information-level) access to remote systems, application service-binding mechanisms innate to the server, and interface aggregation to support the combination of many Web services into a single Web service.

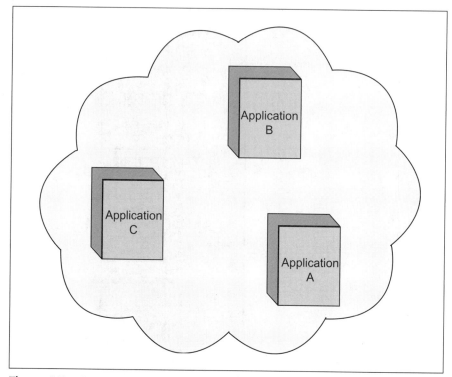

Figure 4.5   Autonomous-distributed solution.

Most adapters were built to support simple information exchange and don't support access to remote application services. These adapters will have to learn how to access application services, abstracting the interface within the integration server. Web services-enabled adapters will emerge sometime in the near future.

However, it does not make much sense to create application service-enabled adapters without an integration server that can process Web services as well as information. This is a bit more complex, but next-generation integration servers are emerging that have the ability to process Web services as well as information, aggregating services within the integration server as required; for example, combining several Web services into one, or passing Web services access between systems. What's more, Web services-enabled integration servers provide enabling mechanisms including WSDL and access to UDDI.

Web services represent an exciting prospect for both application development and application integration. However, like any new concept, it's going to take some time before organizations understand how and where to leverage Web

Missing Pieces

When considering Web services with application integration, there are some missing pieces. For example, Web services don't provide the mechanism to leverage user interfaces. The Web Services User Interface (WSUI) initiative, announced in June 2001, continues to move toward a solution to this problem, but the technical obstacles are significant. In addition, current Web services do not address security well, lacking support for authentication, encryption, and access control. Indeed, Web services do not have the ability to authenticate publishers or consumers of the Web services.

The XML-Based Security Services Technical Committee from the Organization for the Advancement of Structured Information Standards (OASIS) is looking to shore up security within Web services with the Security Assertion Markup Language (SAML). This security standard allows organizations to share authentication information among those they wish to share Web services with as partner organizations. Other emerging security standards include the XML Key Management Specification (XKMS), based on Public Key Infrastructure (PKI).

services in the domain of application integration . . . or in any domain, for that matter. Clearly, first-generation systems are emerging and count on more Web services at work in the near future.

Indeed, organizations need to determine how to move application integration from simple information movement to an application service-sharing infrastructure that provides access to reusable application services—services that allow developers to quickly create robust applications without having to reinvent the wheel. Organizations might find that an aggregation of remotely hosted application services will provide a more efficient and cost-effective paradigm for creating and integrating applications.

Like any other new technology, we must analyze Web services for the real value before pulling it into the enterprise or trading community. Many issues must be considered, including the invasiveness of this technology, the strategic needs of the business, and missing pieces of the standard that are—at this point— mere promises. We'll cover Web services in a lot more detail, later in the book.

UDDI

The Universal Description, Discovery and Integration specification aims to define a common mechanism to both publish and discover information about Web services. IBM, Microsoft, Ariba, and the 63 others that back UDDI hope to create a type of "Yellow Pages" for the Internet.

UDDI is really just a set of databases where businesses can register their Web services as well as locate other Web services they may be interested in leveraging. For example, a company could register a unique program for predicting breakage found in a shipment of glass products, depending on the application service of shipping, point of origin, and destination. That company may publish this information in the UDDI databases, thus allowing other organizations to find this Web service, understand how to access this service programmatically, and understand the interfaces employed.

Scenarios

Before implementing SOAI, we must understand all the processes, application services, and programs that exist within the enterprise. Confronted with such a monumental task, we must initially ask, How best to proceed?

The first step is to break the processes down to their scenarios, or types. For application integration, these types are rules, logic, data, and objects.

A *rule* is an agreed-upon set of conditions. For example, a rule may state that employees may not fly first class on flights of less than 5,000 miles or that all transactions over $1 million must be reported to the government. The rules that exist within a given enterprise are built into the applications in order to control the flow of information. Rules can also be placed in enterprises to control the flow of information between enterprises.

Normally, rules exist in stovepipes—in a single application and accessible by a single department. The challenge of application integration is to provide the infrastructure that will allow the sharing of these rules between organizations. Thus, these rules will become accessible to many applications, either from their current location, or by moving them to a central location.

Rules need to be understood because they affect every aspect of moving data between enterprises, including identifying, processing, and transforming it. In fact, rules processing at the middleware level—through message brokers or process automation tools—will become the first generation of application integration.

Logic differs from rules in that it is simply a sequence of instructions in a program. For example, if this button is pushed, then the screen pops up. The real difficulty in dealing with logic is the consequence of a very basic reality—any ten programmers, given the same set of specifications, may come up with ten slightly different versions of program logic that all function perfectly well. In many ways, logic is as much an art form as a science.

There are three classes of logic: sequential processing, selection, and iteration.

Sequential processing is the series of steps in the actual data processing. Input, output, calculation, and move (copy) are examples of the instructions used in sequential processing. *Selection* is the decision-making dynamic within the program. It is performed by comparing two sets of data and, depending on the results, branching to different parts of the program. *Iteration* is the repetition of a series of steps. It is accomplished with DO loops and FOR loops in high-level languages.

In this context, *data* is nothing more than information that is shared between applications, computers, or humans. Reporting systems, enterprise accounting systems, and human resource systems all share data. Because application services act on data, you need to understand the way in which information is shared at the application service level in order for SOAI to be successful.

Objects are simply data and business services bound as objects. They are bundles of data encapsulated inside an object and surrounded by application services that act upon that data. Objects are so important to SOAI that we will devote much of this chapter to the discussion of the object model and its use within the application integration problem domain.

Objects in systems generally use object-oriented technology, such as C++ or Java. Despite the fact that most objects are service-oriented objects (that is, objects that do something when an interface is invoked; more on these later in this book), the object "mix" may also include distributed objects.

Identifying objects within the problem domain is more complex than identifying business processes. It requires an understanding of the object models used to construct the applications—whether they exist, or, if not, whether they have ever been created. In the absence of the object model, the applications must be re-engineered from the existing code base. (Fortunately, a good set of tools and technologies exist to aid in this re-engineering. Without such tools, the task would demand reading each line of code and creating the object models from scratch.)

Creating object-oriented integration within a B2B problem domain is more than difficult; it may well be impossible. Although its value cannot be disputed, object-oriented integration is a highly invasive process. It demands tight coordination between IT departments within the many different companies that exist in a trading community.

Understanding Service Frameworks

When dealing with Web services, or any service-level integration technology, you must understand the notion of service frameworks and how they differ from more traditional frameworks. This is the idea behind composite applications, which are applications made up mostly of back-end application services.

Service frameworks, in contrast to object frameworks, lack inheritance. Although they provide services, they generally don't provide access to the source code for the distributed objects, making it difficult—though not impossible (depending on the tool or language)—to modify or extend the behavior of distributed objects (e.g., Web services) and service frameworks for an application. As such, service frameworks are the best fit for most application integration problem domains. Distributed object frameworks, including Web services, provide the best example of service frameworks in that they allow applications to invoke application services that are encapsulated in centrally located distributed application services.

Distributed objects, such as those created around CORBA and COM, offer a common approach to create and deploy objects. CORBA-compliant distributed objects are sold through a number of third-party vendors. The Distributed Component Object Model (DCOM) comes with the infrastructure of the Windows operating system. The goal in addressing an integration problem domain is to create a set of distributed objects, using either technology, and then to access those objects either locally or remotely through a well-defined interface from the application that needs a service. For example, distributed objects are built into service frameworks to provide access to accounting functions, financial trading functions, database access functions, and so on. Distributed objects also provide the "plumbing" for easy access to objects that reside on network-connected computers.

As we have noted, object frameworks tend to be tool and language dependent. Distributed objects represent one of the best hopes for frameworks because they offer tool- and language-independent frameworks for applications. C++, PowerBuilder, Delphi, and Smalltalk applications can all access distributed object services.

The ability to mix and match components allows application integration architects to purchase expertise they may not already possess. For example, vertical-market component vendors from the petroleum, financial, and retail industries offer developers specialized functionality that requires little or no custom coding.

In contrast to object frameworks, service frameworks usually contain fewer features and functions than applications, but they provide more services than a simple program function or object (see Figure 4.6). In a number of respects, components are "retro." They adhere more to the modular program model of the past than to object-oriented development.

More Framework Types

Putting aside for now the different types of frameworks that exist, we can examine the three feature categories of frameworks: application service, domain, and support. These categories are consistent among the three framework types.

Application service frameworks, as mentioned in this chapter, encapsulate enterprise application functionality. They provide horizontal functionality across many application integration problem domains. Today most frameworks are examples of application service frameworks. These include the GUI frameworks that come with C++ development tools such as Microsoft Foundation Classes (MFC), Web services, and traditional distributed objects.

Domain frameworks encapsulate expertise for certain problem domains and provide vertical functionality for certain areas of the enterprise (e.g., accounting, marketing, or logistics). These frameworks build common application architectures into a common framework that is shared across applications.

Support frameworks offer native, system-oriented services such as network support, device access, or file access. These frameworks are typically platform dependent.

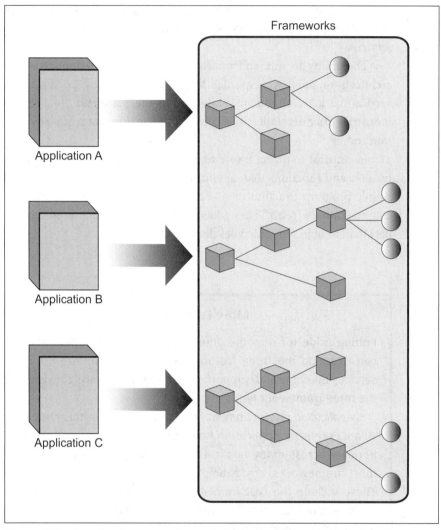

Figure 4.6   Service frameworks contain fewer features than object frameworks.

Moving to Application Services

The road to SOAI is not an easy one, but it may yet be the best route to a solution or to the integration of all applications through the reuse of common application services. Most problem domains that require application integration will likely opt for the other approaches to application integration before attempting SOAI. The former types are easier to deploy and carry less risk. However, "no guts, no glory." Depending on the requirements of the problem domain, the service-level approach, for all its difficulties, could very well turn out to be the "best" solution for the application integration problem. I'm certain it will grow in use as we evolve.

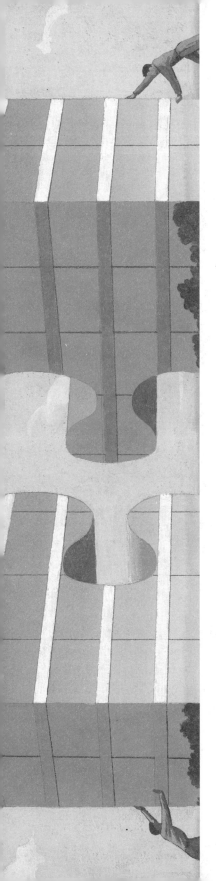

## CHAPTER FIVE

Portal-Oriented Application Integration

In this chapter, we briefly cover the notion of portals; specifically, their use as a form of application integration. Because so much is written about portals, it does not make sense for us to repeat a lot of content here; thus, the chapter is petite.

Focus on the concept of portals, and how we can achieve integration by bringing together information from many different systems within a single user interface.

However, you should also note that portals are not Web services. Indeed, Web services are an enabling technology that may be leveraged by portals. Many are finding the concepts of portals and Web services confusing because both typically bring forward the value of remote applications using a single interface.

Portal-Oriented Application Integration (POAI) allows us to view a multitude of systems—both internal enterprise systems and external enterprise systems—through a single user interface or application. POAI avoids the back-end integration problem altogether by extending the user interface of each system to a common user interface (aggregated user interface)—most often a Web browser (see Figure 5.1). As a result, POAI integrates all participating systems through the browser, although it does not directly integrate the applications within or between the enterprises.

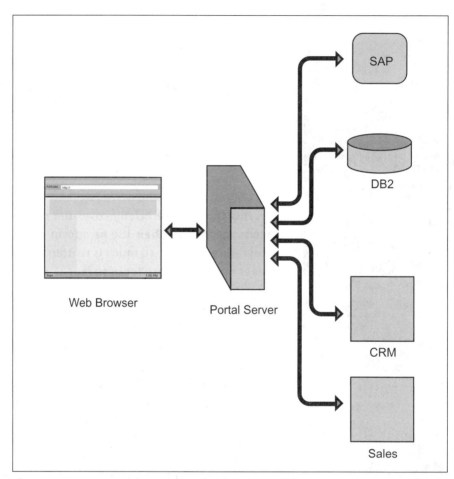

Figure 5.1   Portal-Oriented Application Integration.

Portals have become so common and so much has been written about them that we will cover just the basic concepts here. The important point to remember in the context of application integration is that portals have become the primary mechanism by which we accomplish application integration. Whether that is good, bad, or indifferent doesn't really matter. It is simply the way it is. Trading partners have extended the reach of internal enterprise systems by utilizing the familiar Web browser interface.

**Why Portal-Oriented Application Integration
Deserves Its Own Chapter**

Although the other types of application integration focus on the real-time exchange of information or adherence to a common process model between systems and companies, Portal-Oriented Application Integration is concerned with externalizing information from a multitude of enterprise systems to a single application and interface in support of B2B. That approach goes against the notions of the other types of application integration, which are more real-time and event-driven oriented, so the inclusion in this book of POAI was somewhat of a judgment call.

Although application integration typically refers to the automated movement of information or the binding of processes between two or more applications without the assistance of an end user, it can also occur at the user interface for B2B. Indeed, most examples of B2B information exchange today are also examples of POAI, with digital exchanges leading the way (see the explanation of digital exchanges later in this chapter). Therefore, it's different, but it still belongs within the discussion of application integration.

POAI by Example

An example of POAI is an automobile parts supplier that would like to begin selling parts to retail stores (B2B) using a portal. This portal would allow the retail stores to access catalog information, place orders, and track orders over the Web. Currently, the parts supplier leverages SAP as its preferred inventory control system, and a custom-built mainframe application written in COBOL/DB2 serves as its sales order system. Information from each system is required for the B2B portal, and the portal users need to update those back-end systems as well.

In order to create a portal, the parts supplier must first design the portal application, including the user interface and application behavior, as well as determine which information contained within the back-end systems (SAP and the mainframe) needs to be shared with the portal application. The portal application requires a traditional analysis-and-design life cycle and a local database. This portal application must be able to control user interaction, capturing and processing errors and controlling the transaction from the user interface all the way to the back-end systems.

Although you can employ many types of enabling technologies when creating portals, most portals are built using application servers (discussed in detail later in this book). Application servers provide the interface development environments (IDEs) for designing the user interface, a programming environment to define application behavior, and back-end connectors to move information in and out of back-end systems, including SAP and mainframe systems. Although not integrating the application directly, the portal externalizes the information to the trading partner—in this case, the owner of a retail auto parts store—and also updates the back-end systems—in this case, with orders placed by the store owner or perhaps with the status of existing orders.

Other examples of portals include entire enterprises that are integrated with a single portal application. As many as a dozen companies may provide real-time information for a portal, and hundreds of companies may use that portal, B2B, to purchase goods and services from many companies at the same time. The same type of architecture and enabling technology applies in this case; however, the number of systems integrated with the portal application greatly increases.

Portal Power

The use of portals to integrate enterprises has many advantages. The primary one is that there is no need to integrate back-end systems directly between companies or within enterprises, which eliminates the associated cost or risk. What's more, you usually don't have to worry about circumventing firewalls or application-to-application security, because portals typically do nothing more than Web-enable existing systems from a single enterprise. With portals, you simply connect to each back-end system through a point of integration (user interface, database, application server, etc.) and externalize the information into a common user interface (Web browser). Of course, portals themselves are applications and must be designed, built, and tested like any other enterprise application.

POAI also provides a good facility for Web-enabling existing enterprise systems for any purpose, including B2B and Business-to-Consumer (B2C) selling over the Web. If you need to move information to a user interface for any reason, this is the best approach.

In many application integration problem domains, the users prefer to interact with the back-end systems through a user interface rather than have the systems automatically exchange information behind the scenes (as in data-oriented application integration). Today, more B2B information flows through user interfaces (POAI) than automatically through back-end integration. However, the trend is moving from portals to real-time information exchange, which is the topic of this book. We will eventually remove the end user—who is the most obvious point of latency when considering POAI—from the equation.

The advantages of POAI are clear.

- It supports a true noninvasive approach, allowing other organizations to interact with a company's internal systems through a controlled interface accessible over the Web.
- It is typically much faster to implement than real-time information exchange with back-end systems, such as the data-, service-, and application interface-oriented approaches.
- Its enabling technology is mature, and you can learn from many examples of POAI that exist.

However, there are also disadvantages to portal-level application integration.

- Information does not flow in real time and so requires human interaction. As a result, systems do not automatically react to business events within an enterprise (such as the depletion of inventory).
- Information must be abstracted, most typically, through another application logic layer (e.g., an application server). As a result, some portal-oriented solutions actually add complexity to the solution.
- Security is a significant concern when enterprise data is being extended to users over the Web.

Web-Enabled World

The interest in POAI is driven by the widespread acceptance of the Web as a common platform for e-Business. Today, we purchase products over the Web, update our bank accounts over the Web, even find romance over the Web. Why not exchange information between trading partners over the Web as well?

The notion of POAI has gone through many generations, including single-system portals, multiple-enterprise-system portals, and now, enterprise portals (also known as digital exchanges).

Single-System Portals

Single-system portals, as you might expect, are single enterprise systems that have their user interfaces extended to the Web (see Figure 5.2).

A number of approaches exist to create a portal for a single enterprise system, including application servers, page servers, and technology for translating simple screens to HTML.

Multiple-Enterprise-System Portals

Extending a single-system portal architecture to multiple enterprise systems results in a multiple-enterprise-system portal (see Figure 5.3).

This type of portal represents a classic application server architecture, where information is funneled from several enterprise systems—such as SAP R/3, mainframes, PeopleSoft, and inventory systems—through a single Web-enabled application. Users are able to extract information from these systems and update them through a single Web browser interface accessed over an extranet or over the Web.

Trading Community

When the multiple-enterprise-system portal is extended to include systems that exist within many companies, the result is an enterprise portal (see Figure 5.4).

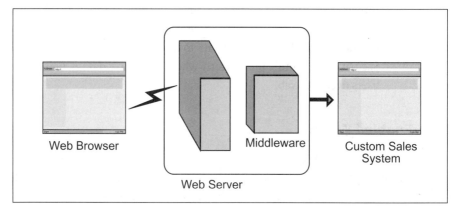

Figure 5.2   Single-system portal.

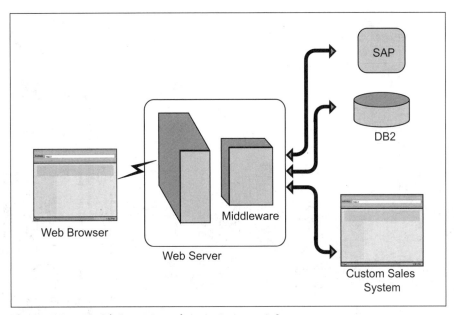

Figure 5.3   Multiple-enterprise-system portal.

Application servers are a good choice for enterprises, funneling information from the connected back-end enterprise systems. However, because hundreds of systems could be connected to this type of portal, it sometimes makes sense to leverage application servers within each enterprise to manage the externalization of information flowing out of the enterprise, then funnel that information through a single master application server and Web server. The result of this structure is the information found in hundreds of systems spread across an enterprise, available to anyone who uses the portal. This is an extremely attractive proposition.

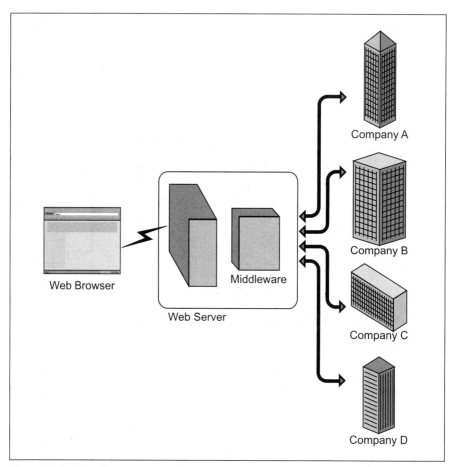

Figure 5.4   Trading community portal.

Portal Architecture

It should be apparent that portals are really Web-enabled applications. Given that reality, it might be a good idea to discuss the architecture and components of portals. The following components comprise portal architecture (see Figure 5.5):

- Web clients
- Web servers
- Database servers
- Back-end applications
- Application servers

Web Clients

The Web client is a PC or any device that runs a Web browser and is capable of displaying HTML and graphics. The Web browser makes requests to the Web server and processes the files the Web server returns. Rather than exchanging messages, the Web client exchanges entire files. Unfortunately, the process is inefficient and resource intensive. Still, with the Web as our preferred common application platform, these drawbacks are also inevitable.

Today, Web browsers need not run on PCs. They can also run on wireless devices such as personal digital assistants (PDAs) and cellular phones.

Web Servers

Web servers, at their core, are file servers. Like traditional file servers, they respond to requests from Web clients, then send the requested file. Web servers are required with portals because the information coming from the application server must be converted into HTML and pumped down to the Web browser using HTTP. HTML, graphics, and multimedia files (audio, video, and animation) have been traditionally stored on Web servers.

Today's Web servers pull double duty. Not only do they serve up file content to hordes of Web clients, but they perform rudimentary application processing, as well. With enabling technologies such as Common Gateway Interface (CGI), Netscape Application Programming Interface (NSAPI), and Internet Server

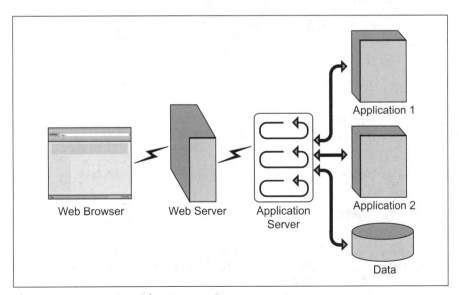

Figure 5.5   Portal architecture and components.

Application Programming Interface (ISAPI), Web servers can query the Web client for information, and then, using Web server APIs, they can pass that information to an external process that runs on the Web server (see Figure 5.6). In many cases, this means users can access information on a database server or on application servers.

Database Servers

Database servers, when leveraged with portals, work just as they do in more traditional client/server architectures—they respond to requests and return information. Sometimes the requests come from Web servers that communicate with the database server through a process existing on the Web server. Sometimes they come directly from Web client communication with the database server via a Call-Level Interface (CLI), such as JDBC for Java or ODBC for ActiveX.

Back-End Applications

Back-end applications are enterprise applications existing either within a single enterprise or across many enterprises. These are typically a mix of ERP systems, such as SAP R/3 or PeopleSoft, custom applications existing on mainframes, and newer client/server systems. Portals gather the appropriate information from these back-end systems and externalize this information through the user interface.

Although the mechanism employed to gather back-end information varies from technology to technology, typically, portal development environments provide connectors or adapters to link to various back-end systems, or they provide APIs to allow developers to bind the back-end systems to the portal technology.

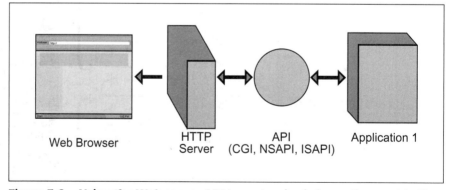

Figure 5.6   Using the Web server API to customize information sent to the client level.

Application Servers

Application servers work with portal applications by providing a middle layer between the back-end applications, databases, and the Web server. Application servers communicate with both the Web server and the resource server using transaction-oriented application development. As with three-tier client/servers, application servers bring load-balancing recovery services and fail-over capabilities to the portal. (Application servers are covered in detail in the context of transactional middleware in Chapter 8.)

What Are Digital Exchanges?

Digital exchanges support the notion of a portal and are loosely defined by a few new vendors. Most digital exchanges are just portal sites set up by a particular industry to support trade within that industry (see Figure 5.7). Anyone can access information through the portal and execute trades, such as the transfer of inventory from one company to another.

Let us say, for example, that a digital exchange is established to create an enterprise for the automotive parts industry. The digital exchange would be able to publish catalogs from various parts suppliers and allow parts-consuming organizations to order parts online. Digital exchanges would also be able to provide information on availability, current price (perhaps bidding between vendors), and logistics, such as when the part will ship and what time it will arrive. This scenario generally accounts for million-dollar trades in support of larger industries. However, smaller digital exchanges are cropping up, such as those that sell day-old bread to retailers. These exchanges, as you might imagine, deal with transactions of less than a thousand dollars.

There are two types of digital exchanges: active and passive. Passive digital exchanges publish catalogs for a particular industry, such as our automotive industry example. They do so with information extracted from a static database and do not support direct interaction with a supplier's information system. At some point, the information is transferred from the operational systems to the digital exchanges and updated as needed. The disadvantage of this method should be obvious. Information published by the digital exchange is not current. Inventory

(continued)

What Are Digital Exchanges? (*continued*)

that shows availability could, in fact, be out of stock—an eventuality that might not be discovered until the supplier organization processes the order.

For this reason, active digital exchanges provide a better solution. Active digital exchanges publish information extracted in real time from the supplier's information systems. The advantage of this approach is up-to-the-minute information presented to the digital exchange user, including up-to-the-second inventory levels. The drawback of this scenario is the investment of time and money required to get an active digital exchange up and running, and integrated with all of the supplier's systems.

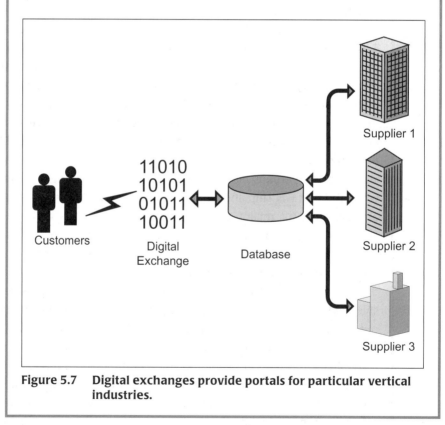

Figure 5.7   Digital exchanges provide portals for particular vertical industries.

Portals and Application Integration

Portals are nothing new. We've been building them since the Web took off and we first understood the value of externalizing existing enterprise data through Web interfaces. That was the birth of B2C e-Business, which led the way to B2B e-Business—which is, after all, what POAI is all about. What is new is the reliance on POAI to support huge transactions and to support enterprises that no longer have to pick up the phone or send a fax to buy, sell, or trade. POAI removes the need for human interaction to support a business transaction. The only requirement is an interaction with a Web browser.

Unfortunately, although they are a necessity today, portals do not support the ultimate goal of application integration—the exchange of business information in real time in support of business events that do not require human interaction. The goals of application integration are to design the user out of the process, thus removing the greatest source of latency in the exchange of information, and to support the new event-driven economy.

## PART II

Application Integration Technology

## CHAPTER SIX

Middleware Basics

This is an introductory chapter, thus not for readers who already have a working knowledge of middleware. Having said that, it's probably not a bad idea for those of you who need a refresher to run through the basics again, including messaging, RPCs, distributed objects, and transaction servers. If you have no need to review these concepts, this can be a jumping-off point for the next several chapters, which cover middleware concepts and technology.

It is important to understand these concepts as we move forward in the book. Many of the more advanced and stylish notions, including Web services, are based on existing middleware models. For example, those who already understand distributed objects will have no problem understanding Web services.

I have devoted the first part of the book to application integration approaches and implementation. In the following chapters, we will concentrate on the technology that makes application integration possible: middleware and standards. This chapter provides an overview of middleware, setting the stage for the following chapters to describe several types of middleware technologies that may assist us in solving the application integration problem.

What Is Middleware?

There are many definitions of middleware. Ultimately, the definition that works best defines middleware in terms of its function. Middleware is a mechanism that allows one entity (application or database) to communicate with another entity, or entities. In other words:

> Middleware is any type of software that facilitates communication between two or more software systems.

Such a broad definition is necessary when you consider that middleware may be as simple as a raw communication pipe running between applications, such as Java's Remote Method Invocation (RMI), or as sophisticated as information-sharing and logic-execution mechanisms, such as Transaction Processing (TP) monitors.

Middleware's import role in the sharing of information means that its importance to the application integration solution is growing more evident. Once it was just a tool for moving information between systems existing within a single enterprise. Now we view middleware as a technology that allows us to move information between multiple enterprises. Middleware conceived and built exclusively for intraenterprise integration presents vendors with a significant challenge, given this new demand on the products.

It is a challenge vendors are anxious to meet. They are aware of the market benefit they will reap by supporting application integration. Of course, in their efforts to claim the marketplace, they are quicker to change their marketing message than they are to change their technology.

Middleware Models

There are two types of middleware models: logical and physical.

The logical middleware model depicts how information moves throughout the enterprise conceptually. In contrast, the physical middleware model depicts both the actual method of information movement and the technology employed.

In order to discuss the logical middleware model, we must first discuss point-to-point and many-to-many configurations, as well as synchronous versus asynchronous. Any examination of the physical middleware model requires a discussion of several messaging models.

Middleware can work in a point-to-point as well as many-to-many (including one-to-many) configuration. Each has its advantages and disadvantages.

Point-to-Point Middleware

Point-to-point middleware uses a simple pipe to allow one application to link to another application: Application A links to Application B. When Application A seeks to communicate with Application B, it simply "shouts down" the pipe using a procedure call, or message (see Figure 6.1).

When compared to other types of middleware, its inability to properly bind more than two applications limits point-to-point middleware. It also lacks any facility for middle-tier processing, such as the ability to house application logic, or the ability to change messages as they flow through the pipe.

There are many examples of point-to-point middleware, including Message-Oriented Middleware (MOM) products (such as MQSeries) and RPCs (such as DCE). While it is possible to link together more than two applications using traditional point-to-point middleware, doing so is generally not a good idea. The purpose of these products is to provide point-to-point solutions, primarily involving only a source and target application. Dealing with more than two applications invites too many complexities. Linking more than two applications with point-to-point middleware requires point-to-point links between all of the applications involved (see Figure 6.2).

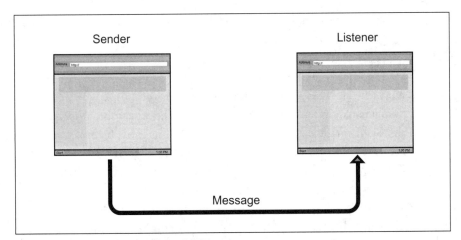

Figure 6.1   Point-to-point middleware.

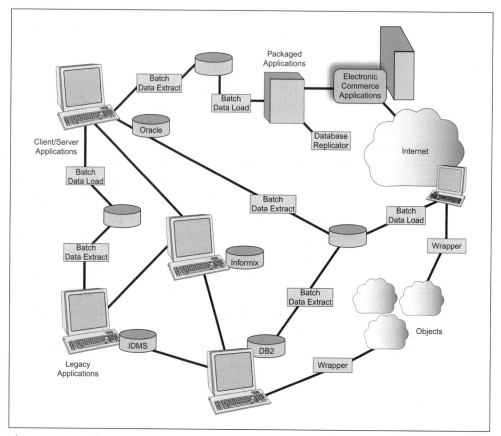

Figure 6.2   Point-to-point middleware does not work well with many applications.

The idea behind the point-to-point model should make it clear that it does not represent an effective application integration solution, given that most problem domains require linking many applications. Perhaps more important, in order to share information in this scenario, applications must be linked and information must be brokered through a shared, centralized server. In other words, sharing information requires a message broker, or transactional middleware.

However, as with all things, these disadvantages are somewhat offset by advantages. The great advantage of point-to-point middleware is its simplicity. Linking only one application to another frees the application integration architect and developer from dealing with the complexities of adapting to the differences between many source and target applications.

Many-to-Many Middleware

As its name implies, many-to-many middleware links many applications to many other applications. This capability makes it the best option for application integration. Being the "best option" makes it the obvious trend in middleware. In addition to this capability to link many-to-many, it is also the most powerful logical middleware model, in that it provides both flexibility and applicability to the application integration problem domain.

There are many examples of many-to-many middleware, including integration servers, transactional middleware (application servers and TP monitors), and even distributed objects. Basically, any type of middleware that can deal with more than two source or target applications at the same time is able to support this model (see Figure 6.3).

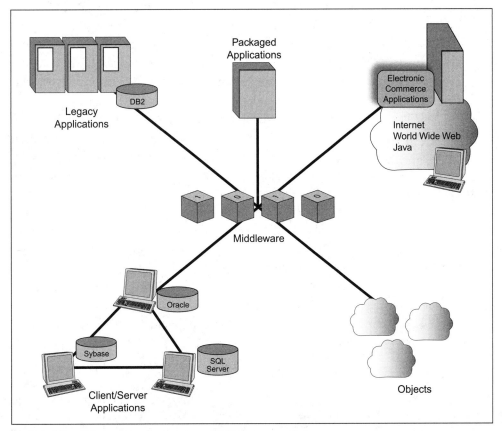

Figure 6.3   The many-to-many middleware model.

While the advantage of the point-to-point model is its simplicity, the disadvantage of the model is its complexity. Although the current generation of middleware products is becoming better at addressing the complexity of linking together so many systems, much work remains. After all, struggling with this complexity falls primarily on the shoulders of the developer.

Synchronous versus Asynchronous

As noted previously, middleware employs two types of communication mechanisms: asynchronous and synchronous.

Asynchronous middleware moves information between one or many applications in an asynchronous mode—that is, the middleware software can decouple itself from the source or target applications. The applications are not dependent on other connected applications for processing. The process that allows this to occur has the application(s) place a message in a queue and then go about its business, waiting for the responses at some later time from the other application(s).

The primary advantage of the asynchronous model is that the middleware will not block the application for processing. Moreover, because the middleware is decoupled from the application, the application can always continue processing, regardless of the state of the other applications.

In contrast, synchronous middleware is tightly coupled to applications. The applications are dependent on the middleware to process one or more function calls at a remote application. As a result, the calling application must halt processing to wait for the remote application to respond. We refer to this middleware as a "blocking" type of middleware.

The disadvantage of the synchronous model rests with the coupling of the application to the middleware and the remote application. Because the application is dependent on the middleware, problems with middleware—such as network or remote server problems—stop the application from processing. In addition, synchronous middleware eats up bandwidth because several calls must be made across the network in support of a synchronous function call. This disadvantage, and its implications, makes it clear that the asynchronous model is the better application integration solution.

Connection-Oriented and Connectionless

Connection-oriented communication means that two parties connect, exchange messages, and then disconnect. Typically this is a synchronous process, but it can also be asynchronous. Connectionless communication means that the calling program does not enter into a connection with the target process. The receiving application simply acts on the request, responding if required.

Direct Communication

In direct communication, the middleware layer accepts the message from the calling program and passes it directly to the remote program. Either direct or queued communication is used with synchronous processing. Direct is usually synchronous in nature, and queued is usually asynchronous. Most RPC-enabled middleware uses the direct communication model.

Queued Communication

Queued communication generally requires a queue manager to place a message in a queue. The remote application then retrieves the message—either shortly after it has been sent, or at any time in the future (barring time-out restrictions). If the calling application requires a response (such as a verification message or data), the information flows back through the queuing mechanism (see Figure 6.4). Most MOM products use queued communication.

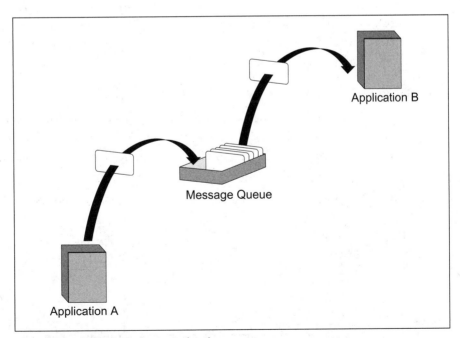

Figure 6.4   Queued communication.

The advantage of the queuing communication model over direct communication rests with the fact that the remote program does not need to be active for the calling program to send a message to it. What's more, queuing communication middleware typically does not block either the calling or the remote programs from proceeding with processing.

Publish/Subscribe

Publish/subscribe (pub/sub) frees an application from the need to understand anything about the target application. All it has to do is send the information it desires to share to a destination contained within the pub/sub engine, or broker. The broker then redistributes the information to any interested applications. For example, if a financial application wishes to make all accounts receivable information available to other applications, it would inform the pub/sub engine. The engine would then make it known that this information was available, and any application could subscribe to that topic to obtain accounts receivable information.

In this scenario, the publisher is the provider of the information. Publishers supply information about a topic, but they don't need to understand anything about the applications that are interested in the information (see Figure 6.5). The subscriber is the recipient, or consumer, of the information. The publisher specifies a topic when it publishes the information. The subscriber specifies a topic that they are interested in. In this scenario, the subscriber receives only accounts receivable information.

Request Response

The request response model is exactly what its name implies. A request is made to an application using request response middleware, and it responds to the request (see Figure 6.6). Examples of request and response middleware include

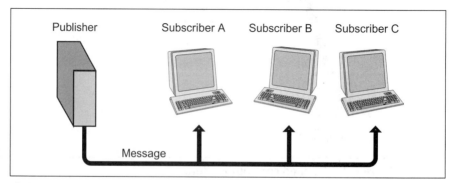

Figure 6.5   The publish and subscribe model.

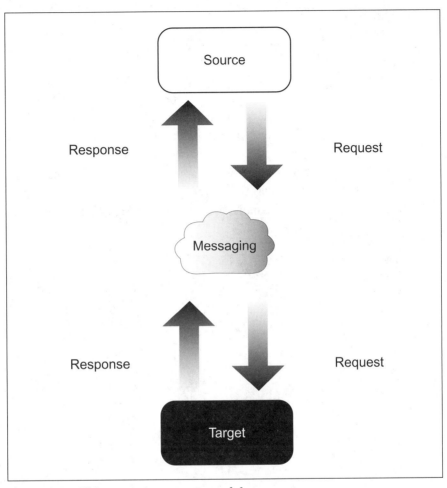

Figure 6.6   The request response model.

any middleware that can facilitate a response from a request between applications, such as integration servers or application servers.

Fire and Forget

The fire and forget model allows the middleware user to "fire off" a message, and then "forget" about it, without worrying about who receives it, or even if the message is ever received. This is another example of an asynchronous approach. The purpose of fire and forget is to allow a source or target application to broadcast specific types of messages to multiple recipients, bypassing auditing and response features. It also allows central servers to fire off messages.

Types of Middleware

The evolution of middleware is changing many of the identifying features that had once made categorizing middleware such a straightforward task. For example, many MOM products now perform publish and subscribe tasks, provide transactional features, and host application logic. The challenge of appropriately categorizing such a product should be plainly evident.

However, even as we acknowledge the difficulty in categorizing middleware, we note that several types of middleware continue to solve particular types of problems. For the purposes of our application integration discussion, we will describe RPCs, MOM, distributed objects, database-oriented middleware, transactional middleware (including TP monitors and application servers), and integration servers (see Figure 6.7).

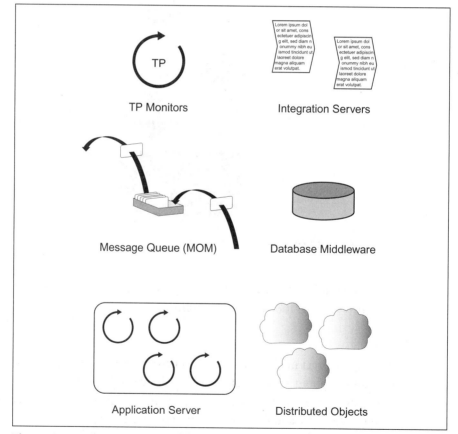

Figure 6.7   **There are many types of middleware, each solving its own set of problems.**

RPCs

RPCs are the oldest type of middleware. They are also the easiest to understand and use. They provide developers with the ability to invoke a function within one program and have that function execute within another program on a remote machine (see Figure 6.8). To the developer, the function executes locally. The fact that it is actually carried out on a remote computer is hidden.

RPCs are synchronous (see the discussion of synchronous functions in the section "Synchronous versus Asynchronous" above). In order to carry out an RPC, the RPC must stop the execution of the program. This quality is what defines RPCs as "blocking middleware." They also require more bandwidth than other types of middleware products because carrying out a remote procedure call requires so much "overhead."

Over the years, RPCs have become a commodity product. For example, most UNIX systems ship RPC development libraries and tools as part of the base operating system. The best known type of RPC is the Distributed Computing Environment (DCE) from the Open Software Foundation (OSF), now the Open Group.

DCE provides a very sophisticated distributed RPC mechanism with many layers of services (such as security, directory, and the ability to maintain integrity between applications). Performance has been a problem with DCE, although the DCE RPC performs as fast as any other RPC. Until quite recently, it worked faster than most implementations of Internet Inter-ORB Protocol (IIOP). The problems are that the DCE directory (Cell Directory Service, or CDS) is not scalable, and administration of a DCE environment can be real ugly. Moreover, for DCE to be effective, it really needs to be deployed everywhere. Very few firms were willing to make a total commitment to DCE.

Despite their simplicity, most RPCs are not well-performing middleware products. To function well, RPCs demand a tremendous level of processing power. Furthermore, many exchanges must take place across a network to carry

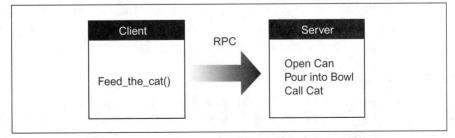

Figure 6.8   **RPCs allow local function calls to execute on remote computers.**

out a request. As a result, they "suck the life" from a network or a computer system. A typical RPC may require 24 distinct steps to complete requests—in addition to several calls across the network. This level of performance limits the benefits of making RPC calls across slower networks, such as the Internet.

RPCs require 10,000 to 15,000 instructions to process a remote request. That's several hundred times the cost of a local procedure call (a simple function call). As is the case with DCE, the RPC software must also make requests to security services to control access to remote applications. Calls to naming services and translation services may be required, as well. All of this inevitably adds to the already-bloated overhead of RPCs.

As we've noted, the advantage of RPCs is simplicity—of the mechanism and the programming. However, when this simplicity is weighed against RPCs' huge performance cost and inability to scale well (unless combined with other middleware mechanisms, such as a TP monitor or message-queuing middleware) it doesn't seem to be such a tremendous benefit.

RPCs are bundled into so many products and technologies that it's difficult to know when they are in use. For example, CORBA-compliant distributed objects are nothing more than an additional layer on top of an RPC. As a result, they rely on synchronous connections to communicate object-to-object (although they now deploy messaging and transaction services as part of the standard). This additional layer translates directly to additional overhead when processing a request between two or more distributed objects.

This structure is the reason distributed objects, although architecturally elegant, generally don't scale, or provide good performance. The Object Management Group (OMG), the consortium of vendors that created CORBA, along with CORBA vendors, are working to solve the performance problem.

Message-Oriented Middleware

RPCs' shortcomings resulted in the creation of MOM to address those shortcomings by the use of messaging. Traditional MOM is queuing software that uses messages—byte-sized units of information that move between applications—as a mechanism to move information from point to point.

Because MOM uses the notion of messages to communicate between applications, direct coupling with the middleware mechanism and the application is not required. MOM products rely on an asynchronous paradigm.

The asynchronous model allows the application to function independently, that is, to continue processing after making a middleware service request. The message is dispatched to a queue manager, which ascertains that the message is delivered to its final destination. Messages returning to the calling application are handled when the calling application finds the time (see Figure 6.9).

Unlike the synchronous paradigm, the asynchronous paradigm does not block the application from processing. Although this model is more complex than the synchronous model, it is more convenient for developers and users. In addition, MOM can ensure delivery of a message from one application to the next for several sophisticated mechanisms, such as message persistence.

Developers find that MOM's use of messages is relatively easy to manage. Messages have a structure (a schema) and content (data). It is possible to think of them as little, one-record databases that move between applications through message-passing mechanisms.

There are two models supported by MOM: point-to-point and message queuing (MQ)—the second being our primary focus here.

MQ has a number of performance advantages over standard RPCs. MQ lets each participating program proceed at its own pace, without interruption from the middleware layer. As a result, the calling program can post a message to the

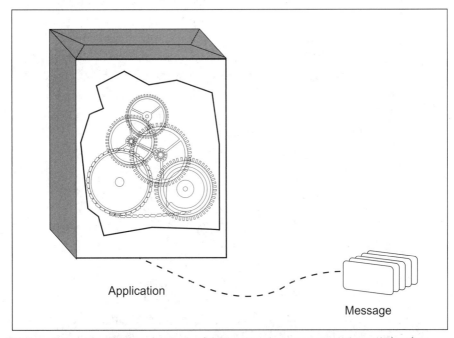

Application

Message

Figure 6.9   Message-oriented middleware does not stop the application from processing.

queue and then "get on with its life." If a response is required, it can get it from the queue later. MQ allows programs to broadcast the same message to many remote programs without having to wait for the remote programs to be up and running.

Because MQ software (e.g., IBM's MQSeries, or Microsoft's MSMQ) manages the distribution of messages from one program to the next (although the program is responsible for putting and pulling messages from the queue), the queue manager can optimize performance by such methods as prioritization, load balancing, and thread pooling.

There is little danger of messages being lost during a network or system failure. Most MQ software allows messages to be declared as persistent or stored to disk during a commit at certain intervals. This ensures recovery from such situations.

Distributed Objects

Distributed objects are classified as middleware because they facilitate interapplication communication. However, they are also mechanisms for application development (in an example of the "middleware paradox"), providing enabling technology for enterprise, or enterprise-wide method sharing. In fact, distributed objects are small application programs that use standard interfaces and protocols to communicate with one another (see Figure 6.10). For example, developers may create a CORBA-compliant distributed object that runs on a UNIX server, and another CORBA-compliant distributed object that runs on an NT server. Because both objects are created using a standard (in this case, CORBA), and both objects use a standard communication protocol (in this case, IIOP), then the objects should be able to exchange information and carry out application functions by invoking each other's methods.

There are two types of distributed objects on the market today: CORBA and Component Object Model (COM). CORBA, created by the OMG in 1991, is more a standard than a technology. It provides specifications that outline the rules that developers should follow when creating a CORBA-compliant distributed object. CORBA is heterogeneous, with CORBA-compliant distributed objects available on most platforms.

COM is a Microsoft-promoted distributed object standard. Like CORBA, COM provides "the rules of the road" for developers who create COM-enabled distributed objects. These rules include interface standards and communication protocols. While there are COM-enabled objects on non-Windows platforms, COM must be considered native to the Windows operating environment, and therefore homogeneous in nature.

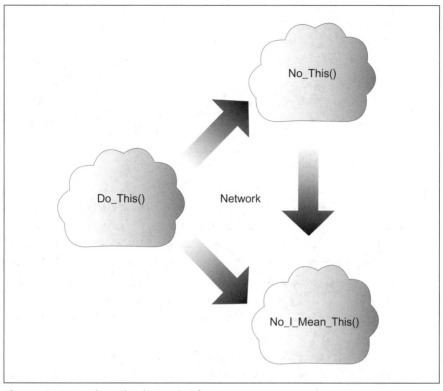

Figure 6.10   Using distributed objects.

Database-Oriented Middleware

Database-oriented middleware is any middleware that facilitates communication with a database, whether from an application or between databases. Developers typically use database-oriented middleware as a mechanism to extract information from either local or remote databases. For example, in order to extract information residing within an Oracle database, the developer may invoke database-oriented middleware to log onto the database, request information, and process the information that has been extracted from the database (see Figure 6.11).

Database-oriented middleware works with two basic database types: Call-Level Interfaces (CLIs) and native database middleware.

While CLIs are common APIs that span several types of databases, providing access to any number of databases through a well-defined common interface, most often we find them working with relational databases. Such is the case with

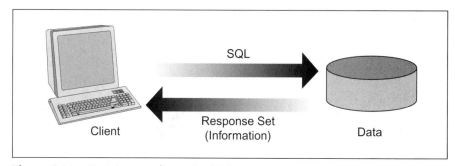

Figure 6.11   Database-oriented middleware.

Microsoft's Open Database Connectivity (ODBC). ODBC exposes a single interface in order to facilitate access to a database. It then uses drivers to accommodate differences between the databases. ODBC also provides simultaneous, multiple-database access to the same interface—in the ODBC architecture, a driver manager can load and unload drivers to facilitate communication between the different databases (e.g., Oracle, Informix, and DB2).

JavaSoft's JDBC is another example of a CLI. JDBC is an interface standard that uses a single set of Java methods to facilitate access to multiple databases. JDBC is very much like ODBC, providing access to any number of databases, and it works from any Java application: applet, servlet, JSP, Enterprise JavaBean (EJB), or standalone application.

Transaction-Oriented Middleware

Transactional middleware, such as TP monitors and application servers, does a commendable job of coordinating information movement and method sharing between many different resources. However, while the transactional paradigm they employ provides an excellent mechanism for method sharing, it is not as effective as simple information sharing—the primary goal of application integration. For example, transactional middleware tends to create a tightly coupled application integration solution, while messaging solutions tend to be more cohesive in nature. In addition, in order to take advantage of transactional middleware, the source and target applications have to be changed.

TP Monitors

In truth, TP monitors are first-generation application servers as well as transactional middleware products. They provide a mechanism to facilitate the communication between two or more applications (see Figure 6.12), as well as a

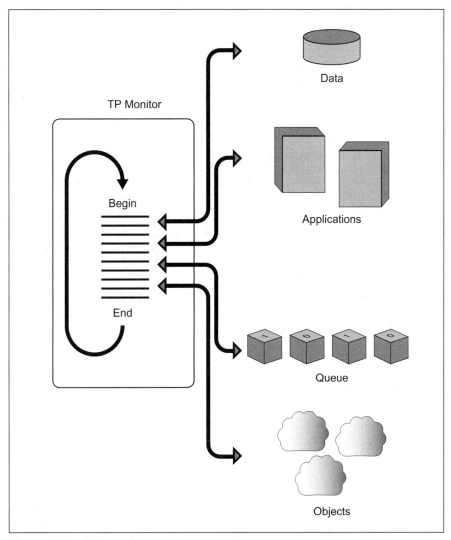

Figure 6.12 TP monitor.

location for application logic. Examples of TP monitors include Tuxedo from BEA Systems, MTS from Microsoft, and CICS from IBM. These products have a long, successful history and continue to process billions of transactions a day.

TP monitors (and application servers) are based on the concept of a transaction—a unit of work with a beginning and an end. The reasoning here is that if the application logic is encapsulated within a transaction, then the transaction either completes or is rolled back completely. If the transaction has been updating remote resources, such as databases and queues, then they, too, will be rolled back if a problem occurs.

Transactions have the advantage of being able to break an application into smaller portions and then invoke those transactions to carry out the bidding of the user, or another connected system. Because transactions are small units of work, they are easily managed and processed within the TP monitor environment. By sharing the processing of these transactions among other connected TP monitors, TP monitors provide enhanced scalability. They can also perform scalability "tricks," such as threading and database connection pooling.

There are two major services performed by the TP monitor. On the one side, a TP monitor provides services that guarantee the integrity of transactions (a transaction service). On the other side, a TP monitor provides resource management and run-time management services (an application service). The two services are orthogonal.

TP monitors provide connectors to resources such as databases, other applications, and queues. These connectors are typically low-level connectors that require some sophisticated application development in order to communicate with these various resources. Once connected, these resources are integrated into the transaction and leveraged as part of the transaction. As a result, they can also recover if a failure occurs.

TP monitors are unequaled when it comes to supporting a high transaction processing load and many clients. They take advantage of queued input buffers to protect against peaks in the workload. If the load increases, the engine is able to press on without a loss in response time. TP monitors can also use priority scheduling to prioritize messages and support server threads, thus saving on the overhead of heavyweight processes. Finally, the load-balancing mechanisms of TP monitors guarantee that no single process takes on an excessive load.

By taking advantage of these features, an application can provide performance as well as availability and scalability.

TP monitors provide queuing, routing, and messaging features, all of which enable distributed application developers to bypass the TP monitor's transactional features. As a result, priorities can be assigned to classes of messages, letting the higher-priority messages receive server resources first.

TP monitors' greatest performance value is in their load-balancing feature, which allows them to respond gracefully to a barrage of transactions. A perfect example of this advantage is end-of-the-month processing. As demand increases, the transaction manager launches more server processes to handle the load even as it kills processes that are no longer required. In addition, the manager can spread the processing load among the processes as the transaction requests occur.

Application Servers

The many new products touting themselves as application servers define the fastest-growing segment of the middleware marketplace. What's interesting about this is that application servers are nothing new (and TP monitors should be considered application servers due to their many common features). Most application servers are employed as Web-enabled middleware, processing transactions from Web-enabled applications. What's more, they employ modern languages such as Java, instead of traditional procedural languages such as C and COBOL (common with TP monitors).

Simply put, application servers provide for application logic sharing and processing, and for connections to back-end resources (see Figure 6.13). These

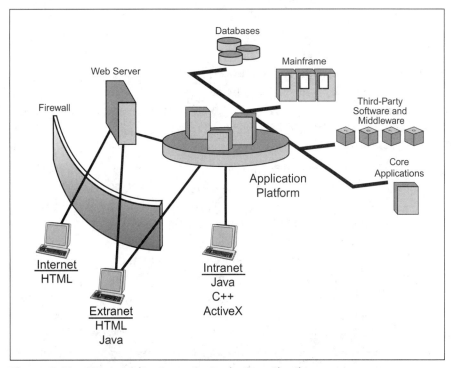

Figure 6.13   The architecture of a typical application server.

resources include databases, ERP applications, and even traditional mainframe applications. Application servers also provide user interface development mechanisms. In addition, they usually provide mechanisms to deploy the application to the Web platform.

Application server vendors are repositioning their products as a technology that solves application integration problems (some without the benefit of a technology that works!). This being the case, application servers, as well as TP monitors, are sure to play a major role in the application integration domain. Many of these vendors are going so far as to incorporate features such as messaging, transformation, and intelligent routing, services that are currently native to integration servers. This area of middleware is in the throes of something more than an evolution. It is in the throes of a genuine revolution.

Integration Servers

Integration servers represent the nirvana of application integration-enabled middleware. At least, the potential of integration servers represents that nirvana. Integration servers can facilitate information movement between two or more resources (source or target applications), and can account for differences in application semantics and platforms. As such, they are a perfect match for application integration (see Figure 6.14).

Integration servers can also join many applications by using common rules and routing engines. They can transform the schema and content of the information as it flows between various applications and databases.

Integration servers, as we have already discussed in previous chapters, are servers that broker messages between two or more source or target applications. In addition to brokering messages, they transform message schemas and alter the content of the messages. They may, indeed, have many additional functions, including a process integration engine and interface, as well as a management mechanism.

The importance of integration servers is a function of their place within the enterprise. In general, integration servers are not an application development-enabling technology. Rather, they are a technology that allows many applications to communicate with one another—without any application necessarily understanding anything about the other applications it shares information with. In short, integration servers "broker" information between applications and databases. By doing so, they broker information between the various source and target systems.

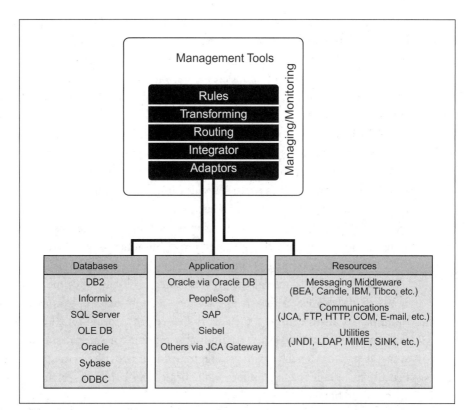

Figure 6.14 **Integration servers are able to share information with a multitude of systems using an asynchronous, event-driven-type mechanism.**

Tough Choices

Ah, wouldn't life be wonderful if there was only one perfect middleware layer choice, one that provided all the features we needed, coupled with unexcelled performance? Well, wake up and smell the coffee. Life may be wonderful, but it's almost never that easy. Before hooking your application to any middleware technology, you need to examine all the technologies and carefully weigh their advantages and disadvantages as they apply to your particular situation.

RPCs are slow, but their blocking nature provides the best data integrity control. For example, while an asynchronous layer to access data may seem to be the best solution, there is no way to guarantee that an update will occur in a timely manner. It is not difficult (especially for us paranoid types) to envision a scenario where an update to a customer database is sitting in a queue, waiting for the database to free up while a data entry clerk is creating a sales transaction using the older data. RPCs may be slow, but they would never allow this kind of situation to occur. When using RPCs, updates are always applied in the correct order. In other words, if data integrity is more important than performance, RPCs may still be your best bet.

Still, as we move forward with application integration, we find that within most enterprises, RPCs are not the best choice. This is a direct consequence of the need for instantaneous processing. We never want to hold up an application while it waits for a trading partner application to respond. As a result, asynchronous middleware is the preferred solution within most enterprises, based on the fact that it does not block an application while it awaits a response from another system. Thus, it supports the notion of long transactions, which are critical to the world of application integration.

MOM vendors contend that synchronous middleware cannot support the needs of today's event-driven applications. Programs simply cannot wait for other programs to complete their work before proceeding. Yet RPCs could provide better performance than traditional store-and-forward messaging layers in some instances. Then again, messaging could provide better performance, because the queue manager offers sophisticated performance-enhancing features such as load balancing.

Middleware remains a great mystery to most people. It is difficult to use, and even more difficult to explain. Most users typically never see middleware plumbing, as they do application development and database products. However, as we go forward, we will see more user interfaces and business layers included with middleware products. The days of the "application program interfaces only" are almost over. Such is the case with newer middleware technologies such as application servers and integration servers that are created from the ground up for application integration. The presence of easy-to-use interfaces will take the power of middleware—at one time, the exclusive domain of the developer—and place it in the hands of the business user.

Clearly, middleware is headed in this direction. It is also how we will ultimately solve the application integration problem.

## CHAPTER SEVEN

Middleware Types and Application Integration: What Works Where?

In this chapter we take a much deeper dive into the world of middleware and look specifically at what types of middleware work for particular types of application integration problem domains.

This is a very important chapter because when architects attempt to solve application integration problems, the trouble they run into is the use of the wrong type of middleware. For example, distributed objects don't work well for problem domains that require a more information-oriented solution, and message-oriented middleware does not support service-oriented solutions. You'll understand the relationships between middleware and application integration solutions by the end of the chapter.

This is a long chapter, but worth the time.

Continuing our discussion from the last chapter, as you may recall, the evolution of middleware is changing many of the identifying features that once made categorizing middleware such a straightforward task. For example, many MOM products now perform publish and subscribe tasks, provide transactional features, and host application logic. The challenge of appropriately categorizing such a product should be plainly evident.

However, even as we acknowledge the difficulty in categorizing middleware, we note that several types of middleware continue to solve particular types of problems. For the purposes of our application integration discussion, we will describe

- RPCs
- MOM
- Distributed objects
- Database-oriented middleware
- Transactional middleware
- Integration servers (covered in the next chapter)

Of course, you can find more in-depth descriptions in many books that focus only on middleware. This chapter focuses on the application of each middleware type in particular application integration problem domains. In other words, which types of middleware solve which problems?

Transactional Middleware and Application Integration

In this section, we will examine those situations in which transactional middleware is a good match for application integration, and we will discuss how to develop application integration around transactional middleware. The first half of the section will be devoted to basic transactional middleware features. The remainder will be devoted to the integration of those features with "traditional" transactional middleware—TP monitors. We will conclude by exploring the new breed of transactional middleware—application servers.

Transactional middleware, including TP monitors and application servers, provides scalability, fault tolerance, and an architecture that centralizes application processing—benefits to distributed computing and application integration that cannot be found in traditional development tools, or even in other types of middleware. Transactional middleware also provides virtual systems and single log-on capabilities. Its strengths often reduce the overall cost of a system.

Transactional middleware can be a good match for application integration because it provides a centralized server capable of processing information from many different resources, such as databases and applications. It ensures delivery of information from one application to the next and supports a distributed architecture (see Figure 7.1). Offsetting transactional middleware's many advantages is the cost of implementation, as well as its intrusiveness, which may preclude its use in many application integration problem domains. For transactional

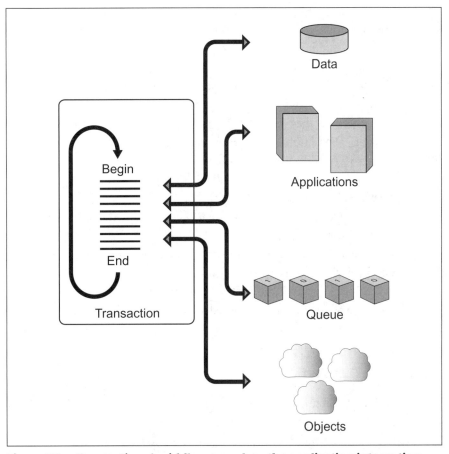

Figure 7.1 **Transactional middleware solves the application integration problem by coordinating the connection of many different resources.**

middleware to be most effective, applications must be altered to use it, an option that is generally forbidden within trading communities.

Despite its invasiveness, transactional middleware is still worth discussing because application servers are a good match for many types of application integration problem domains. Indeed, many application vendors have added application integration features to their products. For example, Portal-Oriented Application Integration, which we discussed in Chapter 5, typically leverages application servers as a mechanism to externalize many applications and data sources through the Web.

Transactional middleware has clear limitations within most application integration problem domains. Although transactional middleware excels at Service-Oriented Application Integration, or at least the sharing of common business logic to promote application integration, none of the current crop of TP monitors or application servers support "out-of-the-box" content transformation or message transformation services—at least not without a lot of programming. Nor do they generally support event-driven information processing. As a result, transactional middleware does not fit well into IOAI. And if method-oriented integration proves to be transactional middleware's only benefit, then much better options may be available to the application integration architect or developer.

Message brokers or traditional message-oriented middleware are better tools for the simple sharing of information between applications. This is not to suggest that transactional middleware is not worthwhile for some application integration projects. However, its greatest benefit is at the application services level. As in all aspects of application integration, architects and developers need to understand the relative advantages and disadvantages of their options so they can make the best choices.

Notion of a Transaction

Transactional middleware is not a new concept. It originated back in the days of the mainframe, at a time when most mainframe databases came with transactional middleware. These were, in fact, TP monitors that managed processes and coordinated access to the database.

To work, transactional middleware requires that complex applications be divided into bite-sized units called transactions. Transactional middleware controls transactions from their beginning to their end, from the client to the resource server and then back again.

In these scenarios, transactions are either all or nothing. Either they work or they do not. A transaction is never left incomplete. As a result, transactional middleware always leaves the system in a stable state. This provides the developer with a consistent and reliable programming model. This stability also makes transactional middleware a natural choice for distributed applications, which must deal with many different databases, queues, and batch interfaces running on heterogeneous platforms (see Figure 7.2).

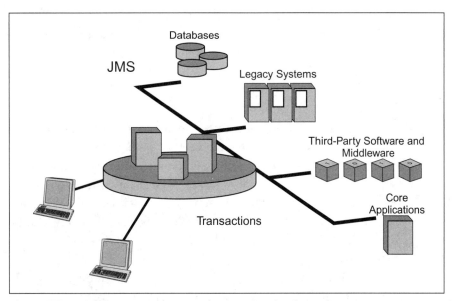

Figure 7.2 **Using transactions to tie together back-end resources.**

The ACID Test

Before delving too deeply into transactional middleware, we must clearly understand the concept of transactions. An easy way to remember the properties of a transaction is to put it to the "ACID" test. That is, a transaction has ACID properties if it is Automic, Consistent, Isolated, and Durable.

Automic refers to the all-or-nothing quality of transactions. Either the transaction completes, or it does not. There is no available middle ground. *Consistent* refers to the fact that the system is always in a consistent state, regardless of whether or not it completes the transaction. *Isolated* refers to the transaction's ability to work independently of other transactions that may be running in the same TP monitor environment. *Durable* means that the transaction, once committed and complete, can survive system failures.

Although the ACID test might oversimplify the concept of a transaction, it provides an easy acronym for remembering the features and functions of transactional middleware.

Developers can count on a high degree of application integrity with transactional middleware—even in heterogeneous environments of very different operating systems and databases. The most important benefit of transactional middleware is that a transaction is always secure. Even when other things go wrong, transactional middleware won't allow those problems to affect any other transaction, application, or data.

Scalable Development

Transactional middleware processes transactions on behalf of the client or node. It can route transactions through many diversified systems, depending on the requirements of the application integration problem domain. For example, it is not unusual for a TP monitor to tie together a mainframe, an NT server, a multi-processing UNIX server, and a file server. Transactional middleware also provides load balancing, thread pooling, object recycling, and the ability to automatically recover from typical system problems. All of this allows this type of middleware to scale to a transaction load that will drive even the largest businesses.

Although transactional middleware is correctly—though only technically—referred to as middleware, it is much more than a simple middleware connection layer. It provides a location for the application code to run and, as a result, a location for business processing and application objects to run. It is also a location where application services can be shared among applications. Transactional middleware can be used to enforce business rules and maintain data integrity, or to create entire applications by building many transaction services and invoking them from the client.

Database Multiplexing

One of transactional middleware's great benefits is its ability to multiplex and manage transactions, thereby reducing the number of connections and processing loads that larger systems place on a database. With transactional middleware in the architecture, you can increase the number of clients without increasing the size of a database server. For example, by using a TP monitor requiring approximately 50 connections, more than 1,000 clients can access the database server.

By "funneling" client requests, transactional middleware removes the "process-per-client" requirement (see Figure 7.3). In such a scenario (also known as database connection pooling), a client simply invokes the transaction services that reside on the TP monitor, and those services can share the same database server connections (threads and processes). If a connection overloads, the TP monitor simply starts a new connection to the database server. This is the foundation of

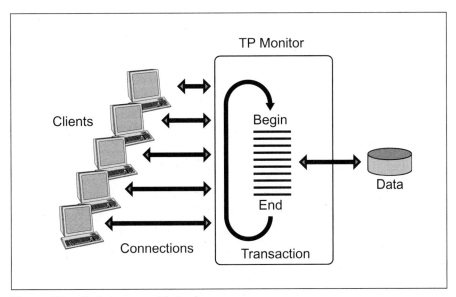

Figure 7.3   Database multiplexing.

three-tier architecture and the explanation for how three-tier architecture can scale to high user loads.

Load Balancing

Load balancing happens when the number of incoming client requests surpasses the number of shared processes the system is able to handle and other processes start automatically. Some transactional middleware can dynamically distribute the process load over several servers at the same time or distribute the processing over several processors in multiprocessing environments.

The load-balancing features of transactional middleware enable it to define "classes" of tasks and therefore prioritize tasks. This capability assures VIP clients of top-notch service. High-priority classes kick up the process priorities. As a rule, developers use high-priority server classes to encapsulate short-running, high-priority functions. Low-priority processes (such as batch processes) run inside low-priority server classes. Developers can also assign priorities by application type, the resource managers required by a transaction, high and low response times, or the fault tolerance of a transaction. By defining any number of parameters, developers can control the number of processes, or threads, available for each transaction.

Fault Tolerance

Transactional middleware was built from the ground up to provide a robust application deployment environment with the ability to recover from any number of system-related problems. Redundant systems guarantee high availability. For example, transactional middleware uses dynamic switching to reroute transactions around server and network problems. The transactions work through a two-phase-commit process that ensures that the transactions complete and guards against transactions becoming lost electrons when hardware, operating systems, or networks fail. Two-phase commit also ensures that reliable transactions can be performed on two or more heterogeneous resources.

If the power fails, transactional middleware alerts all participants in a particular transaction (server, queues, clients, etc.) of the problem. All work accomplished up to that point in the transaction is rolled back, and the system returns to its "pretransaction" state, cleaning up any mess it may have left. Developers sometimes build transactions that automatically resubmit after a failure. The ability to create an automatic-resubmit feature is highly desirable in the context of an application integration problem domain because transactional middleware ensures delivery of the information being shared by the source and target applications. This beneficial feature has not escaped the notice of message broker vendors. Many vendors are now working to provide transactional integrity in their products.

Communication

Transactional middleware is a good example of middleware that uses middleware, including message brokers. Transactional middleware communicates in a variety of ways—including RPCs (specialized for transactional middleware and called transactional RPCs, or TRPCs), distributed dynamic program links (DPLs), interprocess communication, and MOM. Because transactional middleware is simply an API within an application, developers have the flexibility to mix and match a variety of middleware layers and resource servers to meet the requirements of an application or application integration problem domain.

Application Servers

To this point, we've devoted our discussion of transactional middleware to general terms, highlighting the features and functions of TP monitors as prime examples of transactional middleware. We should never underestimate the importance of

TP monitors. Even so, we must also consider a different breed of transactional middleware.

Application servers not only provide a location for application logic and interface processing, they also coordinate many resource connections (see Figure 7.4). They are typically Web-enabled and bring transaction processing to the Web through any number of mechanisms (see the tidbit "Considering Object State Management and Application Servers" later in this section).

The new application servers tend to support Java as both the native language and the development model (although in different ways) as they progress toward the new world of Enterprise JavaBeans, or EJB (described in the section "Enterprise JavaBeans" later in this chapter).

Application servers take many existing enterprise systems and expose them through a single user interface, typically a Web browser. For example, application servers can easily externalize information contained in mainframes, ERP

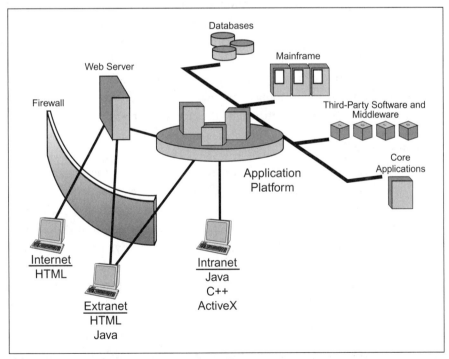

Figure 7.4   Application servers provide both a location for application logic and a mechanism to coordinate connections to remote resources.

applications, and even middleware without a user interface. As a result, developers can gain all the application development capabilities they require, including a programming language and an integrated development environment. This makes application servers ideal for Portal-Oriented Application Integration.

As always, technology gives and technology takes. Where there are strengths, there are also weaknesses. Application servers are not strong players in back-end integration or application-to-application integration, when the information is rarely externalized through a user interface. This weakness is a direct result of the need to code all parts of the information extraction, transformation, and update process, typically through traditional transaction semantics.

Because application servers were created for Web-based transactions and application development, their benefit to application integration is obvious. What makes them invaluable in this context is their ability to perform back-end integration (to bind together several source and target applications through a series of connectors provided by the application server vendors—for example, SAP, PeopleSoft, Baan,—relational databases, and middleware).

In addition to being a mechanism for integration, application servers provide an up-to-date approach to sharing methods. Unfortunately, each application server has its own approach to how this happens. Because of this "individuality," making sound decisions about the selection of an application server—or application servers—for an application integration project requires an understanding of both the category of features and the problem at hand.

Evolving Transactions

Application servers have been used extensively over the years, as have enabling mechanisms such as distributed objects. However, new demands have forced us to re-examine this paradigm, adding up-to-date products such as those built around the notion of processing components with transactionality. This re-examination and development provides us with a dynamic window into the evolution of the technology. And what we see is that the progress is uneven. Despite the development of application servers, TP monitors remain far ahead in performance and reliability. By the same token, application servers have surpassed TP monitors in certain respects, such as having more advanced features (an integrated development environment, for example).

Taking the strengths and weaknesses of application servers into account, we can clearly see their benefit. By placing some or most of the application logic on a middle tier, developers can exert increased control over the application logic through centralization. Such placement increases the ability to scale the application

---

Considering Object State Management and Application Servers

Most application servers use a stateless model to provide component processing environments, enhancing scalability through the recycling of an object in the memory of the application server. Rather than destroy and re-create objects for every connected node, the application server maintains a pool of objects to hand out to any external process-requesting service.

The stateless component model has the advantage of improved scalability. Unfortunately, it also has two major disadvantages: First, it does not support multiple references to the properties of an object. As a result, it does very little to support object reuse through the object-oriented programming model. Second, it has to create a new object for each database request, resulting in a performance hit when object data is loaded from a back-end database.

---

through a set of tricks, such as database multiplexing and load balancing, described previously. The end result is a traditional three-tier client/server computing model (see Figure 7.5), consisting of a presentation layer (the part that presents the information to the client), an application layer (the middle-tier application logic), and a data layer (where the data resides).

The two dominating standards are Java, with its Enterprise JavaBeans initiative (also closely tied to CORBA), and COM+, integrating with products such as Microsoft Transaction Server (MTS) and Microsoft AppCenter.

Enterprise JavaBeans

The primary difference between application servers and traditional transactional middleware (such as TP monitors) is that application servers can function around the notion of transactional components. Nearly every application server that uses this transactional component-type architecture looks to employ EJB as the enabling standard. However, each application server accomplishes this in its own special way.

This awkward reality is partially the result of standards that are still in a state of flux. Sun is working hard to address the issue of an EJB standard and build a certification process.

Although EJBs are really Java-enabled middleware (and therefore a topic to be covered later), their discussion is appropriate in the context of application servers because they add the most value to transactional middleware.

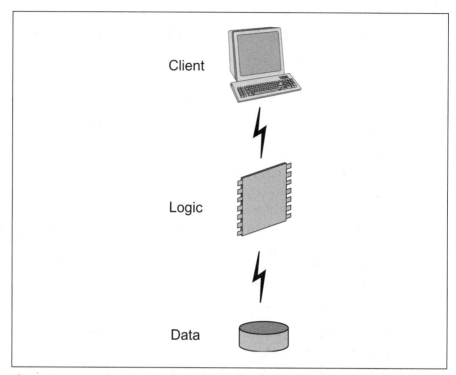

Figure 7.5   Application architecture, using an application server.

The EJB specifications (see www.java.sun.com) define a server-side component model for JavaBeans (see Figure 7.6). EJBs represent specialized JavaBeans that run on a remote server (known as the EJB container). From the architecture point of view, EJBs look very similar to distributed objects such as COM and CORBA.

EJBs use the same architecture as traditional JavaBeans. They can be clustered together to create a distributed application with a mechanism to coordinate processing that occurs within the JavaBeans. As such, they reside on application servers, which process the beans as transactional components.

The EJB model supports the notion of implicit transactions. EJBs do not need to specify the transactional demarcation point in order to participate in distributed transactions. This feature represents an essential benefit to the model. The EJB execution environment automatically manages the transaction on behalf of the EJBs, using transaction policies that can be defined with standard procedures during the deployment process. Of even greater benefit, transactions may be controlled by the client-side applications.

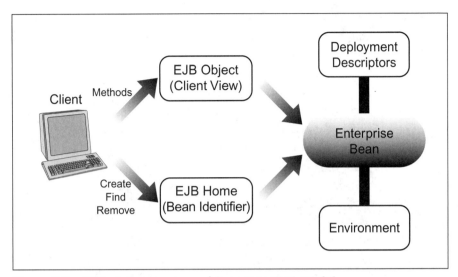

Figure 7.6   EJBs define a server-side component model.

Although the EJB model defines the relationship between an EJB component and an EJB container system, EJBs do not require the use of a specific container system. Any application execution system (such as an application server) can be adapted to support EJBs by adding support for services defined in the EJB specification; services that define the specified relationships between EJBs and a container. The application execution system also provides a portability layer. As a result, EJBs can run in any execution system (EJB container) that supports the EJB standard.

An EJB execution system is called an EJB Server. It provides a standard set of services to support EJB components. EJBs and the EJB Server are analogous to traditional transactional systems. Thus, an EJB Server must provide access to a standard distributed transaction-management mechanism.

An EJB container brings into play the management and control services for a class of EJB objects. In addition, this system provides life-cycle management, transaction control, persistence management, and security services. The larger concept and benefit here is that EJB allows a single vendor to provide both the EJB Server and the associated EJB container.

Transactional COM+ (Using AppCenter)

In a strategy similar to the one employed with EJBs, Microsoft plans to support transactionality through COM+ and AppCenter. AppCenter provides an environment to process transactional COM+ components along with traditional TP monitor features, such as support for ACID, database access, and recoverability.

The sophisticated application server architecture of Windows XP is a notable plus, as are the hundreds of application development tools available for the Windows 2000 platform. However, this may very well be a comment more about what runs on Windows XP than how well something runs.

Component-Dynamic Load Balancing within Windows 2000 supports up to eight connected application servers (nodes). This enables application developers to process one or many COM+ components across a cluster using AppCenter Server. In reality, an AppCenter Server is a Microsoft Transaction Server for transaction support and a Microsoft Message Queue (MSMQ) server for message queuing support all rolled into a single distributed COM+ processing environment. AppCenter acts as a router, using server response time to find the least-busy server to create COM+ components for processing. As a result, it balances the load.

The market for AppCenter consists of those organizations seeking to support both Web- and enterprise-based application processing loads that exceed a single server or symmetric multiprocessing (SMP)-based server.

Component-Dynamic Load Balancing is built to compete with the high-end application servers. These products work primarily with the Enterprise JavaBeans standard from Sun, providing a similar component-processing model on both Microsoft and non-Microsoft platforms. Unfortunately for Microsoft, MTS never got the traction it had hoped to receive. AppCenter is Microsoft's attempt to roll over the existing leaders.

RPCs, Messaging, and Application Integration

Two considerations make our discussion of MOM and RPC-based middleware both brief and possibly irrelevant. First, message-oriented middleware and RPC-based middleware tend to be traditional, point-to-point middleware and therefore ineffective solutions for most application integration projects. Second, there isn't a great deal we can add to what has already been published on the subject.

Because of these considerations, we are confronted with the question, Why devote time and energy to a discussion of this technology if it isn't an effective component of the solution set? The answer is simple and straightforward. We need to understand point-to-point middleware to integrate it within the enterprise. Our discussion will therefore center on the application of this technology to the new application integration space and on the evolution of this technology in support of application integration.

Middleware itself is a common point of integration for source and target systems. Despite the limitations of MOM and RPC-based middleware for application integration solutions, the necessary tradeoffs in both technology and product decisions may make the inclusion of this middleware important to a particular application integration problem domain.

RPCs

As we noted in an earlier chapter, RPCs are nothing more than a method of communicating with a remote computer, a method in which the developer invokes a procedure on the server by making a simple function call on the client (see Figure 7.7). By functioning in this way, RPCs hide the intricacies of the network

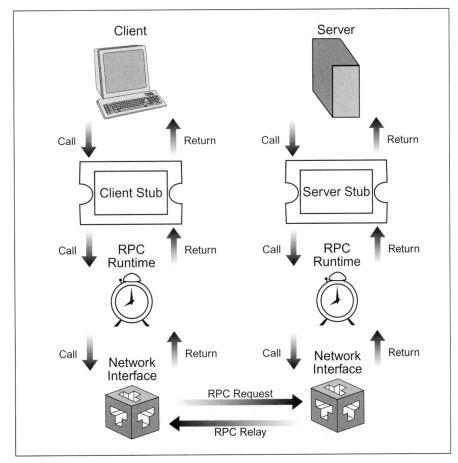

Figure 7.7   Using RPCs.

and operating system. (Remember, the client process that calls the remote function must suspend itself until the procedure completes.)

RPCs are easy to understand and just as easy to use. Even so, they can be problematic when incorporated into an application integration problem domain. The need to stop an application from processing during a remote call could limit the performance of the application. In addition, because RPCs demand a high level of network communication between the client and the server, RPC architecture requires a high-speed network. Most application integration solutions run across the Internet, which is anything but high speed.

RPCs formed the base middleware layers in early client/server systems. Then, as now, they functioned as database-oriented middleware layers. In addition, they are capable of running network operating systems, such as Sun's Network File System (NFS) and Open Software Foundation's DCE. Distributed object technology, such as COM and CORBA, effectively leverage RPCs to provide object-to-object communication.

Message-Oriented Middleware

When bandwidth that can support RPCs is absent, or in a situation where a server cannot be depended upon to always be up and running, message-oriented middleware may be the better choice for an application integration project. Like RPCs, MOM provides a standard API across hardware, operating system platforms, and networks (see Figure 7.8). MOM has the additional benefit of being able to guarantee that messages will reach their destination—even when the destination is not available at the time the messages are sent.

MOM utilizes one of two "macro-messaging" models: process-to-process or message queuing. In the process-to-process model, to exchange messages, both the sending and receiving processes must be active. In the queuing model, only one process must be active because messages can be stored in a queue. The queuing model is best when communication takes place between computers that are not always up and running, over networks that are not always dependable, or when there is a limitation on bandwidth. When taking MOM usage into account, it's no surprise that we see movement from process-to-process to queuing.

Unlike RPCs, which block processing until the procedure call returns, MOM is asynchronous and consequently allows the application to process when the middleware API is invoked. MOM message functions can return immediately, even though the request has not been completed. This allows the application to continue processing, assured that it will know when the request is completed.

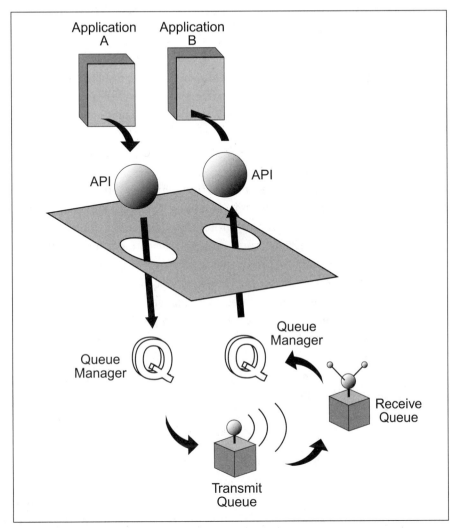

Figure 7.8   MOM provides an API to allow programmers to access its services.

The queuing model works best with transaction-oriented application integration applications that must traverse many platforms. Unlike DCE, the queuing model does not require that the platform be up and running for an application to request services. If the server is down, the request remains in a queue. As soon as the server comes back online, the request is processed. In addition to these queuing features, MOM provides concurrent execution features that allow processing of more than one request at a time.

Aren't Message Brokers MOM?

Of course they are. After all, they use messaging as the primary form of communication. Technically, that makes them MOM. However, for the purposes of this section's discussion, when we refer to MOM, we are referring to more traditional MOM, or message-queuing software. In fact, many people now call message brokers "integration brokers" because of their complexity and specialized purpose of many-to-many application integration.

Queuing software requires that you use an API to change both source and target systems, adapting them to the middleware. They almost always function point-to-point (one application to one application). In contrast, message brokers can connect many applications to many applications. They provide message transformation, routing, and rules-processing services. They can also leverage adapters that minimize the impact on the integrated applications.

Message brokers seem to provide a good fit for application integration. Traditional messaging middleware generally does not. Message brokers are so important to application integration that they deserve their own middleware category, a category we will deal with more completely later in this book.

With all these beneficial features, when should MOM be applied? It is a good choice for store-and-forward communication, or when dealing with applications that are not expected to be reachable at the same time. MOM is a good choice for "defensive communication"—communication between applications when networks frequently fail. MOM is also a good choice for journaled communication—when communication between processes needs to be logged.

Overall, MOM and messaging tend to be better application integration choices than RPC-based middleware. However, if we've learned anything during our examination of application integration solutions, it is that there is no single, objective "best" choice. Most solutions require a certain amount of thoughtful mixing and matching. MOM is no different in this respect. By itself, it does not provide the complete infrastructure necessary for application integration. Message brokers add value to traditional MOM products by providing data and

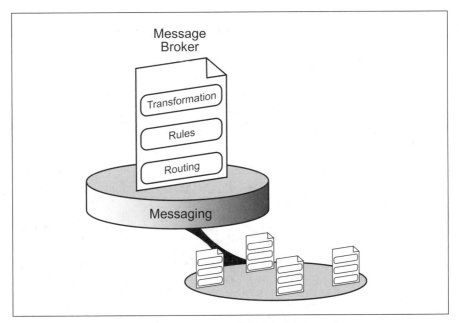

Figure 7.9   Message brokers may use MOM to transport messages.

schema transformation functions, along with intelligent routing and event-driven processing to move information throughout an enterprise. Such a scenario relies on MOM products as little more than functional transport layers (see Figure 7.9).

Examples of MOM

Each MOM product delivers messaging in its own way. Two of the most popular MOM products—MSMQ from Microsoft and MQSeries from IBM—give us insight into how different products approach their tasks.

In the world of MOM, IBM's MQSeries is the proverbial 800-pound gorilla. With a queuing middleware market share of over 65 percent, it can do just about anything it pleases. Although it may not be the most feature-rich messaging middleware product, MQSeries sits atop the application integration world as the preferred messaging layer for moving information throughout an enterprise.

(continued)

Examples of MOM (*continued*)

The most notable benefit of MQSeries is the number of platforms it supports. MQSeries works with IBM OS/390, Pyramid, Open VMS, IBM AIX, NCR UNIX, UP-UX, Solaris, OS/2, Windows NT, SCO UNIX, MacOS, and many others. MQSeries supports all the features of MSMQ, including support for transactions, journaling, message routing, and priorities. MQSeries also provides a common API for use across a variety of development environments. (These interfaces are sold by third-party vendors.)

MQSeries products provide a single, multiplatform API. As a result, messages can be sent from a Windows 2000 workstation and routed through UNIX, VMS, or even a mainframe before reaching their final destination. Platforms running MQSeries work in concert, ensuring that messages are delivered to their destination (see Figures 7.10 a and b). They can also route around network and system failures. MQSeries can be used as a transactional recovery method and a mail transport mechanism, ensuring the delivery of messages.

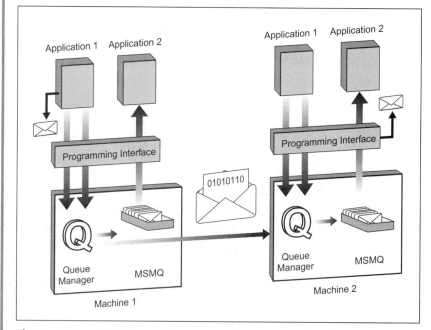

Figure 7.10a   MSMQ provides messaging queuing for Windows.

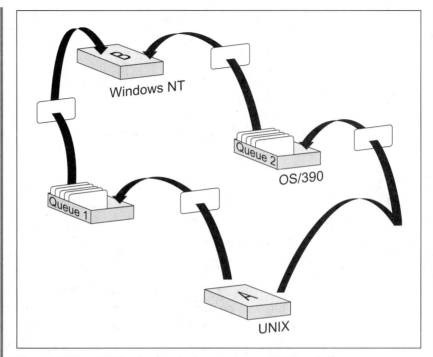

Figure 7.10b   MQSeries is a heterogeneous MOM solution.

MQSeries supports what IBM refers to as an "advanced message framework." This framework consists of three layers: customer application options, a trusted messaging backbone, and comprehensive communication choices (see Figure 7.11). The customer application options provide services such as basic messaging, transactional messaging, workflow computing, mail messaging, option messaging, cooperative processing, data replication, and mobile messaging. Transactional messaging allows developers to coordinate message flow with updates to other resource managers. (For example, several databases on different platforms can be updated at the same time.) The mail-messaging feature allows any Vendor-Independent Messaging (VIM) or Mail API (MAPI) application to transmit e-mail securely and reliably by leveraging the power of MQSeries' messaging infrastructure. MQSeries supports messaging between distributed objects and facilitates cooperative processing between two or more processes.

(continued)

Examples of MOM (*continued*)

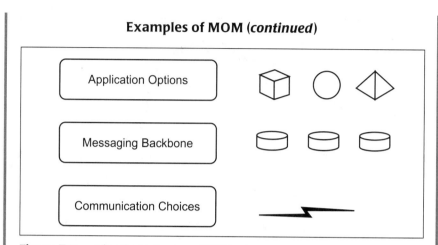

Figure 7.11   The three layers of MQSeries.

MQSeries' messaging backbone guarantees that messages are delivered to their destinations and that the information encapsulated in those messages is secure. Its comprehensive communication choices allow it to leverage any number of protocols and networks for message traffic.

The latest version of MQSeries offers a peek at "things to come" in messaging middleware. Traditional MOM focused on simple A-to-B asynchronous message passing. In an attempt to be competitive with other MOM vendors and other middleware products, MQSeries now provides many value-added services—services never envisioned in the original concept of MOM.

That original concept never included, for example, the encapsulation of transactions. Today, nearly every MOM package takes advantage of the notion of a transaction (a "unit of work"), with the ability to maintain states. MOM can now maintain message persistence and logging, enabling it to provide enhanced manageability and fail-over capabilities.

The best of the queuing products available (like MQSeries) are in the process of reinventing themselves by adding a publish/subscribe engine. It is a smart move. This positive development is intended to gain entry for queuing products into the exploding world of middleware products for information dissemination. Once the playing field is leveled, they will be competitive with existing publish/subscribe middleware from vendors such as TIBCO.

The current MQSeries has taken the leap directly from Version 2 to Version 5, stepping up the IBM installation procedures so that it will be "up to speed" with other IBM products. In the past, MQSeries was notoriously difficult to install. This upgrade should successfully address this frustration. IBM also claims that this new version of MQSeries works better with its DB2, Transaction Server, and other Software Server components. Other new features include Database-Message Resource Coordination (DMRC) and smart message distribution. Long available on a large number of server platforms, MQSeries now supports Windows NT and OS/2, as well.

Before this latest version, MQSeries required a transaction manager or a sophisticated application program in order to combine database updates and messaging activity into a single unit of work. With Version 5.1 and the introduction of DMRC, MQSeries includes MQ and SQL activity support through the new MZBEGIN verb to register a unit of work. Thus, subsequent work can be committed or backed out, depending on whether the procedure succeeds. MQSeries supports the notion of a transaction, without having to employ a TP monitor or application server.

Smart message distribution minimizes the amount of network traffic required to distribute a copy of a single message to multiple users whose queues reside on a single node. MQSeries 5.1 can send a single copy of the message to each target MQ system, using a list of recipients at the target systems. From there, the receiving MQ system produces and queues the copies locally.

In addition, the package includes performance enhancements, such as fast messages (changes to MQSeries' message channel agents to reduce the time and resources required to move nonpersistent messages) and enhancements to internal channel architecture and trusted bindings.

Another significant improvement in this upgrade is MQSeries' ability to support large messages. The previous limit of 4MB per message has been extended to 100MB per message. Additionally, messages may now be built or retrieved in segments and passed by reference.

The publish/subscribe feature in the newest version of MQSeries automates the distribution of relevant information to people and applications. Using the new pub/sub engine, MQSeries developers can ensure

(continued)

Examples of MOM (*continued*)

that clients who subscribe to a particular topic receive exactly what they want. Meanwhile, behind the scenes, MQSeries uses the MQ messaging infrastructure to move the messages throughout the enterprise.

With pub/sub, an MQ-enabled application no longer needs to understand anything about the target application. Now it simply sends the information to be shared to a destination within the pub/sub engine, or broker. The broker can redistribute the information to any interested application.

The real advantage to offering pub/sub is the degree of reliability that MQSeries delivers. The most significant downside is not within the MQSeries environment, but with those pub/sub vendors that now find themselves competing against IBM. TIBCO, which has long dominated pub/sub, might find that MQSeries' new features will finally threaten its "king of the hill" status in the world of finance. In addition, the pub/sub features of MQSeries are the same as many features offered by traditional message brokers, although without schema and content transformation facilities. IBM adopted NEON's message-brokering features and placed them on top of MQSeries as an add-on package—the MQ Integrator.

IBM's ultimate goal is to become the information bus for the enterprise. With this latest release of MQSeries, it takes a giant step toward achieving that lofty goal.

Future of MOM

Despite its shortcomings, MOM still has its place within the enterprise and within some application integration projects. Connecting applications to applications, it is more applicable to EAI than to application integration. Why? MOM requires major changes to source and target applications, which is generally frowned upon in most application integration problem domains. Still, our discussion of MOM has been worthwhile in the context of middleware, because messaging is the basis for many application integration solutions, including message brokers.

RPCs have an even longer shot at becoming the basis of application integration. Their synchronous nature and heavy overhead, as well as their deep impact on source and target applications, will keep RPCs intraenterprise. However, as with MOM, RPCs are a worthwhile discussion, because many application integration solutions leverage RPCs (such as a solution using Java's RMI as a mechanism to enable application-to-application communication).

It is worth remembering: Good technology is always built on the foundation of good technology. Both RPCs and MOM are good technology. They will continue to be the basis of many technology advances.

Distributed Objects and Application Integration

Distributed object technology has been around for nearly a decade. It creates an infrastructure for sharing methods by providing an additional location for application processing and for interoperability among processes. In addition, it provides a standard mechanism to access shared objects, objects that run on any number of servers. As a result, its usefulness to method-oriented application integration should be clear.

As part of the application integration solution set, distributed objects enable architects to create both applications that share common methods and composite applications that support method-oriented application integration. The integration of applications by sharing a common business logic—"application integration nirvana"—lies along this path. But it is hardly a smooth path. As we have already suggested in any number of contexts, the path is always risky and studded with expensive obstacles.

Moreover, take note that Web services, at their core, are distributed objects. Thus, the information discussed in this section is a good primer for our detailed discussion of Web services later in the book. Note the similarities.

What Works?

Distributed objects work best in application integration problem domains where a distributed computing model is in use and a large number of common methods need to be shared. For example, an enterprise may have the following four major applications:

- Customer tracking system (Company A)
- Logistics system (Company A)
- Sales database application (Company B and Company C)
- Inventory planning system (Company C)

Although each of these applications functions independently, they have a number of methods in common, methods that may include

```
Add_Customer()
Edit_Customer()
Delete_Customer()
```

For these methods to be shared, an additional shared application layer must be created (physical or virtual). This layer must possess the enabling technology that allows applications to share methods over the Internet. Application servers, TP monitors, or distributed objects are the best options for such a layer. As we suggested earlier, each has advantages and disadvantages that need to be evaluated.

If method-oriented application integration is the chosen approach, then the application integration architect and developer may seek to create a set of distributed objects that house these common methods. Using a common structure, interface, and communication mechanism (e.g., IIOP or RPCs, which are discussed later in this section), distributed objects provide the enabling technology for sharing these methods (see Figure 7.12).

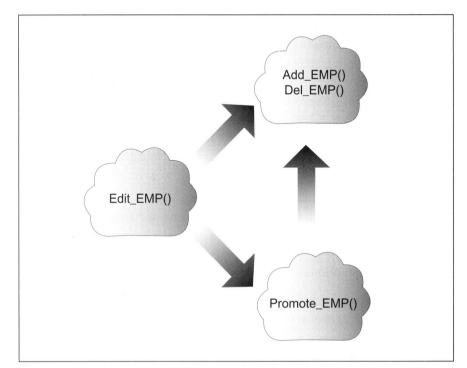

Figure 7.12   Using distributed objects.

What's So Difficult?

Because we have become familiar with the workings of the marketplace, it should come as no surprise that distributed object vendors are quick to suggest that using distributed objects is easy. According to them, it's simply a matter of changing several applications and exposing application methods using distributed object technology for access by other applications or, more commonly, among the distributed objects themselves. What could be simpler? Plenty. For this method to be successful in an application similar to the previous example, the common methods would have to be stripped from all the enterprise applications and redeployed within some sort of distributed object technology. Code would have to be changed everywhere. Each application would need to be tested and then redeployed.

This is a monumental task. It may be worth the effort if it ultimately achieves the business objectives, but it is hardly simple. And it is not a good fit for most application integration problem domains. Distributed object-based application integration is an invasive integration approach. Many changes must be made to accommodate this technology. As a rule of thumb, invasive middleware doesn't cut it when it comes to application integration. But as in all things, there are no absolute rules, and in some cases, this is the right solution.

Before moving forward, however, consider this truism: A solid business case must be made to justify leveraging method-oriented application integration and enabling technology such as distributed objects. Distributed object technology might or might not be simple or worthwhile. The only "objective" way to be sure is to use this calculus: assess what is to be gained from the application integration project against the resources necessary to complete the project. If the resources required far exceed the gain, then other application integration levels are likely to be better approaches. However, if it appears that the return on investment is there, then method-oriented application integration is the most elegant of application integration solutions.

The failure in too many organizations is the absence of strict candor and realism in making such an assessment. Organizations that talk themselves into application integration projects using distributed objects based on exaggerated claims by the media or by vendors are very often in for a rude awakening. Failed distributed object projects outnumber the successes. That's the reality. No hype.

What's So Easy?

Once we understand the disadvantages of distributed objects, we should focus on the many advantages. The greatest advantage of distributed objects is their adherence to an application development and interoperability standard. CORBA, COM+, and Web services (we discuss only CORBA and COM+ in this chapter) are specifications, not technologies. Vendors adhere to the established standard and therefore provide a set of technologies that can interoperate. Because the standard is open and the interfaces well defined, vendors discover that interacting with distributed objects is not difficult.

As distributed object technology continues to mature, vendors add new features that address previously acknowledged shortcomings, such as scalability, interoperability, and communication mechanisms. Distributed objects now provide better scalability through the ability to support transactions. As a result, they offer the same scaling tricks as application servers and TP monitors. OMG now endorses CORBA's Object Transaction Services (OTS). Microsoft expects AppCenter to bring transactionality to COM+. Interoperability continues to improve as common protocols are defined, including CORBA's IIOP and Microsoft's COM+ RPC (loosely based on the DCE RPC). Objects created by different vendors can share information by using a common object-to-object protocol as the least-common denominator. Finally, where traditional distributed objects leverage simple, synchronous communication mechanisms based on the RPC (as is the case with both CORBA and Microsoft), they now provide asynchronous messaging mechanisms, as well. (CORBA provides its own message service as part of the standard, while Microsoft is learning to leverage MSMQ as a way to bring messaging to COM.)

Thus, distributed objects, which were once difficult to deploy and provided few advantages over more traditional alternatives, are now easier to use and provide many more features that benefit an enterprise development technology. In short, distributed objects have become a key enabling technology (in addition to transactional middleware) for method-oriented application integration.

What's a Distributed Object?

Several trends contribute to the potential benefit of distributed objects for application integration.

- The move toward multitier application development. Developers are beginning to realize that the enabling technology of distributed objects "gets them there." Distributed objects give application integration architects and developers the ability to create portable objects that can run on a variety of servers—objects that can communicate using a predefined and standard messaging interface over the Internet. This aspect of distributed objects has remarkable potential for application integration.

- In the recent past, CORBA was the only real standard available (see the "CORBA Internals" tidbit later in this chapter). Microsoft's entry into the distributed object marketplace with COM+ provides a distributed object infrastructure and the ability to tie applications created with traditional tools with a Windows-based operating system. (The Object Request Broker, or ORB, is part of the operating system and therefore a give-away.)

- We learned to bring ORBs to the desktop through the use of application components, such as ActiveX. By mixing and matching components, developers can piece together an application like a jigsaw puzzle. This is the nirvana of application development: the ability to assemble applications the way the Ford Motor Company assembles Mustangs—from prebuilt component parts.

- The rise of the Web renewed interest in distributed objects. Technologies and standards, such as CORBA's IIOP, promise to provide both an enabling technology for dynamic application development and a better application-to-application, object-to-object transport layer. Now that powerhouse Web companies such as Netscape have put their weight behind ORBs, Web developers will increase their rush to ORBs.

The General Idea of ORBs

With so much depending on ORBs, it seems particularly appropriate to address the question, What exactly is an ORB?

Object Request Brokers provide developers with standard objects to communicate with other standard objects, using a standard interface and line protocol. Like traditional objects (such as those found with C++, Java, or Smalltalk), ORBs can access the methods of other ORBs either locally or over a network (see Figure 7.13). ORBs can also exchange data and are platform independent.

A CORBA ORB can pass requests from object to object. One invocation method is for the client to invoke ORB services through the ORB core and the Interface Definition Language (IDL) stub. Another method is through a Dynamic Invocation Interface (DII) stub. A stub provides mapping between the language binding (e.g., C++ and Java) and the ORB services. Specific instructions are given to the ORBs through this process.

At this point, the ORB core moves the request to the object implementation, which receives the message through an up-call, using an IDL skeleton or a dynamic skeleton.

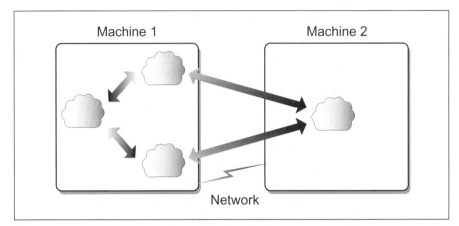

Figure 7.13   ORBs can access methods of other ORBs locally or over a network.

CORBA Internals

My goal is not to add to the already voluminous information available about CORBA. Instead, I hope to provide an overview of distributed objects and their application-to-application integration. If you are considering CORBA (or COM) as the enabling technology for an application integration project, this information should help you.

A CORBA ORB contains four main parts (also see Figure 7.14):

- ORB
- Object services
- Common facilities
- Application objects

These same features exist in other ORBs, such as Microsoft's COM+ and proprietary ORBs.

ORB

The ORB is an engine that shares information with other ORBs. Together, these "engaged" ORBs create a distributed object. ORBs exist as background objects, functioning behind the application. Applications are also layered on top of ORBs, providing the distributed infrastructure. This is the reason ORBs make such effective middleware layers—many

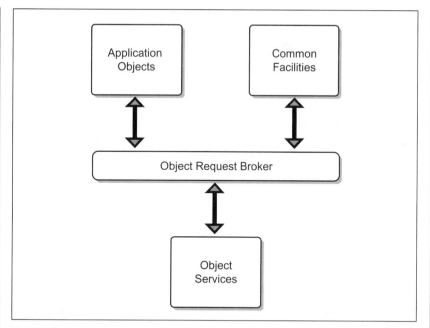

Figure 7.14   Four parts of the CORBA ORB.

communication services already exist in ORB services (such as CORBA-compliant ORBs). Layering also provides heterogeneous application portability and interoperability, the feature that makes ORBs most valuable to application integration.

Object Services

CORBA mandates object services, which are groups of services that leverage object interfaces for communication between services. The basic services that developers expect in an ORB are security, transaction management, and data exchange. Developers use object services as a base class upon which to build applications.

Common Facilities

Common facilities, optional for CORBA, are a collection of services that link with the client. Common facilities allow developers to build component characteristics in CORBA-compliant ORBs. Developers consider common facilities whenever they need to implement CORBA-compliant component-based objects.

(continued)

> **CORBA Internals (*continued*)**
>
> **Application Objects**
>
> Application objects support the application development features of a CORBA ORB, as defined by the ORB developer or application developer. Here "the rubber meets the road" in ORB development—ORBs can be turned into something useful. These features are built into ORB with the IDL, which ensures interoperability with other CORBA-compliant ORBs.

COM+

The dynamic that currently drives the distributed object world—and complicates it—is the emergence of Microsoft's COM+, along with the further development of Microsoft's ORB into COM+. And Microsoft being Microsoft, emotion and power plays are in full view. Although a great ORB debate is raging with high emotion on either side, the bottom line is that COM is as much an ORB as CORBA. Microsoft very effectively devised COM, using its existing Object Linking and Embedding (OLE) model as its basis of design.

ORB provides an object standard that really isn't object oriented (e.g., that has the ability to support inheritance), but then, neither is CORBA. It also provides a common mechanism for inter-ORB communication. COM+ is based on automation (using the COM model), a standard on most Windows desktops and a feature of most Windows-based development tools.

The Realities

As in most things, there is both good news and bad news when considering the role of distributed objects in application integration. Distributed objects do provide application integration developers with an advanced distributed architecture to develop and deploy distributed applications. At the same time, issues remain that make them unsuitable for mission-critical application integration computing. A primary issue is the simple fact that most commercial ORBs don't perform well, even with the transaction and messaging extensions.

When thinking about distributed objects, we must also consider middleware. Most ORBs, both COM and CORBA, use the synchronous communication model. They continue to lack support for asynchronous messaging (although

CORBA and COM+ now provide some asynchronous capabilities). And the ORB code is still not completely portable from platform to platform, especially COM+. (As with other shortcomings, vendors and standards bodies plan to address these problems in new releases of specifications and products.)

So, what can we conclude about distributed objects and application integration? Can they work together? Absolutely. However, as with all things, careful consideration must be employed to make a wise decision. The marriage of technology and application integration is like any other marriage—it's a long-term commitment, and partners have to mesh well to prosper over the long haul. In application integration, the ability to mesh well over the long haul may well be intrinsic to the architecture. Now that we are moving to the next destination of distributed objects, Web services, we have another chance to be successful. Only time will tell.

Database-Oriented Middleware and Application Integration

To a large extent, application integration depends upon database access. This is particularly true for data-oriented application integration. Databases were once proprietary and therefore difficult to access. Now, so many solutions for accessing data exist that we rarely have a problem when we need to retrieve information from or place it into any database. The solutions not only make application integration a much easier proposition, but they also speak directly to the idea that the capability of modern middleware drives the interest in application integration.

However, even with many simplified database access solutions, databases and database-oriented middleware quickly grow complicated. Although database-oriented middleware was once simply a mechanism to "get at" data, it has matured into a layer for placing data in the context of a virtual database—a particular, common database model or format. For example, if we want to view data in a relational database as objects, the database-oriented middleware can map the data so it appears as objects to a source or target application. The same thing can be done "the other way around"—mixing and matching such models as hierarchical, flat files, multidimensional, relational, and object-oriented (see Figure 7.15).

Database-oriented middleware also provides access to any number of databases, regardless of the model employed or the platform upon which they exist. This access is generally accomplished through a single common interface such as ODBC or JDBC, which we will discuss in detail later in this section. Thus,

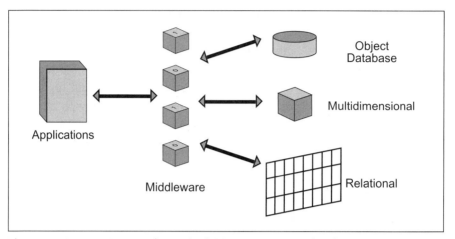

Figure 7.15   Database-oriented middleware allows viewing of data using any model, no matter how the data is stored.

information stored in Oracle, Informix, or DB2 databases can be accessed at the same time through a single interface (see Figure 7.16). By taking advantage of these mechanisms, we can map any difference in the source and target databases to a common model. As a consequence, they are much easier to integrate. (This process also supports the idea of a common enterprise metadata model, presented earlier in this book.)

These examples should make it clear that database-oriented middleware is a major player in the world of application integration. It allows a large number of enabling technologies to process information coming to and going from source and target systems. This ability makes database-oriented middleware the logical choice if a message broker or an application server requires information in a database. Vendors also recognize the advantage of database-oriented middleware. As a result, many application integration products, such as message brokers and application servers, already contain the necessary database-oriented middleware to access the most popular databases. In fact, most message brokers and application servers come prepackaged with the appropriate adapters to access most relational databases, such as Oracle, Sybase, and Informix. To a large degree, database access is now a "problem solved," with many inexpensive and proven solutions available.

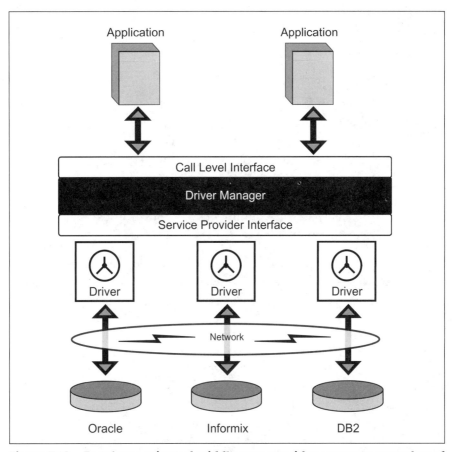

Figure 7.16　**Database-oriented middleware provides access to a number of databases at the same time.**

Nevertheless, we can benefit from understanding the role of database-oriented middleware in the context of application integration in order to get the larger picture. Databases will serve as the primary point of integration for most application integration solutions over the next few years. The bottom line: Your choice of mechanism to move information in and out of databases can make or break your application integration project. That alone makes our examination of database-oriented middleware worthwhile. More than that, integration with more modern middleware solutions is essential and carries with it its own complexities and opportunities.

What Is Database-Oriented Middleware?

Database-oriented middleware provides a number of important benefits (see Figure 7.17), including:

- An interface to an application
- The ability to convert the application language into something understandable by the target database (e.g., SQL)
- The ability to send a query to a database over a network
- The ability to process a query on the target database
- The ability to move a response set (the results of the query) back over the network to the requesting application
- The ability to convert a response set into a format understandable by the requesting application

In addition to these processes, database-oriented middleware must provide the ability to process many simultaneous requests, along with scaling features such as thread pooling and load balancing. These features must be packaged with

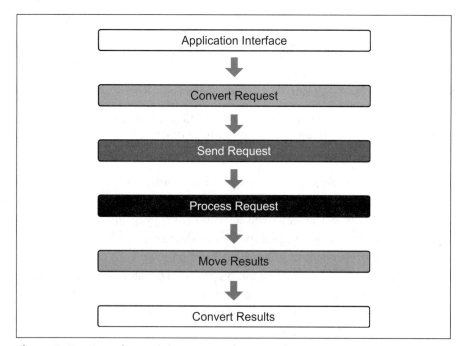

Figure 7.17   Functions of database-oriented middleware.

management capabilities and security features. As in other contexts, vendor approaches to these benefits vary greatly from vendor to vendor and technology to technology.

Types of Database-Oriented Middleware

Again, I have no desire to repeat information that is easily available from other sources. My goal is to provide you with an overview of information that applies to your application integration problem domain.

So, where do we begin? Ultimately, database-oriented middleware is "all the software that connects an application to a database." Any application. Any database. Anytime. Like primitive middleware layers, database-oriented middleware allows developers to access the resources of another computer—in this case, a database server that uses a single, well-defined API. Database-oriented middleware appears straightforward in its architecture, yet each of the many products and standards that make up this market accomplish the basic task in very different ways.

Although several types of database middleware exist, they are all basically native middleware—CLIs and database gateways. For our purposes, native middleware is simply middleware created for a specific database. For example, middleware provided by Sybase to access the Sybase databases from C++ is native database-oriented middleware. Native database-oriented middleware provides the best performance and access to native database features (such as stored procedures and triggers), because the middleware was specifically created for that particular database. The downside to native database middleware is that, once links to a database have been created using native middleware, major renovations are required to change databases.

CLIs, such as ODBC and JDBC, provide a single interface to several databases. CLIs translate common interface calls into any number of database dialects. They also translate the response sets into a common response set representation (see Figure 7.18) that is understandable to the application making the request to the database.

Database gateways provide access to data that was once locked inside larger systems, such as mainframes. They integrate several databases for access from a single application interface. They remap archaic database models (flat files, ISAM, VSAM, and so on) so they appear more traditional, and they translate queries and information as they move in and out of the database gateway software (more on this in "Database Gateways" later in this section).

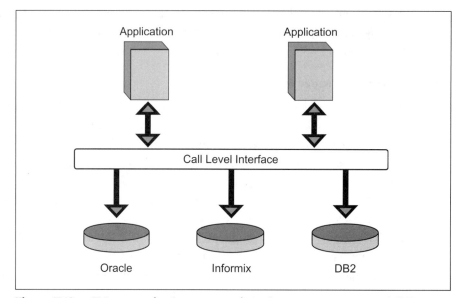

Figure 7.18   CLIs use a single common interface to access several different databases.

Going Native

In addition to ODBC, JDBC, and other database translation interfaces, many other native database-oriented middleware products exist. These are APIs provided by a database vendor or some third party with access to a particular database. In the past, these APIs tended to be older C and C++ libraries. Now, most application integration development tools ship native database-oriented middleware with their products.

Native database-oriented middleware has an advantage over ODBC or JDBC in its ability to provide high-performance database access along with the ability to access features native to a specific database. That's the upside. The downside is that native database-oriented middleware binds the user to that particular middleware vendor, because the application integration application uses calls specific to that particular database.

Database Gateways

Database gateways (also known as SQL gateways) are APIs that use a single interface to provide access to most databases that reside on many different types of platforms (see Figure 7.19). They are similar to virtual database middleware

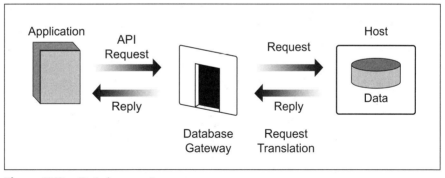

Figure 7.19   Database gateway.

products, providing developers with access to any number of databases residing in environments typically difficult to access, such as a mainframe. For example, using an ODBC interface and a database gateway, developers can access data that resides in a DB2 database on a mainframe, in an Oracle database running on a minicomputer, and in a Sybase database running on a UNIX server. The developer simply makes an API call, and the database gateway does all the work.

Database gateways translate the SQL calls into a standard format known as the Format and Protocol (FAP), the common connection between the client and the server. FAP is also the common link between very different databases and platforms. The gateway can translate the API call directly into FAP, moving the request to the target database, and translating the request so that the target database and platform can react.

A number of gateways are on the market. These include Information Builders' Enterprise Data Access/SQL (EDA/SQL) and standards such as IBM's Distributed Relational Data Access (DRDA) and ISO/SAG's Remote Data Access (RDA).

EDA/SQL

EDA/SQL is a wonderful general-purpose database gateway for several reasons. Among them is its ability to work with most database servers and platforms, bridging many enterprises where dozens of servers might be running on dozens of different platforms, all needing to be accessed from a single application—a perfect fit for application integration. EDA/SQL also has the advantage of using ODBC as the interface rather than a proprietary API. By using ODBC, it can access more than 50 relational and nonrelational database servers.

There are several EDA/SQL components, including the API/SQL, EDA/Extenders, EDA/Link, EDA/Server, and EDA/Data Drivers. API/SQL provides the CLI (ODBC), which allows the developer to access the EDA/SQL resources. EDA/Extenders are redirectors of SQL calls, which route the request across a network. EDA/Link provides the network connections by supporting more than 12 communication protocols. EDA/Server resides on the target database, processing the requests on behalf of the requesting application or integration server. Finally, the EDA/Data Drivers, like ODBC drivers, provide access to more than 50 different target databases.

Ready for Prime Time

The strongest point in support of database-oriented middleware is that the technology is very mature, well tested, and ready for most application integration applications. In other words, database access should not be a major concern for most application integration projects.

Among the problems that remain to be solved for database-oriented middleware is the ability to make it more scalable. Currently, a TP monitor or application server must be employed to multiplex the database connections on behalf of the application or application integration solution. Multiplexing (or connection pooling)—the ability to remove the one-connection-per-request restriction from database-oriented middleware—is becoming part of many database-oriented middleware layers, including JDBC and ODBC.

With renewed interest in nonrelational database models (such as multidimensional, hierarchical, and object-oriented), middleware is learning how to emulate and translate data from model to model. Today we can view a relational database using the object-oriented model and a hierarchical database as a relational database. These emulation and translation services make application integration a much easier proposition because they make it possible to map very heterogeneous environments to a common database model, thus providing an easier starting point for integration. This capability adds the most value to data-oriented application integration.

The world of database-oriented middleware isn't about to undergo drastic change—even as application integration grows in popularity. The simple fact is that solutions to most database access problems already exist.

Isn't it nice to come upon an area of technology where most problems are already solved?

## CHAPTER EIGHT

Java-Based Middleware Standards and Application Integration

What does Java have to do with application integration? The answer is, "A lot." As we move toward middleware standards, we find that most of them, including JMS, JDBC, and JCA, are Java based.

Java is not a "cure-all" for application integration, but there are many related standards that are applicable in more than just a few problem domains. In addition, as Java standards become more accepted, traditional application integration vendors continue to adopt Java-based middleware standards and build them into their products.

This is an important chapter, as is the chapter on JCA (Chapter 10). Once again, just the relevant information will be presented here, including what works where. There are many books on Java middleware you can use as a reference, and you don't have to be a Java expert to get some good information here.

Java-based middleware standards have been with us for some time now, so what is new to tell? To begin with, the standards are always evolving, new capabilities are published monthly, and application integration vendors are moving quickly to support these capabilities.

The latest Java standard, JCA, is clearly a revolution for application integration. We also have JDBC, EJB, JMS, RMI, and even Java-to-XML standards such as JAX. Java is no longer just a language and a virtual machine, but a group of inter-related standards that vendors and architects can leverage within a solution set. In fact, it does not matter if Java is your language or platform of choice. You can mix and match Java and non-Java standards to solve your application integration problems.

Java-Based Middleware Categories

If the idea of Java-based middleware sounds complex, don't be dismayed. It is complex. To simplify the complexity of Java's hype-driven standards and products, we have structured six major categories of Java middleware:

- Database oriented
- Interprocess
- Message oriented
- Application hosting
- Transaction processing
- Connectivity

As you may expect, we'll focus on the standards that are most relevant to application integration: message-oriented, application hosting, transaction processing, and connectivity. See Table 8.1 to see what Java middleware standards are applicable to which type of application integration.

Table 8.1　Java middleware standards compatibility.

	IOAI	BPOAI	POAI	SOAI
Database	X	X	X	
Interprocess		X		X
Message	X	X	X	
Application Hosting		X	X	X
Transaction Processing		X	X	X
Connectivity	X	X	X	

Database Oriented

Database-oriented Java-enabled middleware is the oldest and best supported of these categories. That makes perfect sense—for Java to be successful, it had to access most relational databases. The JDBC specifications have become the ODBC for the world of Java. They are now found in most tools and application servers that support Java.

Interprocess

JavaSoft not only connects to databases, it also provides RMI, a simple synchronous mechanism that allows applets to communicate with one another and invoke one another's methods as needed. For example, you can download an applet that can connect to an Enterprise JavaBean that is running on a remote Web server and use it to invoke a method that updates a database with customer information. This communication can take place in the same machine or over a network. In effect, this creates a "poor man's distributed object." RMI benefits application integration projects by sharing information with other applets and servlets scattered throughout an enterprise.

Message Oriented

Although some traditional message-oriented middleware products like IBM's MQSeries support Java, the real story is a new standard from JavaSoft called Java Message Service. JMS is attracting a critical mass of messaging vendors that seek to bind their products tightly with Java.

JMS adds a common API and provider framework to Java, which enables the Java developer to dispatch and receive messages with other Java-enabled applications or applets that exist anywhere on the network (see Figure 8.1). JMS defines a common set of messaging concepts and programming strategies. It provides a good mix of the messaging features common to most messaging products—important, yes, but hardly revolutionary. The difficulty is to support these concepts and strategies from JMS-compliant vendor to JMS-compliant vendor. If this obstacle is successfully overcome, the resulting products not only will share common characteristics, but will have the ability to share messages, as well—something more traditional message-oriented middleware products have yet to perfect.

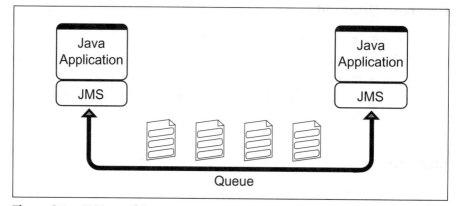

Figure 8.1   JMS provides message transport services for Java.

JMS consists of three major entities: the JMS provider, JMS messages, and JMS domains. The provider implements JMS for a particular product (for example, a Java applet, servlet, bean, or application that supports JMS). JMS messages are sets of messaging interfaces that define a common mechanism and format for moving information between providers.

JMS messages consist of several parts, including the header, properties, and body (see Figure 8.2). The header supports the same set of header fields as traditional messaging products. Both the JMS client and provider use the header to

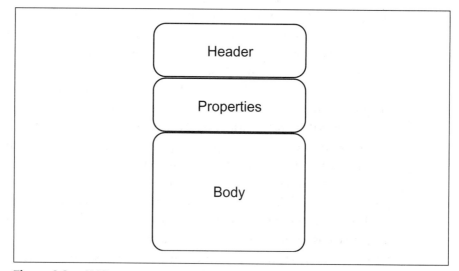

Figure 8.2   JMS message structure.

identify and route messages. JMS message properties allow developers to add information to the standard header, such as application-specific properties, standard properties, and provider-specific properties. The body contains the data that is being transported.

Messaging Models

JMS domains provide for the classification of messaging paradigms, including point-to-point and publish/subscribe. Point-to-point messaging generally relies upon queues to transport messages. Publish/subscribe, as we discussed in Chapter 7, addresses messages to some node in a content hierarchy. Pub/sub is particularly useful to application integration projects because it does not require an understanding about the resource that is being subscribed to. JMS provides client interfaces created for each type of domain.

With these two paradigms available, the question that confronts the architect and developer is, which one to use and when? The answer may be found in a closer examination of the two options. JMS point-to-point messaging defines how a client works with queues. For example, it defines how a JMS-enabled application finds queues, sends a message to them, and/or receives messages from them. JMS can send a message to a specific queue. Asynchronously, the receiving applet or application need not be engaged in order for the message to be placed in the queue; it picks up the message from the queue when it has time.

Point-to-point messaging is best applied when applications need to communicate with one another but, in doing so, do not need to delay the target or source application from processing tasks.

As with traditional queues, JMS queues may contain a mixture of messages. Unfortunately, JMS suffers from the shortcoming of not defining facilities to administer queues. The upside is that this shortcoming is not as significant as it might first appear because JMS implementations leverage static, not dynamic, queues.

Developers should keep several Java concepts in mind when working with JMS queues. Among them are the `Queue object`, `TemporaryQueue`, `QueueConnectionFactory`, `QueueConnection`, `QueueReceiver`, `Queue Sender`, and `QueueSession`. Together, these represent a set of classes that developers can leverage within a JMS-enabled application.

The `Queue object`, the heart of this beast, encapsulates a provider-specific queue name. This object identifies a queue to a JMS method from the client.

A QueueConnection is an active connection to a JMS point-to-point provider. The JMS client leverages the QueueConnection to create instances of QueueSessions, which produce and consume messages.

The TemporaryQueue is created for the duration of the Queue Connection. True to its name, it is a system-defined queue, available only to the QueueConnection object that created it as a temporary storage location. The QueueConnectionFactory creates an instance of a QueueConnection object within a JMS provider. The client uses a QueueReceiver to receive messages that exist in a queue, while in contrast, a QueueSender places messages in a queue.

If the point-to-point model doesn't meet the needs of the project, the JMS pub/sub model probably will. This model uses a content-based hierarchy structure to describe how JMS clients publish messages and subscribe to them from a well-defined node. This model, as we noted in our earlier discussion of middleware models, is superior to simple point-to-point models. It is most practical when considering JMS for use with traditional application integration projects (although either model can be used with application integration implementations).

JMS refers to these nodes as "topics." A topic is, in fact, a small message broker that gathers and distributes messages from other entities (see Figure 8.3). JMS uses topics as quasi-intermediaries. They create messages that are separated logically from subscribers. Topics are adaptive; they adjust as subscribers and publishers appear and disappear.

By drilling down to the next "topic level," we can discern that a topic is nothing more than a Java object that encapsulates a provider-specific topic name.

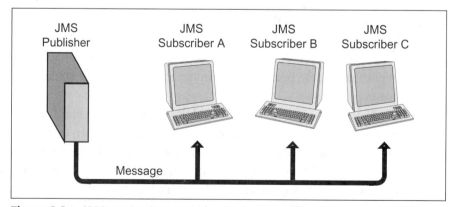

Figure 8.3   JMS can gather and distribute messages throughout an enterprise.

Unlike most pub/sub vendors that group topics into hierarchies, allowing subscribers to subscribe to any part of the hierarchy, JMS places no such restrictions on its users. Instead, it organizes topics and the granularity of subscriptions in a completely open manner. This "openness" is a positive development. Strict pub/sub policies are, by definition, limiting.

JMS and Application Development

Because JMS is just another Java-enabled API, application development comes down to simply linking to and leveraging the proper JMS objects within an application. A JMS application can be created and deployed as a single unit, or JMS clients can be added to an existing JMS-enabled application or applet. Generally, JMS plays an important role in the creation of distributed Java applications and linking non-JMS messages into the world of Java. For example, IBM is in the process of ensuring that its MQSeries is able to exchange messages with JMS. And where Big Blue leads, other MOM vendors are sure to follow.

A typical JMS client application must go through a standard procedure to get up and running. This procedure includes using the Java Naming and Directory Information (JNDI) to find a `ConnectionFactory` object, and then find one or more destination objects. To create a number of instances of a JMS session, the `ConnectionFactory` object is used to create an instance of a JMS connection and the Connections method. Finally, the JMS client must use the Session and the Destinations to create the `MessageProducers` and `MessageConsumers` required for the application. From this point, the connection to the queue or the pub/sub engine is set, and the application may use JMS as a mechanism to transport data into and out of an application.

A number of key issues remain that JMS must address. These include load balancing, fault tolerance, and error notification. We can probably anticipate that JMS-compliant software vendors will build such features into their products. Wouldn't it be nice if they all chose to use a consistent paradigm and mechanism? Sure it would. But don't count on it. As we mentioned earlier in this chapter, no notion of administration is built into the JMS specifications. IBM discovered that a weak administration initially hurt MQSeries, so it responded by fixing the problem. At this point, Java seems to have no such inclination to fix JMS. In addition, security seems to be an afterthought in JMS. Unfortunately, this is hardly unusual in the world of middleware.

Beyond JMS, Java integration with the big MOM products is having a significant impact. With over 65 percent of the point-to-point message-oriented middleware marketplace, MQSeries is MOM's "800-pound gorilla" that will always get its way. Providing Java links will only add value to that domination. IBM is "Java-tizing" just about everything these days. Java is going to be the least common denominator between CICS, Component Broker, and MQSeries—representing the largest enterprise growth area for Java. Although JMS will support smaller systems at first, it is only a matter of time before it supports larger systems, as well.

Application Hosting

Calling application servers "middleware" is a bit ingenuous, to say the least. However, because that is the way they are generally classified, it would be confusing for us to buck the trend. As we discussed in an earlier chapter, an application server is any product that provides a host for application logic and processes all (or part) of an application. For example, interface logic can be defined by using client-side development tools, with all server-side business-logic processes using a remote application server. The benefit of this scenario is that both application logic and access to resources can be shared through a centralized entity (see Figure 8.4).

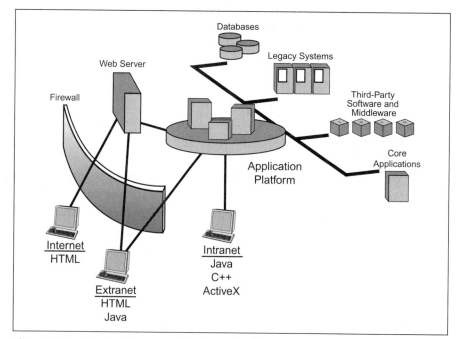

Figure 8.4   Typical Java-enabled application server architecture.

Application servers control access to these environments by using "units of work," or transactions. A transactional paradigm enables them to recover from system- and resource-level problems and to scale to high user and processing loads. To accomplish this, application servers use mechanisms such as multiplexing database requests. However, every product implements these features in unique ways and so should be explored carefully before being used.

These environments include IDEs, which help the developer create the logic for the application server, using an easy-on-the-eyes graphical user interface. They may also provide client-side tools or client-side development features through a partner.

Connectivity

On the connectivity side of things, the JCA specification is the best hope for Java fans. JCA provides application integration technology with the standardized method for integrating EIS with J2EE components, using a common API and a common set of services that developers can employ. JCA is implanted in J2EE containers, and the resource adapters are implemented and provided by EIS (see Figure 8.5).

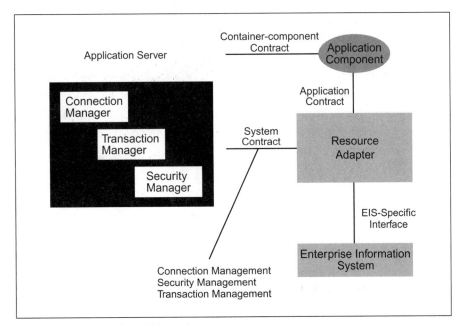

Figure 8.5   A typical JCA environment.

JCA is so important to application integration that we're going to devote Chapter 10 to discussing its current state, as well as its potential.

J2EE

A striking feature of J2EE is that Sun has done a wonderful job of providing middleware services that are part of the standard platform, but at the same time, it has left room for third-party middleware vendors to add value. These middleware services include transactional and messaging middleware services and distributed object services, all in support of Java-enabled distributed application development.

The J2EE platform is made up of the J2EE deployment specification, a set of Internet Engineering Task Force (IETF) standards, and a set of CORBA standards. The middleware built into J2EE includes EJB, Java IDL, JDBC, JMS, Java

---

XML and Java

J2EE provides support for XML through the Java API for XML Processing (JAXP), which provides the ability to verify, create, access, and manipulate XML documents from Java applications.

To manipulate an XML document, the document must first be parsed, validated, and made available through an API, including Document Object Model (DOM) and Simple API for XML (SAX). JAXP supports both APIs. Moreover, the ability to use XSLT framework (see Chapter 11) on the Transformation API for XML (TrAX) is also included in JAXP.

Of course, Java and XML are always evolving, and Sun's Java Community program continues to define many XML-related specifications, including:

- The Java API for XML Messaging (JAXM) enables developers to send and receive XML messages based on the Simple Object Access Protocol (SOAP) with an attachments specification, and contains profiles for ebXML and SOAP-RP.
- The Java API for XML Processing enables developers to process XML documents by providing support for the XML processing standards SAX, DOM, and XSLT.

(continued)

> - The Java API for XML Registries (JAXR) provides a uniform and standard Java API for interacting with XML registries such as UDDI and ebXML Registry/Repository.
> - The Java API for XML-based RPC (JAX-RPC) enables Java technology developers to build Web applications and Web services that incorporate XML-based RPC functionality according to the SOAP 1.1 specification. By using JAX-RPC, Java developers can rapidly achieve Web services interoperability based on widely adopted standards and protocols.[1]

Transaction API (JTA), Java Transaction Service (JTS), and RMI-IIOP. Although each of these middleware mechanisms is important, the most critical features are contained in the transactional component middleware, where EJB adds the most value; in JMS, which provides asynchronous messaging capabilities; and in RMI-IIOP, which provides synchronous object-to-object method sharing.

Transactional J2EE

We've already discussed EJB in detail, and there is extensive EJB literature available, so we will not belabor its value. J2EE provides EJB as a component translation layer that exists inside a container and provides most middle-tier services such as a transaction management layer, security, remote-client connectivity, and database connection pooling.

Fundamentally, EJB is a rudimentary transactional middleware environment that supports two types of components, or beans: session beans and entity beans. In short, session beans are nonpersistent, or transient, and can only link to one client for one session. An entity bean, by contrast, provides persistence.

If you are interested in mixing transactions and Java, you have JTA at your disposal, as well. JTA defines a high-level transaction management specification for distributed transaction processing. In addition, there is JTS, which is an API that provides links with other transactional resources such as TP monitors (e.g., BEA's Tuxedo or IBM's CICS). Although both JTA and JTS are important, they have not gotten the "traction" of EJB, despite their ability to do very different things.

---

[1]Java XML Pack.

Messaging J2EE

JMS is not as well known as EJB, and it provides a very different set of services. Still, it is quickly becoming the messaging middleware standard of choice for many organizations. Moreover, JMS is attracting existing middleware vendors, including IBM, BEA, and Progress Software, which have JMS-enabled their product lines.

Distributed Application J2EE

RMI provides a very simple mechanism to allow both applets and servlets to communicate with one another and invoke one another's methods. RMI is a poor man's distributed object, providing Java developers with the ability to create distributed applications around a simple object-to-object synchronous communication infrastructure. RMI's power is its simplicity. Its weakness has been its difficulty communicating with other distributed objects, including CORBA ORBs. Although both RMI and IIOP are based on TCP/IP (most of IIOP and RMI, actually), they still don't speak the same language.

With the advent of RMI-IIOP, this weakness has been overcome. RMI-IIOP provides developers with an implementation of the Java RMI API over IIOP, allowing them to write remote interfaces between clients and servers, and implement them with just Java technology and Java RMI APIs.

RMI over IIOP is an exciting development because it allows developers to combine the best features of RMI with the best features of CORBA. Until now, we had to "fudge" such connections or depend on proprietary solutions. RMI over IIOP allows us to work entirely within the Java programming language, with no separate IDL or mapping to learn. This approach is much more flexible. It allows us to pass any serializable Java object between application components, including C++ and Smalltalk CORBA ORBs.

This marriage of RMI with IIOP provides more choices for developers who want to mix and match environments. It provides product developers with a better common object-to-object communication mechanism.

Middleware Platforms Emerging

Middleware is becoming a part of platforms. J2EE is simply taking the lead. J2EE is significant in that it is a platform layer that runs within almost all platforms, including Windows XP, Linux, and OS/390. Developers can write an application for J2EE and run it on any operating system that supports J2EE. J2EE applications can communicate with other J2EE applications using the J2EE middleware, as described earlier in this chapter.

Windows XP is another platform that provides native middleware support. Although much more closed and proprietary than J2EE, Windows XP ships with a COM+ ORB, a component transaction layer (based on MTS), a messaging middleware layer (based on MSMQ), and even rudimentary middleware management services. Microsoft dominates the desktop and much of the server marketplace. It knows how to make the use of middleware easy. J2EE and Microsoft Windows XP will battle it out toward the end of the year, once the marketplace figures out they are going after the same e-Business applications.

Middleware is moving from a product-oriented technology to something that is becoming embedded in platforms just like other operating system services (e.g., disk I/O). This is a move in the right direction, considering that popular middleware is retooling for higher-level activities such as process automation, collaboration, and B2B information management. What was unique and innovative technology only a few short years ago is now just another commodity. So goes computing.

Java and Middleware

Basically, everyone is looking to "Java-tize" their middleware of choice, and the product vendors are only too happy to oblige. This is not to say that your application integration technology has to be Java-enabled, only that this should be under consideration. Indeed, many application integration problem domains are not right for Java-based middleware. Again, you have to consider your own requirements.

Java has a tendency to be a religion with some companies. They won't consider non-Java technology. While this is noble, it may not be smart. Most technology solution sets you apply to application integration problems will be a hybrid of both Java and non-Java solutions. In other words, you'll select the best technology for your solution's component parts.

The real advantage of Java is more than the sum of these parts. Java has finally brought about a general consensus on language and platform. Middleware is only adding power to that reality. With the help of heavy-hitter vendors, Java is morphing into a full-blown, enterprise-class application development and processing environment. Middleware support is simply a natural progression of that reality.

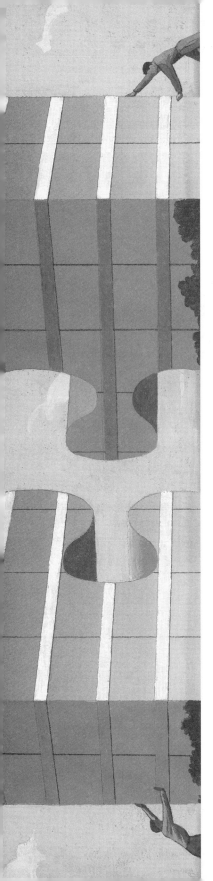

## CHAPTER NINE

Integration Servers and Application Integration

Integration servers are the center of the universe when it comes to application integration. They are not "general-purpose" middleware products such as message queuing or transactional software. Indeed, integration servers were built from the ground up to solve the application integration problem, both intra- and intercompany. Therefore, this chapter is very important, considering that integration servers are part of the solution set for most application integration problems.

As we'll see later in this book, integration servers continue to evolve as the needs of the marketplace evolve. Rather than support simple information exchange between source and target systems, integration servers can now provide support for SOAI using the same integration technology.

Integration servers are sophisticated pieces of software that sit between applications—many applications—intra- or interenterprise, and facilitate the exchange of information and sometimes application services. Integration servers are relatively new and exist solely to solve the application integration problem.

However, while they offer "one-stop shopping" for application integration technology in many respects, the approaches that each integration server vendor takes are very different, and thus solve very different types of problems. Vendors that sell this technology include Mercator, WebMethods, SeeBeyond, and IBM. As such, you need to understand the approaches in order to select the proper technology for your problem domain. Selecting the wrong technology is disastrous. A wrong decision can take many months and many millions of dollars to fix. Hence, the length of this chapter reflects its importance.

Integration Servers Defined

Integration servers can broker information between one or more target entities (networks, middleware, applications, and/or systems) with significantly greater ease than traditional methods, or point-to-point middleware. What's more, they can accomplish this regardless of how the information is represented or accessed. Integration servers can be positioned between any number of source or target systems that exist inside or outside of an enterprise, and broker the information exchange between them. They can account for differences in application semantics and database schemas, and process information by transforming the structure or format of the information so it makes sense to the target application that receives it.

What's more, integration servers provide a mechanism to integrate multiple business processes that, to this point, have remained more isolated than open regardless of whether the business processes are new, old, legacy, centralized, or distributed. Integration servers bridge many different platforms and application development solutions. They can connect to each application and route information between them by using any number of interface mechanisms. More to the point, they are capable of a good deal more than simply routing information. They can provide enhancements such as hosting business functions that build on the existing business functions of the entities they connect.

Integration Server Services

The services provided by integration servers can be put into the following distinct categories:

- Transformation
- Intelligent routing
- Rules processing
- Message warehousing

- Flow control
- Repository services
- Directory services
- Management
- APIs and adapters

The ability of integration servers to leave systems "where they are"—minimizing change while allowing data to be shared—lends tremendous value to application integration. As we've noted time and again, such a capability is critical to application integration, because you typically don't have control over the systems owned by your trading partners. Thus, you need to obtain information housed inside these systems through a nonintrusive point of integration, or perhaps through standards such as EDI and XML. Integration servers fit the bill nicely because they can consume and produce information formatted in a variety of ways.

Integration servers more closely resemble the way business activities "actually work"—providing greater efficiency and flexibility by automating functions currently performed manually, functions such as sending sales reports through interoffice mail or walking data down the hall on a disk. Since integration servers mirror the way business works, their success suggests that the application integration solution, in fact, addresses a business flow problem. Technology such as integration servers functions as the necessary B2B infrastructure.

Why a New Layer?

Traditional middleware such as MOM (message-queuing software and pub/sub engines) solves only part of the application integration problem. Integration servers, by building on top of existing middleware technology, address the other part. This makes integration servers the "middleware of middleware" (see Figure 9.1).

An effective application integration solution contains a number of components that are neither middleware nor applications, but are routing, reformatting, and flow components. Although these components may be placed in an application or middleware, they are a better architectural fit when they are placed in integration servers, providing a central point of integration.

Given all this, exactly what do integration servers offer? As with any new technology, vendors took individual approaches to define products that address

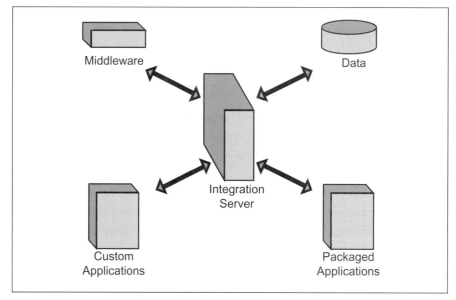

Figure 9.1   **Integration servers can integrate many different types of middleware, as well as applications and databases.**

the integration server problem. Despite this lack of standardization, integration servers share some common components—a transformation layer, a rules engine, and an intelligent routing mechanism, as well as a number of features we will discuss later in this chapter.

The three primary components of integration servers are the transformation layer, the rules engine, and the intelligent routing mechanism.

An integration server is a software system based on asynchronous, store-and-forward messaging. It works simply to manage interactions between applications and other information resources, using abstraction techniques—an application puts (publishes) a message to the integration server. Another application, or applications, consumes (subscribes to) the message (see Figure 9.2).

The application does not need to be session connected in order to work successfully. This eliminates, from the outset, the primary scalability problem associated with most integration technologies. Target systems need not be active. They can receive the information at some future time when they become active.

Integration servers do much more than simply function asynchronously. They extend the basic messaging paradigm by mediating the interaction between the applications, allowing the source and target systems to remain truly anonymous. They also translate and convert data, reformat and reconstitute information, and

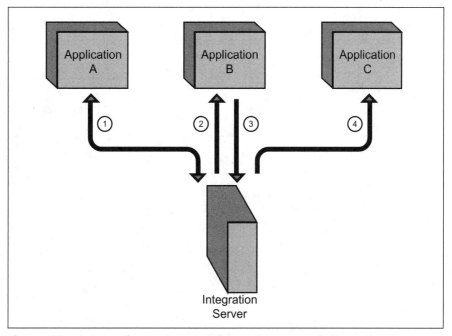

Figure 9.2   Integration servers publish and consume information to provide information flow between applications.

route information to any number of targets (determined by centrally defined business rules that are applied to the message content). They can do this one-to-one, one-to-many, or many-to-many (see Figure 9.3).

To be the solid foundation for a successful application integration strategy, integration servers must offer genuine any-to-any and many-to-many capabilities.

As you might expect, because of the individual approaches vendors take to solve the integration broker problem, not all integration servers are alike. A complete integration-brokering solution demands an underlying messaging system, a brokering layer (or rules engine), a connectivity (adapter) framework, design and development tools, and system management and administration tools. A handful of products currently on the market provide many pieces of the puzzle, but none provide the entire puzzle. A systems integrator is often needed to combine those pieces with the other pieces that are necessary to complete the puzzle.

The success of the finished "picture" depends on the design and architecture of the solution—how well the pieces integrate. This is what determines their scalability. IS organizations need to be thorough about "kicking the tires" to make certain they select the right solution for their application integration initiative.

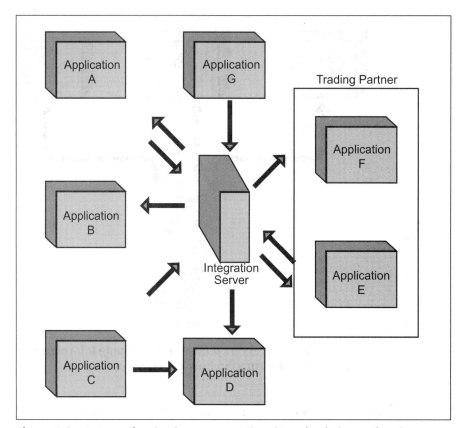

Figure 9.3   Integration brokers can send and receive information from any number of systems, one-to-one, one-to-many, or many-to-many.

Integration servers are different from traditional middleware because of the services they offer above and beyond such products. They certainly use information. Still, it's difficult to fit them into the MOM category. In addition to relying on the concept of a message, they provide value-added services from the uppermost layer in the ISO model, the application layer.

Applications, Databases, and Middleware

Too often, when we consider the details of integration servers, we put the cart ahead of the horse. The first step in an integration server evaluation must include an evaluation of the types of systems to be integrated.

The source and target systems may consist of any number of entities—database servers, Web servers, host applications, user screens, distributed objects, ERP applications, and custom or proprietary applications. The benefit of integration servers rests with their ability to link different types of systems, adjusting to the variations between all source and target systems. They are able to do this by exposing an API (and sometimes an adapter, which will be discussed later in this chapter).

It is also noteworthy that integration servers adhere to a noninvasive application integration model, where the source and target applications don't require many changes to move information among them. Because integration servers are able to leverage many points of integration (including database access, screen scraping, defined APIs, and middleware), in many cases no changes at all are required.

An API is nothing more than the mechanism that allows an application to access the services of an integration server (see Figure 9.4). When using APIs, the developer can create a link between the source or target application interface and the integration server API. This requires creation of a program that binds the application's point of integration to the API of the integration servers, or changing the application to communicate with the integration server using its API.

Doing this has a huge downside. To bind an application to the integration server you must create code to accomplish the task, or change the application to accommodate the integration server API—costly propositions, in terms of both time and money. The inevitable need for testing only adds to the costs.

By contrast, adapters can link deeply into an application or database. They move information to and from source or target applications without the need to create new code (or any code, for that matter). Adapters, which we discussed in the previous chapter and will discuss later, hide the complexities of the integrated applications by managing the movement of information into and out of the application on behalf of the integration server. Adapters leverage points of integration, such as a native interface (e.g., SAP's BAPI). They manage the consumption of information from the source application, converting it into a form that the integration server can understand. On the other end, adapters publish the information to the target application in a form that the target application can understand.

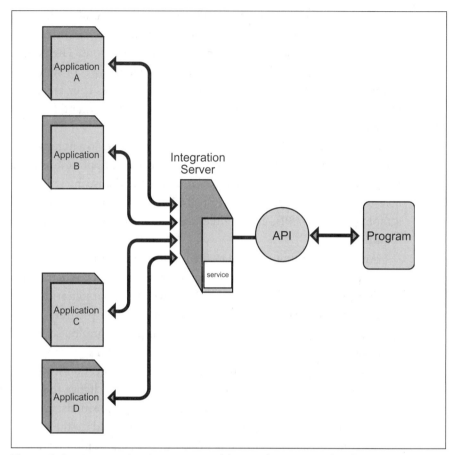

Figure 9.4   Integration servers provide services to applications through an application programming interface or an adapter.

Transformation Layer

The transformation layer is the "Rosetta Stone" of the system. It understands the format of all information being transmitted among the applications and translates that information on the fly, restructuring data from one message so that it makes sense to the receiving application or applications. It provides a common dictionary that contains information on how each application communicates outside itself (application externalization), as well as which bits of information have meaning to which applications (see Figure 9.5).

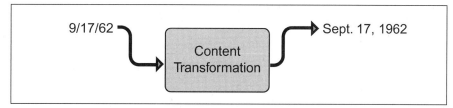

Figure 9.5   The transformation layer.

Transformation layers generally contain parsing and pattern-matching methods that describe the structure of any message format. Message formats are then constructed from pieces that represent each field encapsulated within a message. Once the message has been broken down to its component parts, the fields may be recombined to create a new message.

Most integration servers can handle most types of information, including fixed, delimited, and variable. Information is reformatted using an interface the user integration server provides, which may be as primitive as an API or as easy to use as a GUI.

Message layers generally store application information in a repository (see the section "Repository Services" later in this chapter) that keeps track of the source system, the format of the message, the target system, and the desired format of the target system. Transformation layers are vital because different systems deal with information in such different ways. For example, a SAP system tracks customer information in a manner very different from a Baan system. In order to exchange customer information between the two systems, the information must be reformatted. This reformatting, or transformation, may include a schema conversion and a data conversion. Reformatting ensures consistent application semantics between all integrated source and target applications.

Schema Conversion

A schema conversion (or accounting for the differences in application semantics) is the process of changing the structure of a message and thus remapping the schema so that it is acceptable to the target system. Though it is not difficult, application integration architects need to understand that this process must occur dynamically within the integration server. For example, if a message containing accounts receivable information arrives from a DB2 system on a mainframe, it may look something like this:

```
Cust_No                Alphanumeric     9
Amt_Due                Numeric    9
Date_of_Last_Bill              Date
```

With the following information:

```
AB99999999
560.50
09/17/98
```

The client/server system created to produce the annual report receives the information and must store it according to the following schema:

```
Customer_Number             Numeric    20
Money_Due                Numeric    8
Last_Billed              Alphanumeric    9
```

Clearly, the schema in the client/server system is different from the schema in the DB2 system. Moving information from the DB2 system (the source system) to the client/server system (the target system) without a schema conversion would most likely result in a system error because of the incompatibility of the formats. For the systems to communicate successfully, the information in Cust_No (which is alphanumeric and holds 9 positions) needs to be converted to all-numeric information capable of holding 20 digits or positions. All data that is not numeric (that is, letters) must be translated into numeric data. This can be accomplished either by deleting all characters when translating Cust_No to Customer_Number or by converting characters into numeric representations (A=1, B=2, and so on). This process can be defined within the rules-processing layer of the integration server by creating a rule to translate data dynamically, depending on its content and schema. Moving information from one system to another demands that the schema/format of the message be altered as the information is transferred from one system to the next (see Figure 9.6).

Although most integration servers can map any schema to any other schema, it is prudent to try to anticipate extraordinary circumstances. For example, when converting information extracted from an object-oriented database and placing it in a relational database, the integration server must convert the object schema into a relational representation before it can convert the data within the message.

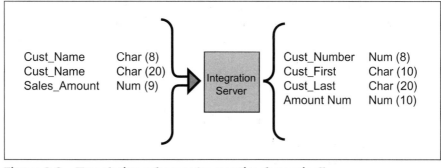

Figure 9.6   Translating schemas/semantics dynamically.

The same holds true when moving information from a relational database to an object-oriented database. Most integration servers break the message moving into their environment into a common format and then translate it into the appropriate message format for the target system. (As we already noted, the rules-processing engine within the integration server allows appropriate programming to take place.)

Data Conversion

In the previous transformation example, information in `Cust_No` (alphanumeric and holding 9 positions) needs to be converted to all-numeric with a capability of 20 positions. The alpha component of `Cust_No` must be dealt with in another manner. It is possible to change the nature of the target application to accept letters, or the alpha component can be either deleted or converted. Deleting characters or converting them into numeric representations are examples of data conversion. The key to successful data conversion is to determine the data formats of the source and target applications, assess the differences between them (for example, which data elements need to be extracted and converted, and where they ultimately need to be placed), and adjust to them. Most integration servers can understand most message schemas through message identifications. Therefore, they automatically convert data to a workable format. However, sometimes it will be necessary to program a rule to address a specific data-type conversion problem. The conversion of numeric information to alphanumeric information (and vice versa) generally requires such a programmed rule.

Although many formats exist within most application integration problem domains, we will confine our attention to the following:

- Alphanumeric
- Binary integers
- Floating point values
- Bit fields
- IBM mainframe floating points
- COBOL and PL/I picture data
- BLOBs

In addition to these formats, there are a number of formatting issues to address, including the ability to convert logical operators (bits) between systems and the ability to handle data types that are not supported in the target system. These issues often require significant customization in order to facilitate successful communication between systems.

In data conversion, values are managed in two ways: carrying over the value from the source to the target system without change, or modifying the data value dynamically. Either an algorithm or a look-up table can be used to modify the data value. One or more of the source application attributes may use an algorithm to change the data or create new data. For example, attributes in the source application may represent "Amount Sold" and hold the value 8. Another attribute, "Cost of Goods Sold," may contain the value 4. However, in the target application, these attributes may have to populate a new attribute, "Gross Margin," which is the amount sold less the cost of the goods sold. In order to make this communication successful, the algorithm "Amount Sold minus Cost of Goods Sold" must be applied.

Algorithms of this type are nothing more than the type of data conversions we have done for years when populating data warehouses and data marts. Now, in addition to using these simple algorithms, it is possible to aggregate, combine, and summarize the data to meet the specific requirements of the target application.

When using the look-up table scenario, it might be necessary to convert to an arbitrary value. "ARA" in the source system might refer to a value in the accounts receivable system. However this value can be determined, it must be checked against the look-up table. Integration servers may use a currency conversion table to convert dollars to yen, which may be embedded in a simple procedure or, more likely, in a database connected to the integration server. The integration server may also invoke a remote application server function to convert the amount.

The application integration architect or developer may encounter special circumstances that have to be finessed. The length of a message attribute may be unknown, or the value may be in an unknown order. In such situations, it is necessary to use the rules-processing capability of the integration server to convert the problem values into the proper representation for the target system.

Intelligent Routing

Intelligent routing, sometimes referred to as flow control or content-based routing, builds on the capabilities of both the rules layer and the message transformation layer. An integration server can "intelligently route" a message by first identifying it as coming from the source application and then routing it to the proper target application, translating it if required. For example, when a message arrives at the integration server, it is analyzed and identified as coming from a particular system and/or subsystem. Once the message is identified and the message schema is understood, the applicable rules and services are applied to the processing of the message, including transformation. Once the information is processed, the integration server, based on how it is programmed, routes the message to the correct target system (see Figure 9.7). This all takes place virtually instantaneously, with as many as a thousand of these operations occurring at the same time.

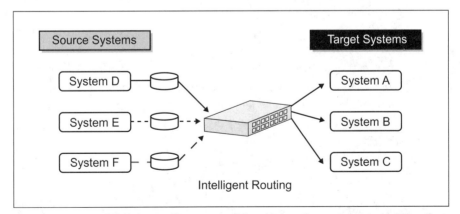

Figure 9.7   Intelligent routing means identifying the message and sending it to the proper destination.

Rules Processing

The rules-processing engine, found within most integration servers, allows the application integration architect and developer to create rules that control the processing and distribution of information. Rules processing is an application development environment supported by the integration server to address the special requirements of integrating applications. By using rules engines, integration servers can implement intelligent information routing and transformation. For example, at times a message will be required by a second target application. At other times, a piece of information will need to be routed to two or more applications. In both these cases, information must be routed to any number of target applications that extract and translate data from any number of source applications. A truly flexible solution requires a rules engine to make these formatting and routing decisions dynamically. Combining a rules engine with a message transformation layer allows such a solution to be realized.

Essentially, a rules engine is an application that resides between applications; one that does nothing more than provide the logic for sharing information. Each rules engine solves an intelligent routing and transformation problem differently. Most have the capability of testing a message to determine its fields and values. Most often, rules engines use traditional Boolean logic (IF, ELSE, and OR) and high-level languages to create rules and associate actions with each rule according to its algorithm.

The rules-processing capabilities of integration servers should not be confused with the capabilities of traditional application servers. Application servers provide a full spectrum of element environments and tools. Most rules-processing engines only provide features sufficient to move a message from any number of source systems to any number of target systems. However, as integration servers have matured, they have begun to provide rules-processing services that rival those of traditional application servers. Pushing the envelope in this direction, some vendors have gone so far as to integrate application servers with integration servers. This strategy combines the best of both worlds while also addressing service-oriented application integration.

Rules processing generally relies on scripting languages rather than on more complex programming languages (such as Java and C++) and on interpreters rather than on compilers. However, as in almost everything about integration servers, the way in which each integration server processes rules varies from vendor to vendor and from integration server to integration server.

Rules are created through either the rules editor (which functions like a program editor) or a wizard. The program editor creates rules by allowing commands to be entered into the integration server. These commands may be stored as a simple text file, or in more sophisticated integration servers, they may be stored within the repository. The rules wizard guides the user through the selection of each rule that is being applied to a particular message, group of information, or events. For example, the wizard may ask if the message should be processed as soon as it comes into the integration server or at a specific time of day. Options such as these are particularly useful for things like updating customer information in a database, when such updates might be better made during off-peak hours. The wizard may also inquire about the transformation of information between the source and target systems, including the logic that may be required. It may create the opportunity to take many variables into account at the same time, such as checking for states and events that other systems may provide. For example, it may not be advisable to update the SAP database if the last update to the database produced an error message or an unstable state. Or certain users might have to be logged on before proceeding with a certain type of message processing. Depending on the need, it may be beneficial to wait for a specific event before extracting information from a source system.

Because rules processing is truly programming, almost anything can be done. Information can be generated based on sales events over a million dollars. Other applications based on the monitoring of events for states can be invoked. Anything that can be programmed can be made part of the rules processing. With rules engines becoming more powerful and vendors providing easier mechanisms to create rules, there is no limit to what is attainable.

Message Warehousing

A message warehouse is a database that, as an option, is able to store information that flows through the integration server. In general, integration servers provide this message persistence facility to meet several requirements: message mining, message integrity, message archiving, and auditing.

Message mining allows the extraction of business data to support decisions, creating the message warehouse as a quasi-data warehouse. For example, it is possible to use the message warehouse to determine the characteristics and amount of new customer information that is being processed through the integration server. All new sales orders for a given period of time can be displayed. Off-the-shelf data-mining and reporting tools work wonderfully for such applications.

Information that is stored in the message warehouse is almost always stored without modification. However, in a few cases, the information must flow through a data warehouse as it would an aggregation or transformation process. The data is combined and altered so that it will make sense to the average business user. In general, application integration architects and application programmers accomplish this through the rules-processing mechanism of the integration server, or they may employ an outside application to alter the message for storage.

Message warehousing can provide services such as message integrity because the warehouse itself provides a natural, persistent state for message traffic. If the server goes down, the message warehouse may act as a persistent buffer, or queue, to store information that would otherwise be lost. Information may then be re-sent or compared with other message warehouses on the network to ensure message transfer integrity. The underlying principle is that of persistent message queuing supported by traditional message-oriented middleware. This also provides state-full messaging, or the ability to maintain states between two or more systems even when using asynchronous messaging, messaging that, by definition, is a cohesive rather than coupled mechanism.

Message archiving enables the integration server user to store months of message traffic in an archive for auditing or other purposes. It allows information to be restored for analysis. Many application integration administrators maintain message archives for just over a year, although no standard currently exists.

Auditing is the use of the message warehouse to determine the health of the application integration solution and to provide the ability to solve any problems that are noted. For example, by using the auditing facilities of an integration server, it is possible to determine message traffic loads, message content variations, and the amount of information requiring transformation. Auditing also tracks information that changes, its state before the transformation, and its state following transformation.

Repository Services

Many integration servers embrace the concept of a repository—a database of information about source and target applications (which may include data elements, inputs, processes, outputs, and the inter-relationships among applications).

Although many experts view repositories primarily as a part of the world of application development, they do not question their value to the world of application integration.

Application integration-enabled repositories, in their simplest form, provide the integration server user with a database of information pertaining to the following:

- Owner of the system (company)
- Location of the system (directory)
- Security parameters
- Message schema information
- Metadata
- Enabling technology
- Transformation information
- Rules and logic for message processing
- Design and architecture information (e.g., UML)
- Object information

The goal is to provide a sophisticated repository that is capable of keeping track of a good deal more than the rudimentary information (such as directory data). It should track more sophisticated information about the source and target systems (such as metadata, message schemas, and even security and ownership). The repository should provide all the information required by the application integration architect and programmer to locate any piece of information within the enterprise and to link it to any other piece of information. The repository must be the master directory for the entire application integration problem domain.

Many concepts of repositories have been taken from the application development world. Rules, logic, objects, and metadata are still tracked within a repository. The difference between the two is that by using the repository with an integration server, other, less sophisticated information—such as encrypted passwords, network addresses, protocol transformation services, and even error code transformations and maintenance information—can also be tracked.

In more sophisticated integration servers, the repository is becoming the axis mundi, able to access both the source and target systems in order to discover necessary information (such as metadata and available business processes). Engaged in this "auto-discovery," the integration server can populate the repository with this or any other information that may be required. Ultimately, the repository will become the enterprise metadata repository, able to track all systems and databases connected to the integration server.

The value of a repository should be clear. With the repository as a common reference point for all connected processes and databases, integrating data and methods is as straightforward as finding their equivalents and joining them together. The repository can also track the rules that the application integration architect and developer apply within the application integration problem domain. Moreover, because the repository knows the schema of both the source and the target systems, it also contains information for the proper transformation of information flowing from source to target. In many cases, this transformation can be automatically defined, freeing the user from ever needing to be involved in the definition of the transformation procedure.

However, repositories remain only the storage mechanisms in this scenario. The integration server must read the information from the repository and carry out the appropriate process. In addition to the integration server engine, the graphical user interface that accompanies most integration servers provides application integration architects and developers with a mechanism to alter the repository, and so alter the behavior of the integration server.

User Interface

One of the wonderful realities of the integration server is that it is middleware "with a face"—or, at least with a graphical user interface. This interface allows the user to create rules, link applications, and define transformation logic (see Figure 9.8).

Although the features and functions of interfaces vary from vendor to vendor, all vendors claim that their product simplifies the application integration process. For some, this claim is something of a stretch. These vendors provide only the most basic features (such as scripting and rudimentary administration) to justify their outlandish claim. However, the newest versions really do simplify the integration process and include such features as wizard systems to define rules and transformation, along with an interface that allows the user to drill down to any level of detail within any connected system. These interfaces can depict an application integration solution, including connected systems, rules, and message routing, using diagrams that bring the entire solution to light. More than simply setting up the solution, these graphical user interfaces also provide

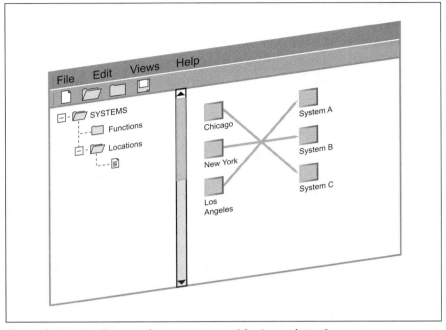

Figure 9.8   The integration server graphical user interface.

administration features, such as the ability to monitor message traffic, the performance of the integration servers, the status of connected systems, and mechanisms to route around problems.

Directory Services

Because integration servers deal with distributed systems, including systems that exist in other organizations, they require directory services to locate, identify, use, and authorize network resources for those systems. Directory services provide a single point of entry for applications and middleware (e.g., integration servers). In doing so, they lend a tremendous benefit to the system. They also support the use of a shared set of standards for directory and naming services. Directory services act as guides among the thousands of resources available to applications and middleware.

Using directory services, the integration server or application integration developer can build applications that are able to intelligently locate resources anywhere on the network. Directories know where to find these resources on behalf of applications. They track them as they are reconfigured, moved, or deleted. For example, an e-mail application can locate a user group, a word processing application can find a printer, and a client/server application can find a database—no matter where these resources exist on the network.

Application objects exist on the network, not on certain servers. Therefore, it is essential that developers share a common infrastructure for locating objects.

At their base, directory services are nothing more than a method of classifying resources on the network in a way consistent with every other method of classification. For example, in biology, biologists classify living things according to kingdom, phylum, class, order, family, genus, and species. Directory services identify and classify all computer systems by moving down a similar hierarchy and by using a naming system to determine the direction of the branches.

A number of directory services exist, including the Domain Name System (DNS), Novell's NetWare Directory System and Directory Services, Netscape Communications' Directory Server, Microsoft's Active Directory, and X.500. DNS enables all Internet users to resolve server names. It has been a tremendous resource for years, but is, unfortunately, limited to that one simple function.

Management

Administration and management of the application integration problem domain is primarily the responsibility of the management layer of the integration server. Because of the level of the technology's maturity and the fact that several enterprise management tools are on the market, too many integration servers are marketed with little or no management.

Application integration solutions require the ability to start and stop source and target applications, as well as the ability to monitor important statistics, such as performance, message integrity, and the general functioning of the entire application integration problem domain. Some integration server vendors are correctly anticipating the needs of application integration management and are creating separate products to address these needs, while enabling existing enterprise management tools to handle the special needs of application integration. These vendors stand to win the lion's share of this growing market.

The management layers of integration servers need to support other features, including the ability to monitor message movement through the system.

These features must include alerts to re-queue throughput, alerts to re-queue availability, and end-to-end performance tracking.

Although it is too early to predict with certainty, it appears that a new generation of management tools built specifically for the application integration marketplace is on the horizon. However, until that generation arrives, users must either depend on what is bundled with the integration server or create their own management infrastructure.

Adapters

Adapters for integration servers have been considered for years; however, as with so many other things, each vendor had its own concept of what an adapter should be (see Chapter 10).

Other Features

Vendors are building other features into their integration servers all the time. These might include version control to track the changes made in integration models (including check in/check out), traditional configuration management capabilities, and impact analysis (the ability to examine how changing information flows will affect a trading community before making the actual changes to the physical flows).

Finally, all integration servers have some sort of amalgamation with a process integration tool that supports functions such as collaboration. Process integration tools place logical abstraction layers on top of existing physical integration flows, allowing users to view application integration from a business-oriented perspective rather than from a technical perspective.

Topologies

Integration servers use a "hub-and-spoke" topology. The integration server, as the hub, rests between the source and target applications being integrated in a configuration that resembles a star (see Figure 9.9). Although this configuration is the most traditional one, new developments suggest the various advantages of leveraging integration servers that use other topologies, such as multihub or federated.

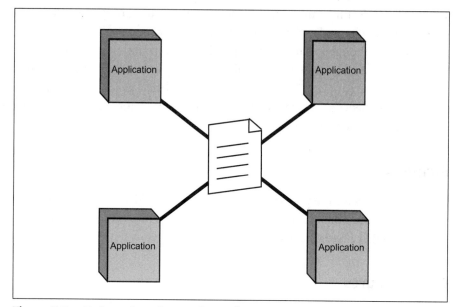

Figure 9.9   Hub-and-spoke configuration.

In the multihub configuration, a number of integration servers are linked, with the source and target applications connected to any of the brokers in the configuration (see Figure 9.10). This configuration can scale, making it possible to integrate virtually unlimited numbers of source and target applications. When more applications need to be integrated than a single integration server can handle, more integration servers can be added to the network.

Like the multihub configuration, the federated configuration supports several integration servers working together to solve an application integration problem. However, federated configurations typically mean that several different types of integration servers, independent of one another, are working in concert to integrate a trading community. This is a common configuration—which makes perfect sense, because most trading partners don't agree on the make and model of integration servers. Therefore, the various integration servers must learn to interoperate. What's important to understand about this configuration is the fact that the source and target applications are statically bound to a particular integration server (see Figure 9.11). The message processing is not shared among integration servers. They typically hand off information, one to another, through a common interchange format such as XML.

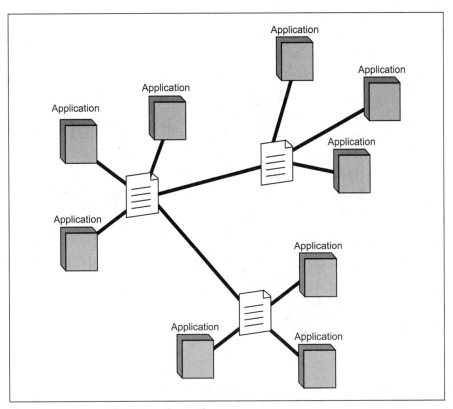

Figure 9.10 Multihub configuration.

The evolution of integration servers is clear. As they become more sophisticated, there is a clear movement away from the simple hub-and-spoke configuration toward the multihub configuration. Unfortunately, this transition is not, and will not be, a smooth one. Some integration servers are able to support multihub configurations. Others are unable to intelligently share the message-processing load. Integration servers that can exist in a multihub configuration become successful by learning to "share the load" with other integration servers on the network. Load-balancing mechanisms that are able to off-load message-processing work to integration servers with available capacity help make it possible to simply add integration servers to the network. They locate the broker, configure it, replicate the repository, and put the integration server to work.

In addition to the ability to scale—a definite requirement for application integration—the multihub configuration provides a fail-safe service. With several

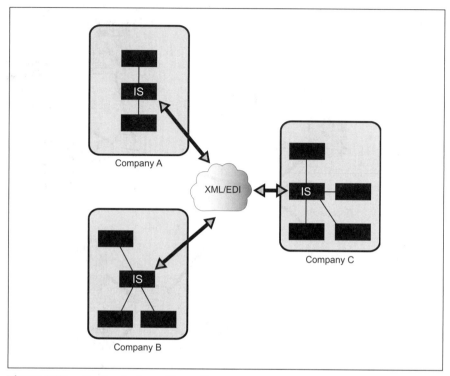

Figure 9.11   Federated configuration.

integration servers sharing the network load, a single failure will not shut down the system. The others can continue processing the information. To say that this is an advantage is a profound understatement. Unfortunately, it is an "uneven" advantage. Many of these fail-safe features vary from vendor to vendor, with some more effective than others. However, an uneven advantage remains an advantage. With the integration server as the beating heart of application integration, it is only prudent to incorporate sound mechanisms to protect it from failure.

The Future of Application Integration and Integration Servers

Integration servers, at least the core engine of integration servers, are destined to become commodity products because many perform only rudimentary functions. In an effort to differentiate their products, many integration server vendors are putting layer upon layer of value-added software on top of the core integration server engine. Thin adapters are giving way to thick adapters. Vendors are learning that it is better to hide the complexities of enterprise systems behind abstraction layers and put a business face on all the "geeky" little details. These abstraction layers save the end user from having to deal with the complexities of the technology and put the end user in a better position to take care of the business at hand.

Given this reality, when all is said and done, integration servers may turn out to be more about business integration than middleware.

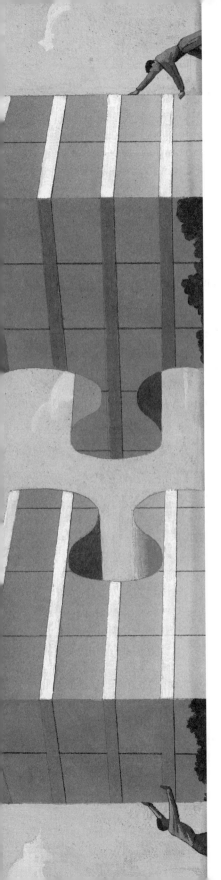

## CHAPTER TEN

Adapters and the J2EE Connector Architecture

There is no question about it: If you're going to do application integration, you're going to need adapters. That's the purpose of this chapter—to explain the notion, architecture, and implementation of adapters.

However, adapters don't stop there. There is a new standard on the rise, the J2EE Connector Architecture, which defines a standard architecture and adapter behavior. This standard gives us the ability to create an adapter once, and then use it anywhere—including most integration and application servers. Clearly this provides the application integration technology consumer with many advantages.

Adapters are powerful; they deal with the ugly details of the underlying application, database, and standards-based (EDI, XML, etc.) interfaces. Believe me, you don't want to have to code through those interfaces on your own. It is always better to buy than to build.

The liberation of information and application services out of back-end systems is the job of adapters. Adapters sit between the source or target applications and the integration server, and account for the differences in the back-end systems by translating requests into something the native source or target application can understand, then they translate the response.

We need adapters for several reasons:

- First, we need some sort of reusable set of software services that can extract and publish information to source or target systems, which saves us from having to build those interfaces as "one-offs" each and every time we do an application integration project.
- Second, we need common interfaces into source or target systems that provide a consistent set of services.
- Finally, we need management visibility into source and target systems' connections. We need this for reliability, as source and target systems are known to go down from time to time, and adapters can manage through those outages.

The simple notion of adapters becomes complicated by numerous vendor varieties, and even the differences between standards. Truth be told, the approaches to adapters outnumber the source or target systems they are looking to connect. Moreover, the use of standards, which is supposed to simplify things, may add more complexity and confusion in the short term. We'll talk more about that below.

The Purpose of Adapters

In the past, when we sought to connect Application A to Application B, or Applications A and B to an integration server, we had to interact with that application using some sort of interface that the application (hopefully) provided. Interfaces into applications and databases vary greatly, including everything from simple well-defined APIs to complex and cryptic exit calls, or perhaps something one level above screen scraping.

After hand-coding the interfaces to the middleware layer a few hundred times, in essence creating mini-applications between the source or target applications and the middleware layer, middleware vendors began to pitch the notion of adapters (see Figure 10.1).

Adapters are layers between the integration server and the source or target application. For example, an adapter could be a set of "libraries" that map the differences between two distinct interfaces—the integration server interface and the native interface of the source or target application—and hide the complexities of those interfaces from the end user or even from the application integration developer using the integration server.

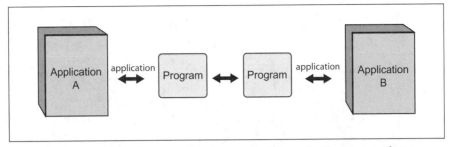

**Figure 10.1   Before adapters, developers had to code the connections
between the application interfaces and the middleware.**

An integration server vendor may have adapters for several different source
and target applications (such as SAP R/3, Baan, and PeopleSoft), or for certain
types of databases (such as Oracle, Sybase, or DB2), or even for specific brands
and types of middleware. Over time, adapters have become more sophisticated.
They began as a set of libraries that developers had to manipulate and evolved
into binary interfaces that require little—if any—programming. Adapters are
also getting smarter, with intelligence placed within the adapter, and with
adapters running at the source and target systems in order to better capture
events.

Two types of adapters exist in the context of integration servers: thin
adapters and thick adapters. These adapters may have two types of behavior:
dynamic and static.

Thin Adapters

Today's most popular integration servers offer thin adapters. In most cases, they
are simply API wrappers, or binders, which map the interface of the source or
target system to a common interface supported by the integration server (see
Figure 10.2). In other words, they simply perform an API-binding trick, binding
one API to another.

Thin adapters have the advantage of being simple to implement. With no
additional, "thick" layer of software between source and target applications, there
is greater granular control. Thin adapters have a number of disadvantages, however. Because using them accomplishes nothing more than trading one interface
for another, thin adapters impact performance without increasing functionality.
And a fair amount of programming is still required. To complicate matters, the
common APIs that are being mapped are almost always proprietary.

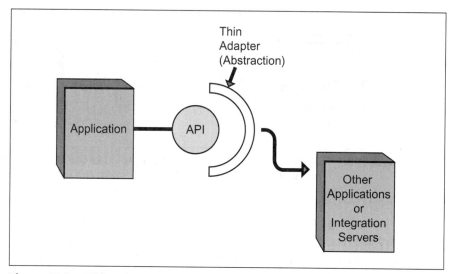

Figure 10.2   Thin adapters don't provide sophisticated layers of software between the source or target systems and the integration server, and are really just simple abstractions on top of existing APIs.

Thick Adapters

Unlike thin adapters, thick adapters provide a significant amount of software and functionality between the integration server infrastructure and the source or target applications. The thick adapter's layer of abstraction makes managing movement or invoking processes painless (see Figure 10.3). Because the abstraction layer and the manager negotiate the differences between all the applications requiring integration, almost no programming is needed.

Thick interfaces accomplish this via the layer of sophisticated software that hides the complexities of the source and target application interfaces from the integration server user. The user sees only a businesslike representation of the process and the metadata information as managed by the abstraction layer and the adapter. In many cases, the user connects many systems through this abstraction layer and the graphical user interface, without ever having to resort to hand-coding.

Repositories are major players in the thick-adapter scenario. As we noted, the repository understands much of the information about the source and target applications and can use that information as a mechanism to interact with the source and target applications on behalf of the integration server.

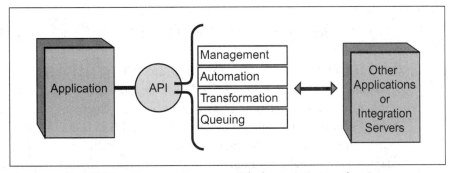

Figure 10.3   Thick adapters place a sophisticated abstraction layer on top of the application interfaces.

In addition, several abstraction layers may be created around the types of applications to be integrated. For example, there may be an abstraction for common middleware services (such as distributed objects, message-oriented middleware, and transactional middleware). There may also be an abstraction layer for packaged applications, and another layer to address the integration of relational and nonrelational databases. This structure hides from the end user the complexities of the interfaces that each entity (middleware, packaged applications, and databases) employs.

Another feature of a thick adapter is the ability to think and process information on its own, independent of the integration server. Processing performed by thick adapters may include

- Simple transformation of application semantics, such as the transformation of a native format to a canonical form.
- Exception-handling routines.
- Information queuing and restart in case of integration server outages.
- Direct routing of information that may not need service from the integration server.

With the many advantages and conveniences of thick adapters, it should come as no surprise that integration server vendors are moving toward them. Their progress is slowed by the fact that thick adapters require a tremendous amount of time to develop, as much as six times that of a thin adapter. Right now, this time investment deters some vendors. However, as application integration becomes more sophisticated, enterprises will continue to look for more sophisticated solutions that require no programming and provide an easy, businesslike method to view the integration of the enterprise.

Static and Dynamic Adapters

As noted earlier, in addition to being thick or thin, adapters are also defined by being either static or dynamic.

Static adapters, the most common adapters in play at this time, must be manually coded with the contents of the source and target systems. They have no mechanism for understanding anything about the schema of connected databases. As a result, they must be configured by hand (i.e., coded) to receive information from the source schema. If the connected database schema changes, static adapters have no mechanism to update their configuration with the new schema.

In contrast to static adapters, *dynamic adapters* "learn" about the source or target systems connected to them through a discovery process that takes place when they are first connected to the application or data source (see Figure 10.4). This discovery process typically means reading the database schema information from the repository (or perhaps the source code) to determine the structure, content, and application semantics of the connected system. More important, dynamic adapters not only learn about the connected system, they also are able to relearn information if something changes within the connected system over time. A dynamic adapter automatically understands when a customer-number attribute name changes.

Type Importers

To address the dynamic nature of source and target systems, many adapters and their connected integration servers provide type importers, mechanisms that read schema information from the source or target systems and automatically define it as an input or an output. As source and target systems change over time, schema information can be reimported as needed.

The use of type importers is important because it saves the end user from having to define by hand—and ultimately risk mistakes—the input and output schema for connected applications.

Type importers can be passive, meaning you have to invoke the initial importing or the reimporting of the schema from the source or target systems. Or they can be active, meaning that importing and reimporting schema (when changed) occurs automatically.

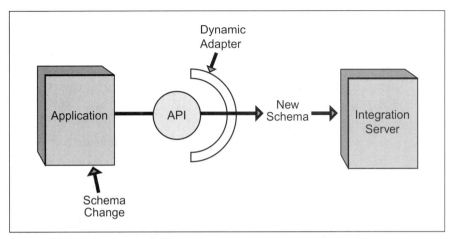

Figure 10.4 **When using dynamic adapters, information such as schema becomes visible to the integration server.**

Centralized versus Distributed Adapters

Two distinct adapter architectures are emerging: distributed and cen-tralized. As the name suggests, centralized adapters run with the inte-gration server. Generally, these are thin adapters that only bind the integration server's API to the API of the source or target application.

Just as centralized adapters are thin adapters, distributed adapters are thick adapters that exist on the integration server as well as on the source or target application. Running an adapter on the application that is being integrated allows many processes of the source or target application to be better determined, such as capturing events, monitoring states, or even restarting the application as required. And because the adapter is in two parts, it is better able to coordinate the transfer of information between the integration server and the source or target application.

Information-Oriented versus Service-Oriented Adapters

Another clear trend in the world of adapters is the movement from simple infor-mation movement to support for service-level application connectivity. As you may guess, each approach requires very different types of adapter technology.

When dealing with simple information, the *information-oriented adapter* merely leverages whatever interface is available to extract information from the source system, and moves that information into the integration server (see Figure 10.5). For example, customer-address information coming from SAP may be transformed to account for differences in application semantics and then published to a target system (or systems), say, PeopleSoft, using the same type of information-oriented adapter.

Service-oriented adapters are a bit more complex. Instead of dealing with the extraction and publication of simple information to source or target systems, service-oriented adapters have to abstract services or application behavior, as well. In other words, they need to expose application functions in a way that they may be abstracted into a composite application as a local function that actually exists on a remote system. Remember, even though the function appears local to the composite application, the application processing occurs in the remote system that is connected through a service-oriented adapter (see Figure 10.6).

In essence, service-oriented adapters take remote function calls within remote systems for other applications, and do so without the applications having to understand anything about each other. Of course, service-oriented adapters have to be linked through some type of integration server or application server to facilitate the extension into the composite applications, and to account for the differences in the applications.

Service-oriented adapters are a result of the interest in SOAI and the use of standards such as Web services, and perhaps some lingering use of more traditional distributed objects. However, creating service-oriented adapters, in practice, is a bit of challenge considering that the adapter has to interact with internal application functions, rather than just application information.

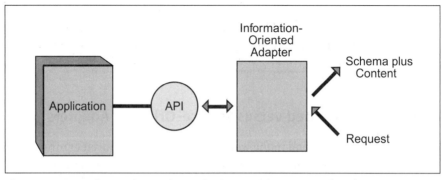

Figure 10.5   **Information-oriented adapters deal only with simple information.**

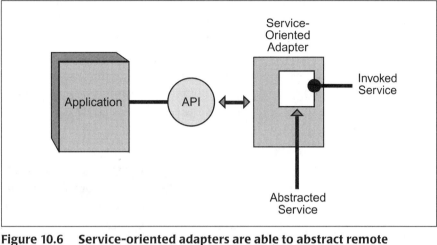

Figure 10.6   Service-oriented adapters are able to abstract remote application services to composite applications that can make use of them.

Interface Types

Not all application interfaces will provide all of the functionality required to create and operate service-oriented adapters, and adapters are always limited by the capabilities of the interfaces that the source or target systems provide. To this end, it's helpful to define interface types that applications and databases provide that fit with service- or information-oriented adapters.

They are

- Static data
- Dynamic data
- Function return data
- Function return service
- Function return abstraction

Static data application interfaces refer to those application interfaces that return simple information within a static record that is difficult—if not impossible—to change. These old types of application interfaces only provide fixed data with visibility into an application and do not provide opportunities for service-level access due to the data-only limitation of this interface. SAP's RFC is an example of a static data application interface. This type of interface works best with information-oriented-type adapters.

Dynamic data application interfaces also provide only data, but they provide data within a dynamic structure that can be defined through the interface call, or within the application or database itself. This means that all types of information can be extracted using this type of interface in a single gulp, and you can define the data that is extracted. Databases are the best example of interfaces that provide dynamic data interfaces, but many applications, including PeopleSoft, do some of this, as well. This type of interface also works best with information-oriented adapters.

Function return data application interfaces provide access to many internal functions, such as an inventory check, but only return responses to those functions; they do not make those functions "remotable" to other applications. This is a bit different from the information-oriented types, such as static and dynamic data, in that you do have access to internal application services, and can even make those services available to other integrated applications. However, you can only extract information as responses to those internal services. SAP's BAPI is a good example of a function return data interface.

Function return service application interfaces provide the adapter with the ability to abstract a static service to the integration server or connected composite application. This is another level over function return data interfaces in that you not only get an answer back from the invocation of a function, you can also bind the remote static function to another application, making it appear as if it were a local function. Any RPC-based application is a good example of a function return service application interface. Web services are another example; indeed, more SOAI products will leverage function return service interfaces, if they are available.

Function return abstraction application interfaces provide the adapter with the ability not only to gain access to a remote service or function, but also to alter that remote service or function to meet the needs of another application or applications. What's unique here is that we can inherit remote services, tossing away what we don't need and adding what we do. What's more, we can do this without changing the code in the serving application. In essence, this is very much like, if not exactly like, object-oriented programming mechanisms.

JCA

As you can read for yourself toward the end of this chapter, JCA (J2EE Connector Architecture) is a standard adapter architecture that provides adapter interoperability between integration servers by offering standard mechanisms for communicating with source or target systems. The purpose of our JCA discussion here is not to provide all of the details about JCA; there are plenty of other places to find more detailed information, including the current spec that can be found at www.java.sun.com. My goal is to provide some basic information and, more importantly, put JCA into perspective, with our discussion in the first part of this chapter taken into consideration. It's also important to understand that JCA is *not* a new set of adapter services. What JCA brings to the table is a standard mechanism to create and deploy adapters . . . something we've yet to provide as an industry.

To understand the need for JCA, we must first understand that, although most application integration technology vendors offer adapters, the adapters they offer are very different and don't work and play well with others. For example, you can't take adapters from WebMethods and make them work with Vitria adapters without a lot of redevelopment on the vendor's side. They are not interchangeable.

It's also important to mention that JCA is Java centric (the J in JCA stands for J2EE), designed to be invoked from a J2EE container. Considering this, it could be an architectural mismatch for those shops that are non-Java. However, it's clearly okay to leverage JCA adapters from non-Java environments. Due to market momentum, most application integration technologies—Java centric or not—will leverage JCA.

Is JCA Thick or Thin?

JCA is a standard adapter architecture that provides adapter interoperability between integration servers by offering standard mechanisms for communicating with source or target systems. So, if JCA is a type of adapter, is it thick or is it thin?

Considering the capabilities of JCA—both existing and proposed—JCA adapters are more thin than thick. They provide a simple abstraction layer on top of the existing source or target application interface. JCA provides some metadata capabilities, based on XML, as well as resource management, but JCA lacks the intelligence to handle exceptions or think on its own when communication with the integration server is absent.

JCA-based adapters may provide these capabilities in the future, but for now, JCA adapters are lean and mean.

Finally, one of the opportunities and challenges of JCA is the notion that packaged application vendors and other third parties will build and support JCA adapters—the idea being that many packaged application and middleware vendors will develop JCA adapters that are usable with a variety of application and integration servers. They are interchangeable, because all JCA developers comply with a single specification and a single set of services and interfaces.

Breaking Down JCA

In the world of JCA, source and target systems (packaged applications, databases, legacy systems, etc.) are known as Enterprise Information Systems (EIS). The idea is that you can communicate with EIS from J2EE through a JCA-compliant resource adapter, which exists within an application server or integration server. Components within the J2EE environment can then interact with the EIS through the resource adapter using the Common Client Interface (CCI) API (see Figure 10.7). You access information through the CCI; in essence, it's an abstraction layer over and above the EIS, sort of a Call Level Interface (CLI) for packaged applications.

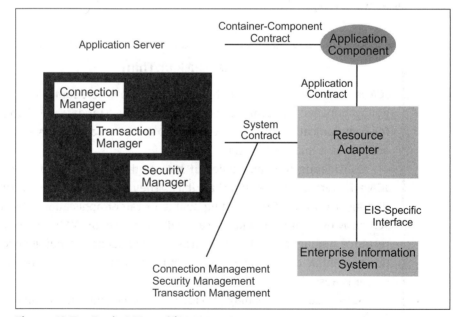

Figure 10.7   Basic JCA architecture.

As we mentioned above, JCA is implemented in a J2EE application server with the resource adapters provided by a JCA adapter vendor or, perhaps, the packaged application or database vendor.

JCAs define a set of elements and services including:

- System-level contracts and services
- CCI
- Packaging and deployment interfaces

System-level contracts and services define the interfaces between the J2EE components and the EIS. They are implemented in the application server and resource adapter, and could be a mix and match of vendors (application server vs. resource adapter). System-level contracts and services define the demarcation line between the J2EE container and the EIS, allowing these components to collaborate on activities such as management of resources, security, and transaction.

The *CCI* defines the properties of a client API that J2EE components (e.g., an EJB) can leverage to connect to and exchange requests and information with the EIS. Moreover, the CCI also allows nonmanaged applications to leverage a JCA resource adapter. Examples of nonmanaged clients include Java applets and application clients.

Finally, the *packaging and deployment interfaces* provide a mechanism that allows resource adapters to plug into J2EE applications.

The JCA standard supports two types of environments: managed environments and nonmanaged environments.

Managed environments support multitier J2EE-based applications that can connect to one or many EISs. In addition, the applications (known as managed applications) may include one or many application components existing within a J2EE container.

Nonmanaged environments support access to one or many EIS systems as well, but do so from nonmanaged application clients, including applets of the Java client application. In this architecture, the Java client connects with the EIS directly, leveraging the resource adapter library.

Understanding JCA Resource Adapters

If JCA is the platform as well as the standard, then JCA resource adapters are the applications that run in that environment. Resource adapters, as we covered briefly above, provide the translation and connectivity information that account for the differences between how the EIS communicates outside itself, and the way JCA needs to communicate to allow for interoperability.

To comply with JCA, all JCA resource adapters and J2EE containers must support system-level contracts. If you remember, a contract defines the rules of the application and the implementation of the interface. What's more, JCA asks that all resource adapters support CCI as their client API, providing a J2EE-based programmatic access to the EIS.

There are two types of contracts: application contracts and system-level contracts. *Application contracts* define the CCI API, or the interface that the J2EE client component (managed or nonmanaged) uses to communicate with the EIS. *System-level contracts*, as the name implies, enable the resource adapters to connect with the system services found in the J2EE container. This allows the resource adapter to manage low-level functions such as transactions and security.

An instance of a service contract is *connection management*, which enables J2EE containers to provide their own services to create and manage EIS connection pools. The purpose of this service is to ensure that there are enough connections to allow for the JCA application integration solution to scale.

The connection management contract provides a consistent application programming practice to create connections for both managed and nonmanaged applications. It also enables CCI-based connection factory and connection interfaces, as well as provides a generic mechanism for J2EE-managed components (security, error handling, etc.). Finally, connection management provides support for connection pooling services that leverage the J2EE container.

What's the Difference Between XA and Local Transactions?

XA transactions support JTA XA resource-based transaction management with JCA-compliant resource adapters. This means that the XA resource interface is implemented through the respective resource adapter. XA transactions allow a transaction to be managed by a single transaction manager that exists outside the domain of the resource adapter.

Local transactions are managed by the J2EE container or sometimes through a J2EE component. Using the JTA UserTransaction interface or the transaction API specific to the EIS, the J2EE container is able to manage resources local to the application and the respective resource adapter.

Another type of service contract is *transaction management*, which extends the J2EE container's transactional middleware capabilities to the resource manager. It's the job of the resource manager to manage the shared EIS resources, specifically, transactions that are managed by the external transaction manager and transactions managed internally that do not interact with external resources.

This is a powerful component of JCA because you can manage transactions across many EIS resource managers, including support for XA transactions and local transactions.

Packaging Your JCA Adapter

When you create a resource adapter, JCA provides a packaging and deployment interface that provides a mechanism for JCA resource adapters to connect to a J2EE container. This process is almost identical to the deployment of EJBs and Web components in a J2EE container.

CCI

CCI provides the ability to write more complex Java interfaces to manipulate an EIS. It's the job of CCI to define an EIS-neutral client API that allows the J2EE components to communicate with many EIS resources at the same time through a single layer of abstraction. In essence, CCI is a remote function call interface for executing information extraction and perhaps method invocation in the EIS.

As we move to more service-oriented type frameworks, CCI will become more important. What's more, the fact that CCI is EIS independent makes it even more powerful because, like the JDBC for databases, you merely program to a single interface, and the differences with the native APIs are accounted for in the JCA resource adapter. The use of CCI is the fundamental advantage of JCA.

Adaptable World

As you can see, adapters are a huge part of application integration. They remove us from the need to deal with the interface details that communicate with a variety of different source and target systems. What's more, adapters provide more consistency from interface to interface because they are, by design, reusable from problem domain to problem domain. However, adapters do not remove the need to have a complete integration solution, including transformation, routing, and process integration. They merely deal with the connectivity to the source or target systems.

Adapters are becoming more important as we look to leverage new standards such as Web services. They need to change from information oriented to service oriented, something that will not happen overnight. There are very different problems to solve as well. What's more, many applications just won't provide service-level access to their internal functions, serving up simple data instead. This is not the fault of the adapter developer, but a limitation of the application interface. As time goes on, a greater number of simple information interfaces will become service based, perhaps even leveraging service-oriented access standards such as WSDL and SOAP.

Emerging standards such as JCA hold the promise of making adapters reusable across applications as well as across vendors. It's going to be some time, however, before we have a critical mass of JCA adapters and all are working and playing well together. In addition, the standard is likely to morph, hopefully to an improved state, accounting for needs such as metadata and scalable communication. Looking forward, it's clear that JCA will include these capabilities in the long term. In the short term, most problem domains will leverage a mix-and-match approach, using both standard and proprietary adapters.

## PART III

Application Integration Standards

## CHAPTER ELEVEN

XML, XSLT, and Application Integration

XML is clearly a component of application integration and not a replacement, as once thought. XML's value is that it promotes a self-defining message structure that most organizations can agree upon, and many application integration architects are using it as a standard format for information exchange.

However, the real value of XML may not be XML itself, but XML derivatives such as ebXML, SOAP, and XML. These standards are still evolving, but they already add value in application integration problem domains.

In this chapter we'll explore the strategic value of XML as well as its transformation standard, XSLT, and their use in the world of application integration. This is a jumping-off point for the following chapters that will explore the ins and outs of XML-related standards.

Since its inception, Extensible Markup Language (XML) was designed as a standard for information interchange on the Internet; thus, its natural application in the world of application integration. Those interested in application integration look to leverage the power of XML, making this new standard a common point of integration for source and target applications.

For some time, XML was a bit confusing. Indeed, I've attended meetings where XML was thought to be the "magic" that will drive application integration, intra- and intercompany, for some enterprises. While XML is a powerful standard for structuring and exchanging information, its value within the world of application integration has proven to be more tactical than strategic. However, this does not mean that we should discount XML; indeed, it will always hold a place as both an information-exchange standard and a jumping-off point for additional standards, including ebXML, RosettaNet, and BizTalk—all covered in this book.

So, What's the Big Deal?

The strengths of XML make it extremely valuable in all types of application integration projects. Still, its real value resides in the world of application integration as the infrastructure for information exchange and management.

XML provides a robust, human-readable information-exchange standard that is not just a consensus choice, but a unanimous one. It can support the exchange of application semantics and information content, providing an application-level mechanism for producing business information that other applications can use without needing to understand anything about the transmitting applications (see Figure 11.1).

XML gets most of its "traction" from this common mechanism for information exchange. More specifically, it gets its traction primarily around two application integration problem domains: intra- and intercompany.

Fundamentally, intracompany application integration is about binding applications and data stores together to solve business problems. Its strength is facilitating the free flow of information from any system to any other system, with each of those systems gaining access to perfect external information in real time. Intracompany typically integrates ERP packages such as SAP, PeopleSoft, and Baan, in addition to Customer Relationship Management (CRM) packages, databases, and older mainframe systems. Intracompany application integration also allows organizations to externalize existing enterprise application information to interested parties through the Web, as evidenced in a portal-based solution.

Knowing, as we now do, that the essence of application integration is the binding of applications and data stores together in order to share information with external and internal information systems, we can see that intra- and intercompany application integration are intrinsically related. Application integration constructs the infrastructure that supports the free flow of information between companies. As such, it is functionally an extension of the intracompany infrastructure that includes enterprise applications existing in other organizations.

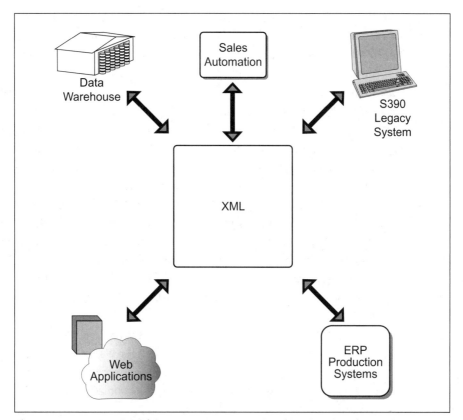

Figure 11.1   XML provides a common mechanism for data interchange that everyone can agree upon.

The design patterns of applications and data stores in the application integration problem domain are similar to those in intracompany application integration problem domains. All that changes is the mechanisms employed to exchange the information, which in an application integration environment are generally less intrusive and more data oriented than in the intracompany application integration environment.

The Value of XML

XML provides a common data-exchange format, encapsulating both data and metadata. This format allows various applications and databases to exchange information without having to understand anything about one other. In order to communicate, a source system simply reformats a message, a piece of information moving from an interface, or a data record as XML-compliant text and moves that information to any other system that understands how to read XML.

Although we can now appreciate XML's value to application integration, it was originally created as a mechanism to publish data through the Web without the originator having to understand anything about the system sending the data. As the application integration problem became more evident, application integration architects and developers recognized the value of applying XML to the problem domain in order to move information between enterprises. The success of XML has led many people to refer to it as the next EDI.

Although XML's benefits sometimes appear revolutionary in scope, as a concept it falls short of being revolutionary. It also falls short of being the panacea for the application solution. We're not suggesting that it does not bring some real value to the application integration solution set. That value simply requires stretching XML far beyond its original intent—which leads to a problem. Stretched too far, XML may be applied in areas where it stands little chance of success.

The overapplication of XML in so many areas of technology diminishes its real value and results in a great deal of unnecessary confusion. Perhaps most damaging is the predictable behavior of many vendors that look to recast XML using their own set of proprietary extensions. Although some want to add value to XML, others seek only to lock in users.

XML's power resides in its simplicity. It can take large chunks of information and consolidate them into an XML document—meaningful pieces that provide structure and organization to the information (see Figure 11.2).

The basic building block of an XML document is the element, defined by tags. An element has both a beginning and an ending tag. All elements in an XML document are contained in an outermost element known as the root element. XML can also support nested elements, or elements within elements. This ability allows XML to support hierarchical structures. Element names describe the content of the element, and the structure describes the relationship between the elements.

An XML document is considered to be "well-formed" (that is, able to be read and understood by an XML parser) if its format complies with the XML specification, if it is properly marked up, and if elements are properly nested. XML also supports the ability to define attributes for elements and describe characteristics of the elements in the beginning tag of an element.

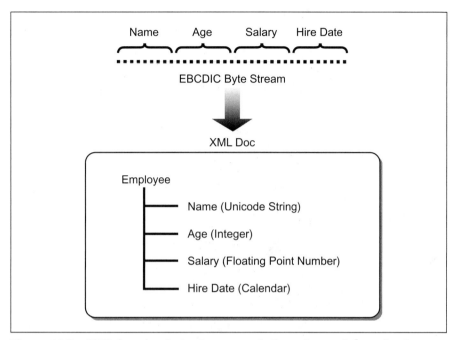

Figure 11.2   XML is a simple text representation of complex or simple data.

For example, XML documents can be very simple, such as the following:

```
<?xml version="1.0" standalone="yes"?>
<conversation>
<greeting>Hello, world!</greeting>
<response>Stop the planet, I want to get off!</response>
</conversation>
```

The Document Type Definition (DTD) determines the structure and elements of an XML document. When a parser receives a document using a DTD, it verifies that the document is in the proper format.

Some XML documents may be DTD specified, contain an internal subset, and possess a more complex structure, such as the following:

```
<?xml version="1.0" standalone="no" encoding="UTF-8"?>
!DOCTYPE titlepage SYSTEM
  "http://www.frisket.org/dtds/typo.dtd"
```

```
[<!ENTITY % active.links "INCLUDE">]>
<titlepage>
<white-space type="vertical" amount="36"/>
<title font="Baskerville" size="24/30"
        alignment="centered">Hello, world!</title>
<white-space type="vertical" amount="12"/>
<!- In some copies the following decoration is
        hand-colored, presumably by the author ->
<image location="http://www.foo.bar/fleuron.eps"
   type="URL" alignment="centered"/>
<white-space type="vertical" amount="24"/>
<author font="Baskerville" size="18/22"
   style="italic">Munde Salutem</author>
<titlepage>[1]
```

XML parsers read XML documents and extract the data for access by another program. Parsers are becoming part of the middleware layer (defined later), able to process XML documents into and out of the middleware infrastructure (see Figure 11.3).

XML metadata can be any attribute assignable to a piece of data; anything from concrete attributes to such abstract concepts as the industry associated with a particular document. XML can also be used to encode any number of existing metadata standards. The binding of data and metadata is a fundamental feature that maximizes XML's benefit to information-sharing scenarios. In fact, it is the feature most consistent with the concept of a common enterprise metadata

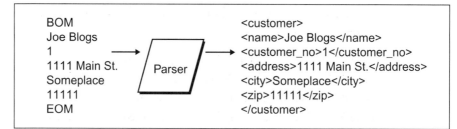

Figure 11.3   XML parsers extract information from XML.

---

[1]www.W3C.org.

repository that is supported throughout an organization or a common metadata layer shared within a trading community. Currently, XML is attempting to establish common metadata standards throughout the Internet in support of B2B, and within the enterprise in support of intracompany application integration.

XML provides individual industries with the ability to define common metadata within their domain. For example, the pharmaceutical industry defines the structure of product data quite differently from the automobile industry. As a result, its metadata definitions must be different as well. XML provides mechanisms such as namespaces (see the description in the "XML Namespaces" tidbit later in this chapter), XML-Schemas, and RDF for defining localized metadata around particular industries, or even between two or more trading partners. These metadata standards are just now emerging and have yet to find wide acceptance within trading communities.

Because XML is independent of any particular type of metadata format, there is little risk that a particular technology vendor will define its own set of metadata tags. In other words, XML cannot be made proprietary to any particular type of data. At least, that's the hope.

What XML Adds

Ironically, XML's real power is not in the technology itself but the fact that everyone seems to agree that XML provides an acceptable common format to allow applications within or between enterprises to exchange critical business information. XML is a momentum technology: Almost everyone concerned with storing or moving information—such as database and middleware vendors—hypes their products with claims of XML support. (Not surprisingly, they support XML in very different ways.)

XML also adds a foundation that other standards can build upon. As we'll explore later in this chapter, XML-enabled standards now exist for transforming information between applications. These standards include Extensible Stylesheet Language Transformation (XSLT, covered later in this chapter), BizTalk, XML for EDI (XEDI), and Commerce XML (cXML). They use XML as their base and expand in a specific direction to address a particular business issue.

What XML Does Not Add

The hype around XML threatens to turn us all into wide-eyed kids at a carnival, ready to eat too much cotton candy and get drawn in to every attraction. We need to step back, take a deep breath, and consider not only what XML does, but what

XML does not do. XML is no exception to the pitfalls of other momentum technologies, in which end users tend to overestimate the capabilities of the technology and thus incorrectly apply them within their problem domain.

One common and dangerous misconception about XML is that it is a substitute for application integration technology such as middleware (including application servers and integration servers). Nothing could be further from the truth! In fact, the opposite is true.

As we already stated, XML is a simple, text-based document format that provides both metadata and information content. Nothing more. Nothing less. You or your vendor must provide the technology to move the XML documents

---

XML Namespaces

A namespace is a collection of names that may be used in an XML document as elements or attribute names. These can identify names with a particular domain and thus avoid redundancy, or allow the use of the same name with two different meanings. Namespaces in XML are identified by a Uniform Resource Indicator (URI), which allows each namespace to be unique. For example, we may have three elements known as "account." The first refers to a frequent-flyer account, the second is a bank account, and the third is a customer account at a hotel. Using namespaces, we can identify these different classes with a different and appropriate URI. Each account name is associated with a particular domain—in our example, the airline URI, the bank URI, and the hotel URI, respectively. For example, we could place the following in the document to associate the element with a particular namespace:

http://www.airline.org.account

http://www.bank.org.account

http://www.hotel.org.account

The importance of XML namespaces in the context of application integration is their ability to define common application semantics between trading partners within a vertical industry. In other words, we can come up with a common notion of a customer, a product attribute, and other properties that are common within a particular vertical industry or trading community.

from application to application. You or your vendor must make any necessary changes to your source and target applications so they can consume and produce XML. In other words, a lot has to occur before you can apply XML to application integration.

In order for applications using XML to be integrated, the applications must externalize the information as XML. Currently, few applications are capable of doing so. In order to be most successful, either the existing applications must change so they produce and consume XML or, better yet, they must leverage XML-enabled middleware technology.

XML-enabled middleware technology manages the extraction of information from the source system (or systems) as well as the conversion of the information into XML (if required) and the placement of the information in the target system (or systems). All this occurs automatically and is transparent to the end user.

XML does not make a good message format for information exchange, either intra- or intercompany. As we noted, XML is text based, and thus information that would normally exist in a binary message as "512 KB" could easily map to an XML document 20 times that size (see Figure 11.4).

Although XML provides a good point of integration when communicating with source or target applications within or between enterprises, moving information using native XML demands a huge overhead. As a result, most middleware vendors still use a binary message format, either proprietary or open, to move XML data and metadata from one system to another.

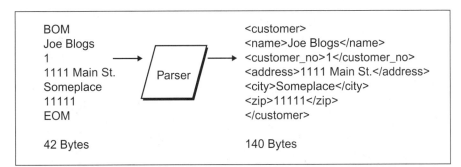

Figure 11.4   Text-based XML is huge, which makes it a difficult format to transport from system to system.

XML Meets Middleware

We have established that XML is a simple, text-based standard and, as such, cannot provide everything needed to integrate disparate applications. It quickly becomes clear that, in order to provide maximum value to the application integration solution set, XML needs middleware (and, conversely, middleware most likely needs XML).

XML's value to middleware is clear. Middleware simply "carries the load." It moves messages that encapsulate or abstract XML and ensures that those messages are understood by any source or target applications that need the information (see Figure 11.5). Middleware may also manage the interfaces with the source or target applications and move information into and out of the applications through an unobtrusive point of integration, such as a database or an API.

Because of XML's value, every middleware vendor, new and old, has declared dominance in the XML space, applying its technology to application integration problem domains. None of us should be surprised that there is a certain degree of "puffery" to these declarations. In truth, it is not particularly difficult to XML-enable a product. Therefore, vendors were able to react quickly, for a change.

XML-enabling a product is simply a matter of embedding a parser within the middleware and teaching the product to read and write XML from and to the canonical message format. In addition, because many of these products already

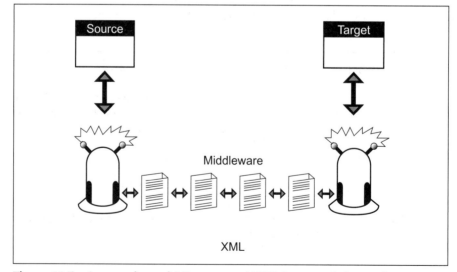

Figure 11.5   Leveraging middleware and XML to move information.

have native connectors to traditional enterprise systems and data stores (such as SAP, PeopleSoft, and DB2), they provide enterprises with the ability to produce and consume XML without impacting the applications.

Integration Solutions

Now that we understand what XML is, what its value is, and how middleware and XML coexist, we can turn our attention to XML-enabled solutions that include the available technology and approaches. In doing so, let's return once again to our macro problem domains: intracompany application integration and B2B application integration.

XML plays a lesser role within the domain of intracompany application integration, but its role is becoming more important. This somewhat-convoluted observation is based on the fact that most systems within an enterprise come under central control. As a result, the integration solutions run deeper and may not benefit from converting information to XML for movement to other applications. Typically, standard information-exchange mechanisms, such as XML, take a back seat to native points of integration and binary messages as a simple matter of efficiency when we consider intracompany application integration. However, as information becomes less centrally controlled, XML will become more important.

Let us look, for example, at a situation in which an enterprise needs to exchange information between its PeopleSoft packaged application, its older COBOL/ISAM applications running on the mainframe, and its new data warehouse. Although there are many ways to approach this problem, most enterprises would use some type of integration server to exchange information between the systems in real time, using whatever native interface the source or target applications provided. There is always the opportunity to convert the data moving between the applications into XML. However, binary messages typically provide better efficiency, as we noted earlier in this chapter.

Although native interfaces currently dominate application integration solutions, we are rapidly moving to a world where most applications and databases will be XML-aware. Therefore, XML will become a common point of integration rather than the hodgepodge of proprietary and complex native interfaces in use today. Taking this reality into account, we recognize that XML is becoming a more prominent player in application integration. Many packaged applications, including PeopleSoft and SAP, are going to leverage XML as the preferred native interface to their systems. Indeed, PeopleSoft has already defined its Open

Integration Framework (OIF) and has outlined how information will move into and out of the PeopleSoft application using XML. SAP is not far behind.

Even as developers build interfaces to new and existing custom applications, XML is becoming the mechanism of choice for producing and consuming information within those systems. Moreover, most database vendors, including Oracle, Sybase, and Informix, are providing mechanisms within their database engines to allow them to read and write XML directly from the database.

XML provides the most value within the domain of intercompany application integration. Here we typically integrate applications that are not under centralized control, and thus difficult to change. As we have explained, XML provides a reasonably good format for information exchange. Perhaps most important, the majority of businesses can agree upon XML as the way information moves into and out of enterprises. XML standards provide additional value by including common metadata layers that may exist between one or more trading partners, and even standard transformation mechanisms such as XSLT.

As we look ahead, the ultimate application integration solution will be some hybrid of intracompany application integration and B2B application integration, providing integration within and between enterprises by using a similar, compatible infrastructure. Getting to this "glorious future" will be accomplished in stages. Enterprises will first learn to integrate their own applications, which entails understanding everything about the source and target systems that they own, and then they will learn to integrate their applications with their trading partners' applications. XML belongs in this mix, but the majority of work in getting to the solution is associated with exploring both problem domains, understanding the requirements, and mapping the correct technology to the solution. In reality, most organizations have just begun the journey down this rather long and expensive road.

XML-Enabled Standards

The XML bandwagon is filling up, joined by many standards organizations. These entities are looking to standardize the way e-Business is conducted, using the common infrastructure they define and vendors provide.

The sad reality is that this bandwagon is overflowing—there are more XML standards organizations than vendors and end users require. Fallout is bound to occur as one or two standards get traction and others do not. The few that appear to be most relevant in the world of XML and application integration include

RosettaNet, XEDI, BizTalk, Extensible Financial Reporting Markup Language (XFRML), XML-Schema, XML Query, and XSLT.

RosettaNet is a consortium of product vendors and end users that defines a framework for data and process interchange with e-Business. Primarily organized for the high-tech industry, RosettaNet outlines standard message data using XML, as well as standardized process flows, to react to standard business events. We feel RosettaNet is so important that we've dedicated a chapter to it (see Chapter 14).

XEDI is a published specification describing how to map traditional EDI to XML and back again.

BizTalk is an industry consortium founded by Microsoft to define a standard XML grammar for XML-based messaging and metadata. Microsoft is providing a BizTalk server to support this standard.

XFRML is a standards push led by the American Institute of Certified Public Accountants (AICPA) to define an XML standard for reporting financial information over the Internet to other interested parties.

XML-Schema is a working group of the W3C that looks to describe a better mechanism to determine the structure of an XML document (see the description earlier in this chapter).

XML Query is another W3C working group looking to create a common set of operations and language syntax for accessing persisted (stored) XML data.

XSLT seeks to provide a standard XML document-transformation mechanism using a stylesheet as a common processing engine. XSLT is important to application integration because schema and information content often must be altered as information flows between applications. We will cover XSLT next.

Using XSLT for B2B Application Integration

Although a number of standards exist for information interchange and process definition, industry standards have yet to emerge for defining common integration server and B2B integration server services such as routing, rules processing, and transformation. In the absence of such standards, individual vendors have created proprietary approaches to these basic information-processing services. As a result, we are confronted with features that are not interchangeable, require specialized training, and do not provide a common framework of services.

Even as we begin to implement standards such as XML, ebXML, RosettaNet, and BizTalk as mechanisms to manage information interchange, we are also looking to create standards that support information processing within the middleware. These standards will define services common to most integration servers and to B2B integration servers, including rules and transformation.

XSLT seeks to fill the need for a standard approach to both rules and transformation processing. Like XML, XSLT is a standard written by the W3C, and it could become the preferred standard mechanism for transforming content and application semantics as information moves from application to application and business to business.

The power of XSLT resides in its simplicity, tight integration with XML, and the completeness of the standard. Although it does not provide every type of out-of-the-box transformation service currently found in most integration servers and B2B integration servers, XSLT provides the infrastructure to create such services through an extensible and declarative programming language. The operative word here is "currently." You can bet the farm that, as this standard evolves, more intracompany application integration and B2B vendors will create their transformation and rules-processing technology to reflect XSLT.

What Is XSLT?

XSLT is a language designed to transform one XML document into another, changing both its schema and content in the process. At its most primitive, XSLT is a text-processing system that enables the programmer to transform XML documents, or, if required, generate other standard markup languages such as HTML (or any text, for that matter).

In previous chapters, we have discussed the need for transformation as information moves between applications, so we will not devote our attention to it here. However, it is important to remember that XML documents are like messages. And because each application has its own unique set of application semantics, documents moving from application to application need to be transformed (see Figure 11.6). Both data structure and content must be semantically correct in order to load into the target application. If the data is not in the proper format, the update operation is likely to fail.

In addition to transforming the schema and content of XML documents, XSLT can perform other types of text-processing and transformation operations, which include creating text-based standard data formats such as comma-delimited files, PDFs, or other industry-standard formats that use text (see Figure 11.7).

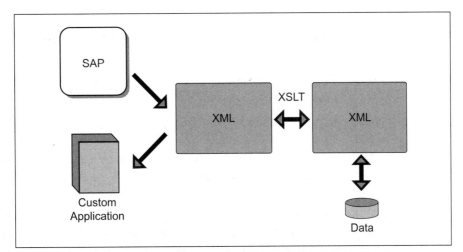

Figure 11.6   You must transform XML as it moves from application to application.

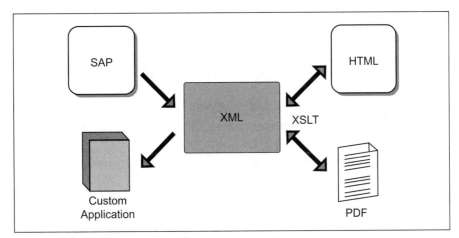

Figure 11.7   XSLT can also create other text-based formats, such as comma-delimited files and PDFs.

Leveraging XSLT Inside Middleware: The Tradeoff

Although XSLT has tremendous promise, a huge disconnect remains between what XSLT provides and what middleware needs to offer in terms of transformation. Still, it is finding its way into more than a few middleware products, including B2B integration servers such as BizTalk Server.

The state of the technology of most integration servers—supporting complex but valuable information transport—is a better fit for binary messaging, which is more efficient than text-based messaging and is easier to manage and process. However, binary messaging does require that specialized systems (such as message-oriented middleware) manage it, and it is not as easily managed by external systems as text-based messaging (e.g., XML).

Because that is the case, to process messages using XSLT, the messages must first be transformed into XML text (or any text) for XSLT transformation and then be transformed back into a binary message. Efficient? Clearly not. Even as a few integration servers look at XSLT as their standard mechanism for transformation, it is apparent that building text processing into existing binary messaging systems will be difficult.

B2B servers, such as BizTalk Server, do not support such sophisticated message-processing operations. As a result, they are able to maintain their messages as XML or EDI text. Therefore, they have a better opportunity to leverage XSLT as their standard transformation mechanism, which they do.

XSLT will fit into some middleware products and not others. XSLT almost certainly will succeed as a standard transformation mechanism in products that already process information as raw text of XML. If XSLT continues to pick up speed, other middleware vendors will inevitably follow the crowd.

Before XSLT existed, most XML developers could only process incoming XML documents by creating custom applications that typically invoked one of two APIs: the Simple API for XML (SAX) and the Document Object Model (DOM).

The SAX API was an event-based interface that used a mechanism through which the parser notified the application of each piece of information in the

---

XSLT and XPath

As the development of XSLT progressed, its creators discovered that there was an overlap between the expression syntax in XSLT for selecting parts of a document and the XPointer language that was being developed for linking one document to another. Taking advantage of this, the creators of XSLT and XPointer decided to combine both efforts, defining a single language known as XPath.

In the world of XSLT, XPath provides a sublanguage encapsulated within the XSLT stylesheet. Most programming operations, including simple calculations or even testing for conditions, can be done using an XPath expression.

---

document as it was read. In the DOM API, the parser interrogated the document and created an object tree structure that represented the structure of the XML document in memory. From that point, a traditional program (e.g., C++ or Java) transformed the tree.

The limitation of both approaches was the same—each time you wanted to transform a new XML document, you had to write a new program.

XSLT provides several advantages over SAX and DOM. XSLT's design is based on the fact that most transformation programs use the same design patterns, and therefore can be automated using a higher-level, declarative language. (Stating that the XSLT language is declarative means that it describes the transformation behavior rather than a sequence of instructions necessary to perform the transformation. In other words, XSLT describes the transformation, then leverages the XSL processors to carry out the deed.) Moreover, when XSLT is used, the requirements of transformation can be expressed as a grouping of rules that define what output should be created when a particular pattern is encountered.

The Mechanisms

Transforming an XML document using XSLT requires two main steps. The first step consists of a structural transformation, during which the data is transformed from the input structure to the output structure (see Figure 11.8). This step may involve selecting data, grouping it, sorting it, or aggregating it, depending on the

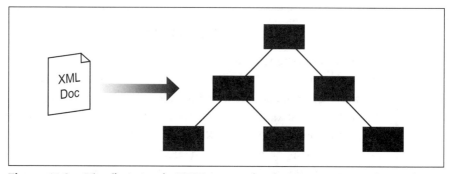

Figure 11.8   The first step in XSLT processing is structural transformation.

needs of the transformation. For example, within an XML document, we can change U.S. dollar values to French francs. Such a transformation would be based on the current conversion rate, either found statically within the transformation program or read from a remote database.

The second step consists of formatting the text so it takes on the new characteristics. In this step, information is placed in a particular type of text structure: XML, HTML, PDF, and so on.

XSLT Processors and Processing

XSLT does not operate directly on the XML text. Instead, it relies on a parser (DOM or SAX compliant) to convert values into an object tree for processing. It uses this tree to manipulate the structure in memory. XSLT enables the user to take advantage of the native language to navigate around the node tree, select nodes, and alter the nodes as the transformation requires.

XSLT processors apply an XSLT stylesheet to an XML source document and thus create a results document—all while remaining consistent with the way processors handle XML through trees. Thus, XSLT must process three trees: the input, stylesheet, and output trees, which we will discuss in more detail later in this chapter.

The XSLT processor applies a stylesheet to an input document and produces an output document. Having the output document be the same kind of object as the input document enables XSLT to carry out a transformation. The stylesheet document defines the transformation to occur.

Again, text documents are not dealt with directly. They are dealt with in object trees that exist in memory. A tree is an abstract data type. There are no predefined ways to represent trees. A tree resembles the W3C's DOM, but without the API, and the structure and processing models of trees are localized to the particular XSLT processor. For example, MSXML3 uses a different structure than the Saxon XSLT processor.

Adhering to the rules of the XSLT specification, the processor must read a stylesheet tree and use it to transform the input document tree to the output document tree. However, no formal rules govern how source documents are read or how output documents are produced.

Most real-world application integration tools are much more complex than this example, and many different types of problem domains will stretch the capabilities of the XSLT processing model (see Figure 11.9), including handling:

- Multiple document inputs.
- Multiple stylesheet inputs.
- Multiple documents outputs.

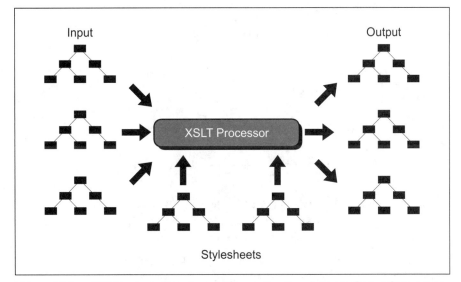

Figure 11.9 **XSLT, when leveraged for application integration, will have to handle complex operations such as processing multiple input, output, and stylesheet documents at the same time.**

Transformation Process

In the domain of XSLT, the stylesheet contains a number of templates expressed as an `<xsl:template>` element with a match attribute. The value of the match attribute is a pattern, and the pattern determines which nodes in the source tree the template rule matches. For example:

```
<xsl:template match="/">
```

Several events occur during a typical transformation. When an XSLT transformation is executed, a stylesheet is applied to evaluate and process a source document. As we discussed earlier in this chapter, the first event to take place is the remapping of the document to a tree that is contained in memory. This prepares the schema and content for the transformation process.

The next step is to find a template rule that matches the root node of the source tree. Then the XSLT processor initiates the contents of the template rule, which, within the stylesheet, is a sequence of elements and text nodes.

For example:

```
<xsl:stylesheet
id = id
extension-element-prefixes = tokens
exclude-result-prefixes = tokens
version = number>
<!- Content: (xsl:import*, top-level-elements) ->
</xsl:stylesheet>
<xsl:transform
id = id
extension-element-prefixes = tokens
exclude-result-prefixes = tokens
version = number>
<!- Content: (xsl:import*, top-level-elements) ->
</xsl:transform>[2]
```

A template rule has the following two parts:

• A pattern that is matched against nodes in the source tree, and a template that can be initiated to form part of the result tree.

---

[2]W3CXSLT Specification; www.w3c.org.

- A template that is initiated for a particular source element to create part of the result tree.

A template can contain elements that specify literal result-element structure. A template can also contain elements from the XSLT namespace that are instructions for creating result-tree fragments. When a template is initiated, each instruction is executed and replaced by the result-tree fragment that it creates. Instructions can select and process descendant source elements. Processing a descendant element creates a result-tree fragment by finding the applicable template rule and instantiating its template. Note that elements are processed only when they have been selected by the execution of an instruction. The result tree is constructed by finding the template rule for the root node and initiating its template.

XSLT Applications

In addition to XSLT's primary purpose in the context of application integration, XSLT has a number of other applications.

Schema Conversions

The main application of XSLT, and the reason for its inclusion here, is for schema conversions as XML documents move between applications, accounting for the differences in the way applications manage data structures.

XSLT is the preferred method of converting data structured within XML. You can leverage XSLT for the following:

- Extracting data.
- Validating data.
- Persisting data.
- Converting attributes to elements.
- Converting elements to attributes.
- Changing the metadata and content of an incoming XML document to create a new outgoing XML document.

Converting XML to Something Else, and Vice Versa

In addition to converting XML document A to XML document B (typically changing its structure and content), XSLT can be a mechanism for reading most types of text files and creating XML or for reading XML and creating most types of text files.

Within the B2B world, the best examples of this are

- Reading EDI from a source application that externalizes information as EDI and converting it to XML.
- Converting XML to EDI so information is accepted in a particular target system.
- Reading other data interchange text, such as comma-delimited data, and converting it to XML.
- Converting XML to a data interchange text format, such as comma-delimited, so information is accepted into particular target systems.
- Reading and writing information to and from nondata text sources, such as PDF documents.
- Publishing information to standard text formats used by publishing systems.

XSLT and Application Integration

XSLT is not the solution to every application integration requirement. It is, however, an important piece in the puzzle. XSLT's great potential lies in its ability to finally provide a standard transformation mechanism that everyone can agree upon, one that does not require application integration architects to relearn technology as they move from vendor to vendor.

There are several other advantages to using XSLT for transformation, including the following:

- A common language for transforming application semantics as text or XML moves between applications.
- A common standard for representing transformation behaviors.
- A common input and output message/document structure.
- Backing from most major B2B and intracompany application integration technology vendors and consultants.

However, there are limitations to consider as well, including the following:

- The slow emergence of vendor support because of the limitations of existing technologies (e.g., moving from binary messaging to XML text).
- The technical limitations, including performance and security, of using text, and only text.
- The fact that not all standards make it, and XSLT could lose momentum and thus lose wide support like so many other standards in the past.

XML and Application Integration

XML and application integration are joined at the hip. Application integration represents the larger problem of moving information between applications and data stores for any business purpose. XML provides a common mechanism for data exchange and integration, with a variety of applications supporting a variety of design patterns.

Even with all the promise and "presence" of XML, we've also learned that it is not a panacea. Users must understand the limits as well as the potential of the technology before leveraging it for their application integration solution. The real power of XML is the notion of the standard information interchange it brings between one or many applications existing within a single organization or within a trading community.

In the next several chapters, we'll take a closer look at important application integration standards based on XML and how they fit into your application integration solution.

## CHAPTER TWELVE

ebXML and Application Integration

There are standards, and there are standards. The ebXML (Electronic Business Extensible Markup Language) standard has evolved over the last few years into something very viable. Today, many organizations leverage ebXML as a B2B collaboration standard; sometimes they just use it within the enterprise.

To keep up with more modern Web services standards, ebXML has been updated to leverage Web services-based facilities such as UDDI and SOAP. Today, ebXML is a full-blown collaboration standard that supports everything from simple information exchange all the way to complex process integration.

One of the notions expressed in the world of ebXML is the concept of collaboration, or the ability to electronically exchange information, ideas, designs, or what have you, all while adhering to a common logical sequence.

What's important about ebXML in the context of application integration is the standard's ability to guide facilitation of information and processes in and between enterprises. Also note how it's one of those standards that is learning to leverage other standards, such as Web services.

While there are many standards that look like ebXML, ebXML is the first horizontal standard designed to address the exchange of information and adherence to interenterprise processes. However, in attempting to reach this lofty goal, ebXML is also a complex standard and takes some understanding before we can comprehend its value to the world of application integration and electronic business.

So, why do we need the ebXML standard? It's really a matter of leveraging the Internet to automate how we do business in real time, leveraging common processes and common information formats. The use of an electronic information standard and enabling technology are driving how we do business, and the interest in standards that provide a common mechanism to do this will only push us further along.

Thus was born ebXML, a collaboration between UN/CEFACT and OASIS. As you can tell by the name, ebXML is built on top of XML, as well as other Internet standards, including Web services, to create an infrastructure for information-based and process-based electronic business. This is a good standard, with growing interest from those doing B2B automation. ebXML provides just enough good technology to make it useful in the real world, without overhyping its capabilities, thus disappointing its implementers.

What is unique about ebXML is that it's a complete standard, addressing:

- Process
- Trading partner management
- Semantics
- Notation
- Security
- Agreements
- Standard information exchange
- Standard information structure

Other standards we discuss in this book, such as Business Process Execution Language for Web Services (BPEL4WS), only address the notion of process and semantics, or other more narrow aspects of application integration between trading partners or internal systems.

However, the aggressiveness of ebXML is also its most limiting factor, because it will take years before the standard finds its way into many enterprises and trading communities. This is due to the amount of work that must occur to get a trading community to leverage ebXML.

ebXML for Trade

The ebXML standard was created to replace EDI (at least that was the idea), or other electronic commerce standards currently in use. Moreover, ebXML looks to create a set of standards that is affordable and will work in small to medium enterprises. The ebXML standard is open, is free to anyone with interest, and does not seem to compete directly with other standards when you consider its application (but it could have some overlap with other process integration standards such as WFMC or BPMI).

At its essence, ebXML is based on process models and encoded in XML; it is also an XML message system to exchange information and a repository to allow information sharing. The message system supports any type of data, including EDI transactions or binary information. In addition to information, ebXML supports trading partner agreements—a fundamental function of EDI partner/profile subsystems—and you may use ebXML to express business services agreements.

As with other standards, ebXML is not a product, but a set of guidelines that allow application and application integration technology vendors to design their products to support it. To date, there are dozens of vendors and products that support ebXML, some in part, some completely. More will be added as the standard matures and adoption continues.

In recent years, it's been clear that ebXML (as well as many other modern Internet standards) has to take on a coexistence strategy rather than a replacement strategy. This is due to the fact that most enterprises are reluctant to shut down their existing B2B systems, such as EDI, until new standards have proven their operational value. Thus, we have another evolution not revolution, which seems to be a common theme as we migrate to newer, but more complex and invasive standards.

ebXML Components

There are several components to ebXML, including:

- Collaboration Protocol Profile (CPP).
- Collaboration Protocol Agreement (CPA).
- Business process and information modeling.
- Core components.
- Messaging.
- Registry/Repository.

CPP describes an enterprise offering using a standard, portable format. This component describes the message-exchange mechanisms as well as business collaborations that are native to the enterprise or trading community. The ebXML standard also describes business processes within CPP, including how partners interact within a trading community. As mentioned in our discussion of process integration earlier in this book, CPP supports intra- and intercompany processes, and public versus private processes, collaborating on both sides of a two-party B2B transaction. For example, when leveraging CPP, a trading community would define all processes between partners—buying parts to build a car, for example—as well as semantic differences, and how processes and data need to interact to support any number of business activities.

CPA describes the particular requirements, facilities, and descriptions for the transaction of trading partner business. It is formed from either manual or automated systems, deriving the intersection of their agreed-upon CPPs. Thus, the CPA becomes the de facto contract between the trading partners, creating "rules of engagement" for a specific collaborative business transaction.

See Listing 12.1 for an example of a CPA.

Listing 12.1

```
<?xml version="1.0" ?>
- <tp:CollaborationProtocolAgreement
  xmlns:tp="http://www.ebxml.org/namespaces/tradePartner
  " xmlns:xsi="http://www.w3.org/2000/10/XMLSchema-
  instance" xsi:schemaLocation="http://www.ebxml.org/
  namespaces/tradePartner http://ebxml.org/
  project_teams/trade_partner/cpp-cpa-v1_0.xsd"
  xmlns:xlink="http://www.w3.org/1999/xlink"
  xmlns:ds="http://www.w3.org/2000/09/xmldsig#"
  tp:cpaid="uri:yoursandmycpa" tp:version="1.2">
<tp:Status tp:value="proposed" />
<tp:Start>2001-05-20T07:21:00Z</tp:Start>
<tp:End>2002-05-20T07:21:00Z</tp:End>
<tp:ConversationConstraints tp:invocationLimit="100"
  tp:concurrentConversations="100" />
- <tp:PartyInfo>
<tp:PartyId tp:type="DUNS">123456789</tp:PartyId<
```

```
<tp:PartyRef xlink:href="http://example.com/about.
  html" /<
- <tp:CollaborationRole tp:id="N00">
<tp:ProcessSpecification tp:version="1.0"
  tp:name="buySell" xlink:type="simple"
  xlink:href="http://www.ebxml.org/processes/
  buySell.xml" />
<tp:Role tp:name="buyer" xlink:type="simple"
  xlink:href="http://ebxml.org/processes/buySell.
  xml#buyer" />
<tp:CertificateRef tp:certId="N03" />
- <tp:ServiceBinding tp:channelId="N04"
  tp:packageId="N0402">
<tp:Service tp:type="uriReference">uri:example.com/
  services/buyerService</tp:Service>
<tp:Override tp:action="orderConfirm" tp:channelId="N08"
  tp:packageId="N0402" xlink:href="http://ebxml
  .org/processes/buySell.xml#orderConfirm"
  xlink:type="simple" />
</tp:ServiceBinding>
</tp:CollaborationRole>
- <tp:Certificate tp:certId="N03">
<ds:KeyInfo />
</tp:Certificate>
- <tp:DeliveryChannel tp:channelId="N04"
  tp:transportId="N05" tp:docExchangeId="N06">
<tp:Characteristics tp:syncReplyMode="none"
  tp:nonrepudiationOfOrigin="true"
  tp:nonrepudiationOfReceipt="false"
  tp:secureTransport="true" tp:confidentiality="true"
  tp:authenticated="true" tp:authorized="false" />
</tp:DeliveryChannel>
- <tp:DeliveryChannel tp:channelId="N07"
  tp:transportId="N08" tp:docExchangeId="N06">
<tp:Characteristics tp:syncReplyMode="none"
  tp:nonrepudiationOfOrigin="true"
  tp:nonrepudiationOfReceipt="false"
```

```
    tp:secureTransport="false" tp:confidentiality="true"
    tp:authenticated="true" tp:authorized="false" />
</tp:DeliveryChannel>
- <tp:Transport tp:transportId="N05">
<tp:SendingProtocol
    tp:version="1.1">HTTP</tp:SendingProtocol>
<tp:ReceivingProtocol
    tp:version="1.1">HTTP</tp:ReceivingProtocol>
<tp:Endpoint tp:uri="https://www.example.com/
    servlets/ebxmlhandler" tp:type="allPurpose" />
- <tp:TransportSecurity>
<tp:Protocol tp:version="3.0">SSL</tp:Protocol>
<tp:CertificateRef tp:certId="N03" />
</tp:TransportSecurity>
</tp:Transport>
- <tp:Transport tp:transportId="N18">
<tp:SendingProtocol
    tp:version="1.1">HTTP</tp:SendingProtocol>
<tp:ReceivingProtocol
    tp:version="1.1">SMTP</tp:ReceivingProtocol>
<tp:Endpoint tp:uri="mailto:ebxmlhandler@example.com"
    tp:type="allPurpose" />
</tp:Transport>
- <tp:DocExchange tp:docExchangeId="N06">
- <tp:ebXMLBinding tp:version="0.98b">
- <tp:ReliableMessaging
    tp:deliverySemantics="OnceAndOnlyOnce"
    tp:idempotency="true"
    tp:messageOrderSemantics="Guaranteed">
<tp:Retries>5</tp:Retries>
<tp:RetryInterval>30</tp:RetryInterval>
<tp:PersistDuration>P1D</tp:PersistDuration>
</tp:ReliableMessaging>
- <tp:NonRepudiation>
<tp:Protocol>http://www.w3.org/2000/09/
    xmldsig#</tp:Protocol>
```

```
<tp:HashFunction>http://www.w3.org/2000/09/
  xmldsig#sha1</tp:HashFunction>
<tp:SignatureAlgorithm>http://www.w3.org/2000/09/
  xmldsig#dsa-sha1</tp:SignatureAlgorithm>
<tp:CertificateRef tp:certId="N03" />
</tp:NonRepudiation>
- <tp:DigitalEnvelope>
<tp:Protocol tp:version="2.0">S/MIME</tp:Protocol>
<tp:EncryptionAlgorithm>DES-CBC</tp:EncryptionAlgorithm>
<tp:CertificateRef tp:certId="N03" />
</tp:DigitalEnvelope>
</tp:ebXMLBinding>
</tp:DocExchange>
</tp:PartyInfo>
- <tp:PartyInfo>
<tp:PartyId tp:type="DUNS">987654321</tp:PartyId<
<tp:PartyRef xlink:type="simple"
  xlink:href="http://contrived-example.com/
  about.html" />
- <tp:CollaborationRole tp:id="N30">
<tp:ProcessSpecification tp:version="1.0"
  tp:name="buySell" xlink:type="simple"
  xlink:href="http://www.ebxml.org/processes/
  buySell.xml" />
<tp:Role tp:name="seller" xlink:type="simple"
  xlink:href="http://ebxml.org/processes/buySell.
  xml#seller" />
<tp:CertificateRef tp:certId="N33" />
- <tp:ServiceBinding tp:channelId="N34"
  tp:packageId="N0402">
<tp:Service
  tp:type="uriReference">uri:example.com/services/
  sellerService</tp:Service>
</tp:ServiceBinding>
</tp:CollaborationRole>
- <tp:Certificate tp:certId="N33">
<ds:KeyInfo />
```

```
</tp:Certificate>
- <tp:DeliveryChannel tp:channelId="N34"
    tp:transportId="N35" tp:docExchangeId="N36">
<tp:Characteristics tp:nonrepudiationOfOrigin="true"
    tp:nonrepudiationOfReceipt="false"
    tp:secureTransport="true" tp:confidentiality="true"
    tp:authenticated="true" tp:authorized="false" />
</tp:DeliveryChannel>
- <tp:Transport tp:transportId="N35">
<tp:SendingProtocol
    tp:version="1.1">HTTP</tp:SendingProtocol>
<tp:ReceivingProtocol
    tp:version="1.1">HTTP</tp:ReceivingProtocol>
<tp:Endpoint tp:uri="https://www.contrived-
    example.com/servlets/ebxmlhandler"
    tp:type="allPurpose" />
- <tp:TransportSecurity>
<tp:Protocol tp:version="3.0">SSL</tp:Protocol>
<tp:CertificateRef tp:certId="N33" />
</tp:TransportSecurity>
</tp:Transport>
- <tp:DocExchange tp:docExchangeId="N36">
- <tp:ebXMLBinding tp:version="0.98b">
- <tp:ReliableMessaging
    tp:deliverySemantics="OnceAndOnlyOnce"
    tp:idempotency="true"
    tp:messageOrderSemantics="Guaranteed">
<tp:Retries>5</tp:Retries>
<tp:RetryInterval>30</tp:RetryInterval>
<tp:PersistDuration>P1D</tp:PersistDuration>
</tp:ReliableMessaging>
- <tp:NonRepudiation>
<tp:Protocol>http://www.w3.org/2000/09/
    xmldsig#</tp:Protocol>

<tp:HashFunction>http://www.w3.org/2000/09/
    xmldsig#sha1</tp:HashFunction>
```

```
<tp:SignatureAlgorithm>http://www.w3.org/2000/09/
  xmldsig#dsa-sha1</tp:SignatureAlgorithm>
<tp:CertificateRef tp:certId="N33" />
</tp:NonRepudiation>
- <tp:DigitalEnvelope>
<tp:Protocol tp:version="2.0">S/MIME</tp:Protocol>
<tp:EncryptionAlgorithm>DES-CBC</tp:EncryptionAlgorithm>
<tp:CertificateRef tp:certId="N33" />
</tp:DigitalEnvelope>
</tp:ebXMLBinding>
</tp:DocExchange>
</tp:PartyInfo>
- <tp:Packaging tp:id="N0402">
<tp:ProcessingCapabilities tp:parse="true"
  tp:generate="true" />
- <tp:SimplePart tp:id="N40" tp:mimetype="text/xml">
<tp:NamespaceSupported tp:location="http://ebxml.org/
  project_teams/transport/messageService.xsd"
  tp:version="0.98b">http://www.ebxml.org/namespaces/
  messageService</tp:NamespaceSupported>
<tp:NamespaceSupported
  tp:location="http://ebxml.org/project_teams/
  transport/xmldsig-core-schema.xsd"
  tp:version="1.0">http://www.w3.org/2000/09/
  xmldsig</tp:NamespaceSupported>
</tp:SimplePart>
- <tp:SimplePart tp:id="N41" tp:mimetype="text/xml">
<tp:NamespaceSupported
  tp:location="http://ebxml.org/processes/buysell.xsd"
  tp:version="1.0">http://ebxml.org/processes/
  buysell.xsd</tp:NamespaceSupported>
</tp:SimplePart>
- <tp:CompositeList>
- <tp:Composite tp:id="N42" tp:mimetype="multipart/
  related" tp:mimeparameters="type=text/xml;">
<tp:Constituent tp:idref="N40" />
<tp:Constituent tp:idref="N41" />
```

```
</tp:Composite>
</tp:CompositeList>
</tp:Packaging>
<tp:Comment xml:lang="en-us">buy/sell agreement between
   example.com and contrived-example.com</tp:Comment>
</tp:CollaborationProtocolAgreement>¹
```

Business Process and Information Modeling is a specification for describing a business process in XML. This includes transactions, document flow, information encryption, binary collaborations, semantics, and such. Processes that leverage ebXML use these specifications when they create CPPs, which are also used to define shared business processes within a trading community.

Core components are a set of ebXML schemas and other components that contain formats for business data, including customer account, amounts, and so on. They are particular to an entity, such as a particular trading partner, but not leveraged as vertical semantics (as with vertical standards within health care and financial services markets).

Messaging, as you may expect, is a standard format for ebXML messages that leverages concepts from messaging middleware, including the ability to transmit information asynchronously or synchronously. This is the visible portion of the CPA and provides specific business rules for processing. ebXML messaging is built inside of SOAP, extending the SOAP protocol by frameworks that support attachments, security, and verifications of delivery.

The ebXML message service provides a mechanism to exchange business messages that does not rely upon proprietary technologies and solutions. The

---

ebXML and BPEL4WS

You may note that this subject has some overlap with BPEL4WS, which is covered in the next chapter. You should also note that BPEL4WS is focused on the process alone, and not a more holistic view of electronic business. In other words, BPEL4WS is general purpose, whereas ebXML is applicable to B2B trading.

---

[1]www.ebXML.org.

message contains structure for message headers used for routing and a payload section for the content. As you may remember, in our message discussion in the middleware chapters (e.g., JMS), we talked about similar structures.

The ebXML message service is broken down, at least conceptually, into three parts:

1. The abstract service interface
2. Functions provided by the messaging service layer
3. Mapping to the underlying transport service (see Figure 12.1)

Registry and Repository services maintain CPPs, CPAs, ebXML components, and other ebXML artifacts such as JAR files, video, WSDL, and semantics. This is a database, when you get right down to it, providing query capabilities that allow users to look for relevant content and even information about trading partners. The services defined by CPPs can be published to UDDI.

This portion of ebXML provides a Web service discovery scenario. Thus, a trading partner would first search for a shared service in UDDI, which may indeed contain reference to a CPP that actually exists in the ebXML Registry, which in turn provides access to information about the trading partner. From there you can use the CPA to create a partnership agreement for B2B transactions. We'll talk more about Registry/Repository services in the next section.

The ebXML Registry provides a core set of services that enable the exchange of information between trading partners. As you may recall, the registry is like a

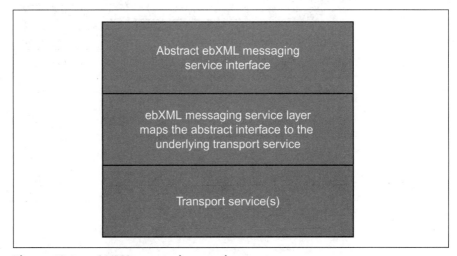

Figure 12.1   ebXML messaging service.

database, allowing a trading partner to place and obtain information pertaining to the interaction between trading partners.

The registry maintains an interface to metadata for a registered item, and access to an ebXML Registry is gained through the use of several APIs (see Figure 12.2). To facilitate semantic recognition of business process and information meta models, the registry provides a mechanism for incorporating human-readable descriptions of registry items. Moreover, you can assign UID keys from other existing business processes and information meta models, such as RosettaNet, and implement them using XML syntax.

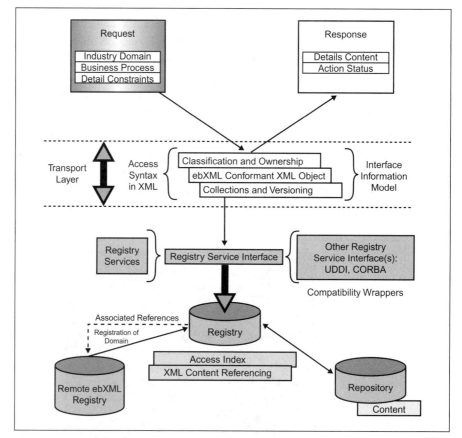

Figure 12.2   Registry architecture.

Comparing XML/edi to ebXML

While not getting the attention of ebXML or the other standards talked about in this section, XML/edi was created to allow enterprises to deploy smarter and cheaper EDI systems and does have some overlap with ebXML, but some complimentary aspects, as well.

The essence of XML/edi is to provide enough intelligence to the electronic mechanism to exchange data that it becomes the framework for B2B commerce. XML/edi is looking to deliver data along with the required process logic, thus it's process aware. Moreover, the notion of XML/edi is to leverage the EDI concept and, indeed, some of the EDI technologies with the understanding that just converting XML to EDI is not enough to satisfy most requirements. In contrast, the ebXML initiative has focused on processes, not just transactions, as well as a central repository. XML/edi guidelines have added two additional key components—*Process Templates* and *Software Agents*—to assist in this type of process, with the idea to provide dynamic processing based on XML notations. Thus, you're encapsulating both data and process into the same documents.

Using XML/edi, XML itself provides the foundation where XML tokens and frameworks are the syntax that transport the other components over the network. The XML tokens replace existing business transactions and enrich the capabilities and transport layers of the Internet. XML/edi uses process templates built using XML that are the glue that binds the XML/edi system together. These templates are globally referenced, or travel along inside the XML as a special section of the document. What is more, they leverage a set of tokens, as well as control and define the business context and processes. ebXML Business Process Meta Model (described later in this chapter) has moved to implement similar mechanisms within the ebXML registry indexing system.

In the world of XML/edi, *Internet repositories* work like ebXML registries, allowing users to manually look up the meaning and definition of trading partner characteristics. This repository provides a semantic foundation for global business transactions, as well as a common mechanism for global access.

ebXML Architecture

Within the world of ebXML there are two views that describe a business interaction:

The first is the *Business Operational View (BOV)*, which addresses the semantics of business data transactions, as well as information interchange. This view includes operational conventions, agreements, and obligations between partners; thus, it relates to how we deal with trading partners and trading communities in general.

The second is the *Functional Service View (FSV)*, which addresses the supporting services and deployment needs of ebXML. There are three major phases associated with the FSV: implementation, discovery and deployment, and runtime (see Figure 12.3).

The *implementation phase* deals with the procedures for creating and executing applications within the ebXML infrastructures. For example, a trading partner wishing to engage in an ebXML-compliant transaction would first obtain copies of the ebXML Specifications. After that, the trading partner would move to understand these specifications, perhaps obtaining additional information such as the trading partners' process information (existing within their business profile) for analysis. In some instances, the trading partner can also submit its own process information to an ebXML-compliant Registry Service. After that, the *discovery and deployment* phase discovers ebXML-related resources and they are self-enabled into the ebXML infrastructure. Next is the *run-time* phase, where the execution of an ebXML process takes place.

FSV leverages information technology aspects of functional capabilities, service interfaces, and protocols. These protocols include the ability for implementation, discovery, deployment and runtime; user application interfaces; data transfer infrastructure interfaces; and protocols for XML interoperability.

Both BOV and FSV (which make up the ebXML architecture) leverage the ebXML Registry to provide distributed services for the sharing of information between trading partners, which allow each entity to find each other and create processes between them. The repository leverages an API to expose its services, thus making the registry accessible from Java and Web-based applications, for example.

Thus, we can conclude that the registry and repository (defined above) are coupled. The registry offers access to services, as well as the information model and reference system. In contrast, the repository provides the physical storage for

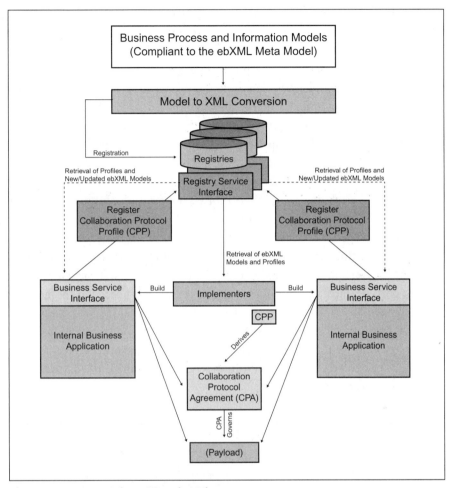

Figure 12.3   Functional Service View.

ebXML. The notion is that all information about all trading partners is contained here and is accessible to any partner (if authorized) looking to create common processes and formats between them.

Business Process Modeling

The ebXML *Business Process and Information Meta Model* is an approach that allows trading partners to define the details to drive a specific business process using standard modeling methodologies. As we already discussed in Chapter 3, a business process defines how trading partners interact, taking on roles, relationships, and responsibilities to facilitate interaction with other trading partners, and creating procedures for how the partners collaborate on business transactions.

The interaction between roles exists as processes that invoke business transactions. Each business transaction is expressed as an exchange of information (business documents) that may be composed from reusable business information objects at the high level. At the low level, business processes can be composed of reusable core processes. Business information objects can be composed of core components.

The *Meta Model* views (support requirements, analysis, and design) provide a set of semantics (vocabulary) for each viewpoint and form. The output from this is a series of artifacts required to facilitate the Business Process and information integration. In other words, this is the semantics portion of this exchange, which defines semantic differences and thus how transformation should occur.

Over and above the view of the Meta Model, the *specification schema* also supports the direct specification of the set of elements needed to configure a run-time system that will execute a set of ebXML business transactions. Thus, we can create a semantic subset of the ebXML Business Process and Information Meta Model by drawing out modeling elements from several of the other views (see Figure 12.4). You can represent the specification schema using the Unified Modeling Language (UML) and DTD.

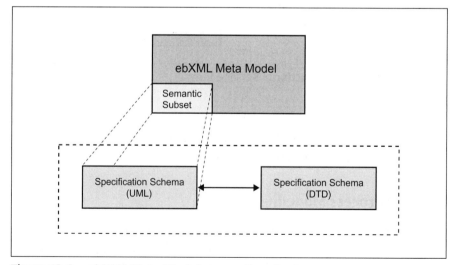

Figure 12.4   ebXML Meta Model, semantic subset.

Business collaboration is a group of choreographed business transactions as defined by the specification schema. In the world of ebXML, each business transaction is implemented using one of many available standard patterns, which define the exchange of messages or other information exchanged between trading partners. Use of a standard pattern is required to carry out the transaction. The specification schema leverages a set of standard patterns, as well as a set of modeling elements that are common to those patterns. The complete specification of business process systems and information in the Meta Model is specified against the specification schema. This information feeds into the formation of the CPPs and CPAs (see Figure 12.5)

EbXML leverages Unified Modeling Language, thus providing a standard modeling methodology and notation to create new business processes. The use of a single approach in and between trading partners is self-explanatory.

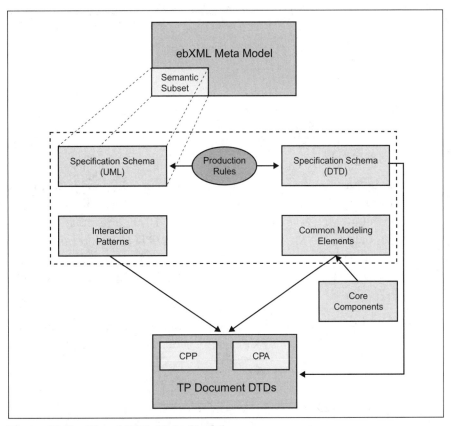

Figure 12.5   The ebXML Meta Model.

> ### Business Process Information Model and CPP and CPA
>
> CPP defines a trading partner's functionality and technical capabilities through an instance of itself and is able to support one or more business processes and one or more roles in each process. We form agreements between two trading partners by defining the conditions under which the two partners will carry out business. The interface between the business process (as well as semantics) and the CPA is the portion of the business process document.
>
> This procedure may be instantiated as XML, which is used to represent the transitional and collaboration layers of the business process and information meta model. The XML is shared between the business process and trading partner information models.

Conformance to ebXML

The ebXML standard, like other standards, is really all about making sure that everyone does things in the same way; thus, there is a need to lay down the law in terms of what it means to be ebXML compliant.

Conformance to ebXML is defined in terms of conformance to the ebXML infrastructure and the technical specifications. The idea is that, if everyone is doing ebXML in the same way, they can exchange information and processes without having to do much extra work. Thus, *conformance* is defined as conformance to an ebXML system that is comprised of all architectural components of the ebXML infrastructure satisfying the minimum conformance requirements.[2] This includes functional and interface requirements in the specification, in particular:

- You shall support all of the functional and interface requirements.
- You shall not specify any requirements that would contradict or cause non-conformance.

---

[2]ebXML Technical Architecture Specification, 2001; www.ebXML.org.

- You may contain a conformance clause that adds requirements that are more specific.
- You shall only contain requirements that are testable.[3]

---

ebXML and UDDI

The relationship between ebXML and UDDI shows how ebXML joins the fast-moving world of Web services. UDDI is a lot like ebXML's Repository, with the fundamental difference being that UDDI aims to create a standard registry for enterprises that seek to leverage common reusable Web services, while ebXML looks to standardize how XML is used in general-purpose process-based B2B integration. The essence of the UDDI model therefore focuses on middleware connectivity using Web services, and using XML only to describe the systems that are available for access using a Web services interface. UDDI does this by maintaining information about the remote services, including profiles and capabilities. This is put into a shared directory that is globally accessible.

There are three types of information that are tracked by UDDI: white, yellow, and green pages. The *white pages* directory allows enterprises to register their names and key services they expose, and whether they will allow other entities to locate and access these services. The *yellow pages* component of the directory categorizes companies by codes (NAICS, United Nation/SPSC codes, and location). The *green pages* contain information about how companies interface with other companies in the registry using XML.

Early on, those creating the ebXML standard and UDDI standard began to make each standard interoperable, integrating ebXML to UDDI. Considering that there is much overlap in the capabilities of each, some are confused as to why two standards must exist. Clearly, they will morph together over time. Indeed, over the next few years, UDDI aims to expand its number of categories and add more complete features to assist in the searching of services within its repository.

---

[3]Ibid.

ebFuture

ebXML is a holistic standard for the automation of electronic business; it covers most bases in terms of enabling technology and has a bright future as a standard to drive trading communities. However, a few missing pieces that I would like to see incorporated into ebXML include

- Vertical processes, or canned processes, leveraged within a particular vertical industry.
- Vertical semantics, or canned data semantics, leveraged within a particular vertical industry.
- Better defined security standards.
- Enhanced synergy with emerging standards, such as Web services.
- Better integration with more traditional standards, such as EDI.

But you can't have everything. As this standard matures, we may see many changes to ebXML, and some of the above issues may be addressed. In the meantime, ebXML is still a good bet for enterprises that want to automate information processes between their trading partners.

## CHAPTER THIRTEEN

BPEL4WS and Application Integration

We are clearly moving toward standards within the world of application integration, both at the information (e.g., XML) and services (e.g., Web services) layers. However, the notion of standards-based process integration, despite a few attempts such as WFMC (discussed in previous books), has not been as well accepted.

With the appearance of Business Process Execution Language for Web Services (BPEL4WS), a derivative of Web services, we have yet another attempt to provide a standard mechanism to define, execute, and share processes. BPEL4WS seems to have more momentum than earlier specifications, with adoptions by most major application integration technology vendors as well as enterprise software vendors. Moreover, its use of Web services and XML-like syntax makes it a natural fit for most consumers of technology. The goal is to provide a standard mechanism to define business processes that span application vendors, platforms, process engines, and application integration technology.

What's important here is that you understand the basics of the specification, what it is, and what it brings to process integration as we defined it earlier in the book, as well as its extension to B2B problem domains. The BPEL4WS specification is the primary reference material for this chapter, and once again we

are going to cover the basics and the relation of this technology to application integration. Thus, you may go directly to the spec for more detail, certainly for more code, but the highlights are covered here.

There are a couple of aspects to process integration standards, including common formats for processes, metadata, and information, and a common set of notations that can span many products. Until now, the use of standards has been widely published but rarely employed. Indeed, most process integration layers— either bound to an application integration technology or not—are proprietary in nature.

The movement of Web services has launched a variety of substandards, or standards that use the notion and enabling technology of Web services in order to define them. BPEL4WS has such a standard. BPEL4WS is focused on the creation of complex processes by joining together local and remote services, thus leveraging the notion of process integration as well as service-oriented Web services.

In the world of BPEL4WS, process is one of two things:

- *Executable business processes* that model actual behavior of a participant in business interaction
- *Business protocols* that use process descriptions specifying the mutually visible message exchange's behavior for each of the parties leveraging the protocol (does not reveal internal behavior)

Process descriptions for business protocols are known as *abstract processes*, and BPEL4WS models behavior for both abstract and executable processes.

To this end, BPEL4WS leverages a well-defined language to define and execute business processes and business interaction protocols, thus extending the Web services interaction model by providing a mechanism to create meta applications—process models, really—above the existing services that exist inside or outside the company.[1]

What's both different and compelling about BPEL4WS is the use of a common syntax that is designed to be transferable from process engine to process engine. This is in contrast to other process integration standards, such as BPMI or WFMC, which are more about approaches than a common language. There is more momentum beyond BPEL4WS, and all technology vendors are declaring support for BPEL4WS.

---

[1]Business Process Execution Language for Web Services, Version 1.0. July 31, 2002.

The BPEL4WS Basics

It's the rule of BPEL4WS to define a new Web service by composing a set of existing services through a process integration-type mechanism with common language control. BPEL4WS is basically a language design to implement the compilation of processes that indicate how the services interface abstractions into the overall execution of the process composition. Indeed, it's designed to be a standard language for process integration. The interface is described as a collection of WSDL portTypes, as is any other Web service (for more information on WSDL, see Chapter 15).

BPEL4WS leverages the concept of message properties used to identify relevant data embedded in messages. Using this mechanism, properties may be viewed in two ways: transparent and opaque:

- *Transparent data* affect the public business protocols (defined below) directly.
- *Opaque data* are primarily associated with back-end systems (affecting business protocols by creating nondeterminism).

The effect of opaque data appears within nondeterminism in the actual behavior of services involved in the business protocols; for example, when creating a protocol to define the purchase of a stock. The broker has a service that receives an order request and responds with either a confirmation of the transaction or a denial, using any number of criteria (e.g., price, number of shares, or buyer's credit). Indeed, the decision process is opaque, but the fact of the decision must exist as a behavior in the *business protocol*.

In essence, the protocol acts as a "switch" within the behavior of the broker's service, although the selection of the branch taken is nondeterministic. To this end, the application of nondeterministic behavior can exist by allowing assignment of the nondeterministic or opaque value to a message property. Thus, the property can then be exploited in defining conditional behavior that captures behavioral alternatives without exploiting the decision processes. The end result is the ability to expose a process to the public, while hiding aspects of the service you would rather not expose to the public.[2]

The applications of this should be readily apparent from our discussion of public versus private processes. Using this mechanism you'll be able to expose

---

[2]Business Process Execution Language for Web Services, Version 1.0. July 31, 2002.

behaviors, but can hide any aspect of the service from outside users, typically other organizations. Thus, you can expose a service with assurances that private or proprietary information won't fall into the wrong hands, or be invoked erroneously.

BPEL4WS defines a model and grammar for describing the behavior of a process using the interactions between the process and its partners. These interactions with the partners occur through Web services interfaces, and the structure of the relationships at the interface level exists in an entity known as a *service link*. It's the job of a BPEL4WS process to describe how these services interact with these partners, defining a more holistic business process, including coordinating logic (sequencing, subprocesses, nesting using outside services, etc.). Within this standard we are able to deal with exception processing and define how individual or composite activities within a process are compensated in cases where exceptions occur.

There are two major concepts to remember when considering BPEL4WS in the context of application integration:

- First, a BPEL4WS process can define a business protocol using the concept of an abstract process, providing a mechanism for identifying protocol-relevant data as message properties using nondeterministic data values hiding private properties.
- Second, it is possible to leverage BPEL4WS to define an executable business process including the logic and state of the process. This mechanism deals with fundamental process integration concepts such as sequencing, subprocesses, and hierarchies.

BPEL4WS exists as an extension of many XML specifications, including:

- WSDL 1.1
- XML Schema 1.0
- XPath 1.0

BPEL4WS and WSDL

Some people confuse BPEL4WS and WSDL; in reality they are very different concepts. First, BPEL4WS leverages WSDL, providing a mechanism to create a coordinating process on top of new or existing Web services defined by WSDL (for more information, see Chapter 15).

WSDL messages and XML schema-type definitions provide the data model leveraged by BPEL4WS processes, and the XPath standard provides support for data manipulation. As mentioned above, all external services are exposed as WSDL services, which is the way Web services work.

Again, at its essence, BPEL4WS is a process modeling mechanism layered on top of the service model defined by WSDL and leveraging a peer-to-peer interaction between the services (see Figure 13.1). Thus, both processes and partners are modeled as WSDL services, with the business processes coordinating the interactions between a process instance and its partners. Indeed, BPEL4WS processes leverage many WSDL services, and it provides the description of the behavior and how these processes interact through a standard Web services interface. Moreover, it's the job of BPEL4WS to define the message exchange protocols leveraged by the business process.

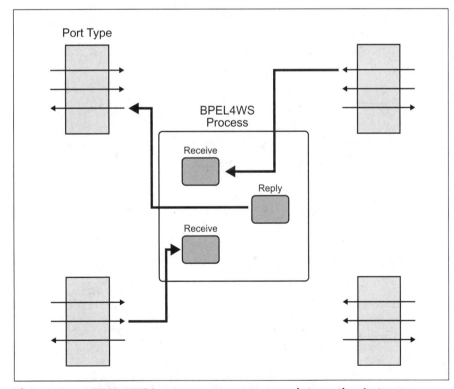

Figure 13.1   BPEL4WS leverages a peer-to-peer interaction between remote or local Web services.

BPEL4WS also leverages WSDL model-based separation between the abstract message contents used by the business process and the deployment information. It's the job of the BPEL4WS process to represent all partners and interactions with these partners in terms of abstract WSDL interfaces.

As I alluded to above, BPEL4WS can be described in two ways: executable business processes and business protocols. Let's dive a bit deeper.

An *executable business process* models the real behavior of a client in an overall business process. This is the meta process that controls the subprocesses, invoking Web services as needed to support the overall process model. No attempt is made to separate externally visible or "public" aspects of a business process for the internals. In short, this is the "meta-application" that sits on top of the subapplications (Web services) invoking services and abstracting their behavior into an overall controller process that looks much like the pattern of a composite application, but without an interface and with characteristics that are consistent with a process.

Business protocols are a bit different, using process descriptions that specify the mutually visible message exchange behavior of each of the parties leveraging the protocol. This is done without revealing internal behavior. The underlying processes that exist in a business protocol are known as abstract processes and are not executable (unlike executable business processes). Abstract process are used to couple Web services interface definitions with behavioral specifications that are leveraged to control the implementation of business roles and define the behavior that each party participating in the protocol can expect from the others.

BPEL4WS Process Syntax

At its essence, the BPEL4WS process itself is a flowchart-like expression of an algorithm.[3] Each step is known as an activity, and there are a bunch of primitive activities (subactivities if you will) that actually

1. Invoke Web services.
2. The caller waits for a message to operate on the service's interface to be invoked by an external service.
3. This generates a response of an input/output operation.

---

[3]Weerawarana, Sanjiva. August 2002. *Understanding BPEL4WS, Part 1.*

4. Waits for a certain amount of time.
5. Copies data from one place to another.
6. Indicates that an error occurred.
7. Then terminates the service.
8. Or else does nothing.

The notation looks something like this:

1. `<invoke>`
2. `<receive>`
3. `<reply>`
4. `<wait>`
5. `<assign>`
6. `<throw>`
7. `<terminate>`
8. `<empty>`

Once we understand how these primitive activities occur, we can create more complex algorithms using structure activities, including:

- `<sequence>` to define the ordered sequence of steps
- `<switch>` to define case statements and thus branching
- `<while>` to define a loop
- `<pick>` to define a program path
- `<flow>` to define a collection of steps

It is the job of BPEL4WS to provide a service aggregation mechanism, and it bunches those services into a single process, but understand that you're creating a new process, as well. To this end, BPEL4WS processes consist of invocations to other services and/or receiving invocations from clients (those that use the service). We do this using the `<invoke>` activity and then the `<receive>` and `<replay>` activities. These are partner processes, and a partner is a service invoked by a process (invoked partners) or a partner that invokes processes (client partners).

Invoked partners, using the `<invoke>` activity, determine the partner to invoke and the innate operation of what operation of which of the partner's portTypes to invoke on that particular partner. It is not unheard of, however, that an invoked partner becomes a client, as well. Thus, we can classify partners as one of three types: services that a process invokes only (invoked partner), services that invoke the process only (client partners), or services that the process invokes and that invoke the process (where either may occur first).[4]

It's the third type that gives rise to the notion of *service link types*; rather than describe the relationship between the service and the process from the view of one of the participants, the service link types represent the view from a third-party declaration of a link between two or more services. Moreover, a service link type is also a collection of roles containing portTypes, defining how these services interact with one another. We use service link types to define partners, which are given a name and a binding to a service link type, and identify the role that the process and partner will play. We use the notion of the *service reference* for the partner to work at runtime, resolving it into a real Web service, and providing a reference for a partner.

Going a bit deeper, a service link type characterizes the relationships between two services through the use of the "role" played by each of the services that exist in the relationship. Moreover, we also specify the portTypes provided by each role. A service link looks like this:

```
<serviceLinkType name="BrokerLink"
     xmlns="http://schemas.xmlsoap.org/ws/2002/07/
        service-link/">
 <role name="Customer">
  <portType name="buy:BuyerPortType"/>
 </role>
 <role name="Broker">
  <portType name="sell:SellerPortType"/>
 </role>
</serviceLinkType>
```

The portTypes of each role originate from a specific namespace, but in some instances both roles of a service link type can be defined in terms of portTypes from the namespace.

Keep in mind that portTypes define abstract functionality by leveraging abstract messages, and ports facilitate access to actual information, communication

---

[4]Ibid.

endpoints, and other deployment-related information, including encryption. Bindings provide the link between the two.

As we began to address in our discussion above, service references provide a mechanism for dynamic communication of port-specific data for services, making it possible to dynamically select a provider for a particular type of service and invoke their methods. Within BPEL4WS, there is a mechanism for correlating messages to stateful instances of a service. Service references are defined as typed references, including port-specific data for a particular service, as well as additional data regarding instance-identification tokens.

For example, a service reference looks like this:

```
<sref:serviceReference
xmlns:sref="http://schemas.xmlsoap.org/ws/2002/07/
  service-reference/">
  <wsdl:definitions> . . . </wsdl:definitions>?
  <sref:service name="qname"/>
  <sref:referenceProperties>?
    <sref:property name="qname">+
      <!- any element content ->
    </sref:property>
  </sref:referenceProperties>
</sref:serviceReference>5
```

Exception Handling

BPEL4WS provides a set of facilities to recover from errors while executing a process or handling exceptions. BPEL4WS makes good use of the exception handling capabilities already built into WSDL. As we described above, you can leverage the `<throw>` and `<catch>` constructs. What's more, you can leverage the notion of compensation, which allows the process designer to implement *compensating actions* for particular irreversible actions. This is supported recursively in BPEL4WS using the notion of *scope*. Scope is essentially a unit of work for compensation. In other words, BPEL4WS supports transactional-type characteristics.

---

[5]Business Process Execution Language for Web Services, Version 1.0. July 31, 2002.

Life Cycle

The model support by WSDL is a stateless client/server model using synchronous or uncorrected interaction. BPEL4WS, however, represents long-running transactions that are stateful in nature. In other words, they have a life cycle that extends well beyond a simple transaction. For example, a cable TV company gets an order, processes the work order, sends out an installer, does the installation, and begins billing the customer. This transaction could take weeks (sometimes months) and is long running. BPEL4WS is able to maintain the state of this process throughout the life cycle, keeping track of when the order came in all the way through to the billing activity. The use of the mechanism in the world of e-commerce is the most logical application, driving long-term durable transactions between trading partners. Coupled with the public versus private process features of BPEL4WS, it's clear that this is a process specification created for both internal and external use.

BPEL4WS can also create process instances, or many copies of the same process or subprocesses, as required to solve the business problem. When creating a process instance using BPEL4WS, the creation is implicit, thus activities that receive messages can be annotated to indicate that the occurrence of that activity creates a new instance of the process. To accomplish this, each business process should contain at least one "start activity." If one start activity executes, the use of correlation sets is not limited.

You can kill instances of business processes when the controlling business process completes, or when a fault reaches the process scope and is either handled or not handled, or when a process instance is explicitly terminated by a terminate activity. These are simple nesting-type constructs and should not be unfamiliar to most developers.

Message Properties

There are two parts to the data encapsulated in BPEL4WS messages:

- Application data
- Protocol-relevant data

Business protocol data is the correlation token leveraged in correlation sets. This includes security, transaction, and message protocols. This data is embedded in the application-visible message parts, in contrast to the infrastructure protocols, which add implicit parts to the message types representing protocol headers. Message properties are defined as a way of naming and representing distinguished data elements encapsulated within a message.

Correlation

When executing a business process instance, one or many communications occur with partners that are part of the process. In some cases, correlated conversations that involve more than two entities or leverage a lightweight transport infrastructure with a correlation token exist inside the application data moving between parties. Thus, in many instances, it is necessary to provide additional application-level mechanisms that match message and conversation inside the business process instances.

To this end, BPEL4WS addresses correlation scenarios, providing a declarative mechanism that specifies correlated groups of operations inside an instance of a service, and a set of correlation tokens can be defined as a set of properties shared by all messages inside a correlated group. This is known as a *correlation set*, which is instantiated inside the scope of an instance of a business process.

Data Handling

Within BPEL4WS the maintenance of the state of the business process requires the use of a state variable known as *containers*. The data from the state is extracted and combined in interesting ways to manage the process behavior requiring data expression. BPEL4WS uses XML data types and WSDL messages as an enabling mechanism for data handling, as do traditional Web services.

The difference between abstract and executable processes is in the way data is handled within a process. Abstract processes don't have the same capabilities to manipulate the values contained in message properties, which are limited to the use of a nondeterministic value to reflect outcomes of private behavior. In contrast, executable processes are permitted to use a full range of data manipulation and assignments features, but cannot use nondeterministic values.

BPEL4WS by Example

So, now that we know some of the details behind BPEL4WS, perhaps it's best to walk through an example to bring the concepts home. Let's return to our broker example.

When receiving an order from a client, the broker example creates three process instances that are required to carry out the order (see Figure 13.2):

1. Booking the order into the order management system
2. Executing the trade
3. Deducting the amount of the trade from the client's cash account

In the world of process integration, as you may remember from the previous chapter, some processes can proceed in parallel; there are control and data dependencies that exist between the tasks running in parallel. For example, you can't execute a trade before booking the order, and then and only then can you deduct the amount of trade from the client's cash account.

The WSDL portType offered by the service to its clients (`bookOrderPT`), and other WSDL definitions required by the business process, are included in the same WSDL document. For example, the portTypes for the Web services serving up trade calculations, execution information, and accounting services are defined there, as well. BPEL4WS creates a process defined as an abstract process by referencing the portTypes of the services involved in the process. This facilitates reuse of the process definitions through multiple deployments of the processes.

Moving further through our example, the service link types represent the interaction between the trading system and each of the parties with which it

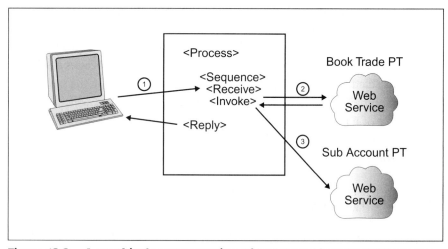

**Figure 13.2   A graphical representation of our example BPEL4WS process
to book the purchase of a stock.**

interacts. Remember, we can use a service link type to represent dependences between services, and each service link type defines up to two "role" names and lists the portTypes that each role supports for the process. For our scenario, two link types—`BookOrderLT` and `ExecTradeLT`—list a singe role because, in the corresponding service interactions, one of the parties provides all the invoked operations. In this case, the `BookOrderLT` service link abstracts the connections between the process and the requesting client, where the order booking service offers a service operation `BookOrder`. What's more, the `ExecTradeLT` service link represents the communication between the booking order service and the execute trade service.

Value of BPEL4WS

BPEL4WS, from the survey in this chapter, has the potential to become a language-based standard for process integration, allowing models to be created on one tool or application integration technology, and transferred one to another without having to make changes to the code. The reality is that it will take some time before BPEL4WS becomes a standard process integration solution, albeit it has the momentum right now.

You should also remember that BPEL4WS does not bring a lot to the table in terms of functionality, but the promise of standards could finally bring many enterprises to process integration—those that previously avoided this technology due to its proprietary nature. Standards, however, are only as good as the number of people who leverage them. That's the variable yet to be defined.

## CHAPTER FOURTEEN

UCCnet and RosettaNet: Supply Chain Integration Standards

The power of supply chain integration is something we've just begun to understand. Product-intensive companies such as Wal-Mart, Ford, Boeing, and many others all wrestle with the problem of linking to customers and suppliers in real time, providing a mechanism to automate the exchange of information such as orders, payments, logistics, and so on.

We will cover supply chain integration in great detail in Chapter 17. However, we will begin our discussion here by looking at the two of the most significant supply chain integration standards: UCCnet and RosettaNet. Each has its own set of industries for which it is applicable (UCCnet for retail supply chains, RosettaNet for high-tech manufacturing), and each has its own way of approaching supply chain integration, which is even more interesting.

What you want to focus on with this chapter are both the basics of the standards and architectures, and the enabling technologies they employ. Note their similarities and differences.

The need to exchange information between companies has been an issue with product-intensive companies for decades, as we seek to automate the business processes, either formal or informal, between trading partners. The problem has been in the use of common infrastructures or standards to drive these efforts, which eliminate the need for each trading community to create their own one-off solution.

Thus, the recent focus has been on creating standards that define not only how one or two companies work together, but also how entire micro-economies of suppliers and partner organizations exchange common product data in real time to automate business processes and information exchange between hundreds of business entities.

Granted, we have been automating supply using enabling chains for years. The use of EDI is a major cost savings. However, in recent years, we've focused on technologies and standards that bring additional value to trading communities such as

- Catalog services
- Reusable processes
- Prebuilt processes
- Common transport layers
- Transaction capacities
- Legal compliance
- Metadata

Indeed, we are moving toward a world where, no matter what industry you're in, there is a standard that defines how you interact with trading partners. For now, most of these standards—including the two we highlight in this chapter—are in the category of "up and coming," but that's better than "new and unknown."

Categories of Standards

Keep in mind there are many types of standards out there, but they have a tendency to fall into one of the following categories:

- Process-based
- Service-based
- Message-based

Process-based standards, such as ebXML and RosettaNet, approach trading communities by creating common processes that span enterprises. Typically these prebuilt processes determine how they carry out business activities, such as depleting inventory, logistics, order validation and verification, and so on.

The advantage of process-based standards is that they go well beyond simple information exchange (albeit they may still provide an information exchange infrastructure). They also provide a mechanism to define and drive a common process, as well as precanned processes that you don't have to create, just bind to internal processes (see Figure 14.1). Moreover, they typically provide common metadata and information exchange infrastructures.

Service-based standards, as you may have guessed from the name, are standards that provide access to common services in support of a trading community. Web services-based standards, including BPEL4WS, fall into this category, providing access to common services in support of e-Business. For example, a Web service that is globally accessible calculates shipping costs and applicable taxes for sending goods overseas.

The advantage of service-based standards is that we share not only common processes, but also real application services that span multiple companies. There are many other places in this book where we make the case for sharable services. The disadvantage is that services have a tendency to be more invasive, and it's difficult to get other organizations inside a trading community to alter their systems to expose services. To this end, it may be a better choice to leverage a Web services network and centralized server that host Web services for access to many entities. Thus the services do not have to exist in just one enterprise, and they are more accessible and considered neutral.

Message-based standards focus on the exchange of information between organizations. The notion is to define a common message (sometimes an XML

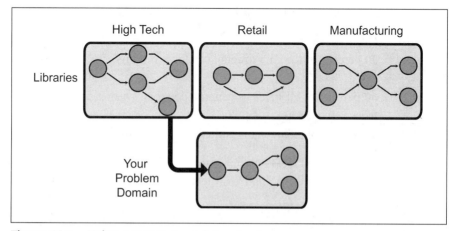

Figure 14.1   Using process-based standards.

document) and leverage that to define how these trading partners communicate. EDI is an example of a message-based standard, providing a common, universally understood format for exchanging order and payment information. However, message-based standards are also a part of more sophisticated enabling standards such as ebXML.

The advantage of message-based standards is the ease of implementation due to their sheer simplicity. Basically, all trading partners decide to leverage a message-based standard, and then begin exchanging information. The disadvantage is that message-based standards don't address important aspects of supply chain integration, including common processes.

UCCnet: The Basics

Retailers and their key suppliers have begun driving toward collaborative networks that will reduce their costs by reducing inventories, and improve revenue by preventing stock-outs. These new trading relationships often expand and extend software touch-points beyond traditional supply chain technology, such as EDI.

A key enabler for these relationships is agreement between trading partners on both the technology used to transmit the information and, more importantly, the business data itself. One area that is receiving significant attention in the market is business data synchronization for items.[1]

For example, suppliers incorrectly fill a large number of purchase orders because the retailer did not use the correct material number. As a result, the wrong material is sent, increasing inventories and damaging revenue. A.T. Kearny conducted a study that found as much as:

- 30 percent of the data in retail catalogs contains errors that cost from $60 to $80 each
- 60 percent of all invoices generated errors, with each invoice error costing from $40 to $400
- 43 percent of all invoices resulted in deductions

As a subsidiary of the Uniform Code Council (UCC), UCCnet has developed a neutral industry source where retailers can locate product and partner

---

[1]Mercator UCCnet documentation.

information regardless of which manufacturer published it. Known as the *GLOBALregistry*, this hub-based architecture provides item synchronization services among all participants of the supply network. This capability is delivered by communicating all information through industry standards for transport, UCC-defined formats, and processes.

The adoption of large players on the retail side, such as Wal-Mart, Lowe's, Food Lion, SuperValu, and Ace Hardware, has driven increased adoption rates on the supplier side thus far. For example, when Wal-Mart announced that its Tier 1 suppliers must now subscribe to the UCCnet, the result was a significant increase in participation due to the many suppliers who have relationships with Wal-Mart. Bottom line is that retail participation drives the explosive growth rate of the GLOBALregistry because they drag their suppliers into the UCCnet.

There are three major areas of service that make up UCCnet:

- A standard database for products and locations.
- Access to updated trading information.
- The use of standards for both storing and retrieving this information.

The use of UCCnet's GLOBALregistry provides a single database for product and trading partner information and is endorsed by EAN International and many of the world's leading industry organizations. Using this database, companies can publish and transmit their product information, providing trading partners with access. Moreover, the use of EAN.UCC standards provides a set of technical standards to ensure integrity of the data throughout the supply chain.

So, how does a trading partner become part of UCCnet? Just subscribe. A full-service subscription provides access to:

- *GLOBALregistry* for storage of data relating to the products you are trading, including the attributes for each item. This is the common registry for use when exchanging information with trading partners.
- *Item Synchronization* for the publication of current industry-compliant data to the GLOBALregistry, thus making this information available to the trading partners.
- *SYNCpoint*, which is a Web browser interface providing the trading partner with the ability to synchronize EAN.UCC item information with other suppliers. This also includes access to business applications and services.
- *M2M*, which provides the message transport mechanism for UCCnet.

UCCnet Components

There are four main components supporting this standard:

1. *Protocol support.* UCCnet currently supports two techniques to connect to their hub. The first of these is called the UCCnet Technical Application Programming Interface (UTAPI). This technique is being deprecated, so should not be considered when developing strategy.
2. *Partner and message management.* This includes the ability to set up links to the GLOBALregistry, ensure that messages sent/received adhere to the standard, provide a record of sent/received messages for nonrepudiation and auditing, and the ability to drill down into message payloads as a business user interface. Also required is the ability to route messages to appropriate post offices based on the content of the message.

   The *UCCnet Technical User's Guide* contains an example of the payload used by UCCnet items. As you can see from the *User's Guide*, it is a complex XML-based payload. We describe this in additional detail below.
3. *Process management support.* Currently UCCnet is a stateless B2B standard. However, with the acquisition of RosettaNet, and emerging business needs, we should expect that a public process will be defined for UCCnet transactions. The UCC (UCCnet's parent organization) has proposed an ebXML-based version of stateful UCCnet transactions as a first step toward adding this functionality. As a result, the ability to lay a process layer on top of the transaction flow for public processes will be needed.
4. *Application integration capabilities.* In order for organizations to gain business benefit from connecting to UCCnet's hub, they must be able to harmonize the various applications in their portfolio. This requires core application integration capabilities.

UCCnet Message Set

UCCnet uses a DTD message structure to define the valid building blocks of an XML document (how they exchange information). The UCCnet message structure uses several of the features leveraged by the EAN.UCC Message Architecture, including the separation of messages into three layers:

1. Transport
2. Command
3. Data/Document

The *transport layer* deals with the technology required to get the message from point A to point B. A message includes all necessary information such as recipient, sender, associations, identifier, and so on. This dynamic information is always changing.

In terms of UCCnet this layer is customized for the applications, meaning it's proprietary to UCCnet. There are future plans to move to ebXML and Web services standards, including SOAP.

The *command layer* defines the function and operation, and how each should be performed when a particular message is received. This is also dynamic and is associated with a grouping of messages or a single message.

And finally, the *document/data layer* describes what information the command acts upon. This typically appears as an identifier to the specific document (e.g., the Global Trade Item Number, or GTIN, or the Global Location Number, or GLN). This information is persistent from transaction to transaction.

Global identifiers identify persistent data objects in the system. This is required because we have data from so many trading partners at the same time. This allows commands to use references to these documents in lieu of the entire structure.

UCCnet leverages these identifiers, which are kept in a central location, unique to the UCC. However, they do not exist for other documents, including price brackets, prices, and so on. The end result is a set of identifiers that is globally accessible, but still easy to create and track.

For example, we may use a concatenation of properties to create a unique identifier. We can take the owner's GLN, an owner-generated identifier, and a document type, and create this structure.[2] Thus, as long as the owner makes sure the entity ID (created by the owner) is unique, the three concatenated elements, taken as a whole, would provide a unique identifier for the document for which it was created. For example:

Type: `PriceBracket`
GLN: `9090909090909`
Identifier: `X90909`

Thus, the above is considered unique as long as the trading partner does not create another `PriceBracket` with the same identifier. Thus we can consider

---

[2]UCCnet. *Technical Users Guide;* page 9.

this globally unique. In the world of UCCnet, this concept is known as `typed EntityIdentification`.

The notion of *document reuse* in the world of UCCnet is when a particular business entity is able to reuse a variety of different business processes, including the ability to reuse an item and its GTIN. In this scenario, you may reference a GTIN in the context of pricing information or other documents, meaning it's reused within other business processes. You may also apply this concept to other types of entities, such as EDI or XML.

UCCnet: A Contender?

UCCnet is one of those standards that's powerful enough to be useful, but not too complex to use. It's a vertical standard, and only applicable in a single industry—product-intensive companies—and has a strong foothold with retailers.

As we have seen above, UCCnet provides two basic services: data synchronization and a global registry of product information required to support a basic trading community. This standard provides a unique way to identify products, which has been haphazard in the world of retail.

Users of UCCnet are a "Who's Who" in retail, including Wal-Mart, Wegmans Food Markets, and Ralston Purina. Moreover, trading exchanges such as Transora leverage UCCnet to support catalog services, as in GlobalNetXchange.

In the future we will likely see UCCnet join forces with other, more horizontal B2B standards, such as BPEL, ebXML, and RosettaNet. Indeed, we are seeing convergence today with this and other supply chain standards. For a while, however, these standards are going to be more vertically focused.

Clearly, the number of retailers and suppliers leveraging UCCnet is increasing quickly as they realize what UCCnet is and what it is not. It's correct to consider UCCnet a public utility, thus neutral. Considering all this, it has a bright future.

RosettaNet

RosettaNet, in its basic form, is just another trading community standard. However, its innovative approach to managing trading communities at both the information and process levels makes it particularly important to application integration and supply chain integration.

The RosettaNet consortium was created to define standard processes and interfaces to manage supply chains within the high-technology industry. Building on the successes of RosettaNet, a movement is now under way to leverage the same or similar standards in other industries. The innovation within the RosettaNet community has been in defining how other trading community standards, typically structured around verticals, will operate.

For all its strengths and innovations, RosettaNet is still in its early stages of development. A proof-of-concept prototype, running in early 2000, demonstrated that the concept will work. Indicators point to enough interest from the partners to make production systems inevitable. At this point, things bode well for RosettaNet.

RosettaNet History

RosettaNet was officially formed in 1998 to standardize e-Business activities in the high-technology industry (e.g., computer manufacturing and reselling). It defined open interfaces between manufacturers, distributors, resellers, and other participants in the supply chain. Indeed, close to 300 vendor members are participating in the development of the RosettaNet standard. (More information about RosettaNet is available at www.rosettanet.org.)

The high-technology industry provided a good testbed for the RosettaNet concept. The industry uses many of the same component suppliers (semiconductors, ICs, peripherals, etc.) and thus could quickly agree about information formats. Catalyzing RosettaNet's development was the perception that EDI had largely failed because of its expense, its proprietary nature, and its inability to adapt to changes in B2B processes. In addition, EDI was weak at real-time information exchange and was unable to keep up with high-volume information flows (although XML has not yet proved its viability here, either).

What's RosettaNet?

Despite the common belief that RosettaNet is all about XML, it is not. RosettaNet is a set of standard mechanisms—processes, really—that allow companies to agree upon the processing of standard business transactions. XML was added to take the place of EDI as a mere data interchange standard.

Because RosettaNet is about processes rather than data, the most important aspect of RosettaNet is the development of common Partner Interface Processes (PIPs) and common dictionaries. RosettaNet provides a master dictionary to define properties for products, partners, and business transactions. This master dictionary, coupled with an established implementation framework, can be used to support the application integration dialog. PIPs provide alignment within the overall supply chain process, allowing businesses to interact at a number of levels to support the processes of common trading communities.

For example, PIP2A2, Query Product Information, defines a common process between companies. Because each company adheres to this common process, or PIP, there is no confusion about what this particular process does. Common semantics and common mechanisms automatically carry out the process.

The real value of RosettaNet is the common agreement on "which processes do what, and where." Although we long ago established processes for executing common business activities, there has been little agreement about common processes that exist between companies or a common set of application semantics (dictionaries). It should be apparent that, as we have suggested, RosettaNet is less about technology and all about creating PIPs, which are really contracts or agreements.

Fundamentally, creating PIPs is a matter of understanding a process in detail, finding a way to make it more efficient, and defining it by using the standard PIP framework that RosettaNet offers. The process to create PIPs is depicted in Figure 14.2.

The stages to the process include

- Business process modeling
- Business process analysis
- PIP development
- Dictionaries

Those who want to leverage RosettaNet use business process modeling to identify and quantify the properties and behaviors of a particular business process. This is a laborious process of documenting what happens while selling a product, checking inventory, or shipping a product to a customer. Each stage is a process, and each stage may have hundreds of steps. Each step must be inventoried, defined in detail, and completely understood, with the goal of automating the process based on an agreement between companies. The output of this effort is a model that reflects every detail of a particular process using a common framework.

Business Process Analysis

Once the business process model is understood, we must realign the process in the form of a PIP target list. This step determines how much value this process will have when automated by RosettaNet.

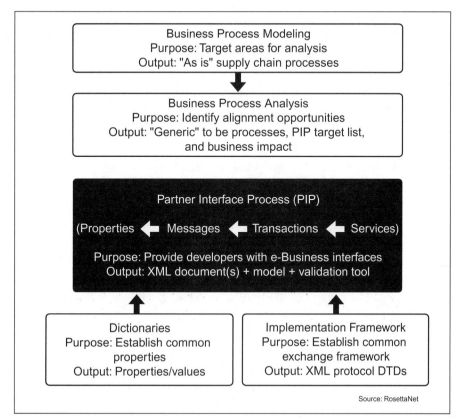

Figure 14.2   RosettaNet development process.

PIP Development

Each PIP provides a common business/data model and documents that enable system developers to leverage RosettaNet interfaces. Each PIP includes

- XML documents using a particular DTD, specifying PIP services, transactions, and messages, including dictionary properties
- Class and sequence diagrams in the Unified Modeling Language (UML)
- A validation tool
- An implementation guide

Dictionaries

During the development of RosettaNet, two data dictionaries were created to provide a common set of properties that exist within PIPs—a technical properties dictionary and a business properties dictionary. The technical properties dictionary provides the technical specifications for all product categories. The business properties dictionary describes attributes used to define supply chain partner companies and business transaction properties. These dictionaries, when bound to the RosettaNet Implementation Framework (exchange protocol), become the basis for each PIP.

It's the PIP

The real value of PIPs is the ability to allow manufacturers to seamlessly add new products to their partners' catalogs—for example, adding a new part number using a common format and information interchange standard.

A PIP specification (see Appendix A for an example) comprises three views of the e-Business PIP model.

The Business Operational View (BOV) provides the semantics of the business data entities and their exchange flow between roles during normal operations. The content of the BOV section uses the PIP Blueprint document created for the RosettaNet business community.

The Functional Service View (FSV) defines the network component services, agents, and functions required to execute PIPs. These include all transaction dialogs in a PIP protocol. The FSVs are semantically derived from the BOV and include two major components: the network component design and the network component interactions.

The Implementation Framework View (IFV) defines the network protocol message formats and communication requirements between protocols supported by network components. These messages are exchanged when software programs execute a PIP.

There are several categories, or clusters, of PIPs, such as the following (see the tidbit "RosettaNet PIP Clusters and Segments" for a complete listing):

- Cluster 1: Partner, Product, and Service Review
- Cluster 2: Product Introduction
- Cluster 3: Order Management
- Cluster 4: Inventory Management

As you might expect, there are several subcategories within each cluster (see the tidbit "RosettaNet PIP Clusters and Segments," and the tidbit "Published RosettaNet PIPs within Clusters and Segments"). Note that Clusters 1 through 3 are extensions, or a rehashing, of processes already specified in EDI during the past quarter century. Also, Cluster 4 PIPs are much like the VICS Collaborative Planning, Forecasting, and Replenishment standards administered by the Uniform Code Council.

RosettaNet PIP Clusters and Segments

Cluster 1: Partner, Product and Service Review
    Segment A: Partner Review
    Segment B: Product and Service Review
Cluster 2: Product Introduction
    Segment A: Preparation for Distribution
    Segment B: Product Change Notification
Cluster 3: Order Management
    Segment A: Quote and Order Entry
    Segment B: Transportation and Distribution
    Segment C: Returns and Finance
    Segment D: Product Configuration
Cluster 4: Inventory Management
    Segment A: Collaborative Forecasting
    Segment B: Inventory Allocation
    Segment C: Inventory Reporting
    Segment D: Inventory Replenishment
    Segment E: Sales Reporting
    Segment F: Price Protection
    Segment G: Ship From Stock and Debit/Credit (Electronic Components)
Cluster 5: Marketing Information Management
    Segment A: Lead/Opportunity Management
    Segment B: Marketing Campaign Management
    Segment C: Design Win Management (Electronic Components)
Cluster 6: Service and Support
    Segment A: Warranty Management
    Segment B: Asset Management
    Segment C: Technical Support and Service

Published RosettaNet PIPs within Clusters and Segments

Cluster 0: RosettaNet Support
    Segment A: Administration
        PIP0A1: Notification of Failure
Cluster 1: Partner, Product and Service Review
    Segment B: Product Review
        PIP1B1: Manage Product Information Subscription
Cluster 2: Product Introduction
    Segment A: Preparation for Distribution
        PIP2A1: Distribute New Product Information
        PIP2A2: Query Product Information
        PIP2A5: Query Technical Information
        PIP2A8: Distribute Product Stock Keeping Unit
Cluster 3: Order Management
    Segment A: Quote and Order Entry
        PIP3A3: Transfer Shopping Cart
        PIP3A4: Manage Purchase Order
        PIP3A5: Query Order Status
        PIP3A6: Distribute Order Status

The Technology

RosettaNet's technology is nothing new or revolutionary. Its implementation is based on CommerceNet's OBI specification, XML, X12 EDI, and PKCS#7 digital signatures.

The OBI specification was established to allow companies to use the Internet to purchase products that might not be part of their core business, such as coffee for the office coffee machine. OBI uses HTTP for communication between companies, Secure Socket Layer (SSL) for security services, PKCS#7 for digital signatures, and X12 for purchase orders.

The RosettaNet communication model specifically defines the behavior that should occur within the OSI application and session layers, dividing the application layer into the action, transaction, process, service, agent, message handling, transfer, and security layers (see Figure 14.3).

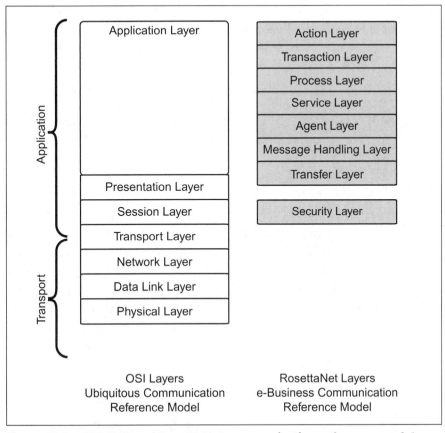

Figure 14.3   **ISO/OSI and RosettaNet communication reference model.**

The *action layer* provides business actions that act upon or in conjunction with accompanying information.

The *transaction layer* provides transaction monitoring for sequences of message exchanges that support a unit of work. Either every party commits to the transaction or the transaction is rolled back completely.

The *process layer* encapsulates the conditional choreography of a transaction for executing a PIP.

The *service layer* provides network resources that perform network and business-related functions.

The *agent layer* provides a communication interface for other applications.

The *message handling layer* provides asynchronous delivery of information.

The *transfer layer* provides a mechanism for information transfer between uniquely named network resources.

The *security layer* allows for a secure communication connection, which leverages digital signatures to implement authorization and authentication.

RosettaNet uses OBI as a subset of its enabling technology, adding more functionality within the data formatting area. It leverages XML rather than EDI (OBI was created to use EDI) to move information from point to point. (Although many EDI-like semantics are maintained, XML was selected for its compact and simple nature, and its acceptance in the market.)

PIP Communication

As we noted earlier in this chapter, the fundamental requirement of a PIP is to exchange business data between trading partners. RosettaNet-compliant networked applications receive data using a standard format that all systems and humans in the loop can understand.

Those who created RosettaNet PIPs created RosettaNet messages by using the set of elements and codes defined in the RosettaNet business and technical dictionaries. The set exists as a baseline from which PIP teams create message-exchange specifications and precisely define the values and codes that are assignable to each of the data elements—all of which are part of the PIP implementation guidelines.

These guidelines are sent as a document from RosettaNet to trading partners and RosettaNet solution partners. The guidelines define the vocabulary, structure, and allowable data element values and value types for each message exchange.

Moreover, PIP specifications enable the development of interoperable applications. Each message has three parts: the Preamble Header, the Service Header, and the Service Content. This information is typically packaged for exchanges as MIME messages.

PIP Message Structure

RosettaNet business messages consist of a message header and a message body, and both the header and body are a well-formed XML document. The header and body are encoded inside a multipart/related MIME message. The message preamble section of the MIME message contains elements that are global to the RosettaNet service, and those that are common to the Service Header and Service Content. This information is specified as a DTD that is common across all messages.

The message header is also specified using a DTD that is also common across all messages. There is a separate DTD or XML schema for each message, and that DTD or XML schema is used to validate the body of the messages. The idea behind a common message header DTD that is separate from the message content DTD is to support the logical segmentation of validation steps, which include validation of grammar, sequence, schema, and content. Grammar and sequence validations are performed against the message header DTD, and validation of message content is deferred until the schema validation step. When this mechanism is used, the message header may be valid even when the content is not. RosettaNet has this structure in place so trading partners can send failure messages. The message content is specified in individual PIPs, and each PIP has one or more "actions" that are defined by the schemas or DTD contained in the message.

RosettaNet Networked Application Protocols

RosettaNet leverages most native Internet protocols, including HTTP and TCP/IP. The TCP/IP protocol provides the functionality defined for the transport layers. Sockets and SSL are OSI session layer protocols.

RosettaNet and B2B Application Integration

It is a safe bet that RosettaNet will shape the way we view intercompany process integration as it supports the goal of supply chain integration. To date, it is the most sophisticated standard available. This sophistication is due to the fact that it takes both processes and data into account, defining common processes and points of integration within a vertical industry. Other trading community standards have yet to deliver both layers—and won't, unless they can get everyone on the same page for both application semantics and technology.

Sometimes we forget that even in the world of high technology we still have to deal with the psychology of people. The real strength of RosettaNet is not the technology, it is the fact that this organization got many people in a larger vertical industry (high technology) to define and agree upon a standard. What's more, it has succeeded at clearly defining the value of using such a standard as well as how new technology, including XML, fits into the framework. To its credit, RosettaNet built upon past success, reusing what worked with EDI.

The future is clear in RosettaNet. As organizations seek to open automated trade, they have to agree upon processes and semantics, an agreement that has thus far been frustratingly elusive.

Supply Chain Standards Moving Forward

As we move toward a more real-time enterprise and a real-time economy, the use of supply chain standards will become more pervasive. Indeed, we can foresee a day when all information systems within a trading community exchange information and leverage common processes, thus automating all aspects of the supply chain, including ordering, billing, shipping, production, and logistics.

As we move forward with supply chain integration, the challenge is to get everyone on the same set of standards. Standards bodies are competing for hearts and minds, and movement toward standards is slow. It's clear that most enterprise architects understand that some standards can be risky, but to not move toward standards is to not move the organization forward.

To this end, we will see a slow adoption of standards over the years, but it's going to be steady. Moreover, you have to remember that application integration, the focus of this book, and supply chain integration go hand in hand. You have no hope of getting your supply chain under control if your current information systems are not integrated, and thus able to expose and consume information.

We must also consider the notion of synergy with horizontal standards, such as Web services and ebXML. Most supply chain integration standards, including the two we discussed in this chapter, will continue to leverage these standards; thus, you need to factor that in to your architecture and technology choices. Remember, everything is inter-related.

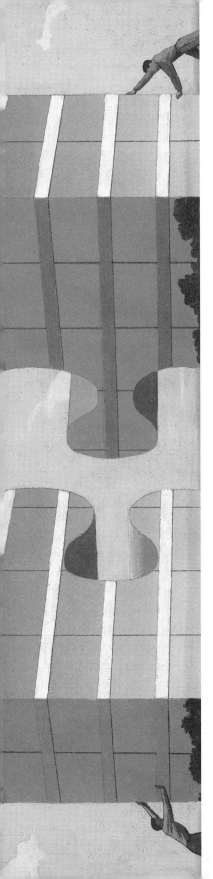

## CHAPTER FIFTEEN

SOAP, WSDL, and UDDI, Oh My . . . Web Services Foundations and Application Integration

So, you want to do Web services? This chapter talks about the foundation standards: SOAP, WSDL, and UDDI. What's important about these Web services components is the fact that most vendors (IBM, Sun, BEA, Microsoft, etc.) can agree upon these standards as the foundation for their own Web services strategies; thus, we have the chance of interoperability.

Be clear that we will focus on how these standards apply to the notion of application integration. There are hundreds of books that provide additional information in much more detail. Also note that there will be more opinion in this chapter than in the other chapters on standards.

Web services is the latest notion to take the information system development world by storm as major vendors (including Microsoft, HP, and Sun) announce their Web services strategies. The press promotes Web services as the biggest paradigm shift since the Web itself. At the same time, rank-and-file IT professionals are trying to understand just what Web services are, and assess their value within the enterprise and application integration.

The idea of Web services is exciting: the ability to create new applications by aggregating the services of many other applications that exist locally or remotely on the

Internet. However, there are a number of issues to consider when looking at Web services:

1. Keep in mind: This is an old idea with new wrapping. If you remember the promise of distributed objects of almost a decade ago, the concept is the same: provide the infrastructure for applications to exchange information, as well as leverage methods encapsulated within those applications. Web services simply put a newer, sexier architecture and enabling technology into the mix—most importantly, adding the word "Web."

2. Standards overload still prevails. As in the days of distributed objects, vendors see a hot space emerge, and all stake their own claims in the Web services space, publishing their own proprietary standards that they call "open." Thus, a shakeout is inevitable before we understand which standards will become "standard." This will only delay acceptance of Web services. Today, caution is needed from those who look to address application integration using Web services. Things could change and they may be stuck holding the bag.

Despite the usual drawbacks of emerging technology, Web services—at least the notion of Web services—is an interesting technology for the world of inter- and intracompany application integration. Web services hold the promise of moving beyond the simple exchange of information—the dominating mechanism for application integration today—to the concept of accessing services that are encapsulated within old and new applications, in and between companies. This means we can not only move information from application to application, but also create composite applications, leveraging any number of back-end application services found in any number of applications, local or remote.

Key to this concept is figuring out how Web services fit into the existing application integration technology and approaches. For example, when is the use of Web services appropriate, and how do we determine cost-effectiveness? Keep in mind: Implementing Web services is bound to be an invasive process, thus expensive when compared to enabling systems for simple information exchange. For more information on how Web services fit with application integration, see Chapter 4 on Service-Oriented Application Integration.

SOAP

Simple Object Access Protocol (SOAP) defines the Extensible Markup Language (XML)-based message format that Web service-enabled applications use to communicate and interoperate with each other over the Web. The heterogeneous environment of the Web demands that applications support a common data encoding protocol and message format. SOAP is a standard for encoding messages in XML that invoke functions in other applications. It is analogous to Remote Procedure Calls (RPCs) used in many technologies, such as DCOM and CORBA, but eliminates some of the complexities of using these interfaces. SOAP enables applications to call functions from other applications, running on any hardware platform regardless of operating system or programming language (see Figure 15.1).

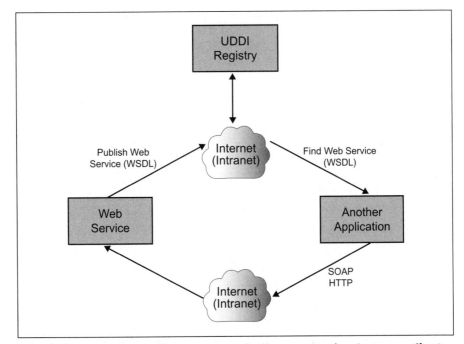

Figure 15.1   SOAP provides a communication mechanism between client and server.

Integrating the World with .NET . . . Again

Ever since the beginning of modern computing, we have sought out mechanisms that allow applications to access both the services and data of other applications, no matter where they exist. Indeed, it has been the whispered goal of developers to create applications so open and so well architected that other applications could access their value without having to understand anything about them.

This was the goal of the distributed object movement of the early 1990s. Common Object Request Broker Architecture (CORBA), Component Object Model (COM), and a handful of other, more proprietary instances of distributed objects promoted technology that promised open access to application services and information. That is, if we would only do things their way.

We are about to see another attempt to reach application development nirvana with the advent of the .NET strategy from Microsoft. Once again, we have another framework for doing something we've been trying to do for years. What's changed? In a word: the advent of the "Internet," and I don't mean the Web.

Integration Obstacles

Over the last few years, there has been a new interest in application integration, or allowing applications to share information and processes between and within enterprises. This has proven to be a difficult problem to solve, because differences in systems, both at the platform and application levels, are difficult to work around. For example, the simple structure of a customer record is different from application to application, and processes are exposed differently (if they are exposed at all).

Enter a new breed of application integration technology, including products that work from the inside out, or from the enterprise to the trading community, and those that work from the outside in. While we're clearly getting better and allowing very different applications to exchange information (and sometimes processes), achieving total integration is still out of reach.

We can define total integration as the ability to have many applications network-connected, exchanging information and sharing processes without having to understand anything about the applications they are interacting with. Indeed, the application would only need to leverage a common infrastructure for locating, understanding, and invoking remote application services.

The uses for this type of integration are endless and include creating composite applications, or applications that aggregate the processes and information of many applications. For example, using this paradigm, application developers simply need to create the interface and add the application services by binding the interface to as many Internet-connected application services as required.

.NET to the Rescue

The concept of .NET is to provide this total integration. .NET defines Internet-connected applications as Web services. You can think of Web services as methods exposed by a company or software program that are both discoverable and accessible by other programs or organizations in need of a particular service; for example, purchasing a product, reserving a flight, and calculating tariffs—discrete business services that have value to many organizations.

.NET is an architectural vision, more than actual technology. However, pieces have already emerged, such as Universal Description, Discovery and Integration (UDDI), and a host of tools forthcoming from Microsoft that provide the opportunity for total integration. What is more, SOAP provides .NET with a standard way to expose objects through firewalls, business to business.

The UDDI specification aims to define a common mechanism to both publish and discover information about Web services. Those that put UDDI together (IBM, Microsoft, and Ariba, and 63 others) look to create a type of "Yellow Pages" for the Internet. The first generation of the specification is out now. (See the "UDDI" section later in this chapter for more details.)

Critical Success Factors

Okay, understanding that .NET, at its core, is really nothing new, what are the chances that .NET will influence application development going forward? What are the chances that it will change the way businesses

(continued)

Integrating the World with .NET . . . Again (*continued*)

think about integration, inside and outside? Before any of this happens, a few things need to occur:

First, developers must widely accept the .NET way of doing things. I am not sure Microsoft has captured the hearts and minds of most developers. Java still makes up a large part of enterprise development, for example. If Microsoft is to succeed here, it has to show capabilities at the enterprise level not yet seen within Microsoft development tools.

Second, Microsoft must become heterogeneous. Let's face it, most enterprises will not give up their Sun boxes for Windows 2000 just yet. Microsoft needs to demonstrate it has the ability to work with the enemy, as well as deal with the frustrations of integrating many very different platforms. Finally, the .NET standard must be controlled by many companies, not just Microsoft. That lack of control may frustrate Microsoft, but without the perception of this standard being open, it doesn't have a chance.

WSDL

Web Service Description Language (WSDL) is a collection of metadata about XML-based services used for describing what businesses do and how to access their services electronically. Based on SOAP, WSDL specifies the procedures to discover functional and technical information about Web services over the Internet.

A WSDL document is comprised of a number of elements:

- Type definitions, for data elements (normally using XML Schema).
- Message definitions, which comprise one or more typed data elements.
- Operation definitions, which are abstract descriptions of actions supported by the service, and which define what are the input and output messages.
- PortType definitions, which list the set of operations supported by the Web service.
- Binding definitions, which describe the binding between the portTypes and protocols (e.g., SOAP or HTTP GET/POST).
- Service definitions, which list the set of bindings.

Thus, we can say that WSDL provides a standard approach for Web services providers and those who use the services, or a standard agreement between users and services on interfaces. WSDL provides an automated mechanism to generate proxies for Web services using a standard language. This standard is analogous to Interface Definition Languages (IDLs) found in both COM and CORBA. In other words, it's a simple, standard contract between client and server.

WSDL defines an XML grammar for describing network services as a collection of communication endpoints that can exchange information. The WSDL services definition provides a recipe for automating the way applications communicate (see Figure 15.2).

Within the world of WSDL, services are a collection of network endpoints, also known as ports, and the abstract definition of endpoints. This mechanism provides for the reuse of abstract definitions, or messages. Messages are abstract descriptions of information flowing from application to application, and messages are separated from the data format bindings. PortTypes, another WSDL entity, are abstract connections of an operation, which are an abstract description of an action that is supported by the service. Bindings are a concrete protocol and data format specification for an instance of a portType.

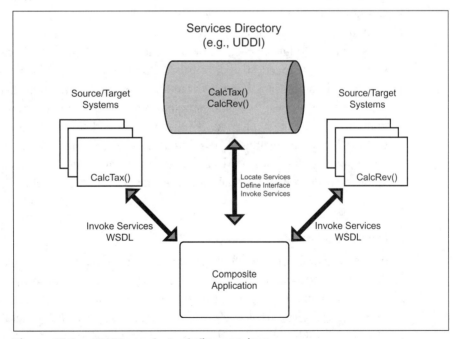

Figure 15.2   WSDL works to define services.

Waiting for Application Integration Standards to Mature Could Be a Terrible Mistake

We've all seen the press: "Web services will change the way we integrate applications." "Web services will revolutionize distributed computing." Can the industry afford to wait for this magical group of standards that hold the promise of revolutionizing the way we integrate and build applications? Can you afford to wait, when the waiting itself could prove harmful to the overall health of your company? To answer those questions, you must weigh the value of a standard with the downside of the delays due to arcane internal politics within the standards organizations.

We've been here before. If you're as old as me (I'll be 40 this year), you remember the component programming "revolution" that promised to eliminate the need for custom development, as applications would be built out of prebuilt software components. You may also remember the two competing component standards, OpenDoc and ActiveX, that were to take us down the road to component nirvana. Many application development projects stalled as developers and architects waited to see how the standards would evolve and who would win; in the end, neither standard really made much of a difference in the way we do development today. In fact, most of those who waited for ActiveX or OpenDoc have moved on to Java-based standards.

Other examples include the evolution of the distributed object standards of the early 1990s, something that never really caught on for the majority, but did delay projects as those looking to leverage the CORBA or COM standards waited for the standards to mature . . . and they are still waiting today. Those are just a few of many examples where we stopped work to wait for standards that never evolved, or evolved too late in the game.

Factoring in Standards

Clearly, the industry is waiting for standards in the world of application integration, and for good reason. The solutions today are largely proprietary. The vendors responded with standards around XML, Java, and Web services. They are in the process of defining the second generation of these standards to fill in the missing pieces. For example, the Web

Service Interoperability Organization (WS-I) as well as the Web Services Security standards (WS-Security) promise to normalize the competing Web services standards in use today.

Current issues surrounding the leveraging of proprietary standards are being replaced with the frustration of having to wait for—and deal with—the emerging Web services standards. Indeed, there is clear evidence that the sloth of the Web services standards organizations is holding up application integration projects. Confused end users wait for the standards to emerge and mature, fearing that implementing now could mean selecting the wrong technology and standard.

The lack of progress in Web services standards development results in a slow-up of the adoption of Web services in both intra- and inter-company integration markets. Of course, the slow movement of end users causes vendors to suffer in the short term. The long-term effects are even more worrisome. In some cases, developers spend more time dealing with standards committees than dealing directly with the IT issues of their employer. In short, we begin to think robotically, allowing standards committees to replace traditional innovation. This phenomenon has negative outcomes:

- First, because the larger players typically drive standards, their proprietary religious beliefs usually take precedence. The genesis of the standards you adopt could actually be created in the halls of Microsoft, IBM, or Sun, and not by a group of end users. This has been my experience in the past.
- Second, if you wait for some standard to emerge and do not actively engage in work on your organization's IT issues, then you run the risk of falling behind your competition in creating your application integration infrastructure. Application integration is becoming largely strategic to organizations as they learn to deal with business events, such as selling a product, in real time. The value of application integration in the world of B2B is also becoming well known.
- Finally, standards are not solutions, and they are not designed for your particular business domain. What's more, they are only implemented within products, and are of no value unless they are bound

(continued)

> ## Waiting for Application Integration Standards
> ## to Mature Could Be a Terrible Mistake (*continued*)
>
> to an enabling technology. Thus you run the risk that, when the standards finally emerge, they won't provide the anticipated value you seek, or the vendor won't implement a standard in such a way to solve your ultimate problem.
>
> ### Happy Medium
>
> It's not the purpose of this chapter to knock standards; they continue to be a very important part of IT. There are many that work, including ODBC, JDBC, J2EE, XML, and XA. However, there are many that are on the scrap heap, including AD/Cycle, Open Unix, and OpenDoc.
>
> We can't let standards define our strategic technology as we move forward. Instead, we must leverage mature standards, when and where they make sense, to solve today's problems. To this end, it's important to understand your own needs, and then look for viable options. If standards meet those needs as part of an enabling technology, all the better. The key is that you solve your problem, and not leverage a particular standard to do it. That's "management by magazine" at its worst.
>
> What's more, we can't let standards hold us up. If you always wait for the next magic bullet, you may not be serving the needs of your end users. We have to understand that the focus of IT is to solve the business problems of the company using whatever technology is available to do so. Today.

UDDI

The Universal Description, Discovery and Integration (UDDL) Business Registry is a standard for cataloging and publishing WSDL descriptions of Web services that are available over the Internet. In much the same way as people peruse common Yellow Pages for a particular service, commerce systems can search the UDDI registry and find Web services, download the parameters for interaction, and effectively interact with the discovered Web service using SOAP (see Figure 15.3).

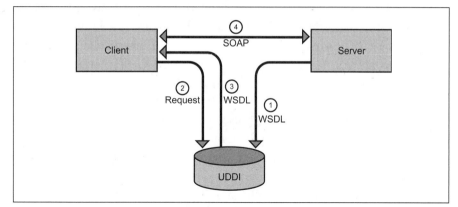

Figure 15.3   UDDI is a standard for tracking and exposing WSDL for intercompany integration.

UDDI Business Registry is an implementation of the UDDI specification. A UDDI business registration consists of three components:

1. *White pages.* Address, contact, and known identifiers.
2. *Yellow pages.* Industrial categorizations based on standard taxonomies.
3. *Green pages.* The technical information about exposed services (e.g., WSDL documents).

UDDI specifications consist of an XML schema for SOAP messages and a description of the UDDI API specification—the latter is actually a SOAP specification. The API defines methods for both inquiry and publishing services.

The UDDI invocation model is this:

1. A programmer uses the UDDI Business Registry (either via a Web interface or using the inquiry API) to locate the business entity information for the business partner advertising the Web service.
2. The programmer drills down to find the advertised Web service and obtains the binding templates (WSDL documents).
3. The programmer prepares the program based on the WSDL specifications.
4. At runtime, the program invokes the Web service as planned, using the binding obtained from the WSDL document.

The UDDI specification aims to define a common mechanism to both publish and discover information about Internet-accessible services that the UDDI folks call Web services. You can think of Web services as methods exposed by a company or software program that are both discoverable and accessible by other programs or organizations that are in need of a particular service; for example, purchasing a product, reserving a flight, calculating tariffs—discrete business services that have value to many organizations.

Those that put UDDI together (IBM, Microsoft, and Ariba, together with 63 others) are looking to create a type of Yellow Pages for the Internet. The first generation of the specification is out now.

UDDI is really just a set of databases where businesses can register their Web services as well as locate other Web services they may be interested in leveraging. As an example, a company has a unique program for predicting breakage found in a shipment of ceramics, depending on the method of shipping, point of origin, and destination. That company may publish this information in the UDDI databases, allowing other organizations to find this Web service and understand how to access this service programmatically, as well as the interfaces employed (e.g., OAG BODs). Other examples would include the ability to create orders within a particular supplier's system through UDDI-registered Web services, as well as the ability to make payments by accessing Web services found in banking systems.

The core component of the UDDI project is the UDDI business registration database. This is really a large XML file that describes a business entity and any Web services that exist within that entity. The UDDI Business Registry can be used at a business level to determine if a particular trading partner has a specific Web service interface. You can locate companies in a given industry that provides a particular type of service. For example:

```
Airlines -> XYZ Air ->  Reserve_Flight()
```

The folks that wrote the UDDI specification describe UDDI as the next layer on the stack, with SOAP below it, and XML below that and above native network protocols (HTTP and TCP/IP). The UDDI spec describes a conceptual cloud of Web services, as well as an API to define a simple framework for describing any kind of Web service. The spec is made up of several documents, including an XML schema that defines a SOAP-based API for both registering and finding Web services.

Using the UDDI discovery services allows entities to register information about the Web services that are exposed for use by other Internet-connected businesses. By doing this, information is added to the UDDI Business Registry through a Web interface or through a defined registry protocol.

The UDDI Business Registry is a distributed database, which provides virtual centralization. There are multiple root nodes that synchronize data in near time, allowing businesses to register with one database, and have that information available in all UDDI databases within minutes. UDDI is taking this approach due to the large number of entities that may be using the databases at a single point in time, as well as protection against database failure.

Once the information is inside of the registry, other UDDI-enabled programs, or UDDI-aware programmers, can both discover and use Web services. Using this mechanism, the partner can determine if the service exists and is compatible with native enterprise systems. You may locate specific services through UDDI directly, or through online marketplaces and search engines that can peek into UDDI databases as a data source. As we move forward, the UDDI gang promises that this will be more of an automated process.

What UDDI looks to bring to the table is nothing new. We've been looking to create standard infrastructure to share program services, both intra- and inter-company, for some time. This was clearly the basic goal of distributed object standards, including the Object Management Group's (OMG's) CORBA specification (see www.omg.org). However, while a few B2B implementations exist, CORBA requires more time and effort than many organizations are willing to invest, and has no registry or discovery mechanisms to provide a clearinghouse for Internet-accessible methods. What's more, CORBA has a tendency to bind applications tightly together; UDDI is more loosely coupled. Loosely coupled application integration is a better fit for B2B.

Other recent attempts to create B2B method-sharing standards using a more contemporary approach include Hewlett-Packard's e-Speak. Like UDDI, e-Speak was designed specifically with B2B in mind and shares many of the same goals. However, e-Speak has not captured much interest from the B2B development community, and new standards such as UDDI will have to overcome many of the same obstacles.

UDDI will succeed, and provide value for the new real-time B2B marketplace, if it can quickly show successful implementations. Moreover, UDDI must learn to attract developers with excellent tools and support. Clearly, Microsoft will play a role in doing that. Finally, UDDI will need to stand the test of time. The simple fact is that most information technology standards don't exist in the long term, and UDDI will have to prove itself with both viability and market share. In the short term, count on a confusing battle with other B2B application integration standards that provide many of the same features as UDDI. This is the future of the IT marketplace, and there is a land grab occurring right now.

Web Services as an Enabling Standard

Web services, and all the substandards that support it, have a bright future in the world of application integration. If nothing else, they provide the option to apply Service-Oriented Application Integration. While Web services is not the only standard that applies in this area, it's the only one that people are paying attention to today. Indeed, we are in danger of misapplying Web services, using it within problem domains where it does not belong. That's the trouble with new standards that receive a lot of press. Project leaders, architects, and even vendors want to apply it to areas where it won't be successful.

Clearly, you need to consider the value of Web services to the world of application integration and its proper use within an enterprise or trading community. As we move forward, you can be sure Web services will find its proper place in the application integration stack.

CHAPTER SIXTEEN

Other Standards

The purpose of this chapter is to touch on those standards that are relevant to application integration, and thus worth exploring, but not in depth. Once again, the focus will be on the application of these standards to application integration. Greater detail can be found in other publications.

Keep in mind as we conclude our discussion of standards that this is a dynamic area, things are changing, and today's flavor of the month may be outdated in a short order. Standards can be risky, and only a few make it the distance. This doesn't mean you shouldn't employ standards. Just factor the dynamics into your solution decisions.

There are holistic standards, such as ebXML, BPEL4WS, and RosettaNet, which are more strategic, and then there are tactical standards, such as the ones we will describe in this chapter. This does not diminish the importance of these standards. They could be critical to many enterprises and to application integration in general.

Most of these standards are security based and look to provide a standard set of security services to Web services and Web-based communication in general. We still have a long way to go in that area. What's interesting is the number of security standards that are out there. Clearly, we won't need all of them at the end of the day, and it will be interesting to see how they shake out. Let's take a look at some of the most popular.

WS-Security

The WS-Security specification proposes a standard set of SOAP extensions that can be leveraged when building secure Web services to implement confidentiality, or the ability to leverage Web services without having to worry about others getting into your business.

WS-Security is designed as the base for the construction of a wide variety of security models, which includes

- PKI
- Kerberos
- SSL

Moreover, WS-Security provides support for multiple security tokens, multiple trust domains, multiple signature formats, and multiple encryption technologies.

This standard defines three main mechanisms:

1. Security token propagation
2. Message integrity
3. Message confidentiality

Each of these technologies do not provide a complete security solution, and WS-Security is a building block that can be used in conjunction with other Web service extensions and higher-level application-specific protocols to leverage a wide range of security and encryption technologies. You may use these independently (e.g., to pass a security token) or tightly integrated; for example, signing and encrypting a message and providing a security token hierarchy associated with the keys used for signing and encryption.[1]

The importance of leveraging this standard in the world of application integration is obvious, as we seek ways to exchange messages between enterprises with the assurance that others outside the trading partners won't have access to them. The support for multiple security standards is an added value as well, considering the number of organizations that may be involved and the diverse security technologies that may be in place.

---

[1]Web Services Security (WS-Security) Specification. http://www-106.ibm.com/developerworks/webservices/library/ws-secure/.

XML Encryption

XML Encryption offers a point-to-point security solution for applications that need to exchange structured data in a secure way; thus, this security standard is aimed at data exchange. This is one of the most important standards when it comes to application integration, because many companies leverage XML as a common format, and XML, being just text, must have some sort of security mechanism, or else the data is out there for all to see.

XML Encryption attempts to address areas that are not addressed by SSL, including the encryption part for the data being exchanged, and secure sessions between applications. Using this standard, each side of the exchange is able to maintain secure or insecure states as they exchange information, one to another; for example, exchanging XML-encrypted files that can be seen by one party but not the other. XML Encryption is not limited to just XML; it can also secure binary data.

XML Signature

Before we understand what *XML Signature* is, we must first understand what digital signatures are. A *digital signature* leverages encryption technology to support nonrepudiation, or the ability to validate that a party has "signed off" on a particular document. This is a binding legal agreement, such as ordering custom-built products. Digital signatures, in general, rely on public key cryptography, applying a signing encryption algorithm with a private key. The receiver can validate the signature by using a verification encryption algorithm, and thus the generated value should match up. If the information is different, then they won't match and the signature will be invalid.

This is important in the world of application integration when considering work flow issues, or the movement of information between parties, and the validation of that information as signed off by the parties. What's more, some data exchange operations may rely on digital signatures, as well; for example, the ability to do electronic business with a clear understanding that agreements digitally signed are as good as signed work orders or purchase orders.

XML Signature is the specific syntax that represents a digital signature over any digital content. XML Signatures can be applied to any digital content, including XML, an HTML page, binary-encoded data (such as a GIF), XML-encoded data, and a specific section of an XML file.

There are three types of XML Signatures:

1. Enveloped
2. Enveloping
3. Detached

An *enveloped signature* is a signature on a document, where the XML Signature will be embedded within the signed document. An *enveloping signature* is a signature where the signed data is embedded within the XML Signature structure itself. A *detached signature* is a signature where the signed entities and signature are separate from each other.

Once we understand digital signatures, we also need to understand how an application might create and verify a signature. All PKI systems provide APIs that allow you to leverage process signatures, but it would be much more efficient if this code was reusable. To address this issue, the OASIS Digital Signature Services (DSS) Technical Committee is to create a specification for a set of Web services that can create and validate XML Signatures.

Missing Pieces of Web Services

When considering Web services with application integration, there are some missing pieces. For example, Web services don't provide the mechanism to leverage user interfaces. The Web Services User Interface (WSUI) initiative, announced in June 2001, is moving to solve this problem, but the technical obstacles are significant. Also, current Web services do not address security very well, lacking support for authentication, encryption, and access control. Indeed, Web services do not have the ability to authenticate publishers or consumers of the Web services.

The XML-Based Security Services Technical Committee from the Organization for the Advancement of Structured Information Standards (OASIS) is looking to shore up security within Web services with the Security Assertion Markup Language (SAML). This security standard allows organizations to share authentication information among those they wish to share Web services with as partner organizations. Other emerging security standards include the XML Key Management Specification (XKMS), based on Public Key Infrastructure (PKI).

XKMS

XML Key Management Specification addresses the need to enable parties to obtain the correct encryption keys. It is made up of two parts: The XML Key Information Service Specification (X-KISS) and the XML Key Registration Service Specification (X-KRSS).

The *X-KISS specification* defines a protocol for a Trust service that resolves public key information encapsulated in XML-SIG elements. This protocol's point system delegates the tasks required to process the elements. The purpose of this protocol is to minimize the pain of application implementation by abstracting the clients from the complexity and syntax of the PKI leveraged to create a trusted link.

The *X-KRSS specification* allows a Web service that accepts registration of public key data. Once registered, the public key may be used with other Web services, including X-KISS.

Each protocol exists in terms of structures expressed in the XML schema language and SOAP.[2]

SAML

Security Assertion Markup Language is an XML framework for exchanging security information over the Internet and enables disparate security systems to interoperate using a single security mechanism. SAML resides within a system's security mechanisms to enable exchange of identity and entitlement with other services. It defines the structure of the documents that transport security information among services.

SAML has the following components:

- Assertions and request/response protocols
- Bindings (the SOAP-over-HTTP method of transporting SAML requests and responses)
- Profiles (for embedding and extracting SAML assertions in a framework or protocol)
- Security considerations while using SAML (highly recommended reading)
- Conformance guidelines and a test suite
- Use cases and requirements[3]

---

[2]*XML Key Management Specification (XKMS)*. March 2001.

[3]Byous, Jon. *Single Sign-On Simplicity with SAML: An Overview of Single Sign-on Capabilities Based on the Security Assertions Markup Language (SAML) Specification*. 2002.

SAML provides technology that supports a single sign-on using XML. Using SAML authentication, you can sign-on and receive a SAML authentication assertion as a response to the request. This authentication assertion is simple XML and is transportable using SOAP.

XHTML

Extensible HTML (XHTML) provides a compromise between traditional HTML and XML. Now in a working draft at the W3C, XHTML is thought by its creators to be the ultimate replacement for HTML. XHTML leverages XML for structure and extensibility, enabling authors to use language subsets.

Although it's too soon to tell if XHTML will set the Web world on fire, it does offer a nice compromise between the power of XML and the existing features and functions of HTML. In addition, it brings structure to HTML, which has been drifting off in many directions for some time now. This will be a big deal for site builders, so it is important to understand this new technology and its impact on your site. I recommend that you also visit www.w3c.org/TR/xhtml1 for further developments.

Why Another Standard?

With XML out there, along with DHTML, SSL, XSL, and other cryptic acronyms, why do we need yet another Web-born standard?

There are two reasons:

First, XHTML is built from the ground up as an extensible language. The extensibility depends on the XML requirement that the XHTML-compliant Web documents be well formed (conform to the standard, basically). This greatly eases the development and integration of new elements within the document.

Second, XHTML is built from the ground up for portability, and XHTML can run within a number of containers, including devices such as personal digital assistants (PDAs) and WebTV. Let's face it, folks, HTML is a mess, and portability across browsers is difficult enough, without considering portability across static devices.

From a practical point of view, site builders who already understand HTML won't have much of a learning process to understand XHTML.

What's more, there is already a base of authoring tools that make creation of XHTML documents simple. (I'll talk about those below.)

One of the things I like most about XHTML is that it requires well-formed documents and won't accept sloppy coding. For example, you are required to stick to lowercase-only coding, and you have to use end tags—no exceptions. You have to validate your code against three Document Type Definitions (DTDs) defined by the W3C. DTDs, as you may remember, are collections of XML declarations that define a legal structure. We got away with sloppy coding for years because browsers have been too forgiving, but to support portability, these constraints must exist.

The specification provides a definition of strictly conforming XHTML documents using the XHTML namespace found at www.w3c.org. A strictly conforming XHTML document is a document that supports only the facilities described in the XHMTL specification. This means it must meet the following criteria:

First, the XHTML document must validate against the XHTML DTD, as mentioned above. Second, the root element of the document must be <html>. Third, the root elements of the document must designate the XTHML 1.0 namespace. Finally, you must include a DOCTYPE declaration in the document before the root elements. The public identifier included in the DOCTYPE declaration must refer to the XHTML DTDs.

For example:

```
<!DOCTYPE html PUBLIC "-//W3C//DTD XHTML 1.0 Strict//EN"
   "http://www.w3.org/TR/xhtml1/DTD/strict.dtd">
<html xmlns="http://www.w3.org/TR/xhtml1">
 <head>
  <title>Title Goes Here</title>
 </head>
 <body>
  <p>Moved to <a href="http://xxxx.org/">xxxx.org
  </a>.</p> </body>
 </html>
```

(continued)

XHTML (*continued*)

When using XHTML, all elements must either have closing tags or be written in a special form, and all the elements must nest. Although overlapping is illegal with traditional SGML, it works with most SGML-based browsers that have chosen to ignore the rules.

For example, here is an example of a correctly nested element:

```
<p>it's raining today <em>paragraph</em>.</p>
```

Here is an example of overlapping elements.

```
<p>it's raining today <em>paragraph.</p/em>
```

XrML

Extensible Rights Markup Language (XrML) defines a content-centric access control mechanism that uses a digital rights methodology. Long story short, it defines XML languages that may be leveraged to specify rights and conditions to control access to digital content and services. For example, XrML is able to define who can view a particular resource and under what circumstances.

Playing the Standards Game

Now that we are closing out our discussion of standards, we can look back and see that the number of standards, even redundant standards, is as complex and difficult to understand as the array of application integration products on the market today. The trick is to understand their value, size up their market viability, and see if there is a strategic fit into your problem domain. Then, you must find products that support them.

Remember, standards are not products or solutions. They simply provide a common data format, process mechanisms, or service-based framework that many people can agree upon. Application integration products, such as application servers and integration servers, are where the rubber meets the road. How they support a standard that is strategic to your situation should be examined, along with other application integration mechanisms they provide. This rule goes for all standards reviewed in this section of the book.

This is not to say that standards are always helpful. Clearly, they are not. Some can lead you down dead-end streets as standards lose momentum and die. Some may not provide all of the functionality you need, and thus prolong the time it takes to complete an application integration project. Sometimes they only serve to complicate your application integration solution.

Still, it's important that we have standards, and continue to promote and develop the ones that make sense. By doing this, we can easily exchange information, processes, and services, without having to do close coordination between enterprises or departments. The real payoff is years away, but the investment must be made today.

PART IV

Advanced Topics

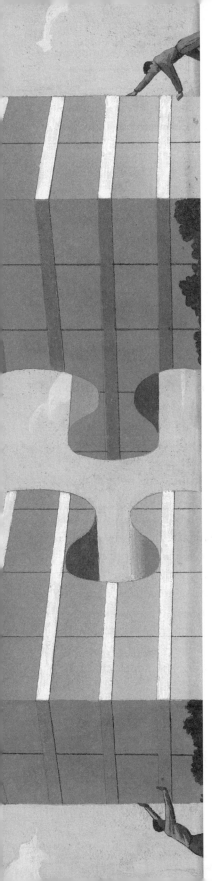

## CHAPTER SEVENTEEN

The "Verticalization" of Application Integration Technology

It has been a clear trend in the world of application integration to customize solutions for particular problem domains, such as vertical industries. This means providing specific connectors, formats, transformation, and behaviors that have value for verticals such as finance, manufacturing/retail/distribution (MRD), telecommunications, health care, and other areas that have particular application integration requirements, inter- or intracompany.

Typically, vertical application integration solutions are built around standards such as RosettaNet, UCCnet, and ebXML (see in-depth coverage in Part III) for MRD; HIPAA for health care; and GSTP, Omgeo, and SWIFT for finance. However, we'll spend the most time on supply chain integration as a concept, which is becoming more important as we move closer to the real-time economy.

What you need to get out of this chapter is the simple fact that application integration is no longer just about connecting one application to another; sometimes it is a business application unto itself, with the support of an underlying application integration infrastructure including the use of well-defined interoperability standards and mandatory behaviors. By the time this book is published, this will be even more apparent, which is why this is a long, but very important, chapter.

Clearly, middleware is taking on properties that are more business application-like, something that flies in the face of the traditional middleware role of linking one application to the next. At the time middleware first appeared, EAI had not yet emerged as a new set of technologies and a new discipline, so the notion of domain-specific middleware seemed a bit far-fetched.

Today, it's a new world. As we look to add more value to application integration, many application integration technology vendors have announced their movement into more vertical domains, including finance, health care, and manufacturing.

So, why create vertical-specific subsystems for application integration? It's really about providing more out-of-the-box value to the end user, moving well up the stack to business process and logic layers, and creating reusable behavior applicable to a vertical business domain such as finance, health care, manufacturing/retail/distribution (MRD), and telecom. Moreover, specific standards-based connectivity and transformation solutions provide value, such as HIPAA processing for health care, or GSTP (Global Straight Through Processing) TFM (Transaction Flow Manager) connections for finance. We can also add supply chain integration to that list using standards such as ebXML, RosettaNet, and EDI.

This is a bit of a paradigm shift for traditional application integration technology vendors that dealt with primitive technology such as routing and transformation rather than specific business applications containing both business logic and business application schemas. While vendors did deal with vertical domains, in most cases, they applied custom one-off solutions, with few components transferable to similar problem domains. The end users had to foot the bill for the custom development work as well as absorb future maintenance costs.

Application integration vendors have to understand much more than the connectivity technology. They must understand business requirements to support a true business application. As such, the industry is rethinking what ultimately drives application integration, and it is moving toward a solutions-oriented type of offering. These product offerings do things that would previously be described as "unnatural acts," moving from general-purpose horizontal middleware to the subsystems that are vertical specific.

To understand the shift in thinking, it's helpful to refer to a reference model (see Figure 17.1). As with any layered model, the lower levels are the most primitive in function.

Resource adapters, the lowest level of services in the stack, provide the connectivity into any number of source or target systems using standards such as

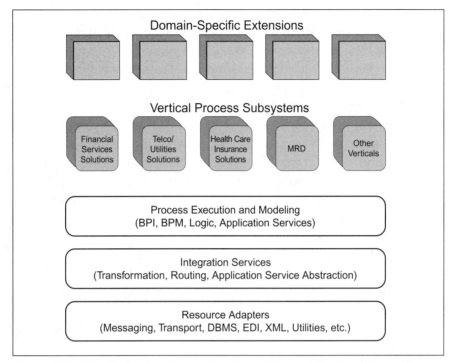

Figure 17.1   Vertical subsystems sit on top of the application integration stack.

XML, EDI, Web services, or JCA, or more likely, proprietary packaged application interfaces or direct database access. Furthermore, you may have specialized vertical-oriented adapters here including connections to the GSTP TFM adapters, HIPAA, EDI, ebXML, RosettaNet, and so on. The common pattern is consumption and production of both information and schema and, in some cases, adhering to a standards-based processing requirement. This is also where service-oriented access occurs.

Integration services, which encompass traditional integration server functions, would include the transformation and routing of information that make the information sharable among many different applications and standards. New here is the abstraction of application services, using newer standards such as Web services or perhaps distributed objects.

This layer enables the integration server to employ remote application behavior and fit this behavior inside a composite application or business process. Service-Oriented Application Integration is valuable to vertical markets that are considering the reusability aspect of this paradigm, and thus the reusability of business applications that may now be combined with more traditional application integration capabilities.

Process execution and modeling is, in essence, the business process modeling, management, and integration layer. The purpose of this mechanism is to provide a platform for modeling and process execution that orchestrates the movement of information and the invocation of remote application services in support of a business application—in this case, a vertical application that applies to many problem domains within a vertical market and can be extended for a particular application.

Reusable processes are the fundamental value of vertical subsystems within the world of application integration. They are canned process models that, when connected to specific resources (e.g., packaged applications), provide a quick solution for a vertical need.

In additional to reusable processes, we also have the opportunity to create reusable verticalized application services as well. Better yet, we can leverage reusable verticalized application services that others build and make available to us. Again, this is the promise of Web services.

Finally, this layer provides business activity monitoring (BAM) capabilities, or the ability to monitor processing in real time, making adjustments as required. This is particularly important with vertical domains such as finance, where adjustments in processing and visibility into transactions or groups of transactions are important during runtime.

Vertical process subsystems are the vertical applications created within the process execution and modeling layer. (Keep in mind, in some cases, they may have specialized processing that needs to occur at the resource adapter layer.) This is where the vertical behavior resides, and thus is the ultimate value for the end user. These are, in essence, the business applications that have as much to do with business information processing as application integration. The value of these systems is that they are nearly complete out of the box. While they typically require some domain-specific extensions (see the next paragraph), they should provide most, if not all, of the functionality to service a specific vertical market application requirement.

Domain-specific extensions, as you may expect, are extensions to the pre-canned processes that customize these processes for a specific implementation. In many cases, they will connect precanned verticalized processes with enterprise processes, or even trading community processes. Within some projects, vertical subsystems are connected together, along with the enterprise processes; for example, leveraging GSTP connectivity and processing along with ISO 15022, Omgeo, and transaction matching in the finance vertical market.

A Huge Shift in Thinking

The movement toward verticalization is nothing new, but it is a new trend in the world of application integration. The challenge is the shift in thinking. Implementing vertical subsystems, in most cases, means implementing business applications—not general-purpose application integration technology. This is a huge change from how traditional technology and service providers approached application integration, and it will require the technologist to work with the domain experts to create the ultimate solution. Moreover, we also need to understand that this is complex stuff that requires complete solutions. Simply providing connection into a "standards cloud" (e.g., ebXML) does not make a vertical subsystem. You must consider the behavior, as well—the vertical business functions that must bind with vertical connectivity.

Today's application integration technology vendors are jumping on the vertical bandwagon, bundling service offerings or creating partnerships (perhaps an empty press release from time to time) as a means to sell an application integration product. Perhaps the approach should be to merge application integration with vertical needs and, ultimately, business applications. It's all about solving the ultimate business problem at the end of the day. The more value you bring to the solution, the more likely you are to produce a quick return on investment.

Approaching Finance with STP

In the world of high finance, the battle cry these days is "Straight Through Processing" (STP). STP is not so much about reautomating manual clearing of trades as it is the initial automation of this process. Today it takes days to clear trades, and there is a mandate to reduce this process to hours, even minutes.

Integration is the key here—as it is within all of the verticals we are going to talk about—connecting existing systems to these STP systems, which will allow financial institutions to communicate with other financial institutions in real time, exchanging trade clearing data.

There are many standards around STP today, the largest being GSTP and Omgeo, with a common characteristic of providing a central server to clear trades (TFM for GSTPA and CTM for Omgeo)—a server accessible over the Internet. Let's take a quick look at each, and then the concept behind SWIFT.

GSTPA

The *Global Straight Through Processing Association (GSTPA)* initiative was designed with the intention of "organizing and promoting the efficient electronic flow of cross-border trade information, on trade date." It is based upon the concept of the Transaction Flow Manager—a central virtual matching utility that matches trade information sent in by participants and directs message flow, while keeping participants up to date on the trade status. Having said that, the GSTPA initiative officially ended its existence. However, there are a few installations around with banks clearing trades on GSTPA.

Omgeo

Omgeo Central Trade Manager (CTM) is a new service designed to automate the post-trade confirmation process and the early stages of settlement. Omgeo LLC, the company that provides this service, is a joint venture owned equally by the Depository Trust & Clearing Corporation (DTCC) and Thomson Financial. Omgeo CTM builds upon the existing Oasys services provided by Thomson Financial. Oasys is an electronic trade confirmation (ETC) service used by Broker Dealers (BDs) and Investment Managers (IMs) to exchange trade confirmation information. Oasys has a large user base of approximately 2,000 firms around the world. Omgeo hopes to migrate its Oasys user base to the CTM service over time, and Oasys has now been rebranded "Omgeo Oasys."

Omgeo CTM is basically the Oasys service with the addition of a central matching facility. There are, of course, more facilities and functions in the new service than in Oasys, and some major differences—primarily the ability of CTM to send SWIFT settlement instructions on behalf of the investment manager. However, Omgeo CTM is essentially used for the same purpose as Oasys—the exchange of block and allocation trade confirmation information between broker dealers (the sell side) and investment managers (the buy side). In concept, Omgeo CTM is also similar to the GSTPA TFM service and will compete with it directly.

The participants in Omgeo CTM are broker dealers and investment managers. Custodians are not direct participants and will not be customers of Mercator GSS for Omgeo. Broker Dealers are called Executors in CTM, with Investment Managers referred to as Orderers. Securities matched in CTM are equities-based and debt-based instruments.

Matching in the Omgeo Central Trade Manager is a two-stage process and occurs at both the block level (called Trade Level in Omgeo) and the allocation level (called Trade Detail). There are 21 message types defined within the CTM process. Each message can be used by either the orderer or the executor. There are no Investment Manager-specific or Broker Dealer-specific messages. Omgeo provides a complete data dictionary of fields used in Omgeo CTM. Document Type Definitions (DTDs) for all messages are also included, as well as sample XML.

Message flow and trade state management is the same for both IMs and BDs, although this needs to be confirmed with Omgeo. Messages are based on the ISO 15022 standard and use the enhanced MT511 message protocol. Messages are expressed in XML tag-delimited syntax.

There is no restriction on the order that messages can be sent to the CTM. Either an IM or a BD can initiate the process. (Currently within Oasys there is a definite sequence of message entry—a lock-step process.) Matching in the CTM occurs when enough information has been received for it to take place.

After MATCH AGREED status is reached, trades cannot be modified. Participants cannot cancel one side or the whole trade after MATCH AGREED unless both parties agree to cancel their sides. Participants (both IM and BD) can operate at the Block and Allocation or Allocation-only level. Thus, if they operate at the Allocation-only level, they just need to input Trade Detail (allocation) information. Matching still occurs at the block level, but the CTM constructs a pseudo block message(s) from information contained in the Trade Detail messages.

There are two levels of message validation—synchronous and asynchronous. Synchronous validation looks at the structure of the message only. It will pass or fail, and either a Valid or an Invalid message will be returned to the participant. This is the equivalent of a SWIFT ACK or NAK. Asynchronous validation happens after synchronous validation and validates the content against the existing trade-side data. The CTM does not send a message to the participant after an error has been found at asynchronous validation level.

The only proactive messages that are sent to the participant from the CTM after synchronous-level validation are a Valid or an Invalid message. The participant must send retrieve or query messages to the CTM to obtain the status of individual or multiple trades.

The CTM generates Notification of Business Exceptions, which indicate a problem with the trade. These are time-based alerts and are generated against an Omgeo-defined table of timeouts for different business processes. Participants have to send request messages to obtain these statuses.

There are two connection methods available to the CTM—the "Direct Interface," which is a real-time API-based connection running on Solaris 2.6 and NT 4.0 SP5, and the "Import/Export Adapter," which is a file-based connection method. This second method sits between the Direct Interface and the participant's systems. The Direct Interface provides authentication and encryption (40- to 128-bit) services. It uses a leased line to get to the Omgeo network and does not format messages or interpret incoming messages.

There is a mechanism called "Update Guard" that prevents a record from being updated once it has already been updated. This involves the exchange of Update Guard information between the participant and the CTM.

Matching at the CTM (at both block and allocation) occurs at two levels— level 1 matches, which are mandatory field matches (quantity, trade date, security ID, etc.), and level 2 matches, which are profile driven by the Investment Manager.

It is not clear from the CTM specification how profiles are updated by the Investment Manager. Two profiles can be set up—for equity-based and debt-based instruments.

There are a number of value-added services that can be optionally used with Omgeo CTM. These include Securities ID cross-referencing against Telekurs and Exshare data, SSI enrichment for either party using the Omgeo Alert service, and the automatic generation and sending of settlement instructions to the Custodian via the SWIFT network (messages supported are the 7775 MT521, MT523, and MT592 and the 15022 MT541, MT543, and MT515).

Investment Managers must be direct participants to use the CTM. However, for Broker Dealers, a bridge exists between the Oasys network and the CTM environment. Therefore, Broker Dealers who are existing users of Oasys can still continue to use Oasys to send confirmation messages to IMs who are participants in Omgeo CTM. It also means that IMs who join Omgeo CTM get access to a ready-made community of about 1,000 brokers. The initial target market for Omgeo CTM is the Investment Management community.

SWIFT

The Society for Worldwide Interbank Financial Telecommunication was established in 1973 in Belgium as an industry-owned co-operative. SWIFT provides secure and reliable messaging between financial institutions worldwide. Set up to provide a global and highly secure telecommunications network to exchange messages between financial institutions, it has offices in 15 countries. In 2001, it had over 7,455 live users in 196 countries and carried 1,534,000,000 messages.

SWIFT is made up of three categories of users—members, submembers, and participants. Full-fledged members must also become shareholders. Banks, eligible broker/dealers, and regulated investment managers may qualify as members. Member-owned financial organizations (ownership or control must be more than 50 percent) can qualify as submembers. Other recognized and regulated financial organizations may become participants.

SWIFT is governed by a board of directors elected from the membership. SWIFT is solely a carrier of messages between financial institutions. The information in these messages is issued and controlled exclusively by the sending and receiving institutions. SWIFT does not hold assets or manage accounts on behalf of customers. Given its importance in the financial community, SWIFT plays an important role in the global fight against money laundering.

SWIFT messaging serves four main markets:

1. Payments: In 2001 this constituted over 60 percent of the SWIFT message traffic
2. Securities: 29 percent of the message traffic (this is the fastest growing)
3. Treasury: 7 percent of the message traffic
4. Trade Finance: 3 percent of the traffic

Messages emanating from Europe make up 58 percent of the total traffic, with North America at 19 percent, Asia Pacific 12 percent, and the rest of the world 11 percent.

The SWIFT network offers a standardized form of exchanging messages in a highly secure environment. Messages can be exchanged either as a single transaction or in bulk. It has over 230 different message types with a standardized format. It also provides standardized bank identifier codes (BICs) and cross-referenced clearing codes of financial institutions. Third-party service providers (such as GSTPA, CLS, and Crest) use SWIFT's network to conduct their own business.

Traditionally, SWIFT has served the financial community through FIN, its store-and-forward messaging service. FIN is accessed over an X.25 connection. It provides message-processing facilities, including validation to ensure messages are formatted according to SWIFT message standards, delivery monitoring and prioritization, and message storage and retrieval.

As the financial industry evolves, so do its messaging needs. Access to FIN is to be replaced by an IP-based protocol SIPN (Secure IP Network) called SWIFTNet.

SWIFTNet has interactive capabilities. Customers will be able to access SWIFTNet via a number of interfaces:

- *SWIFTAlliance Gateway (SAG).* SAG offers a single window to access all SWIFTNet services that provide centralized automated integration with different in-house applications, and service-specific interfaces such as Axion4 gateway and CLS gateway. SAG handles connectivity of customer applications to the SIPN. Typically, a customer application (client) exchanges messages via SAG with a central application (server). The design of SAG embeds SWIFTNet Link and SWIFTNet PKI (Public Key Infrastructure).
- *SWIFTAlliance Access (SAA).* This is a multiplatform, multinetwork interface designed to connect single or multiple destinations to SWIFT, telex, fax, and private networks. SAA is designed for high-volume users.
- *SWIFTAlliance Entry (SAE).* Designed for low-volume users, this is a low-cost, easy-to-install SWIFT interface.
- *SWIFTAlliance Webstation.* This is a browser facility to access SWIFT services available over SWIFTNet.
- *SWIFTNet Link.* This mandatory software product provides access to all SWIFTNet services.
- *SWIFTNet PKI.* This is mandatory security software and hardware installed alongside SWIFTNet Link.
- *TrustAct.* This is SWIFT's new Internet-based messaging service for securing B2B e-commerce.
- *e-paymentsPlus.* This builds on TrustAct and allows banks to offer secure end-to-end online payment service to their corporate clients.
- *SWIFT Messages & Services.* Messages use the SWIFT FIN standard, which defines syntax and validation criteria. It has adopted the ISO15022 standard for some of its messages.

SWIFT provides over 230 different messages split into three main message types. These are

1. User to User Messages, exchanged between financial institutions; further split into more than nine categories covering a variety of markets (e.g., securities, trade finance, and treasury markets). Some of the most widely used messages are in category MT100s and MT500s.
2. System Messages, sent from SWIFT to user and vice versa.
3. Service Messages, exchanged between SWIFT and users, mainly for communication purposes.

For every message that is sent to SWIFT, it will send a message back to the user acknowledging successful acceptance (or otherwise) of the sent message. These messages are known as ACK (successful) or NAK (unsuccessful) messages. For a NAK, it will inform the user of the reason for failure by an error code.

ACK/NAK messages are "pushed" to the users; i.e., they are mandatory. There is no charge for ACK, but NAK attracts a tariff to discipline senders to send properly formatted messages.

In addition to ACK/NAK (for messages coming into SWIFT), there is another level of outgoing messages (from SWIFT). UAK (positive user acknowledgment) is sent by the user on successful acceptance of the message sent by SWIFT, and UNK (negative user acknowledgment) is sent when the user has not successfully accepted the output from SWIFT. UAK/UNK are optional and chargeable. Messages are uniquely referenced for traceability and searchability.

An important facet of SWIFT's service is security; responsibility and liability surround the security issue, which focuses on three areas: network and connectivity, terminals security at the client end, and messages. Once the message enters the SWIFT network, SWIFT guarantees delivery of the message in a predefined time. If it fails to do so, it will make good any losses incurred by the user. SWIFT guarantees 24x7 availability. In turn, users must abide by the agreed-upon terms and conditions in order to use SWIFT services. For example, a user must be able to receive (i.e., be logged on to the SWIFT network) for at least seven hours each working day between 8 a.m. and 6 p.m. local time to receive delivery of messages.

Additional services SWIFT provides include the BIC database, an integrated database of banks, and cross-referenced financial institutions' clearing codes. It also provides a facility for users to copy messages to third parties.

So how does SWIFT differ from other STP machines, such as GSTPA or Omgeo? SWIFT is solely a carrier of messages between financial institutions. It provides a trusted mechanism to exchange high-value payment messages between financial institutions. It validates, authenticates, stores, and forwards. The decryption of messages only happens in memory. SWIFT does not hold assets or manage accounts on behalf of customers. It does not clear or settle transactions. It is purely a secure pipe to transport messages from source to destination.

Unlike GSTPA or Omgeo, SWIFT does no additional processing. What one party sends, the counter party receives without SWIFT altering anything. Securities transactions matched in GSTPA or Omgeo would most probably use SWIFT messages to convey settlement instructions. SWIFT *does* have a matching machine—Accord—but this is limited to providing matching services for Treasury products.

Approaching Health Care with HIPAA

The *Health Insurance Portability and Accountability Act* (HIPAA) was passed to help facilitate better availability of health insurance for individuals and families, to combat fraud, and to develop security standards for health care record information. HIPAA is Public Law 104-191, signed into effect on August 21, 1996, by President Clinton.

It is defined as

> An act to amend the Internal Revenue Code of 1986 to improve portability and continuity of health insurance coverage in the group and individual markets; to combat waste, fraud, and abuse in health insurance and health care delivery; to promote the use of medical savings accounts; to improve access to long-term care services and coverage; to simplify the administration of health insurance; and other purposes.[1]

HIPAA has several purposes. HIPAA limits exclusions for pre-existing conditions that can be used to deny coverage. It ensures the proper transfer of patient information to a new insurer. It also prevents discrimination in enrollment based on a person's health status. Another part of HIPAA directs the Secretary of

---

[1]www.hipaa.org.

Health and Human Services to develop and implement a set of uniform standards for the electronic exchange of health care information. In general, HIPAA:

- Limits exclusions for pre-existing medical conditions.
- Provides a process for the transfer of information concerning prior coverage to a new insurer.
- Ensures individual rights for enrollment in health care coverage when situations change.
- Prohibits discrimination in enrollment based on health status.
- Directs the development and implementation of a uniform standard for EDI of health care information.
- Guarantees availability of coverage for small employers.
- Preserves, with narrow pre-emptive provisions, the state's traditional role in regulating health insurance, including the ability to offer greater protection.
- Expands the ability for combating fraud and claims abuse in the delivery of health care.
- Provides tax benefits for self-employed individuals and small businesses.
- Authorizes limited experimentation with medical savings accounts.

HIPAA has some teeth! The fines and penalties provided for in the law can call for imprisonment up to ten years for willful violation and fines up to $250,000.

Penalties for violation can include fines against individuals and institutions; failure to comply with standards may result in a $100 fine per occurrence (to a maximum fine of $25,000 per year). Willful disclosure of identifiable health information can result in a $50,000 to $250,000 fine per incident. In addition, the individual responsible for disclosure may face imprisonment of one to ten years, as well as a possibility of forfeiture of assets.

HIPAA has a large impact on information technology resources. Section 1173 of the act promotes standards to enable electronic exchange of data. This section directs the establishment of standards for Unique Health Identifiers, Code Sets, and Security Standards for Health Information, Electronic Signature, and Transfer of Information among Health Plans. HIPAA Standards and Guidelines have been implemented. The EDI Standard used for HIPAA is the X12 4010 standard and the X12 4010A (Addenda). Changes to the HIPAA standard were addressed and passed in October 2002 by the ANSI Standards Committee.

Who is affected by HIPAA and subject to compliance regulations? The list includes Fiscal Intermediaries, also known as claims processors, Health Plans, Employers, and Health Care Providers. The definition of a health care provider was specifically spelled out in the Federal Register as it applies to HIPAA: "any other person furnishing health care services or supplies" (other than those under the statutory definition of provider) "that maintain or transmit automated health information."

Security and technology standards were developed to meet the following guidelines:

- The strategy must be comprehensive and encompass all aspects of the data interchange.
- The standard must be technology-neutral to allow any organization using any technology to implement it.
- The technology must be scalable to allow an organization to grow and develop.
- The compliance timeline for HIPAA implementation is short. Once the proposed rules are reviewed and published, institutions will have 24 to 36 months, depending on their size, to implement the standards.

Approaching Manufacturing, Retail, and Distribution with Supply Chain Integration

The difference between supply chain integration and application integration is in their relationship to one another. One is the rail, the other is the train. Application integration, as we've discussed, requires placing new approaches and technologies around the process of extending the reach of applications, enabling them to exchange information with other applications that exist in other organizations. Supply chain integration represents the enabling processes that run on top of the infrastructure that application integration creates (see Figure 17.2). Whereas application integration is about a tactical process that depends heavily upon technology, supply chain integration is more about strategy.

The symbiosis of supply chain integration and application integration is clear. The technology, the approaches, and even the benefits are much the same. A tightly coupled supply chain is dependent upon the success of application integration, along with such application integration technology as message brokers,

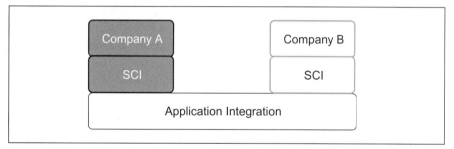

Figure 17.2   Application integration creates the infrastructure that allows supply chain integration (SCI) to work.

application servers, and standards such as XML, EDI, ebXML, UCCnet, and RosettaNet (covered in Part III of this book).

Supply chain integration is a well-known and time-proven concept. There is significant literature dealing with it, so I will not cover it exhaustively here. My purpose is to understand the basic notion of supply chain integration and its usefulness in the context of application integration.

Value of the Chain

Supply chain integration may well represent the Promised Land. But as with most Promised Lands, the road leading to it is hardly smooth or straight. A substantial commitment to technological and organizational change must be made for supply chain integration to work. Companies with little corporate patience, companies with little corporate vision, and companies looking for short-term gains need not apply. There is risk aplenty on the road to this Promised Land. This glory bus is only for organizations willing to confront the risk, willing to face new and changing technological approaches, willing to absorb significant short-term expenses, and willing to invite the need to layer into other organizations not under their direct control—other organizations that could even include a competitor or two.

No foolproof method for integrating a supply chain exists. However, organizations can take steps to ensure that they minimize the risks. The smart strategy is to plan for the long term, implement in the short term, and "keep your eye on the ball"—the business reasons for supply chain integration. The most difficult trick may be keeping the technology in perspective. It is there to be controlled, not to be worshipped. Ultimately, it is the tool, not the master. Finally, organizations must make wise decisions. They must avoid the carnival barkers in the technology marketplace. They need to base their decision making on what adds the most value to the chain, not on what glitters or what is trendy. You'll find the term "Supply Chain Acceleration" attached to many products these days; few have anything to do with supply chain integration.

It is a fool who does not respect the risks involved. Every organization should feel the weight of these risks. However, the remarkable opportunity that supply chain integration represents is beginning to outweigh the risks. We are fast approaching a point of critical mass where the greater risk might well be in failing to integrate.

Organizations can no longer afford the luxury of perceiving their operations as if they existed in a vacuum. No organization is an island, to paraphrase a quote. Every organization needs to collect comprehensive, accurate, and timely information throughout the supply chain.

Once this information is gathered, it must be analyzed in order to better comprehend the causes and effects of the business environment on the core business. Once such an analysis has been accomplished, the resulting knowledge will allow the organization to make informed business decisions and to utilize information as a mechanism to gain market share.

Supply Chain Entities

Within the notion of a supply chain there are several entities, including:

- Supplier
- Consumer
- Supplier systems
- Consumer systems
- Private information
- Public information
- Private processes
- Public processes

Suppliers are those organizations that supply a good or service as part of the supply chain. An example would be lumber providers for housing construction. It's the role of the supplier, in a supply chain, to accept an order and provide information back as to how the order will be completed. Suppliers typically receive payment.

Consumers are those organizations that use the good or service to meet some business need, such as building a car or perhaps providing logistics services. It's the role of the consumer to place orders, providing order information. Consumers typically pay suppliers.

Supplier and consumer systems are those systems that consume and produce information to carry out the defined roles of the supplier and consumer. These can be mainframes, Enterprise Resource Planning (ERP) systems, client/server systems, Web-based systems, or anything that can produce information of value to the supply chain and receive information as appropriate.

In addition to the information systems themselves, you also have the notion of private and public information. *Private information* is information that is not to be shared within the supply chain; examples would be employee information or sales data. It is critical when dealing with a supply chain that you mark data as private or else risk having sensitive information get outside of the organization. In contrast, *public information* is information that is sharable and not sensitive, such as order information or payment verifications.

In addition to information, you also have the concepts of public versus private processes. Like public and private information, *private processes* are processes that are intracompany and do not have anything to do with the supply chain. *Public processes* are shared, with participation by multiple organizations. Public versus private processes are very important in the world of application integration because they map to Process-Oriented Application Integration and are controllable within the process engines found in prevailing application integration technology. What's more, they may link to emerging and existing standards that define processes for supply chains, including RosettaNet and ebXML.

Defining Your Supply Chain

Supply chains support the flow of goods and services from their origin to their endpoint—the customer. The components of the supply chain may include the original suppliers, multiple production operations, logistics operations, retailers, the customer, and even the customer's customer. For example, an organization that builds birdhouses has a supply chain that includes the lumber company that processes trees into lumber, the plant that turns the lumber into birdhouses, the company that supplies the paint for the birdhouses, the logistics department that ensures the availability of supplies, the sales staff, the shipping department, the retailer, and the customer who ultimately purchases the birdhouse (see Figure 17.3). As we suggested earlier, not all of these organizational components may be under the direct control of the organization that heads the value chain.

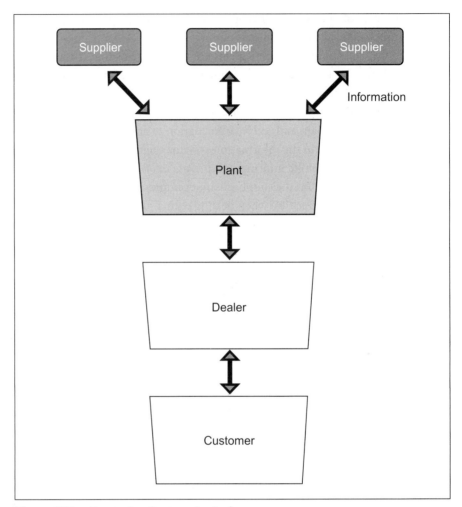

Figure 17.3   Example of a supply chain.

Supply chains include many concepts, such as the following:

- Collaborative planning and forecasting
- Design collaboration
- Coordinated manufacturing
- Coordinated distribution management

These concepts represent such sophisticated processes that a number of large software companies, such as Manugistics and I2, have established a strong market in selling software to address them. Moreover, supply chain simulation software, such as that sold by Gymsym, provides users with the ability to model supply chains before they go into production. Even getting to this preliminary point depends upon a sound application integration infrastructure.

The supply chain determines the speed of operation and time to market, as well as the inventory an organization must carry at any given time. Supply chain management determines the overall cost of goods sold as well as customer service and satisfaction. Supply chain management relies on the planning and the control of the flow of goods and services, information, and money throughout the supply chain.

One more aspect to consider in understanding the need for supply chain integration involves the systems that enable these functions. These applications constitute possible data sources for a supply chain integration solution: In the enterprise domain, the inefficiencies spring from lack of process visibility among the functions. These functions are supported by applications, and a supply chain integration strives to tie these applications and processes together in a coherent, seamless whole to improve internal operations and minimize costs. These applications can be provided by a great variety of vendors and generally include complex, high-value engines for the generation of forecasts and plans for the management of operational processes.

Often, these applications are a world unto themselves without much exchange of information, even among applications from the same vendor. Carrying information from one system to another encompasses time-consuming and error-prone operations that may span a few enterprise functions or may be geographically scattered.

Having said all that, it becomes easier to understand and predict the problems that can arise from process isolation. For example, imagine that a discrepancy between demand forecast and actual orders placed is not communicated to production in an acceptable time: Either excess capacity or lost opportunity will result. Similar problems can be drawn, for example, from a production control that has poor communication with inventory control and procurement, or even between these functions.

In general, process isolation leads to:

• Higher buffer inventories. Lack of timely visibility into procurement, demand, and production results in a higher operational risk; managers tend to stock up to reduce this risk.
• Slower response to market demand. Information that is not reported in a timely manner or addressed by the different functions of the enterprise results

in lower customer satisfaction, loss of opportunity (when the required goods cannot be delivered on time or at all), or excess capacity and high levels of finished inventory. Certainly, processes and systems have been devised to eliminate this problem, but the reality is that enterprises are still plagued by interprocess inefficiencies and miscommunications.

- Forecasting methods have evolved into extremely sophisticated applications. However, these forecasts are only as good as the data they are fed and are only useful if their output becomes actionable information that is communicated to the appropriate enterprise function in time for action. The most accurate forecast is useless if its information is not acted upon in a timely manner.

- The ERP revolution has promised near-perfect control of enterprise processes with efficient process integration. Yet, problems associated with process isolation still persist. ERP implementations place a significant burden on enterprises that chose to pursue them without a correspondingly high benefit. For example, several ERP implementations at different groups of the same firm have resulted not only in process silos, but also in application isolation, higher maintenance, and usage risks without a significant return on investment.

Often, enterprises spend significant effort and money in business process engineering, ERP systems, supply chain execution systems, supply chain planning systems, or other more-or-less integrated combinations thereof, only to realize that they still have difficulty decreasing their costs or affecting gains on the customer satisfaction front.

Forecasting and Supply Chains

Forecasts are approximated estimations of the behavior of the business environment—not accurate representations. Although forecasts are used for long-range planning, they must be revised periodically with fresh data. This data can be historical (e.g., revise the forecast for the upcoming three months based on all the data available up to today) or forward looking. The former example has limited accuracy and puts enterprises in constant reactive mode in the face of changes in the business environment. The latter increases the accuracy of the forecasts and decreases the extent to which organizations react to their environment: Proactively responding to clients' needs or supplier peculiarities becomes a possibility. Clearly, access to the best data provides better forecasts; that's its link with application integration. Moreover, this information must come from multiple systems, both intra- and intercompany.

Although the ability to detect changes in the business environment provides for a considerable competitive advantage, it is necessary to make this information actionable and communicate it to the appropriate function for follow-up. This function may be internal to the enterprise or may be at a business partner (for example, change orders communicated to suppliers).

Although simple, this view of a value chain points to some needs in terms of information sharing that can have an adverse affect on the efficiency of the chain.

- Deficiencies in responding to demand can have an amplified propagation through the chain. For example, suppliers vying to completely fulfill a forecasted demand by the customer will duplicate the orders.
- Long lead times or infrequent availability may result in high inventory buildups.
- High inventories may also exist as hedging against poor visibility into availability.
- Slow response to demand (latency) spikes or dips generated by the primary customer may propagate through the chain and result in abnormally long lead times, a glut of capacity, high inventory, and so on.

The collection of data into the data core of a supply chain integration solution presents two distinct problems: a technical problem and a business problem. Both are related to the attractiveness of the solution to the participants in a chain—what is compelling in a solution to create an incentive for partners to participate, above and beyond the value statements mentioned above. To this end it is important to ensure that participation in a supply chain integration solution be economical and that it introduce little to no risk into the participant's organization; that is, the collection mechanism should be quick and easy to install and simple to maintain. In a further stage, participants may decide to deploy their own solution in order to manage their respective relationships and chain.

A well-crafted supply chain integration and management system must create such a level of interdependency in a trading partnership that customers become locked in to such an extent that the cost of switching (not just the cost of goods but the cost of maintaining the relationship, as well) is so high that there is a permanent damper in the intent to switch to an alternate supplier. In a well-implemented supply chain integration environment, the flow of materials and monies is frictionless and the cost of altering the environment by substituting participants is potentially high. A well-crafted system will create an environment in which it is easy to add or delete a participant but difficult to replace an existing relationship.

Particularly in the extended enterprise domain, supply chain integration is not meant as:

- Visibility into each and every process. This would result in redundant information that would be hard to maintain and update (or even make sense of). Tracking every bit of data leads to high installation and maintenance costs without a corresponding increase in value
- Free-for-all visibility whereby any participant in the chain can view every bit of process data of every other participant. This adds little value to the chain and is bound to increase the potential for conflict and mistrust. A supplier may not be interested in sharing availability information about scarce or strategic components and may want to trade them outside of the supply chain integration framework. Likewise, a customer may not publish demand for a set of components that make up a strategic element of its product, and a supplier at a given tier may not wish to share availability information with potential competitors in the same tier.
- Demand. Suppliers add great value from having visibility into their clients' forecasts as well as into their orders. This allows for more accurate and timely fulfillment, better operations planning, improved purchasing, and so on.
- Supply. Visibility into supply (inventory and production capacity) adds great value to suppliers and to customers. The former can plan replenishment deliveries to the client according to this information, and the latter can plan their production and sales in the face of the known availability at the suppliers. This set is broken up into two subgroups:
    - Inventory
    - Production
- Distribution. This data should satisfy the question, "Where is my order?" and it should allow for effective order tracking and monitoring of times of delivery. In simple terms—and from an IT perspective—a supply chain integration solution hinges on a few components:
    - Integration. This addresses a need that follows the nature of the problem: connecting a variety of systems across firewalls and integrating their data into a coherent whole (which is the concept behind this book).
    - Workflow management. This component solidifies the value of the solution. For example, the need to escalate and process an exception alert can only be addressed appropriately with some workflow management system. An exception—for example, a discrepancy between forecasted and

actual demand—may trigger a workflow that spans the full value chain and may require a great deal of human intervention. Only a robust and configurable workflow management system can adequately address this need.

- Data core. A data core wrapped in a standardization layer, which contains the set of data that represents the state of the supply chain, should represent data in a standardized format. It should also constitute the layer upon which more sophisticated uses are configured (e.g., workflow management and analytics).

- Configurability. Supply chain integration solutions must be configurable to address these quirks of the business environment in which they are deployed. Solutions that have too rigidly defined workflows (or too loosely defined ones, for that matter) are unlikely to address the realities of most value chains.

Questions to Ask When Considering a Supply Chain Solution

When considering a supply chain integration solution, users must consider a series of issues that have deep, long-range impact on their operations and in the performance of the solution.

1. Does the solution integrate only internal systems, or does it allow for partners to share their process information (e.g., information about actual demand, or changes in forecasted demand)? A true supply chain integration solution will allow for integration of information across the extended enterprise—that is, across firewalls—because as much value as it adds, integration of internal systems is an EAI problem, not a supply chain integration problem.

2. How scalable is the solution? A well-designed solution will allow for the addition and removal of trading partners participating in the solution, as well as for the addition and removal of internal systems at one participant or another. The solution must be scalable enough to grow or contract with the chain.

3. How strong is the transformation of the integration component? Given the multitude of systems involved in a chain that is three

(continued)

**Questions to Ask When Considering a
Supply Chain Solution (*continued*)**

or four main tiers deep, this becomes an important consideration, and light transformation capabilities are unlikely to suffice.

4. How invasive is the solution? A solution that requires writing
   wrappers, interfaces, or changes to existing systems is clearly not
   attractive. A solid solution must allow for the deployment of
   agents that carry the right adapters to the internal systems from
   which it will source data.

5. To what extent does the workflow management component
   allow for human intervention? Full automation is a sure recipe
   for disaster: Following the very old law of "garbage in, garbage
   out," there are only so many "IF" and "ELSE" statements that can
   be programmed into a workflow manager before it runs out of
   computable options and botches a job. A well-crafted system will
   allow for rich, configurable human intervention. For example, it
   must allow for the creation of user interface screens in which
   users can view supporting, contextual information that allows
   them to make a decision, and exceptions not handled by the predefined rules must be brought to the appropriate user for decision and routing. Truly, a supply chain integration system is a
   robust way of marrying decision support with operational management, not just a decision support system or an operational
   system, and certainly not a reporting and analysis tool.

6. Participants in a supply chain that are far removed from the
   main client (and owner of the hub) may also want to ask what is
   the compelling reason for them to participate in the solution.
   Take, for example, an automotive supply chain. When faced with
   the costs of installing and maintaining a new solution, a supplier
   of springs for car seats may have little incentive to participate in
   a supply chain integration solution because this business represents only a small fraction of their revenue. The costs and risks
   may not justify participation. On the other hand, participants
   who are closer to the end customer (say, the assembler of dash-
   boards in the example above) are more compelled to participate

for the opposite reasons. Thus, the manner in which data is sourced from the different participants in a supply chain integration solution must make participation economically compelling.

7. The maintenance of visibility relationships poses an interesting problem to each participant in a supply chain. Generally, supply chain integration solutions are point to point. An enterprise must maintain several systems to exchange information with several clients, which introduces and amplifies the IT risks of having to deploy and maintain a great number of relationships. A solution to this problem at enterprises that maintain a great number of relationships is to pass deployment through a hub. The hub acts as a node in each chain and functions as the central point through which an enterprise manages the relationships it maintains with suppliers and clients.

What may catch your attention is that the questions above lead strongly to integration as the cornerstone of a supply chain integration solution. Although there is enough in a solid supply chain integration solution to differentiate it from an application integration solution, the reality is that supply chain integration without a very robust integration and transformation layer is simply not possible.[2]

Extending Applications

Now that we understand some of the higher-level concepts, let's now focus on how supply chain integration relates to application integration.

To consider supply chain integration is, in reality, to consider extending the enterprise. Just as an extended family might include aunts, uncles, second cousins, and other distant relatives, the extended enterprise comprises all of the members in a company's supply chain, such as the various legal units within the company, suppliers, supplier vendors, and customer organizations.

Extending the enterprise demands leveraging technology, such as application integration-enabled middleware and traditional application development tech-

---

[2]Mercator White Paper. 2002. "Supply Chain Visibility." www.mercator.com.

nology. For example, common network infrastructures must be in place, such as those offered by VANs, proprietary wide area networks (WANs), or the Internet. A significant benefit of the Internet is its ability to level the playing field for smaller organizations seeking to leverage the power of supply chain integration. By taking advantage of the common links of the Internet and the common platform of the Web, organizations can become part of a set of informally connected systems.

Although some organizations may fight against this evolution, they are fighting a losing battle. The Internet has, on a fundamental level, already accomplished the task by creating its own natural supply chain.

Consider a typical direct-order apparel company. Consumers access the company's Web site, where they are able to browse the available merchandise. The consumer can get an immediate price for an order, including tax and shipping charges, along with a ship date, the estimated time of arrival, and a confirmation number to track the order as it progresses through the chain. The value this capability provides to the consumer is the ability to shop without sales pressure and time constraints, with an enormous amount of information about the costs, timing, and status of the order. These benefits are part of the reason that online storefronts are doubling their sales every year and, in the process, adding value to the concept of the supply chain.

Web-enabled commerce benefits the company as well as the consumer. With orders collected directly from the consumer, point-of-sale data is immediately available to the supply chain systems. This data provides real-time feedback to various points within the organization's business processes. For example, suppliers are made aware of the demand for a particular garment, enabling them to adjust production. Sales departments know the success or failure of a product line before its effect reaches the bottom line. A company that has automated its own business processes and integrated its systems with the systems of the supply chain partners becomes part of a team, and can build a mechanism for dealing automatically with the volatility of the most aggressive markets.

Binding the Home System to a Stranger's

The integration of information and business functions is only the first step in effective supply chain management and application integration. Those individuals responsible for automating the supply chain must analyze the available information to determine the required courses of action. The best systems automatically trigger a corresponding transaction by evaluating conditions and providing decision makers with sufficient data to make effective decisions.

The flow of information must be unimpeded among all members of the supply chain. All communication barriers must be removed. The degree of difficulty in creating links to members—and opening this flow of information—ranges from very low to very high. Most members have information systems in place. This is the upside. The downside is that the types of information retained and the standards they rely upon vary greatly. For example, many information systems are proprietary and fail to provide points of integration. In addition to being difficult to integrate with the supply chain, such proprietary technology results in higher cost and diminished value.

The Internet provides the supply chain with an inexpensive network for sharing information between members. As we have seen, the Web provides the additional benefit of linking unknown users (e.g., customers) into the supply chain. Those responsible for integrating supply chains should look to the Web-enabled customer base as a mechanism to extend supply chain integration, not simply as a link to it.

The Process

Although the Big Four consulting firms promote a number of methodologies for creating an automated supply chain, the process is really just like traditional system development—with a twist.

The first step is to automate and optimize all of the major business processes within each member organization. Attempting to integrate a supply chain before the members have their core systems in place will be costly, frustrating, and futile. The second step is to extend the enterprise to incorporate all members in the supply chain. This is the most difficult and time-consuming part of the process. This step requires psychology as well as technology. Once your members' hearts and souls are in the right place, you will find that application integration technology and techniques add the most value.

At the heart of this process is a system architecture-and-design effort that extends the enterprise systems to all the member organizations. Not only is the enterprise being automated (and the process flows, object models, database models, and so on being created), but the way in which all of this integrates with other systems in other organizations is being defined. (In a way, this integration method is analogous to the integration process outlined for the types of application integration.) The end result is a common information infrastructure that integrates all member business systems with those of customers and suppliers.

Once such an infrastructure is in place, the new family of application integration technology—message brokers and application servers—creates the best new opportunity to take command of the supply chain problem. Using message brokers, supply chain integrators can bind systems, even custom proprietary systems belonging to a trading partner, with their own enterprise systems. This is not significantly different from addressing any other integration problem in the enterprise. In this case, the problem domain is simply extended to include the relevant systems owned by the trading partners (see Figure 17.4). Here, you must rely on what we've learned in this book—first defining the infrastructure for integration, then defining the processes that control communication between the systems.

Throughout the process, organizations should look for opportunities to add value to the supply chain system, such as real-time decision support to increase responsiveness—for example, defining triggers to automatically perform business processes, such as reordering inventory, increasing the marketing budget for a best-selling product, or informing management of other issues that need to be addressed. Other examples include evaluating an organization's leveraging systems to automatically select suppliers based on price and availability, freeing the staff from performing a complete analysis of the business drivers.

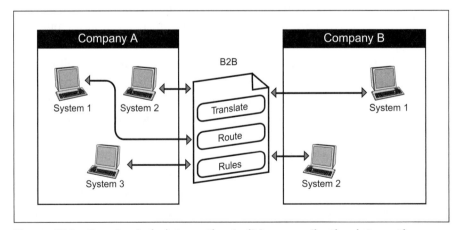

Figure 17.4   Supply chain integration builds on application integration techniques and technologies.

This type of sophisticated processing lends itself well to the process integration or collaboration aspect of application integration; that is, the ability to create a workflow/process integration layer on top of existing interenterprise processes. A real-time solution brings with it the greatest degree of flexibility, because changing a process or a flow is a simple matter of dragging icons around on a screen.

Near-time decision support information is important, as well. Almost all supply chain systems need to leverage the power of data warehousing technology to provide decision makers with the information they need to drop a product line, increase promotional activities, or normalize the number of participants in the supply chain.

As I've suggested, in addition to the technical issues these solutions raise, there is a human component to the process. Supply chain integration is not complete unless it is accompanied by an investment in re-educating and reorienting employees, suppliers, and other interested parties. Too often "techies" forget about the "soft" aspects of supply chain integration only to discover that these soft aspects are as vital to the process as the hard aspects.

Absent from this process is the ability for all players in the chain to make enterprise-wide commitments to creating and managing a complex organization and business system that better fits the needs of the market. Organizations that are doing this today will own the market in the future.

Supply Chain Technology

Although some organizations are using new application integration-enabled or traditional middleware to tie custom systems together with those of their supply chain members, many others are looking to ERP packages as points of integration. ERP provides members in the supply chain with a common application layer to exchange information through well-defined interfaces, business logic, and repositories. Unfortunately, getting all members of the chain to run the same ERP application—or any other application, for that matter—is an almost impossible task.

ERP systems are designed to provide their owners with a system for planning, controlling, and monitoring an organization's business process. What's more, ERP systems offer easy, system-to-system integration through standard mechanisms for communication. They also build a common understanding of what the data represents and a common set of rules (methods) for accessing the data. However, traditional ERP systems are not necessarily supply chain systems.

Supply chain systems must deal with the complexity of integrating information from any number of disparate systems that span multiple organizations. Although some properties of ERP systems are appropriate for use with the supply chain, others are not. Typically, ERP systems exist within a single organization, using a single database as the point of integration with internal organizations. As a result, there is a single database and network protocol standard; thus the enterprise system is able to work with other departmental systems without having to deal with complex integration problems.

When supply chains integrate external systems, it is nearly impossible to get all member organizations to agree on a set of standards (e.g., network protocol, database architecture, and process integration). Because of this difficulty in arriving at a unanimous agreement, the best solution is moving information from system to system using layers and layers of middleware, gateways, and adapter technology. In most cases, very little processing can be shared among the members. As a result, the supply chain system architecture can grow exceedingly complex and confusing.

Because of this reality, two problems need to be solved. The first is getting all member organizations to agree upon a single communication standard and a single set of application semantics. Although it might appear that communication would be an easy problem to solve, it rarely is. Some of the member organizations, especially the smaller manufacturing concerns, face significant costs to get their systems ready to link to others in the chain. Once everyone is ready, the second problem must be addressed—all members need to agree upon a common communication mechanism and middleware approach, allowing all member systems to seamlessly access processes and data in the extended enterprise.

As difficult as these two problems might appear, implementing the solutions is often more difficult.

These difficulties will not be overcome anytime soon. The value that the new application integration technology brings to this problem domain is the ability to integrate many of these systems without requiring that significant changes be made in the systems owned by any of the trading partners. Instead of an organization having to change the database, the application, and possibly even the network, application integration-enabled middleware can adapt each system into the larger system by accounting for the differences in data and methods within a middle tier (see Figure 17.5).

The middleware best suited for supply chain systems is represented by integration servers and application servers. Because message brokers are message

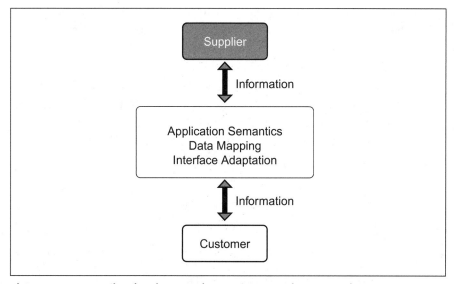

Figure 17.5 **Application integration technology is able to link many different systems in the supply chain by not requiring that changes be made to the source or target systems.**

oriented and asynchronous, they're able to move information from system to system without requiring that all systems be up and running at the same time.

Application semantics is another issue that organizations must confront. Although most organizations can agree upon relational databases, few can agree upon a common schema and architecture that can be shared across the chain. Supply chains solve this problem either by forcing a common data architecture among the members, or by using message brokers or data translation middleware to adapt the data to various models and schemas. The latter is, as in other contexts, the path of least resistance.

It's a Vertically Aligned World

The merger of application integration technology and vertical-specific applications and application integration standards is a natural evolution. Indeed, most application integration technology vendors are working toward providing a common application integration infrastructure along with a specific vertical extension. Sometimes these are mere libraries of code, sometimes completed bolt-on or standalone applications. The objective is to provide additional value to the end user, making the application integration technology that much more valuable.

As we move forward we are going to see these "high-in-the-stack," vertically aligned applications become more widespread, and with the rise of vertical standards, such as HIPAA and STP, these will become even more important. The downside is the additional complexity, and the fact that many need to get their own application integration house in order before attempting to move toward a vertical solution. You have to move up the stack, never down the stack.

## CHAPTER EIGHTEEN

12 Steps to Application Integration

So, now that we know most of the technical details about application integration, the question arises: How do we leverage this technology within our enterprise? The answer to this question is more about "methodology" than "silver bullet," and it's clear that there is much work to be done to make application integration work within your company. The purpose of this chapter is to tie everything together for you, providing you with a step-by-step procedure, which, if followed, will ensure success in your enterprise.

Our "12-step program" for integrating applications relies upon a practical approach to application integration. We reuse some of the activities we've learned with traditional database design, application design, and development. Many times, we use the same design patterns to bind applications together as we did to build them. After all, there is no need to reinvent the wheel if the result will only confuse an already-complex process.

This pragmatic approach relies on familiar concepts and terms such as metadata, schemas, object-oriented modeling, object-oriented analysis and design, patterns, and good old requirements-gathering techniques. Although these are not the only activities in an application integration project, the following steps should be considered when approaching application integration:

1. Understand the enterprise and problem domain.
2. Make sense of the data.

3. Make sense of the processes.
4. Identify any application interfaces.
5. Identify the business events.
6. Identify the data transformation scenarios.
7. Map information movement.
8. Apply technology.
9. Test, test, test.
10. Consider performance.
11. Define the value.
12. Create maintenance procedures.

In this chapter, we concentrate on steps 2 and 3 because we begin to define the models that will serve as the basis for our application integration solution at those steps. These steps are also unique to our approach.

Step 1: Understand the Enterprise and Problem Domain

Sounds simple, huh? Too bad this is the most complex and time-consuming part of the entire process. However, it is unavoidable. At some point, the problem domain must be studied, both freestanding and in the context of the enterprise. Understanding the problem domain requires working with many organization heads to get a handle on the structure and content of the various information systems, as well as the business requirements of each organization—how they do business, what's important, and, perhaps more importantly, what's not.

This process is a basic requirements-gathering problem. It requires interfacing with paper, people, and systems to determine the information that will allow the application integration problem to be defined correctly so that it can be analyzed, modeled, and refined. Only then can the appropriate solution set be employed.

The quality of the information gathering at this step leads directly to and impacts the success of steps 2 and 3.

Step 2: Make Sense of the Data

We begin with the data for a couple of reasons. First, most application integration projects exist only at the data level. This reality alone justifies the quest to understand what exists in the databases scattered throughout an enterprise. Second, even if the application integration project works at the service, application interface, and user interface levels, it is still necessary to understand the databases. Face it. There's no getting around this step.

Ultimately, the implementation of IOAI comes down to understanding where the data exists, gathering information about the data (e.g., schema information), and applying business principles to determine which data flows where, and why.

There are three basic steps that must be followed to prepare for IOAI implementation:

1. Identify the data.
2. Catalog the data.
3. Build the enterprise metadata model, which will be used as a master guide for integrating the various data stores that exist within the enterprise.

In short, implementing an application integration solution demands more than the movement of data between databases and/or applications. A successful solution requires that the enterprise also define both how that information flows through it and how it does business.

Identify the Data

Unfortunately, there are no shortcuts to identifying data within an enterprise. All too often, information about the data, both business and technical, is scattered throughout the enterprise and of a quality that ranges from "somewhat useful" to "you've got to be kidding me!"

The first step in identifying and locating information about the data is to create a list of candidate systems. This list will make it possible to determine which databases exist in support of those candidate systems. The next step requires the determination of who owns the databases, where they are physically located, relevant design information, and such basic information as brand, model, and revisions of the database technology.

Any technology that can reverse-engineer existing physical and logical database schemas will prove helpful in identifying data within the problem domains. However, while the schema and database model may give insight into the structure of the database or databases, they cannot determine how that information is used within the context of the application.

The Data Dictionary

Detailed information can be culled by examining the data dictionaries (if they exist) linked to the data stores being analyzed. Such an examination may illuminate such important information as:

- The reason for the existence of particular data elements
- Ownership
- Format
- Security parameters
- The role within both the logical and physical data structure

While the concept of the data dictionary is fairly constant from database to database, the dictionaries themselves may vary widely in form and content. Some contain more information than others. Some are open. Most are proprietary. Some don't even exist—which is often the case with less sophisticated software.

Integrity Issues

When analyzing databases for IOAI, integrity issues constantly crop up. In order to address these, it is important to understand the rules and regulations that were applied to the construction of the database. For example, will the application allow the update of customer information in a customer table without first updating demographics information in the demographics table?

Most middleware fails to take into account the structure or rules built into the databases being connected. As a result, there exists the very real threat of damage to the integrity of target databases. While some databases do come with built-in integrity controls, such as stored procedures or triggers, most rely on the application logic to handle integrity issues on behalf of the database. Unfortunately, the faith implicit in this reliance is not always well placed. Indeed, all too often it is painfully naive.

The lack of integrity controls at the data level (or, in the case of existing integrity controls, bypassing the application logic to access the database directly) could result in profound problems. Application integration architects and developers need to approach this danger cautiously, making sure not to compromise the database's integrity in their zeal to achieve integration. Perhaps this is where a decision to use another application integration level as a primary point of integration might be considered.

Data Latency

Data latency—the characteristic of the data that defines how current the information needs to be—is another property of the data that needs to be determined for the purposes of application integration. Such information will allow application integration architects to determine when the information should be copied, or moved, to another enterprise system, and how fast.

While an argument can be made to support a number of different categories of data latency, for the purpose of application integration within the enterprise, there are really only three:

- Real time
- Near time
- One time

Real-time data is precisely what it sounds like—information that is placed in the database as it occurs, with little or no latency. Monitoring stock price information through a real-time feed from Wall Street is an example of real-time data. Real-time data is updated as it enters the database, and that information is available immediately to anyone, or any application, that requires it for processing.

While zero-latency real time is clearly the goal of application integration, achieving it represents a huge challenge. In order to achieve zero latency, application integration implementation requires constant returns to the database, application, or other resource to retrieve new and/or updated information. In the context of real-time updates, database performance must also be considered—while one process updates the database as quickly as possible, another process must be simultaneously extracting the updated information.

The successful implementation of zero latency presents architects and developers with the opportunity to create such innovative solutions as SOAI, where business processes are integrated within the application integration solution. In many cases, SOAI makes better sense than IOAI solutions, because it allows data and common business processes to be shared at the same time. The downside to SOAI is that it is also the most expensive to implement.

Near-time data refers to information that is updated at set intervals rather than instantaneously. Stock quotes posted on the Web are a good example of near-time data. They are typically delayed 20 minutes or more, because the Web sites distributing the quotes are generally unable to process real-time data.

Near-time data can be thought of as "good-enough" latency data. In other words, data only as timely as needed.

Although near-time data is not updated constantly, it still faces many of the same challenges as real-time data, including overcoming performance and management issues.

One-time data is typically updated only once. Customer addresses or account numbers are examples of one-time information. Within the context of application integration, the intervals of data copy, or data movement, do not require the kind of aggressiveness needed to accomplish real-time or near-time data exchange.

The notion of data typing goes well beyond the classification of the data as real-time, near-time, or one-time. It is really a complex process of determining the properties of the data, including updates and edit increments, as well as the behavior of the data over time. What do the applications use the particular data for? How often do they use it? What happens with the data over time? These are questions that must be addressed in order to create the most effective application integration solution.

Data Structure

Another identifying component of data is data structure. How information is structured, including the properties of the data elements existing within that structure, can be gleaned from a knowledge of the data format. Likewise, length, data type (character or numeric), name of the data element, and type of information stored (binary, text, spatial, etc.) are additional characteristics of the data that may be determined by its format.

Resolution of data structure conflicts must be accomplished within such application integration technologies as integration brokers and/or application servers. Different structures and schemas existing within the enterprise must be transformed as information is moved from one system to another.

Catalog the Data

Once the logical and physical characteristics of the databases to be integrated are understood, it is time to do the "grunge" work—data cataloging. In the world of application integration, data cataloging is the process of gathering metadata and other data throughout the problem domain. Once accomplished, it is possible to create an enterprise-wide catalog of all data elements that may exist within the enterprise. The resulting catalog then becomes the basis of understanding needed to create the enterprise metadata model—the foundation of IOAI.

For most medium to large enterprises, the creation of this data catalog is a massive undertaking. In essence, it demands the creation of the "mother of all data dictionaries," a data dictionary that includes not only the traditional data dictionary information, but also all the information that is of interest to application integration—system information, security information, ownership, connected processes, communication mechanisms, and integrity issues—along with traditional metadata such as format, name of attribute, and description.

While there is no standard for cataloging data within application integration projects, the guiding principle stands clear: The more information, the better. The catalog will become both the repository for the application integration engine to be built and the foundation to discover new business flows. It will also become a way to automate existing business flows within the enterprise.

While data catalogs can be made using index cards or paper, electronic spreadsheets (e.g., Microsoft Excel) or PC-based databases (e.g., Microsoft Access) provide more attractive alternatives. Remember that a data catalog is not the enterprise metadata. It is the foundation of the metadata. Therefore, there is no need to expand the data catalog into a full-blown metadata repository until it is completely populated.

It is an understatement to suggest that this catalog will be huge. Most enterprises will find tens of thousands of data elements to identify and catalog even while reducing redundancies among some of the data elements. In addition to being huge, the data catalog will be a dynamic structure. In a very real sense, it will never be complete. A person, or persons, will have to be assigned to maintain the data catalog over time, assuring that the information in the catalog remains correct and timely, and that the architects and developers have access to the catalog in order to create the application integration solution.

Build the Enterprise Metadata Model

Once all the information about all the data in the enterprise is contained in the data catalog, it is time to focus on the enterprise metadata model. The difference between the two is sometimes subtle. It is best to think of the data catalog as the list of potential solutions to your application integration problem and to think of the metadata model as the IOAI solution. The metadata model defines not only all the data structures existing in the enterprise, but also how those data structures will interact within the application integration solution domain.

Once constructed, the enterprise metadata model is the enterprise's database repository of sorts: the master directory for the application integration solution. In many cases, the repository will be hooked on to the integration broker and used as a reference point for locating not only the data, but also the rules and logic that apply to that data. However, the repository is more than simply the storage of metadata information. It is the heart of the ultimate application integration solution, containing both data and business model information.

The metadata repository built with the processes outlined in this chapter will not only solve the IOAI problem, it will also provide the basis for other types of application integration. As in the world of client/server and data warehousing, the process builds up from the data to the application (and from the application to the interface, if necessary). This "hierarchical" flow identifies IOAI as the foundation for the larger application integration solution.

Logical Model

Just as with traditional database design methods, the enterprise metadata model used for IOAI can be broken into two components: the logical and the physical. And, just as with the former, the same techniques apply to the latter. Creating the logical model is the process of creating an architecture for all data stores that are independent of a physical database model, development tool, or particular DBMS (e.g., Oracle, Sybase, or Informix).

A logical model is a sound approach to an application integration project in that it will allow architects and developers to make objective IOAI decisions, moving from high-level requirements to implementation details. The logical data model is an integrated view of business data throughout the application domain, or data pertinent to the application integration solution under construction. The primary difference between using a logical data model for application integration versus traditional database development is the information source. While traditional development, generally speaking, defines new databases based on business requirements, a logical data model arising from an application integration project is based on existing databases.

At the heart of the logical model is the Entity Relationship Diagram (ERD). An ERD is a graphical representation of data entities, attributes, and relationships between entities for all databases existing in the enterprise.

Computer-Aided Software Engineering (CASE) technology is but one of the many tools to automate the logical database modeling process. Not only do these tools provide an easy way to create logical database models, they can also build logical database models into physical database models. In addition, they create the physical schema on the target database(s) through standard middleware.

Physical Model

The myriad of database types in any given enterprise minimizes the importance of the physical enterprise model because, with so many database types, the physical model will rarely be used. The reason is clear—there is simply no clear way to create a physical model that maps down to object-oriented, multidimensional, hierarchy, flat-file, and relational databases, all at the same time. However, if those databases are to be integrated, some common physical representation must be selected. Only then can the model be transformed as required. The necessity of the physical model is only for those times when it is possible to map the logical to the physical—that is, those times when an enterprise uses a homogeneous database approach, usually "all relational." The input for the physical model is both the logical model and the data catalog. When accessing this information, consider the data dictionary, business rules, and other user-processing requirements.

Normalizing the Enterprise

Before the logical—and sometimes physical—database is completed, it is desirable to normalize the model. This is a process of decomposing complex data structures into simple relations using a series of dependency rules. Normalization means reducing the amount of redundant data that will exist in the database or, in the case of application integration, in the enterprise. It is a good idea to do this in both the logical and physical database design, or the application integration redesign.

When considered within the context of application integration, the normalization process is very complex and risky. Because there can be no control over most of the databases that are being integrated, normalizing the logical enterprise metadata model often results in a new version of the model that has no chance of being implemented physically. This result violates an essential credo of application integration: Whenever possible, it is best to leave the applications and databases alone. Changes to databases inevitably translate into expense and risk. Furthermore, most enterprises employ a chaotic mosaic of database technology, making it technically unfeasible to accomplish such changes without rehosting the data. This is almost always completely out of the question.

However, the issue remains: Are changes to be made to source and target databases, or not? Generally, it is wise to normalize the logical enterprise metadata model to discover areas within the enterprise that may benefit from changes in their data structures. Changes to databases may allow the enterprise to reduce the amount of redundant data and thus increase the reliability of the integrated data. Remember, the notion of IOAI is to perceive all the information within the enterprise as a single source of information and, in turn, to make that huge amount of enterprise information as efficient as possible through processes such as normalization.

Step 3: Make Sense of the Processes

Once the enterprise data is understood, and baseline information such as the enterprise metadata model has been created, the decision must be made as to how to approach the enterprise business model. This decision will depend on how the particular application integration problem domain is addressed. This view of the enterprise at the process or service-oriented level requires understanding and documentation of all business processes and how they relate to each other, as well as to the enterprise metadata model.

As with the database analysis procedures outlined previously, it is desirable to use traditional process-modeling techniques, such as object modeling (e.g., the Unified Modeling Language, or UML) to create business processes. What's more, instead of creating the business processes from a set of application requirements, it is preferable to document existing business processes and methods to better understand what they do and, therefore, how to integrate them at the service-oriented level through a composite application.

Process Integration

We already stated that identifying processes that exist within an enterprise is a difficult task, requiring the analysis of all the applications in the enterprise that exist in the application integration problem domain. The task is made even more difficult due to the possibility that many entities embrace numerous types of applications over a number of generations of technology.

Once the applications in the problem domain have been analyzed, the enabling technology employed by each application within the problem must be identified. With applications in the enterprise dating from as long ago as 30 years, this step will uncover everything from traditional centralized computing to the best distributed computing solutions. Once this identification has been made, the next step is to determine ownership of the processes and, subsequently, develop insight into those processes—for example, why information is being processed in one manner versus another, or why multiple arrays are used to carry out a particular operation. In most cases, ownership will rest with the application manager, who determines when the application is to be changed and for what reason(s).

Finally, the documentation for the application will need to be found. In a small number of instances, applications have been well documented and well updated as they have matured. The vast majority of the time, applications are poorly documented, or the documentation has not been updated to keep up with the maturation of the application. Proper documentation has a profound impact on SOAI. Therefore, even if documentation is nonexistent, it is imperative that baseline documentation be created as the application integration solution is put into place. This is an area of significant expense as applications are opened in order to be understood and their features documented.

Process identification is important to the SOAI project life cycle. Without understanding the processes, moving forward is like a guessing game or playing blind man's bluff. There can never be real certainty that the enterprise is being accurately integrated. While data is relatively easy to identify and define, processes are much more complex and difficult.

Process Cataloging

In the same way that IOAI requires a data-level catalog, SOAI requires a "process catalog"—a list of all business processes that exist within an enterprise or, at least, within the problem domain. For example, if an application integration architect needs to understand all the processes that exist within an inventory application, he or she will read either the documentation or the code to determine which processes are present. Then, the architect will enter the business processes into the catalog and determine the purpose of the process, who owns it, what exactly it does, and the technology it employs (e.g., Java or C++). In addition, the architect will need to know which database a particular business process interacts with as well as its links to the metadata model. The catalog will require other information as well, such as pseudocode, data flow diagrams, and state diagrams, which define the logic flow for the particular process. In the world of traditional, structured programming, this would mean a flowchart, or pseudocode. However, in the world of object-oriented development, this refers to the object model. Thus, it is important not only to identify each process but to understand how the logic flows within that process.

Other information may be maintained in the catalog as well, information that may include variables used within the processes, object schemas, security requirements, and/or performance characteristics. Each process catalog must maintain its own set of properties, custom-built for each specific application integration problem domain.

The Common Business Model

If the enterprise metadata model is the end state for IOAI analysis, then the common business model is the end state for SOAI. Simply put, the common business model is the aggregation and high-level model of all objects, methods, properties, procedural logic, batch processing, and everything else in the enterprise that processes information.

The common business model is assigned this name (and not the "object model") for one reason: In order for it to document and account for such a wide array of techniques and technologies, the model must remain, at least at first, an independent paradigm. Many of the applications written in the last ten years use the object-oriented paradigm for both programming and design. However, most traditional applications (those older than ten years) use a structured application-programming paradigm, as well as structured design. The common business model must remain independent of both.

Having an independent paradigm results in a simplification of the business processes in the enterprise or the application integration problem domain. The common business model does not map out a complex, detail-oriented model, but rather a high-level understanding of the processes in the enterprise along with their functions and features—all with an eye toward those that may be combined or reused.

Business modeling is important for another reason, as well. The ultimate goal of application integration is to move beyond the simple integration of applications to the much more complex integration of business process flow analysis and design. Thus, the business model provides the basis of understanding that allows for the creation of a proper business process flow that is necessary within the enterprise. To accomplish this, the current state and the desired state—along with a plan to get from one to the next—must be documented.

For the sake of clarity, application integration architects should use the Unified Modeling Language to define the common business model. Using UML affords application integration architects a twofold benefit. First, an abundance of tools is available to create and maintain UML. Second, a deep pool of information exists regarding leveraging UML for a variety of purposes.

The real challenge to creating a common business model is scope. The temptation—and thus, the trap—to rearchitect and redesign each source and target application is very real. However, creating a business model is not an application development problem. It is an application integration problem. The application integration architect must recognize that the purpose of the common business model is to document existing processes, not to change the source and target applications. While it is certainly possible to rewrite everything from scratch in order to integrate the enterprise, such an endeavor would largely outweigh the value of application integration.

Leveraging Patterns for Service-Oriented Application Integration

Patterns are always interesting. More than interesting, they are also useful in the context of SOAI. They enable the application integration architect to identify common business processes among the many business processes that already exist within the enterprise. Or they may be used to identify new processes in need of integration. Using patterns in this way is simply borrowing them from the world of application architecture and applying them to the world of enterprise architecture—a perfect fit.

Patterns arise over and over during considerations of application integration architecture. Patterns formalize and streamline the idea of application integration—to build once at the application level and then reuse throughout the solution domain. Patterns describe recurring design problems that appear in certain design contexts. They describe generic schemes for the solution of the problems, solution schemes created by defining their components, responsibilities, and relationships.

A three-part schema is part of every pattern: context, problem, and solution. *Context* describes the circumstances of the situation where the problem arises or which circumstances have to be true for the pattern to be valid. For example, an object uses data from an external system. The *problem* is what is addressed by the pattern. The challenge for the architect or designer is to capture the essence of the problem or what design issues define the problem. For example, changing the state of the object means that the object and the external data are inconsistent. As a result, there is a need to synchronize the external data and the object. The resulting *solution* is the well-proven and consistent resolution of the problem.

Types of Patterns

All patterns are not created equal. There are types, or categories, of patterns to be used in specific situations in the application integration problem domain. For example, some patterns assist application integration architects in structuring a system into subsystems, while others allow the architect to refine the subsystems and applications and the ways in which they interact. Some patterns assist application integration architects in determining design aspects using pseudocode or a true programming language such as C++. Some address domain-independent subsystems or components, or domain-dependent issues such as business logic. Clearly, the range of patterns makes it difficult to define neat categories for them. However, there are three useful, and generally accepted, categories: architectural patterns, design patterns, and idioms.

Architectural patterns are complex patterns that tend to link to particular domains. They provide application integration architects with the basic system structure—subsystems, behavior, and relationships. It would not be unfair to consider these architectural patterns as templates for application integration architecture, defining macro system structure properties. *Design patterns* are not as complex as architectural patterns. They tend to be problem domain independent. These patterns provide application architects with a means of refining the subsystems and components, and the relationships between them. The goal in using these patterns is to find a common structure that solves a particular problem. An *idiom* is a low-level pattern coupled with a specific programming language. It describes how to code the object at a low level.

Pattern descriptions, or micro-methods, provide specifications for deploying the pattern. They give application architects problem-independent analysis and design methods that are found in traditional, object-oriented analysis and design methodologies such as UML.

Application-to-Application Integration

Patterns, as recurring phenomena, provide application integration architects with a methodology for defining and solving recurring problems. They allow application architects to create reusable solutions that can then be applied to multiple applications. The ensuing information is too often kept "in the architect's head," where it is either forgotten or simply unavailable when the problem arises again. Unfortunately, application integration architects, even the good ones, tend to be poor documentation generators.

Extending the previous concept, it becomes clear that patterns do a good job of recording design experience across a development group. They level the playing field, providing every team member with access to this valuable information. Application integration developers and application architects may create a database of architecture patterns—with search features and links to code and models.

Patterns also provide a standard vocabulary and a base set of concepts for application integration development and application architecture. For this reason, terms used to represent concepts should be carefully chosen. Thoughtful terminology results in greater efficiency because terms and concepts no longer have to be explained over and over. When endowed with a common terminology, patterns provide a natural mechanism for documenting application architectures. The vocabulary should be consistent across many projects. If this consistency is adhered to—and the patterns are accessible and understandable to all members of the application development teams—then patterns can be employed with striking success.

Patterns allow application integration developers and application architects to build complex architectures around predefined and proven solutions because they provide predefined components, relationships, and responsibilities. While patterns don't provide all the design detail necessary to solve a problem at hand, they do define a starting point. Moreover, they provide application integration architects with the skeleton of functionality.

Using patterns, application integration architects can manage software complexity because all patterns provide predefined methods to solve a problem. For example, if the problem is integrating an enterprise, there is no need to reinvent the wheel. The task is simply to find the pattern that describes the problem and then to implement the solution. (This assumes that only sound patterns with working solutions are captured.)

The Value of Patterns

Patterns add value to the application integration architecture and the software development life cycle. They have the potential to increase the quality of most system development and to provide effective integration without increasing cost. However, they are not necessarily the panacea for all that ails the system. Patterns should not be assumed to be a mechanism for replacing a sound methodology, or a sound process. Patterns are able to become part of each, and in many instances, some pattern-oriented enterprise architecture is already taking place. Patterns simply formalize the process, filling in the gaps and providing a consistent approach.

There are those who describe patterns as the "second coming" of enterprise architecture. As comforting as that assertion might be, there is no evidence to validate it. Patterns are, simply, another available tool to be used. What is more, patterns are valuable only if they are practiced consistently for all applications in the enterprise. Capturing patterns for a single application is hardly worth the effort. Application integration architects need to establish the infrastructure for patterns, creating standard mechanisms to capture and maintain the patterns over the long haul, refining them when necessary.

Finally, patterns only provide an opportunity for reuse within the application integration problem domain. They are not a guarantee of success. Object-oriented analysis and design methodologies formalize the way reusable elements (objects) are implemented. Patterns define architectural and design solutions that can be reused. There is a difference. Patterns need not be linked to object-oriented analysis, design, or implementation languages. Nor do they need rigorous notation, a rigid process, or expensive tools. Patterns can be captured easily on 3x5 index cards or a word processor. The ideal way to capture patterns in the context of application integration is within the process catalog described previously. Doing so allows both process information and pattern information to be gathered at the same time.

Again, the concept of patterns is a very simple one. However, patterns, as described by the pattern community, are often too difficult to understand and use. The depth and range of academic double-speak regarding patterns has "spooked" many application architects. Hopefully, as with other technologies based on complex theory, patterns can be freed of the shackles of academia and be made available to the masses so they can become a primary tool for integration at the service level.

Step 4: Identify any Application Interfaces

In addition to seeking common methods and data to integrate, it is important to take note of the available application interfaces in support of application interface-level application integration, or integration with application interfaces and other application integration levels.

Interfaces are quirky. They differ greatly from application to application. What's more, many interfaces, despite what the application vendors or developers may claim, are not really interfaces at all. It is important to devote time to validating assumptions about interfaces.

The best place to begin with interfaces is with the creation of an application interface directory. As with other directories, this is a repository for gathered information about available interfaces, along with the documentation for each interface. This directory is used, along with the common business model and the enterprise metadata model, to understand the points of integration within all systems of the application integration problem domain.

Application Interface Directory

The application interface directory can be thought of as a list of business processes that are available from an application—packaged or custom made. It must, however, be a true application (database, business processes, or user interface) and not a database or simple middleware service. The application interface directory expands on the enterprise metadata model, tracking both data and methods that act upon the data.

Application Semantics

The first portion of the application interface directory is a list of application semantics. These establish the way and form in which the particular application refers to properties of the business process. For example, the very same customer number for one application may have a completely different value and meaning in another application. Understanding the semantics of an application guarantees that there will be no contradictory information when the application is integrated with other applications. Achieving consistent application semantics requires an application integration "Rosetta Stone" and, as such, represents one of the major challenges to the application integration solution.

The first step in creating this Rosetta Stone is to understand which terms mean what in which applications. Once that is accomplished, you have taken the first very difficult step toward success.

Business Processes

Business processes are listings of functions or methods provided by the application. In some applications, such a listing is easy to determine because the business processes are well documented and easily found by invoking the user interface. However, in other applications, determining these processes requires a search through the source code to discover and understand the various methods and functions available.

As with application semantics, it is critical to understand all business processes that are available within a particular application. Once understood and documented in the application interface directory, it is possible to determine the particular combination of processes to invoke in order to carry out a specific integration requirement. For example, in an application that contains as many as 30 business processes for updating customer information, it is vital to know which process wants to invoke what, and why.

Step 5: Identify the Business Events

The next step is the identification of all relevant business events that occur within an enterprise. This means when something—an event—happens, then there is a resulting reaction. For example, a customer signing up for credit at an online Web store represents an "event." It may be desirable to capture this event and make something else happen, such as running an automatic credit check to ensure that the customer is credit-worthy. That consequence may kick off a chain of events at the credit bureau and return the credit status of the customer, which typically fires off still other events, such as notifying the customer through e-mail that the credit application is accepted or denied. These events are generally asynchronous in nature but can be synchronous in some instances.

This should make clear that, in attempting to understand an application integration problem domain, a real attempt should be made to capture the business events that may take place within the domain. It is important to understand what invoked a business event, what takes place during the event, and any other events that may be invoked as a consequence of the initial event. The end result is a web of interrelated events, each dependent upon the other. Currently, this web exists through automatic or manual processes. In the application integration solution set, all these events will be automated across systems, eliminating the manual processing entirely.

Step 6: Identify the Data Transformation Scenarios

With an existing understanding of the data and application semantics that exist within an application integration problem domain, it is good to get an idea about how schema and content of the data moving between systems will be transformed. This is necessary for a couple of reasons. First, data existing in one system won't make sense to another until the data schema and content is reformatted to make sense to the target system. Second, it will ensure the maintenance of consistent application semantics from system to system.

Step 7: Map Information Movement

Once the preceding steps have revealed all the information available, it is time to map the information movement from system to system—what data element or interface the information is moving from, and where that information will ultimately move.

For example, the customer number from the sales databases needs to move to the credit-reporting system, ultimately residing in the customer table maintained by the credit system. This knowledge enables us to map the movement from the source system (the sales system), to the target system (the credit system). It should be noted where the information is physically located, what security may be present, what enabling technology exists (e.g., relational table), and how the information is extracted on one side to be placed on the other.

It is also necessary to note the event that is bound to the information movement. Or, if no event is required, what other condition (such as time of data, real time, or state changes) causes the movement of information from the source to the target. (This process is typically more relevant to cohesive systems than coupled systems, because coupled system are usually bound by coupled services, which is where the data is shared rather than replicated. Mappings need to be adapted to the application integration level that is being used to integrate the systems.)

Step 8: Apply Technology

Many technologies are available, including application servers, distributed objects, and message brokers. The choice of technology will likely be a mix of products and vendors that, together, meet the needs of the application integration solution. It is very rare for a single vendor to be able to solve all problems—not that that reality has ever kept vendors from making the claim that they can.

Technology selection is a difficult process, which requires a great deal of time and effort. Creating the criteria for technology and products, understanding available solutions, and then matching the criteria to those products is hardly a piece of cake. To be successful, this "marriage" of criteria and products often requires a pilot project to prove that the technology will work. The time it takes to select the right technologies could be as long as the actual development of the application integration solution. While this might seem daunting, consider the alternative—picking the wrong technology for the problem domain. A bad choice practically ensures the failure of the application integration project.

Step 9: Test, Test, Test

Testing is expensive and time consuming. To make testing an even more "attractive" endeavor, it is also thankless. Still, if an application integration solution is not tested properly, then disaster looms large. For example, important data can be overwritten (and thus lost). Perhaps worse, erroneous information could appear within applications. Even without these dire eventualities, it is necessary to ensure that the solution will scale and handle the other rigors of day-to-day usage.

To insure proper testing, a test plan will have to be put in place. While a detailed discussion of a test plan is beyond the scope of this chapter, it is really just a step-by-step procedure detailing how the application integration solution will be tested when completed. A test plan is particularly important because of the difficulty in testing an application integration solution. Most source and target systems are business critical and therefore cannot be taken offline. As a result, testing these systems can be a bit tricky.

Step 10: Consider Performance

Performance is too often ignored until it's too late. A word of advice: Don't ignore performance! Application integration systems that don't perform well are destined to fail. For example, if processing a credit report for a telephone customer takes 20 minutes during peak hours, the application integration solution does not have business value.

While most application integration solutions won't provide zero latency with today's technology, the movement of information from system to system, or the invocation of common business processes, should provide response times under a second. What's more, the application integration solution should provide that same response time under an ever-increasing user and processing load. In short, the application integration solution must scale.

So, how do you build performance into a system? Design for performance, and test performance before going live. Remember, performance is something that can't be fixed once the application integration solution has been deployed. Performance must be designed from the ground up. This means the architecture of the application integration solution needs to provide the infrastructure for performance, as well as the selected enabling technology. It is possible to make some adjustments before the solution is deployed using traditional performance

Making Application Integration Scale

Let's face it: Many application integration solutions are not scaling to meet enterprise needs. End-user organizations are finding that their application integration solution that worked so well at the department level is falling down when stepping up to the enterprise. So, what did they do wrong? There are many reasons why performance/scaling, in the world of application integration, has just become an issue.

First, most existing application integration problem domains are small—less than six source and target systems. The message or transaction rate is also small—typically less than ten messages per second. Now, with application integration taking more of a B2B and enterprise-wide focus, problem domains are growing larger, and the number of source and target systems are growing well past six with message rate requirements moving past the 100-message-per-second range. The hard fact is that both the architectures and technologies leveraged for smaller problem domains may not work in larger ones. We saw this in the world of client/server development, and we are seeing it again within application integration.

Second, most application integration projects are tossed together without much architectural thought, including scalability planning. As I work with many application integration architects and projects, I'm hard-pressed to find project leaders who have any idea of how their solution will scale in both performance and capacity to meet future requirements. They seem content with just getting the technology up and running.

Third, and expanding upon the previous point, most application integration projects fail to perform adequate performance testing and almost never create performance simulation models. Solutions should be put through their paces, including simulated and increasing transaction loads being placed on the middleware, as well as simulating additional source and target systems. The cost of testing application integration solutions, of course, is high because the solution sets are so complex. However, clearly it's much better to find out that your solution won't scale before rather than after it's placed into production.

(continued)

Making Application Integration Scale (*continued*)

Finally, application integration technology vendors, with just a few exceptions, have done a poor job in creating technology that scales. The focus has been on adding features and functions in order to make the final cuts with end-user organizations, rather than focusing on operational efficiency. Scalability is not yet a sexy concept in the world of application integration. While everyone says they can scale, the fact is that few can. Claims are only verifiable through expensive testing.

Performance Anxiety

Issues such as message rates, transactions per second, and interface/adapter performance must be taken into account when considering performance engineering and application integration. Determining performance within an application integration problem domain is very complex, because there are so many variables to consider; for example:

- Message consumption rate from source system.
- Number of transformations required and duration.
- Message splitting or combining required.
- Rules-processing cycles for each message.
- Message production rate to target system.

This, of course, is just an instance of what occurs as application integration solutions operate. You need to consider the fact that many message consumption, transformation, splitting, combining, and production operations occur simultaneously. As such, you must consider how each operation consumes resources (processor cycles, memory, storage, etc.), and how the application integration solution behaves as the message rate and number of integrated systems increases. The dynamics may surprise you.

The most reliable approach to performance in the design of an integration solution is to select the technology, test, and then do a simulation model to make an educated assessment of how well it will perform. Using simulation tools, it is possible to determine the time it will take for a message or a transaction to move between applications. This simulation must test the various entities of the system at the component (e.g., server) and system (e.g., integrated systems) level to ensure the overall performance of the application integration solution. Just as a chain is no stronger than its weakest link, an integration solution is no more efficient than its slowest-performing component. Testing identifies problem components before the solution is actually implemented.

Making an application integration solution scale comes down to selecting the correct approaches and enabling technology for the problem domain. For example, if message rate is going to be a limiting factor, it is important to select a technology that can distribute message processing among any number of connected message brokers. If transaction load and database access integrity is the limiting factor, then transactional middleware may be a better fit.

There is no hard-and-fast rule about designing a system to scale. The first step is to determine your requirements and then back the appropriate architecture and technology into those requirements. Putting the technology first is a very costly example of putting the cart ahead of the horse. And, once again, simulation tools and performance models are your first stop in determining scalability of your application integration solution. If we consider application integration for what it is, a strategic solution, than ignoring performance and scalability is simply not logical.

models, such as those developed over the years within the world of distributed computing. Finally, it is necessary to run some performance tests to ensure that the system performs well under a variety of conditions. For example, how well does it perform at 100 users, 500 users, 1,000 users, and even 10,000 users? What about processing load? What happens to performance as you extend the application integration solution over time?

Step 11: Define the Value

With the hard part out of the way, it's time to define the value of the application integration solution, to determine the business value of integrating systems. In this scenario, the method of determining value is generally evaluating the dollars that will be saved by a successful application integration solution. Two things should be considered here: Soft- and hard-dollar savings. Hard dollars, simply put, represent the value of the application integration solution that is easily defined by the ability of the solution to eliminate costly processes, such as automating manual processes, reducing error rates, or processing customer orders more quickly. In contrast, soft-dollar savings are more difficult to define. These savings include increased productivity over time, retention rate increase due to the ability to make systems work together for the users, and customer satisfaction (based on ease of use) with an organization with integrated systems.

Of course, defining value in a particular system can be based on any criteria and will differ from problem domain to problem domain, and from business to business.

Step 12: Create Maintenance Procedures

Last but not least, it is necessary to consider how an application integration solution will be maintained over time. Who will administer the message broker server? Who will manage security? Who will monitor system performance and solve problems?

In addressing the need for ongoing maintenance, a good idea is to document all of the maintenance activities that need to occur—and assign people to carry them out. Remember, an application integration solution represents the heart of an enterprise, moving vital information between mission-critical systems. As such, it is also a point of failure that could bring the entire enterprise to its knees.

With that happy thought in mind, this might also be a good time to consider disaster recovery issues, such as redundant servers and networks, as well as relocating the application integration solution should a disaster occur.

Method or Madness?

As I noted at the outset of this chapter, we have not (and could not) defined everything you must do to create a successful application integration project. My goal has been to outline the activities that may be necessary for your application integration project. Unlike traditional application development, where the database and application are designed, application integration solutions are as unique as snowflakes. When all is said and done, no two will be alike. However, as time goes on, common patterns emerge that allow us to share best practices when creating an application integration solution. We still need to travel farther down the road before we can see the entire picture. But we're getting there. We're getting there.

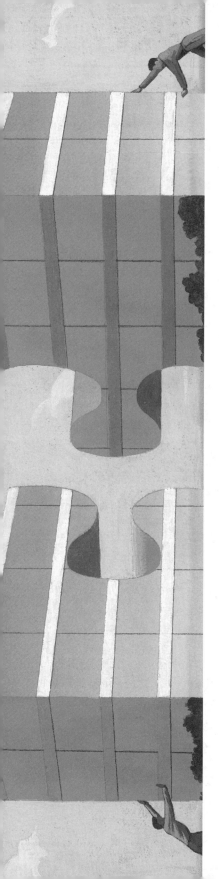

## CHAPTER NINETEEN

Leveraging Ontologies and Application Integration

It's a judgment call as to the proper placement of this chapter in the book. It clearly could go with our earlier discussion of metadata. However, this is a fairly new topic in the context of application integration—indeed, an advanced topic. Thus, here is where it stays.

Truth be told, ontologies are nothing new, and the use of ontologies within the notion of application integration is nothing new either, no matter if we called it ontology or something different. However, the recognition that ontologies play a major role in the logical understanding of the problem domain—if not the solutions, as well—is something new. If we understand the ontologies, then we clearly understand how to solve the information integration problem by turning very different schemas and data structures into views and mappings that are more meaningful to both end users and application integration architects.

If you don't understand application semantics—simply put, the meaning of data—then you have no hope of creating the proper application integration solution. You must understand the data to define the proper integration flows and transformation scenarios, and provide service-oriented (such as Web services) frameworks to your application integration domain, meaning levels of abstraction.

393

This is where many application integration projects fall down. Most application integration occurs at the information level. So, you must always deal with semantics and how to describe semantics relative to a multitude of information systems. There is also a need to formalize this process, putting some additional methodology and technology behind the management of metadata, as well as the relationships therein.

To this end, many in the world of application integration have begun to adopt the notion of ontology (or the instances of ontology: ontologies). *Ontology* is a term borrowed from philosophy that refers to the science of describing the kinds of entities in the world and how they are related. Ontologies are important to application integration solutions because they provide a shared and common understanding of data (and, in some cases, services and processes) that exists within an application integration problem domain, and how to facilitate communication between people and information systems. By leveraging this concept we can organize and share enterprise information, as well as manage content and knowledge, which allows better interoperability and integration of inter- and intracompany information systems. We can also layer common ontologies within verticals, or domains with repeatable patterns.

The view of ontologies was best summarized by Quine, who claimed that the question ontology asks can be stated in three words: "What is there?"—and the answer is, "Everything."[1] In the context of information-oriented integration, each information system is regarded as a "theory" that recognizes the existence of a set of objects: its own ontology.

At its essence, ontology is a conceptual information model.[2] Ontologies describe things that exist in a problem domain. This includes properties, concepts, and rules and how they relate to one another, which supports a standard reference model for information integration (the link to application integration), as well as knowledge sharing. We leverage ontologies in the science of application integration because they support human understanding of information. This use is self-explanatory within the context of application integration. Ontologies also provide the ability to facilitate information-based access and information integration across very different information systems. We achieve this by formalizing the application semantics between intra- and interorganizational information resources.

---

[1]Quine, W.V. 1948. "On What is There." In "Review of Metaphysics," Vol. II, No. 5; reprinted in *From a Logical Point of View* (1961).

[2]Akkerman. January 15, 2001. "What are Ontologies?—An Executive Summary."

Ontologies: A Deeper Dive

When dealing with application integration, as you know by now, we are dealing with much complexity. The notion of ontologies helps the application integration architect prepare *generalizations* that make the problem domain more understandable.[3] In contrast to abstraction, generalization ignores many of the details and ends up with general ideas. Therefore, when generalizing, we start with a collection of types and analyze commonalities to generalize them.

Clearly, semantic heterogeneity and divergence hinder the notion of generalization, and as commonalities of two entities are represented in semantically different ways, the differences are more difficult to see. Thus, ontological analysis clears the ground for generalization, making the properties of the entities much more clear. Indeed, ontological analysis for application integration encourages generalization. Thus we can say, "Within an ontological framework, integration analysis naturally leads to generalization."[4]

Considering that statement, it's also clear that application independence of ontological models makes these applications candidates for reference models. We do this by stripping the applications of the semantic divergences that were introduced to satisfy their requirements, thus creating a common application integration foundation for use as the basis for an application integration project.

Returning to the core problem we wish to solve within application integration domains, we are looking to achieve semantic interoperability between very different systems. The solution to this problem is based on our ability to leverage formal ontologies required to account for the different types of ontologies for any business reason. For example, we can leverage *resource ontologies* to define semantics used by our SAP systems, but we may also use *personal ontologies* to define the semantics of a user or a user group. In addition, we have the notion of *shared ontologies*, which are common semantics shared between any numbers of information systems.[5]

The best approach to developing an ontology is usually determined by the eventual purpose of the ontology. For example:

---

[3]Partridge, Chris. 2002. "The Role of Ontology in Semantic Integration."

[4]Ibid.

[5]Cui, Zhan, Dean Jones, and Paul O'Brien. 2002. "Issues in Ontology-Based Information Integration."

- When developing a resource ontology, it is best to adopt a bottom-up approach, defining the terms used by the resource and then making generalizations to the terms.
- When developing personal ontologies, we look at the essence of the user or user group, top down or bottom up.
- When developing a shared ontology, it is best to use a top-down approach, defining the general concepts first, and working down to the detail.

Once we define the ontologies, we must account for the semantic mismatches that occur during translations between the various terminologies. Therefore, we have the need for *mapping*.

Creating maps is significant work that leverages a great deal of reuse. The use of mapping requires the "ontology engineer" to modify and reuse mapping. Such mapping necessitates a mediator system that can interpret the mappings in order to translate between the different ontologies that exist in the problem domain. It is also logical to include a library of mapping and conversion functions, as there are many standards transformations employable from mapping to mapping.

Finding the Information

One of the benefits of leveraging ontologies is the fact that no matter where the information resides, we can understand and map information relevant to the application integration scenarios. Ontologies allow you to differentiate between resources, which is especially useful when those resources have redundant data (e.g., customer information in almost all enterprises). Thus, in order to make better sense of the data and represent the data in a meaningful way, terms defined in ontologies allow the application integration architects to fully understand the meaning and context of the information. Again, this is ontology's value within application integration.

When considering schemas, local to remote source or target systems, the application of ontologies is leveraged in order to define the meaning of the terms used in some domain. Although there is often some communication between a data model and the attributes, both schema and ontologies play key roles in application integration because of the importance of both semantics and data structures.

If you've ever seen an application or database schema, you know this to be true:

- The terms we leverage in schemas are often cryptic.
- If ontologies are not bound to the technology, they can better represent the meaning of the data.
- This makes application integration technology much more productive.

However, you must also take the time to define a relationship between the ontologies and the physical application or database schema: the purpose of mapping as we mentioned above. Remember, no matter how the information is structured physically, or how the schema is represented, the mapping must occur to leverage ontologies properly.

Another important notion of ontologies is *entity correspondence*. Ontologies that are leveraged in more of a B2B environment must leverage data that is scattered across very different information systems, and information that resides in many separate domains. Ontologies in this scenario provide a great deal of value because we can join information together, such as product information mapped to on-time delivery history, mapped to customer complaints and compliments (see Figure 19.1). This establishes entity correspondence.

To gather information specific to an entity, we need to leverage different resources to identify individual entities, which vary widely from each

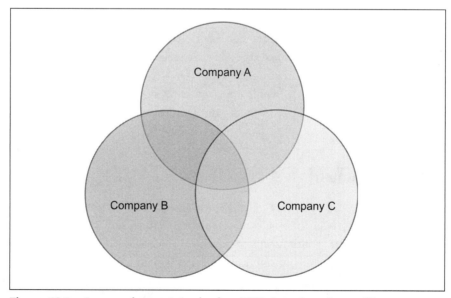

Figure 19.1   Leveraging ontologies in a B2B domain using entity correspondence.

Ontology and Mapping Servers

So, how do you implement ontologies in your application integration problem domain? In essence, some technology—either an integration broker or applications server, for example—needs to act as an *ontology server* and/or *mapping server*.

An ontology server houses the ontologies that are created to service the application integration problem domain.[6] There are thee types of ontologies stored: shared, resource, and application ontologies. *Shared* ontologies are made up of definitions of general terms that are common across and between enterprises. *Resource* ontologies are made up of definitions of terms used by a specific resource. *Application* ontologies are native to particular applications, such as an inventory application.

Mapping servers store the mappings between ontologies (stored in the ontology server). The mapping server also stores conversion functions, which account for the differences between schemas native to remote source and target systems. Mappings are specified using a declarative syntax that provides reuse.

---

physical information store. For example, when leveraging a relational database, entities are identified using keys (e.g., customer number). Within the various information systems, many different terms are used for attributes. The notion of ontologies, in this scenario, allows us to determine whether entities from different applications and databases are the same or noncrucial to fusing information.

Ontology Treatment

Ontologies have a wide range of applications. These include horizontal ontologies and vertical ontologies. *Horizontal ontologies* are general in nature, such as space-time relationships. These are common ontologies that span multiple domains, are not applicable to any single vertical space, and provide a

---

[6]From the DOME Project.

mechanism to organize and standardize information content. We've employed this type of ontology for years in the form of object models, hierarchies, taxonomies, and, in many cases, XML vocabularies.

Vertical ontologies, which also incorporate features from horizontal ontologies, are domain specific, such as natural languages for health care or financial services. Vertical ontologies not only define data in terms of semantics native to a particular vertical industry, they also contain rules and formal computer languages that can perform certain types of run-time automated reasoning. This means we understand the metadata, and have logic bound to the metadata, as well.

The use of vertical ontologies, which extend the capabilities of horizontal applications, is where the most value exists. As we learn to define these ontologies as common frameworks for specific business requirements, and define the reuse of such frameworks applicable across multiple like-domains, we also learn to apply languages and reasoning techniques. Ultimately this provides repeatable information formats, rules, and logic that, in turn, enable application integration architects to leverage existing solutions rather than form them from general-purpose middleware and application development technology.

RDF and Ontologies

Resource Description Framework (RDF), a part of the XML story, provides interoperability between applications that exchange information. RDF is another Web standard that's finding use everywhere, including application integration. RDF was developed by the W3C to provide a foundation of metadata interoperability across different resource description communities and is the basis for the W3C movement to ontologies such as the use of Web Ontology Language (OWL).

RDF uses XML to define a foundation for processing metadata and to provide a standard metadata infrastructure for both the Web and the enterprise. The difference between the two is that XML is used to transport data using a common format, while RDF is layered on top of XML— defining a broad category of data. When the XML data is declared to be of the RDF format, applications are then able to understand the data without understanding who sent it.

(continued)

RDF and Ontologies (*continued*)

RDF extends the XML model and syntax to be specified for describing either resources or a collection of information. (XML points to a resource in order to scope and uniquely identify a set of properties known as the schema.)

RDF metadata can be applied to many areas, including application integration. One example would be searching for data, and cataloging data and relationships. RDF is also able to support new technology (such as intelligent software agents and exchange of content rating).

RDF itself does not offer predefined vocabularies for authoring metadata. However, the W3C does expect standard vocabularies to emerge once the infrastructure for metadata interoperability is in place. Anyone, or any industry, can design and implement a new vocabulary. The only requirement is that all resources be included in the metadata instances using the new vocabulary.

RDF benefits application integration in that it supports the concept of a common metadata layer that is sharable throughout an enterprise or between enterprises. Thus, RDF can be used as a common mechanism for describing data within the application integration problem domain.

Web-Based Standards and Ontologies

The use of languages for ontology is beginning to appear, built on reasoning techniques that provide for the development of special-purpose reasoning services. In fact, the W3C is creating a Web standard for ontology language as part of its effort to define semantic standards for the Web. The *Semantic Web* is the abstract representation of data on the World Wide Web, based on the Resource Description Framework standards (see the "RDF and Ontologies" tidbit) and other standards still to be defined. It is being developed by the W3C, in collaboration with a large number of researchers and industrial partners.

In order for the Semantic Web to function, computers must have access to structured collections of information and sets of inference rules that they can use to conduct automated reasoning. This notion is known as knowledge representation. To this end, and in the domain of the World Wide Web, computers will find the meaning of semantic data by following hyperlinks to definitions of key terms and rules for logically reasoning about data. The resulting infrastructure will spur the development of automated Web services such as highly functional agents.[7] What's important here is that the work now being driven by the W3C as a way to manage semantics on the Web is applicable, at least at the component level, to the world of application integration, much like XML and Web services.

An example of the W3C contribution to the use of ontologies is the *Web Ontology Language*. OWL is a semantic markup language for publishing and sharing ontologies on the World Wide Web. OWL is derived from the DAML+OIL Web Ontology Language and builds upon the RDF. OWL assigns a specific meaning to certain RDF triples. The future Formal Specification, now in development at the W3C, specifies exactly which triples are assigned a specific meaning and offers a definition of the meaning. OWL only provides a semantic interpretation for those parts of an RDF graph that instantiate the schema. Any additional RDF statements resulting in additional RDF triples are allowed, but OWL is silent on the semantic consequences of such additional triples. An OWL ontology is made up of several components, some of which are optional, and some of which may be repeated.[8]

Using these Web-based standards as the jumping-off point for ontology and application integration, it's possible to define and automate the use of ontologies in both intra- and intercompany application integration domains—domains made up of thousands of systems, all with their own semantic meanings, bound together in a common ontology that makes short work of application integration and defines a common semantic meaning of data. This, indeed, is the goal.

Extending from the languages, we have several libraries available for a variety of vertical domains, including financial services and e-Business. We also have many knowledge editors that now exist to support the creation of ontologies, as well as the use of natural-language processing methodologies. We have seen these in commercially available knowledge mapping and visualization tools using standard notations such as UML.

---

[7]Berners-Lee, Tim, James Hendler, and Ora Lassila. May 2001. "The Semantic Web," *Scientific American.*

[8]Web Ontology Language (OWL) Guide Version 1.0, www.w3c.org.

Types of Vertical Ontologies

Moving forward with the notion that the application of ontologies in the vertical domains is where the most value exists, it's feasible to further define types of ontologies, or architectural approaches. For our purposes we can define them as:

- Information based
- Behavior based
- Process based

Information-based ontologies are the most basic of the architectural approaches. They simply define common information properties, concepts, rules, and how they relate one to another, using standard reference models that support information integration as well as knowledge sharing for a vertical domain. Information-based ontology is required in all domains, no matter if you leverage behavior-based or process-based ontologies. What is more, information-based ontologies typically require a repository.

Behavior-based ontologies define terminologies and concepts relevant to a particular application service that is repeatable across multiple vertical domains. A problem example of this is HIPPA processing, which is made up of common sets of functions as well as common sets of semantics. The purpose of this type of ontology architecture is to define standard semantic meaning around Service-Oriented Architecture (SOA), thus providing better reuse from problem domain to problem domain. It is interesting to note that the concept of semantics is missing from the current Web services-based standards, and the use of behavior-based ontologies is something that would fill that gap (for more information about this subject, see "The Web Services Scandal" by Jeffrey Pollock in the August 2002 issue of *Application Integration Journal*).

Process-based ontologies define terminologies and concepts around coordinating processes that are relevant to a vertical domain. This differs from behavior-based ontologies in that the process coordinates the use of both behavior (remote functions) and information (information passing between systems). However, like behavior-based ontologies, we are again looking to define standard semantic meaning to common processes that are transferable among vertical domains, such as Straight Through Processing (STP). Moreover, process-based ontologies define inputs, outputs, constraints, relations, hierarchies, sequences, subprocesses, and process control semantics.

Abstraction and Ontologies

When dealing with abstraction, certain characteristics of the objects are coded in the databases in such a manner that the set of characteristics is representative of real-world objects.[9] Depending on the importance of the information, or need for detail, the set of characteristics are defined as more or less detailed. This is, in essence, the notion of abstraction and ontologies.

To this end, in some instances, object-oriented modeling may be employed to define ontologies by defining information at different levels of abstraction. We define this by suggesting a number of specializations. In each specialization, a number of additional characteristics are required, thus increasing the level of detail in the original object. Being an object-oriented model, each specialization inherits the characteristics of the more generic object class. Using this model, you can mix and match ontologies for use inside of your application integration problem domain.

When using this type of ontology model, ontologies are translated into classes, and all classes have special operations for navigation in the ontology tree. This model can support both single and multiple inheritance.

Object abstraction and object-oriented modeling are helpful in creating ontologies for application integration. The support of inheritance is especially useful, considering the opportunity for reuse, as well as abstraction layers that offer various levels of detail.

Value of Ontologies

While there is no free lunch here, the use of the ontologies concept within modern application integration techniques and technologies seems to be a good match. Indeed, today we are already leveraging certain aspects of ontologies within most application integration projects, whether we understand the con-

---

[9]Fonseca, Frederico, Max Egenhover, and Clodoveu David. 1999. "Ontology-Driven Information Integration."

cept or not. The value here is to recognize ontologies as a concept that formalizes the management and integration of information, services, and processes . . . formalizing something we are already doing informally.

The real significance of ontologies—leveraging the reusable aspects—is within vertical domains where the use of common metadata, services, and processes has the most worth. Once we get semantics under control within vertical systems (more often, a collection of systems), application integration—or linking a common set of semantics to back-end systems—won't be as daunting as this process is today. What's more, the application of standards such as Semantic Web and OWL will make ontologies that much more attractive.

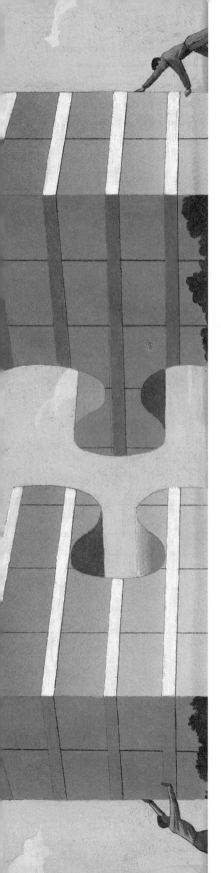

## CHAPTER TWENTY

Application Integration Manifesto

This chapter really sums up the concepts presented in the entire book, with a few new concepts added to make it worth the read, summarizing common patterns required into a manifesto, or features you're going to need when you solve your application integration problem.

The value of this chapter is that you can leverage it as a checklist as you select your application integration solution and customize it for your problem domain.

This by no means is the end of the line with application integration features and functions. As we progress and learn more, features and function will appear that provide value, as well as new enabling technology standards. This is an ongoing evolution, like everything else with technology.

If application integration is a critical success factor for most enterprises today, then the approaches and technologies leveraged within these problem domains should have some common features that will make the implementation of application integration technology successful. Indeed, we see common patterns within most strategic implementations of application integration technology, including transformation and routing, transaction control, information management, and metadata management. These tactical components may extend well beyond a single product, but have more to do with the requirements driving the selection of the solutions or technologies than the needs of the existing programs and systems.

Within many other types of technologies is a common set of patterns that distinguishes that technology as unique and of high value. These patterns provide discipline, and repeatable solutions allow us to approach each application integration problem domain with ease.

Repeatable solutions require knowledge of implementation strategies. To this end, it's a logical conclusion that a set of policies will provide those looking to implement application integration within their enterprise with rules to the game, or a manifesto.

The goal of this manifesto is not to create static rules and regulations governing application integration solutions, but to provide a set of solution patterns that are applicable to the application integration problem, be they complex or simplistic. While some patterns will bring value to your particular problem domain, other won't have the same impact. However, you must also consider issues you'll have to deal with in the future and look at application integration for what it is: strategic infrastructure.

Please note that this manifesto is independent of standards such as ebXML, XML, JCA, and JMS, instead focusing on the core functionality. How you implement the technology in your organization, including enabling technology and standards, will be up to you and, indeed, will change over time. This manifesto is a long-term set of policies that are independent of technology and standards.

As part of this manifesto, we will consider some features or patterns as mandatory, something that you really should have in your application integration solution stack to meet your current requirements as well as requirements that will emerge in the future. It's important that you understand this, or you will have the ungodly task of ripping out infrastructure and interfaces, and rebuilding them using another set of technologies. In other words, it's better to make sure your solution set of choice lives up to your expectations now and into the future. Hence, they must live up to the manifesto.

Mandatory

As I alluded to above, these features are mandatory due to their importance in solving the application integration problem, or a complete stack of features that will allow you to approach most problem domains. Keep in mind that, while some features won't find service in some application integration projects, you'll need them as part of your infrastructure as your problem domain changes and grows in scope. In other words, the notion here is to create an application integration technology stack that serves the application needs of your enterprise now and into the future. This is very important when you consider the cost of replacing the technology or, more importantly, the strategic issues of not having the proper application integration infrastructure to react to changes in the industry.

Connectivity

The heart of any application integration technology stack is the ability to extract information and invoke remote services contained in remote information systems—one or many. This is the fundamental jumping-off point for application integration. The value of this type of technology is the ability to connect to complex (and perhaps archaic) systems and manage the production of information and services out of those systems, and at the same time, publish information to those systems as needed.

We can define *connectivity* as any pattern of technology, typically software systems, that connects into source or target systems through some type of point of integration (see Figure 20.1).

We need connectivity for several reasons:

- First, we need some sort of reusable set of software services that can extract and publish information to source or target systems, which saves us from having to build those interfaces as "one-offs" each and every time we do an application integration project.
- Second, we need common interfaces into source or target systems that provide a consistent set of services.

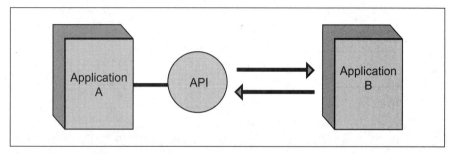

Figure 20.1   Connectivity.

- Finally, we need management visibility into connections to source and target systems' connections. We need this for reliability, as source and target systems are known to go down from time to time, so we can manage through those outages.

Support for Information-Oriented Connections

When dealing with simple information, information-oriented connectivity merely leverages whatever interface is available to extract information from the source system and move that information into the integration server. For example, customer address information coming from SAP may be transformed to account for differences in application semantics, and then published to a target system (or systems), say, PeopleSoft, using the same type of information-oriented connectivity.

Information-oriented connections offer certain advantages.

- First, we're dealing with simple information, so we usually don't have to change source and target systems. Most applications, certainly databases, already know how to produce and consume simple information.
- Second, we don't need to manage complex issues such as state, logic, and sequencing because there is no notion of behavior, just information.
- Finally, this approach is easy to understand and is in wide use.

In many cases, the information-oriented approach is the correct solution. Using service or business process integration to integrate systems is contraindicated for many problem domains when looking at the business problems they are trying to solve. In fact, you'll find that service and business process integration approaches to application integration are overapplied.

Accessing information within databases and applications is a relatively easy task, accomplished with few—if any—significant changes to the application logic or database structure. This is a tremendous asset because altering applications is not possible in many problem domains, such as supply chains, where you are likely dealing with systems that are beyond your direct control.

However, the straightforward appearance of information-oriented connectivity should not create the impression that it is simple. It is not. Migrating data from one system to another sounds straightforward and reasonable enough, but in order for information-oriented connectivity to actually work, architects and developers need to understand all integrated systems in detail.

Application semantics make this problem even more complex. Typically, application semantics in one system are not compatible with other systems—the semantics are so different that the two systems just can't understand each other. For example, sales accounting practices might be different, as well as invoice numbers and customer sales data. Thus, Information-Oriented Application Integration is not just about moving information between data stores, but also managing the differences in schema and content (see the "Transformation" section later in this manifesto).

Support for Service-Oriented Connections (a.k.a. Web Services)

Service-oriented connectivity is a bit more complex, but nonetheless important. Instead of dealing with the extraction and publication of simple information to source or target systems, service-oriented adapters have to abstract services or application behavior as well. In other words, they need to expose application functions in a way that they may be abstracted into a composite application as a local function that actually exists on a remote system (see Figure 20.2). Remember, even though the function appears local to the composite application,

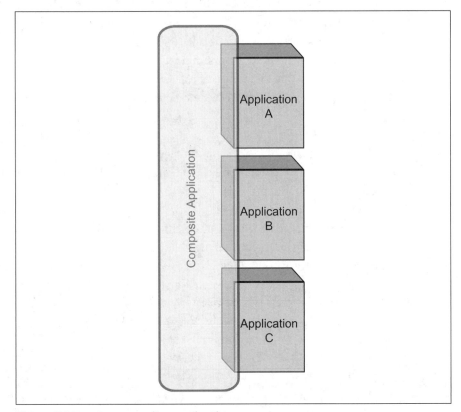

Figure 20.2   A composite application.

the application processing occurs in the remote system that is connected through a service-oriented connectivity subsystem (adapter).

In essence, service-oriented connections take remote function calls within remote systems for other applications, and do so without having the applications understand anything about each other. Of course, service-oriented connections have to be linked through some type of integration server or application server to facilitate the extension into the composite applications, and to account for the differences in the applications, including semantics and enabling technology.

Service-oriented connectivity is a result of the interest in service-oriented architectures and the use of standards such as Web services, and perhaps some lingering use of more traditional distributed objects. However, creating service-oriented connectivity, in practice, is a bit of a challenge considering that the "connection" has to interact with internal application functions, rather than just application information. You're extending the behavior of that application to other applications, making the application functions appear native.

Service-oriented connectivity allows enterprises to share common application services as well as information. Enterprises accomplish this sharing either by defining application services they can share, and therefore integrate, or by providing the infrastructure for such application service sharing. Application services can be shared by hosting them on a central server, or by accessing them interapplication (e.g., through distributed objects or Web services).

Support for Coupling

Coupling, in the context of application integration, is the binding of applications together in such a way that they are dependent upon each other, sharing the same methods, interfaces, and, perhaps, data.

In essence, coupling is the tight binding of one application domain to the next. As a consequence of this requirement, all coupled applications and databases will have to be extensively changed to couple them. Further, as events and circumstances evolve over time, any change to any source or target system demands a corresponding change to the coupled systems, as well. Coupling creates one application and database out of many, with each tightly dependent upon the other. Service-Oriented Application Integration clearly leverages coupling in how applications are bound together.

Support for Cohesion

Cohesion is the "act or state of sticking together," or "the logical agreement." Cohesively integrated applications and databases are independent from one another. Changes to any source or target system should not directly affect the others. In this scenario, information can be shared between databases and applications without worrying about changes to applications or databases, leveraging some type of loosely coupled middleware layer to move information between applications and make adjustments for differences in application semantics.

You need to consider the tradeoffs. Cohesion provides the greatest flexibility as the application integration solution moves into the future, but it is not always the right fit. Some problems domains (e.g., service-oriented solutions) are better addressed with coupling.

Systems can be added to, changed, or removed from a cohesive application integration solution without typically requiring changes to any other system in the problem domain. Integration brokers provide the technology infrastructure of most cohesive application integration solutions. They are able to account for the differences between systems, accommodating differences in application semantics within a middle-tier process.

Despite cohesion's flexibility, if common business processes are to be reused, then a coupled approach provides more value. Distributed objects, transaction processing monitors, application servers, and, of course, Web services provide a good technology solution for a coupled application integration solution.

Support for Transaction-Oriented Connections

Transactional connections require that complex application requests be divided into bite-sized units called transactions. Transactional middleware, a component of an integration server or an application integration solution set (integration server, application server, or a combination), controls transactions from their beginning to their end, from the client to the resource server and then back again. It's important that we deal with transactions at the connection level because the remote functions contained in source or target systems must participate in the transaction.

In these scenarios, transactions are either all or nothing. Either they work or they do not. A transaction is never left incomplete. As a result, transactional middleware always leaves the system in a stable state. This provides the application integration architect with a reliable integration model to support transactional business solutions.

Support for Abstraction

The notion of abstraction, in terms of connectivity, lets us think about collections of data or services as abstract entities, thus represented in a form that is most useful to the integration server or the application integration architect. It's this notion that provides for the grouping of related pieces of information independent of their physical location and structure, as well as defining and understanding what meaningful operations can be performed on the data or services.

In other words, abstraction in its use with connectivity and application integration allows us to redefine the look, feel, and behavior of certain data sets and application services that are local to source or target systems. This means we can represent the data set or application service in a manner that best fits the needs of the application integration problem you are attempting to solve.

This also means enforcing certain restrictions on the use of the data or service, based on the needs of the application integration scenario, as well as streamlining the task of reasoning about the data or service. We've employed this concept with great success in the world of object-oriented technology for years.

What's more, we need to separate the implementation from the abstraction itself, so we can change the internal representation and/or implementation without changing the abstract behavior, and so people can use the abstraction in terms of connectivity without needing to understand the internal implementation.[1]

Transformation

The transformation layer is the "Rosetta Stone" of the system. It understands the format of all information being transmitted among the applications and translates that information on the fly, restructuring data from one message so that it makes sense to the receiving application or applications. It provides a common dictionary that contains information on how each application communicates outside itself (application externalization), as well as which bits of information have meaning to which applications.

Transformation layers generally contain parsing and pattern-matching methods that describe the structure of any message format. Message formats are then constructed from pieces that represent each field encapsulated within a message. Once the message has been broken down into its component parts, the fields may be recombined to create a new message.

Most integration servers can handle most types of information, including fixed, delimited, and variable. Information is reformatted using an interface that

---

[1]Goldman, Kenneth J. 1996-97. "Data Abstraction."

the user integration server provides, which may be as primitive as an API, or as easy to use as a GUI.

There are a few aspects to the notion of transformation:

Support for Differences in Application Semantics

Accounting for the differences in application semantics is the process of changing the structure of a message, and thus remapping the structure and data types so that it is acceptable to the target system. Although it is not difficult, application integration architects need to understand that this process must occur dynamically within the integration server.

This process can be defined within the rules-processing layer of the integration server by creating a rule to translate data dynamically, depending on its content and schema. Moving information from one system to another demands that the schema/format of the message be altered as the information is transferred from one system to the next.

Although most integration servers can map any schema to any other schema, it is prudent to try to anticipate extraordinary circumstances. For example, when converting information extracted from an object-oriented database and placing it in a relational database, the integration server must convert the object schema into a relational representation before it can convert the data within the message. The same holds true when moving information from a relational database to an object-oriented database. Most integration servers break the message moving into their environment into a common format and then translate it into the appropriate message format for the target system.

Support for Differences in Content

Related to the concept of accounting for the differences in application semantics, accounting for content changes is another important aspect of transformation. In short, it's the reformatting of information so that it appears native when sent to a target system. The information needs to appear native, requiring that changes be made to source or target systems.

Although many formats exist within most application integration problem domains, we will confine our attention, for the purposes of this manifesto, to the following:

- Alphanumeric
- Binary integers

- Floating point values
- Bit fields
- IBM mainframe floating points
- COBOL and PL/I picture data
- BLOBs

In addition to these formats, there are a number of formatting issues to address, including the ability to convert logical operators (bits) between systems and the ability to handle data types that are not supported in the target system. These issues often require significant customization in order to facilitate successful communication between systems.

In data conversion, values are managed in two ways: carrying over the value from the source to the target system without change, or modifying the data value dynamically. Either an algorithm or a look-up table can be used to modify the data value. One or more of the source application attributes may use an algorithm to change the data or create new data.

Algorithms of this type are nothing more than the type of data conversions we have done for years when populating data warehouses and data marts. Now, in addition to using these simple algorithms, it is possible to aggregate, combine, and summarize the data to meet the specific requirements of the target application.

When using the look-up table scenario, it might be necessary to convert to an arbitrary value. "ARA" in the source system might refer to a value in the accounts receivable system. However this value may be determined, it must be checked against the look-up table. Integration servers may convert dollars to yen using a currency conversion table, which may be embedded in a simple procedure or, more likely, in a database connected to the integration server. The integration server may also invoke a remote application server function to convert the amount.

The application integration architect or developer may encounter special circumstances that have to be finessed. The length of a message attribute may be unknown, or the value may be in an unknown order. In such situations, it is necessary to use the rules-processing capability of the integration server to convert the problem values into the proper representation for the target system.

Support for Abstract Data Types

Transformation mechanisms also need to support abstract data types (ADTs), allowing different representation of data and behavior to meet the requirement of the application integration scenario.

ADTs provide a mechanism with a clear separation between the interface and implementation of the data type, including the representation of the data, or choosing the data structure, and the operations of the data

The interface with the abstract data type is created through an associated operation. What's more, the data structures that store the representation of an abstract data type are invisible to the integration view. The ADT also includes any operations, or algorithms, contained with the ADT.

The internal representation and execution of these operations is changeable at any time and won't affect the interface to the ADTs. Thus, a completely different representation is possible for sets storing information in the ADT.

Having said all that, ADTs consist of:

- An interface, or a set of operations that can be performed
- The allowable behaviors, or the way we expect instances of the ADT to respond to operations

The implementation of an ADT consists of:

- An internal representation—data stored inside the source or target system's variables
- A set of methods implementing the interface
- A set of representation invariants, true initially and preserved by all methods

Information Routing

In addition to transformation, information routing is another core feature that provides a mechanism to move information from system to system. We have a few scenarios that apply, including:

- One to one
- Many to many
- Many to one

It's important that your integration technology can route information from many systems to many systems, as well as split information coming from one system to be sent to multiple targets, and combine information coming from many systems for a single target. While this sounds simple, the application of the mechanism is far from simple. We must introduce the notion of behavior to operate on this information.

Intelligent Routing

Intelligent routing, sometimes referred to as flow control or content-based routing, builds on the capabilities of both the rules layer and the semantic transformation layer. An integration server can "intelligently route" a message by first identifying it as coming from the source application and then routing it to the proper target application, translating it if required.

For example, when a message arrives at the integration server, it is analyzed and identified as coming from a particular system and/or subsystem. Once the message is identified and the message schema is understood, the applicable rules and services are applied to the processing of the message, including transformation. Once the information is processed, the integration server, based on how it is programmed, routes the message to the correct target system. This all takes place virtually instantaneously, with as many as a thousand of these operations occurring at the same time.

Filters

In addition to intelligent routing, it's important to provide the notion of filtering, as well. In the world of application integration, filters are software subsystems that are able to analyze content and selectively leave out specific information based on content or, perhaps, source or target information.

Filters are important to application integration due to the complexity of information coming from source systems and the need to simplify that information before it's processed in the integration server or sent to the target system. The notion of filtering is well defined, and the act of filtering is a mandatory feature.

Persistence

In addition to processing information in flight, application integration technology requires that information consumed from a source system and published to a target system be persisted native to the application integration technology.

Persistence can take many forms, including simple logging to track the progress of information flowing from application to application, or even the invocation of remote application services (e.g., Web services). Or it can be more sophisticated, such as the ability to track and maintain state for long-term, durable business transactions, or even to provide some decision support capabilities through message warehousing.

Logging

Logging is the physical storage of information and processing that takes place on that information in a physical file or database that is local to the application integration technology. Its purpose is threefold:

- Auditing
- Fail-safe
- Transaction tracking

Auditing refers to the technology's ability to keep track of all information and service invocations during a specific period of time, and report on both the information and processing at any time for any reason. Auditing is very important because we need to keep track of the movement of information in support of business transactions, transactions that may have to be examined in the future to determine discrepancies or, perhaps, to track problems down within the application integration solution.

Auditing logs record all information that flows in and out of the integration server, as well as any transformation, filtering, or validation operations. We also track how other external systems operate on the data, such as those connected to the application integration technology using distributed standards such as Web services. Remember, the core issue that auditing attempts to address is accountability of the application integration solution for normal business processing.

What is more, auditing may be used to determine the health of the application integration solution and provide the ability to solve any problems that are noted. For example, by using the auditing facilities of an integration server, it is possible to determine message traffic loads, message content variations, and the amount of information requiring transformation. Auditing also tracks information that changes, the state of information before the transformation, and its state following transformation.

Fail-safe is another issue to address when considering logging. This means the information processed by an application integration solution is not only interesting from a business perspective, but is also required to recover the system in the event of a network or server malfunction. It's the role of a fail-safe logging mechanism to record and track information flowing in and out of the system, persisting the information as it's processed. By persisting the information during processing, the fail-safe mechanism is able to pick up where it left off after hardware and software failures, perhaps rolling the application integration processing back so the source and target systems are not left in an unstable or unreliable state.

Similar to fail-safe logging, *transaction tracking* logs the functioning of the integration server in support of transactions, including two-phase commit as well as short- and long-term transactions. This also relates to transaction controls (presented later).

Message Warehousing

A bit different from general-purpose persistence as described previously, a message warehouse is also mandatory. A message warehouse is a database that, as an option, is able to store information that flows through the integration server. In general, integration servers provide this message persistence facility to meet several requirements: message mining and message archiving.

Message mining allows the extraction of business data to support decisions, creating the message warehouse as a quasi-data warehouse. For example, it is possible to use the message warehouse to determine the characteristics and amount of new customer information that is being processed through the integration server. All new sales orders for a given period of time can be displayed. Off-the-shelf data-mining and reporting tools work wonderfully for such applications.

Information that is stored in the message warehouse is almost always stored without modification. However, in a few cases, the information must flow through a data warehouse as it would an aggregation or transformation process. The data is combined and altered so that it will make sense to the average business user. In general, application integration architects and application programmers accomplish this through the rules-processing mechanism of the integration server (or they may employ an outside application to alter the message for storage).

Message warehousing can provide services such as message integrity because the warehouse itself provides a natural, persistent state for message traffic. This also provides state-full messaging, or the ability to maintain states between two or more systems even when using asynchronous messaging; messaging that, by definition, is a cohesive rather than coupled mechanism.

Transactionality

Transactionality is mandatory for all application integration solutions for obvious reasons. We must ensure the delivery and processing of certain business information and, in doing so, need to support the notion of a transaction.

As we discussed above when considering connectivity, transactional application integration solutions require that complex applications be divided into bite-sized units called transactions. Transactionality controls transactions from their beginning to their end, from the client to the resource server and then back again.

An easy way to remember the properties of a transaction is to put it to the "ACID" test. That is, a transaction has ACID properties if it is Automic, Consistent, Isolated, and Durable.

Automic refers to the all-or-nothing quality of transactions. Either the transaction completes, or it does not. There is no available middle ground. *Consistent* refers to the fact that the system is always in a consistent state, regardless of whether it completes the transaction or not. *Isolated* refers to the transaction's ability to work independently of other transactions that may be running in the same TP monitor environment. *Durable* means that the transaction, once committed and complete, can survive system failures.

Although the ACID test might oversimplify the concept of a transaction in the context of connectivity, it provides an easy acronym for remembering the features and functions of transactional connections.

Moreover, we must provide transactional control between systems that may not, unto themselves, support transactions. And clearly we must also provide support for transactions between systems that are transactional in nature and provide nesting transaction support and support for transactional standards such as two-phase commit.

Application integration architects can count on a high degree of application integrity with transactional connectivity—even in heterogeneous environments of very different operating systems and databases. The most important benefit of transactional middleware is that a transaction is always secure. Even when other things go wrong, transactional middleware won't allow those problems to affect any other transaction, application, or data.

To this end, we can divide transactions into three types, all mandatory: short-term, long-term, and state management.

Short-Term Transactions

Short-term transactions are typically business transactions with a short duration, such as purchasing a book online. The payment is made, the product is shipped, the accounting database is updated, and it's over.

Most transactions, as you may have guessed, are short-term transactions due to the nature of how we do business. These transactions have the following characteristics:

- These transactions are durable for a short period of time, typically less than a day.
- Small amounts of simple data such as invoices, SKUs, and customer data make up these types of transactions.
- These transactions are numerous, typically more than 1,000 an hour for many businesses.

Long-Term Transactions

Long-term transactions, in contrast to short-term, are durable for a long period of time, perhaps months or years. These transactions are more difficult to track due to the complexities of monitoring transactional conditions over such a duration. Examples of long-term transactions are the construction of a house or office building, or collaboration in the development of a product or service. These types of transactions have the following characteristics:

- They are durable for a long period of time, typically more than a day.
- They support complex data, perhaps tracking special metadata just for a particular transaction.
- They are few in number, typically less than 10 a day, and in some cases much fewer.

State Management

Finally, state management is another mandatory feature. This refers to the ability of the application integration solution to track the current state of an application integration transaction through long- and short-term transactions.

State retention is important to application integration due to the number of integration transactions that may be running at an instance in time, and making sure that all sync points are recorded during the duration. Applications entering or exiting the transaction will have context as to how they participate in both the production and consumption of information as well as remote service management.

Process Awareness

Process awareness integration is a strategy as much as a technology, providing your organization with the ability to interact with any number of systems—inside or outside the organization—by integrating entire business processes both within and between enterprises; it is also mandatory.

Indeed, process awareness integration delivers application integration by dealing with several organizations and internal systems, using various metadata, platforms, and processes. Process awareness integration even deals with people and other non-IT-related entities that may participate in a process. Thus, process awareness integration technology must be flexible, providing a translation layer between the source and target systems and the process awareness integration engine. Moreover, process awareness integration technology needs to work with several types of technologies and interface patterns.

Process awareness integration is really another complete layer on the stack, over and above more traditional application integration approaches, including Information-Oriented and Service-Oriented (Web services) Application Integration. This includes the following:

- A single instance of process awareness integration typically spans many instances of traditional application integration, including information and services.
- Application integration typically means the exchange of information between two or more systems without visibility into internal processes. Process awareness integration defines a master application that has visibility into many encapsulated application services and application information.
- Process awareness integration leads with a process model and moves information between applications and invokes internal application services in support of that model.
- Process awareness integration is independent of the source and target applications. Changes can be made to the processes without having to change the source or target systems.
- Application integration is typically a tactical solution, motivated by the requirement for two or more applications to communicate. Process awareness integration is strategic, leveraging business rules to determine how systems should interact and better leverage the business value from each system through a common abstract business model.

Thus, process awareness integration is the science and mechanism of managing the movement of data, and the invocation of application services in the correct and proper order to support the management and execution of common processes that exist in and between organizations and internal applications. Process awareness integration provides another layer of easily defined and centrally managed processes that exist on top of a set of processes, application services, and data within any set of applications.

It's mandatory that a process awareness integration layer bound to an application integration solution support

- Processes
- Subprocesses
- Hierarchies
- Inheritance
- Service control
- Information movement

Support for Modeling

Modeling is the ability to create a common, agreed-upon process between computer systems, automating the integration of all information systems to react in real time to business events such as increased consumer demand, material shortages, and quality problems.

Support for Monitoring (a.k.a. Business Activity Monitoring)

Monitoring is the ability to monitor all aspects of the business and enterprise or trading community to determine the current state of the process in real time.

Support for Optimization

Optimization is the ability to redefine the process at any given time in support of the business and thus make the process more efficient.

Support for Abstraction

Abstraction is the ability to hide the complexities of the local applications from the business users and have the business users work with a common set of business semantics.

Need for Rules

It's important to note that the above manifesto is a set of mandatory features you should employ within your application integration solution and implementation of that solution within your problem domain. The purpose is to serve not only your current application integration requirements—inside and outside the organization—but also the application integration requirements that you may encounter in the future. In other words, it's a checklist of features you must have in order to ensure success now and in the future. Fail to follow this manifesto, and you will run the risk of failure.

Glossary

Note: Some terms are taken directly from
www.messageq.com *(with permission).*

Advanced Program-to-Program Communication (APPC):
IBM's solution for program-to-program communication, distributed transaction processing, and remote data access across the IBM product line.

application interface-level EAI: Refers to the leveraging of interfaces exposed by custom or packaged applications. Developers leverage these interfaces to access both business processes and simple information. Using these interfaces, developers are able to bundle together many applications, allowing them to share business logic and information. The only limitations that developers face are the specific features and functions of the application interfaces.

Application Link Enabling (ALE): A SAP R/3 technology that combines business process with middleware. ALE provides a robust distributed architecture for SAP, giving transparent distributed access to both SAP data and processes. The ALE architecture is also essential for moving information to non-SAP systems and, ultimately, supporting the entire EAI effort.

Application Programming Interface (API): An interface that enables different programs to communicate with each other.

application servers: Servers that provide not only for the sharing and processing of application logic, but also the connections to back-end resources. These resources include databases, ERP applications, and even traditional mainframe applications. Application servers also provide user interface development mechanisms. Additionally, they usually provide mechanisms to deploy the application to the platform of the Web.

asynchronous communication: A form of communication by which sending and receiving applications can operate independently so that they do not have to be running or available simultaneously. An application sends a request and may or may not wait for a response. See also *nonblocking communication.*

automatic binding: Describes the action when an RPC client stub locates a specific server on a list of servers.

backbone: A series of connections that forms a major communication pathway within a network.

bandwidth: The amount of data that can be sent through a connection; usually measured in bits per second. A fast modem can move about 15,000 bits in one second (about a page of English text).

binding: The association of a client and a server.

BizTalk: An industry initiative headed by Microsoft to promote XML as the common data exchange language for application integration.

blocking communication: A synchronous messaging process whereby the requestor of a service must wait until a response is received.

buffered queue: A message queue that resides in memory.

Business Application Programming Interface (BAPI): Provides an object-oriented mechanism to get at the underlying proprietary SAP middleware technology, such as RFCs. In addition to providing access to the data and processes, a benefit once possible only by means of specific methods, a BAPI allows access to the SAP Business Objects held in the Business Object Repository (BOR), encapsulated in their data and processes.

Business Component API: Allows internal and external applications to invoke business rules encapsulated within PeopleSoft as well as simple access data. This interface provides a high-level abstraction layer hiding the complexities of the PeopleSoft system from those that invoke the Business Component API.

Business Process Execution Language for Web Services (BPEL4WS): An XML-based language for describing portable business processes.

Business Process Integration-Oriented Application Integration (BPIOAI): Approaching applications integration by controlling information flow and service invocation through a business process.

business process management: The concept of shepherding work items through a multi-step process. The items are identified and tracked as they move through each step, with either specified people or applications processing the information. The process flow is determined by process logic, and the applications (or processes) themselves play virtually no role in determining where the messages are sent.

Business Process Modeling Language (BPML): An extensible markup language developed by the BPMI as a means of modeling business processes.

Business to Business (B2B): The exchange of information and application services between two or more companies in support of business.

common business model: The aggregation and high-level model of all objects, methods, properties, procedural logic, batch processing, and everything else in the enterprise that processes information.

Common Object Request Broker Architecture (CORBA): An object model standard maintained by the OMG. It is a competing object model of COM/DCOM and JavaBeans.

Common Programming Interface-Communications (CPI-C): IBM's SNA peer-to-peer API that can run over SNA and TCP/IP. It masks the complexity of APPC.

communication middleware: Software that provides interapplication connectivity based on communication styles such as message queuing, ORBs, and publish/subscribe.

communication protocol: A formally defined system for controlling the exchange of information over a network or communication channel.

Component Object Model (COM): Microsoft's standard for distributed objects; an object encapsulation technology that specifies interfaces between component objects within a single application or between applications. It separates the interface from the implementation and provides APIs for dynamically locating objects and for loading and invoking them. See also *Distributed Component Object Model.*

Computer-Aided Software Engineering (CASE): An automated set of tools that allows a system designer to model a computer system or database before actually programming the system or creating the physical database.

connectionless communication: Communication that does not require a dedicated connection or session between applications.

data-level EAI: The process—and the techniques and technology—of moving data between data stores. This can be described as extracting information from one database, perhaps processing that information as needed, and updating it in another database. While this sounds direct and straightforward, in a typical EAI-enabled enterprise, implementing EAI might mean drawing from as many as 100 databases and several thousands of tables. It may also include the transformation and application of business logic to the data that is being extracted and loaded.

data-level integration: A form of EAI that integrates different data stores to allow the sharing of information among applications. It requires the loading of data directly into the database via its native interface and does not involve the changing of business logic.

data transformation: A key requirement of EAI and message brokers. There are two basic kinds of data transformation: Syntactic translation changes one data set into another (such as different date or number formats), while semantic transformation changes data based on the underlying data definitions or meaning.

data warehouse: A database that receives relevant information from several operational databases. Data warehouses are almost exclusively used for decision support.

database middleware: Allows clients to invoke SQL-based services across multivendor databases. This middleware is defined by de facto standards such as ODBC, DRDA, and RDA.

digital certificate: An electronic "credit card" that establishes your credentials when doing a business transaction over the Internet.

directory services: A way for clients to locate services. Usually contained in a single system image of available servers.

Distributed Component Object Model (DCOM): Microsoft's protocol that enables software components to communicate directly over a network in a reliable, secure, and efficient manner. DCOM is based on the DCE-RPC specification and works with both Java applets and ActiveX components through its use of the COM object model.

Distributed Computing Environment (DCE): From the Open Software Foundation, provides key distributed technologies such as RPC, distributed naming service, time synchronization service, distributed file systems, and network security.

Document Object Model (DOM): A programming interface specification developed by the W3C allowing a programmer to create and modify HTML pages and XML documents as objects.

Electronic Business XML (ebXML): A project to use XML as a standard and secure way to exchange business data between companies.

Electronic Data Interchange (EDI): A standard for sharing information between trading partners in support of supply chain integration.

Enterprise Application Integration (EAI): The unrestricted sharing of information between two or more enterprise applications. A set of technologies that allows the movement and exchange of information between different applications and business processes within and between organizations.

Enterprise JavaBeans (EJB): An architecture for setting up program components written in Java.

Entity Relationship Diagram (ERD): A graphical representation of a conceptual or physical database design.

Extensible Markup Language (XML): Like HTML, a subset of Standard Generalized Markup Language (SGML), a standard for defining descriptions of structure and content in documents. However, whereas HTML is concerned with the presentation of information on a Web page (without context or dynamic behavior), XML provides context and gives meaning to data.

Extensible Stylesheet Language (XSL): A simple, declarative language that programmers use to bind rules to elements in XML documents and so provide behavior.

fault-tolerance: The ability of a system to recover from typical system problems, such as network or processor failures.

gateway: A hardware and/or software setup that performs translations between disparate protocols.

groupware: A collection of technologies that allows the representation of complex processes that center around collaborative human activities. It is a model for client/server computing based on five foundation technologies: multimedia document management, workflow, e-mail, conferencing, and scheduling.

heterogeneity: A typical enterprise information system today includes many types of computer technology, from PCs to mainframes. These technologies include a wide variety of different operating systems, application software, and in-house-developed applications. EAI solves the complex problem of making a heterogeneous infrastructure more coherent.

HIPAA (Health Insurance Portability and Accountability Act): A government mandate that deals with protecting health insurance coverage for people who lose or change jobs, as well as the standardization of health care-related information systems and how information flows between them. HIPAA is based on EDI X.12.

Hypertext Markup Language (HTML): The set of markup symbols inserted in a file intended for display on a World Wide Web browser. The markup instructs the Web browser how to display a Web page.

information: Machine-readable content or data that is in the correct format to be processed by an application or system.

Information-Oriented Application Integration (IOAI): An approach to application integration where the source and target systems exchange information in real time.

integrity: In a client/server environment, integrity means that the server code and server data are centrally maintained and therefore secure and reliable.

intelligent routing: Sometimes referred to as "flow control" or "content-based routing," intelligent routing builds on the capabilities of both the rules layer and the message translation layer. In this scenario, the message broker can identify a message coming from the source application and route it to the proper target application, translating it if required.

Intermediate Document (IDOC): A structured information set providing a standard format for moving information in and out of a SAP system. In this regard, it represents a concept similar to EDI, but IDOC is not a standard. It is possible to invoke an RFC at the SAP level and get an IDOC as a result.

Internet Inter-ORB Protocol (IIOP): A standard that ensures interoperability for objects in a multivendor ORB environment.

Inter-Process Communication (IPC): A mechanism allowing applications to communicate with one another at the process level.

invasive integration: An implementation approach that requires changes or additions to existing applications—the opposite of *noninvasive integration.*

Java 2 Platform, Enterprise Edition (J2EE): A Java platform designed for highly scalable computing.

Java Database Connectivity (JDBC): An API specification for connecting Java programs to databases.

Java Message System (JMS): An API for Java that supports message queuing.

legacy application: An older application that serves a valuable purpose in an organization, but is not considered state-of-the art in terms of technology.

load balancing: Automatic balancing of requests among replicated servers to ensure that no server is overloaded.

Logical Unit 6.2 (LU6.2): IBM's device-independent process-to-process protocol provides the facilities for peer-to-peer communication between two programs and also supports asynchronous networking.

message broker: A key component of EAI, a message broker is an intelligent intermediary that directs the flow of messages between applications, which become sources and consumers of information. Message brokers provide a very flexible communication backbone and such services as data transformation, message routing, and message warehousing.

Message-Oriented Middleware (MOM): Used for connecting applications running on different operating systems, most commonly through the use of message queuing.

message queuing (MQ): A form of communication between programs. Application data is combined with a header (information about the data) to form a message. Messages are stored in queues, which can be buffered or persistent. Message queuing is an asynchronous communication style and provides a loosely coupled exchange across multiple operating systems. See also *buffered queue* and *persistent queue.*

message routing: A super-application process where messages are routed to applications based on business rules. A particular message may be directed based on its subject or actual content.

message warehousing: A central repository for temporarily storing messages for analysis or transmission.

method-level EAI: The sharing of the business logic that may exist within the enterprise. For example, the method for updating a customer record may be accessed from any number of applications, and applications may access each other's methods without having to rewrite each method within the respective application.

middleware: Software that facilitates the communication between two applications. It provides an API through which applications invoke services, and it controls the transmission of the data exchange over the network. There are three basic types: communication middleware, database middleware, and systems middleware.

nonblocking communication: An asynchronous messaging process whereby the requestor of a service does not have to wait until a response is received from another application.

noninvasive integration: An implementation approach that does not require changes or additions to existing applications.

normalization: The process of organizing information into tables in such a way that the result of using the information is always unambiguous.

Object Management Group (OMG): A consortium of object vendors and the founders of the CORBA standard.

object middleware: Allows clients to invoke methods or objects that reside on a remote server. This middleware revolves around OMG's CORBA and Microsoft's DCOM.

Object Request Broker (ORB): Software that allows objects to dynamically discover each other and interact across machines, operating systems, and networks.

OpenDoc: A set of shared class libraries with platform-independent interfaces.

Open Database Connectivity (ODBC): A Windows-standard API for SQL communications.

Open Integration Framework (OIF): Clearly outlines the options that are available to those looking to integrate with PeopleSoft, including up-to-date mechanisms such as XML and its latest Business Component API appearing with PeopleTools 8.

Organization for the Advancement of Structured Information Standards (OASIS): A nonprofit international consortium whose goal is to promote the adoption of product-independent standards for information formats.

patterns: Formalize and streamline the idea of EAI—to build once at the application level and then reuse throughout the solution domain. Patterns describe recurring design problems that appear in certain design contexts. They describe generic schemes for the solution of the problems, solution schemes created by defining their components, responsibilities, and relationships.

persistent queue: A message queue that resides on a permanent device, such as a disk, and can be recovered in case of system failure.

Portal-Oriented Application Integration (POAI): Approaching application integration by aggregating the information contained in many back-end systems within a portal.

process automation: Sometimes referred to as "workflow," process automation is the science of managing the movement of data and the invocation of processes in the correct and proper order. Process automation provides another layer of easily defined and centrally managed processes (or workflows) that exist on top of an existing set of processes and data contained within a set of enterprise applications.

public key infrastructure (PKI): Allows users of public networks to exchange data using a public and private cryptographic key pair that is obtained and shared through a trusted authority.

publish/subscribe (pub/sub): A style of interapplication communication. Publishers are able to broadcast data to a community of information users or subscribers who have issued the type of information they wish to receive (normally defining topics or subjects of interest). An application or user can be both a publisher and a subscriber.

Relational Database Management System (RDBMS): A type of database that represents physical data storage as a set of tables with columns and rows, and is able to link (create a relation) through columns that two or more tables have in common.

Remote Data Access (RDA): The ability to link to a database residing on a remote system, and requesting information from that database.

Remote Function Call (RFC): An interface for SAP callable from a multitude of platforms, development environments, and applications. The R/3 Automation Software Development Kit provides RFC libraries, RFC Dynamic Link Libraries (DLLs), and user dialogs, in addition to an error-processing facility. Documentation and sample programs for RFCs are included in this software, allowing access to SAP processes and data from standard software such as MS Excel, PowerBuilder, Visual Basic, C++, and Java. Even more beneficial is the ability to access RFCs using other, more "standard" Microsoft interfaces such as COM, COM+, and OLEDB.

Remote Procedure Call (RPC): A form of application-to-application communication that hides the intricacies of the network by using an ordinary procedure call mechanism. It is a tightly coupled synchronous process.

Resource Description Framework (RDF): A part of the XML story, provides interoperability between applications that exchange information.

RosettaNet: An organization set up by leading information technology companies to define and implement a common set of standards for B2B application integration.

router: A special-purpose computer or software package that handles the connection of two or more networks. Routers check the destination address of the packets and decide the route to send them.

scalability: The ability of an information system to provide high performance as greater demands are placed upon it, through the addition of extra computing power.

Semantic Web: An intuitive standard created by Tim Berners-Lee providing a mechanism for the Web to address semantics.

server: A computer or software package that provides specific capabilities to client software running on other computers.

Service-Oriented Application Integration (SOAI): The process of joining applications together by allowing them to share services between them.

Simple Object Access Protocol (SOAP): An XML- and text-based mechanism allowing applications to invoke remote Web services.

sockets: A portable standard for network application providers on TCP/IP networks.

SQR: A reporting tool that's a part of all PeopleSoft applications.

stored procedure: A program that creates a named collection of SQL or other procedural statements and logic that is compiled, verified, and stored in a server database.

Straight Through Processing (STP): Occurs when a transaction, once entered into a system, passes through its entire life cycle without any manual intervention. STP is an example of a zero latency process, but one specific to the finance industry, which has many proprietary networks and messaging formats.

Structured Query Language (SQL): The standard database query language for relational databases.

synchronous communication: A form of communication that requires the sending and receiving applications to be running concurrently. An application issues a request and waits until it receives a response from the other application.

System Network Architecture (SNA): A network architecture from IBM found in the more traditional mainframe technology.

systems middleware: Software that provides value-added services as well as interprogram communication; for example, transaction processing monitors are required to control local resources and also cooperate with other resource managers to access nonlocal resources.

transaction processing (TP) monitor: Based on the premise of a transaction. A transaction is a unit of work with a beginning and an end. The reasoning is that if application logic is encapsulated within a transaction, then the transaction either completes or is rolled back completely. If the transaction has been updating remote resources, such as databases and queues, then they too will be rolled back if a problem occurs.

transactional middleware: Provides an excellent mechanism for method sharing; it is not as effective when it comes to simple information sharing, the real goal of EAI. For example, transactional middleware typically creates a tightly coupled EAI solution, where messaging solutions are more cohesive in nature.

Transmission Control Protocol/Internet Protocol (TCP/IP): The network protocol for the Internet that runs on virtually every operating system. IP is the network layer, and TCP is the transport layer.

trigger: A stored procedure that is automatically invoked on the basis of data-related events.

two-phase commit: A mechanism to synchronize updates on different machines or platforms so that they all fail or all succeed together. The decision to commit is centralized, but each participant has the right to veto. This is a key process in real-time transaction-based environments.

Unified Modeling Language (UML): A standard set of notations and concepts to approach object-oriented analysis and design.

Universal Description, Discovery and Integration (UDDI): An XML-based registry for Web services, allowing remote users to discover and invoke Web services whether they are known or not.

user interface-level EAI: Using this scenario, architects and developers are able to bundle applications by using their user interfaces as a common point of integration (which is also known as "screen scraping"). For example, mainframe applications that do not provide database- or business process-level access may be accessed through the user interface of the application.

Web services: Application services that are made available to local or remote applications through well-defined interfaces and communication protocols.

Web Services Description Language (WSDL): An XML-based language used to describe how to invoke a Web service, analogous to an Interface Definition Language (IDL), used with traditional ORBs.

Web Services Interoperability (WS-I): An organization of several IT industry companies aimed at creating Web services specifications that all companies can use.

Web Services Security (WS-Security): A proposed IT industry standard addressing security when data is exchanged as part of a Web service.

workflow: Software used to automatically route events or work items from one user or program to another. Workflow is synonymous with "process flow," although traditionally "workflow" has been used in the context of person-to-person information flows.

World Wide Web Consortium (W3C): An industry consortium that seeks to promote standards for the evolution of the Web.

XA interface: Set of function calls, split between the transaction manager and the resource manager. Allows the resource manager to tell the transaction manager whether it is ready to work with a transaction or whether it is in an unresponsive "resting state."

X/Open: An independent open systems organization. Its strategy is to combine various standards into a comprehensive integrated systems environment called Common Applications Environment, which contains an evolving portfolio of practical APIs.

XML: See *Extensible Markup Language*

XML Query Language (XQL): A way to locate and filter the elements and text in an XML document.

Xpath: A language that describes a way to create and process items with XML.

XSL Transformations (XSLT): A standard way to describe how to transform the schema and content of an XML document.

zero latency: No delay between an event and its response.

Zero Latency Enterprise (ZLE): An enterprise in which all parts of the organization can respond to events as they occur elsewhere in the organization, using an integrated IT infrastructure that can immediately exchange information across technical and organizational boundaries.

zero latency process: An automated process with no time delays (i.e., no manual re-entry of data) at the interfaces of different information systems. Straight Through Processing (STP) is an example.

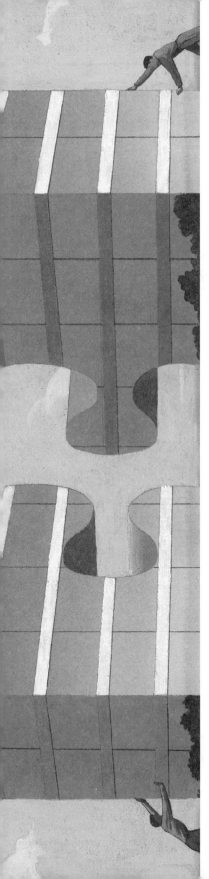

PIP™ Specification— PIP1A2: Maintain Account

Cluster 1: Partner, Product and Service Review
Segment A: Partner Review

Beta 01.00.00B
18 May 2000

RosettaNet

Contents

1 Document Management

1.1 Legal Disclaimer

RosettaNet™, its members, officers, directors, employees, or agents shall not be liable for any injury, loss, damages, financial or otherwise, arising from, related to, or caused by the use of this document or the specifications herein, as well as associated guidelines and schemas. The use of said specifications shall constitute your express consent to the foregoing exculpation.

1.2 Copyright

©2000 RosettaNet. All rights reserved. No part of this publication may be reproduced, stored in a retrieval system, or transmitted, in any form or by any means, electronic, mechanical, photocopying, recording, or otherwise, without the prior written permission of the publisher. Printed in the United States of America.

1.3 Trademarks

RosettaNet, Partner Interface Process, PIP and the RosettaNet logo are trademarks or registered trademarks of "RosettaNet," a non-profit organization. All other product names and company logos mentioned herein are the trademarks of their respective owners. In the best effort, all terms mentioned in this document that are known to be trademarks or registered trademarks have been appropriately recognized in the first occurrence of the term.

1.4 Acknowledgments

This document has been prepared by Edifecs Commerce (http://www.edifecs.com, http://www.CommerceDesk.com) from requirements in conformance with the RosettaNet methodology.

1.5 Prerequisites

The audience should be familiar with the RosettaNet User's Guide, "Understanding a PIP Blueprint." This document can be downloaded from the RosettaNet EConcert Document Library at the following web address.

http://www.rosettanet.org/usersguides/

1.6 Related Documents

- RosettaNet IT Technical Dictionary
  http://www.rosettanet.org/techdictionaries/
- RosettaNet Business Dictionary
  http://www.rosettanet.org/businessdictionary/

1.7 Supply Chain Requirements

This PIP includes design and technology requirements utilized in the supply chains listed below.

1. Information Technology (IT)

1.8 Document Version History

Version	Date	PIP Specification Development
Beta 01.00.00A	11 May 2000	RosettaNet: approved, untested, published Specification
Beta 01.00.00B	18 May 2000	Edifecs Commerce: incremented Spec version to correspond with DTD version update—due to change in the Response Document which had two lines repeating at the end of the physical address element: Address line 1 and City Name.

2 Introduction

Partner Interface Process™ (PIP) Specification comprises the following three views of the ebusiness PIP model.

1. **Business Operational View (BOV).** Captures the semantics of business data entities and their flow of exchange between roles as they perform business activities. The content of the BOV section is based on the PIP Blueprint document created for RosettaNet's business community.
2. **Functional Service View (FSV).** Specifies the network component services and agents and the interactions necessary to execute PIPs. The FSV includes all of the transaction dialogs in a PIP Protocol. The purpose of the FSV is to specify a PIP Protocol that is systematically derived from the BOV. The two major components within the FSV are the network component design and network component interactions.
3. **Implementation Framework View (IFV).** Specifies the network protocol message formats and communications requirements between peer-protocols

supported by network components in the RosettaNet Implementation Framework. These messages are exchanged when software programs execute a PIP; RosettaNet distributes these as XML Message Guidelines.

3   Business Operational View

3.1   Business Process Definition

Maintenance of account information includes such activities as updating ship-to and bill-to locations as well as updating relationships between ship-to and bill-to address. This Partner Interface Process (PIP) supports both customer and vendor account types. For an explanation of these account types, please refer to PIP1A1, "Request Account Setup."

Example

Assume that "ABC Distributor" purchases product from "Acme Manufacturer." If ABC Distributor decides to open a new warehouse, they would initiate this PIP to report the new warehouse location to Acme Manufacturer. Acme would update the customer account in their system with the new location and provide an acknowledgment back to ABC. Conversely, Acme may add a new address to which purchase orders should be sent. As a result, Acme would use this PIP to advise ABC of this new address. ABC would add the purchase order address to the vendor account and acknowledge the addition(s) back to Acme.

This PIP was also designed with the understanding that the Account Provider determines what, if any, of the updated account information is accepted and reflected in their system. Thus, referencing the example, ABC might report the new warehouse location and a new bill-to location to Acme. However, Acme must review the updates and decide which information to change in their system. If Acme finds that ABC's new bill-to location already exists in their system, then Acme would reject that portion of the request and notify ABC of the rejection. This PIP was designed to allow an Account Provider to accept part of a request and reject part of a request, so that the recipient could reject the bill-to, but accept the warehouse location within the same PIP.

3.2   PIP Purpose

The purpose of this PIP is to support a process whereby trading partner account information can be maintained.

3.3   PIP Business Process Flow Diagram

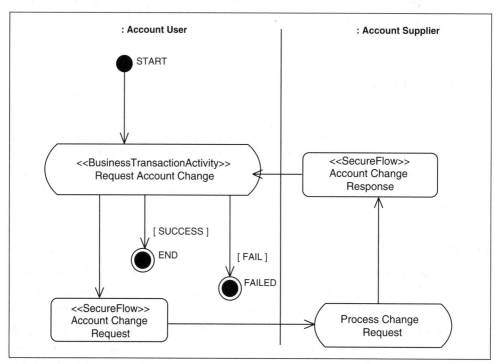

Figure 3.1   Maintain Account

3.4   PIP Start State

The start state is comprised of the following conditions.

- The account type is defined to be a Customer or a Vendor.
- The account has been setup.

3.5   PIP End States

End states are comprised of one or more conditions.

END

- Account Change Response received.
- One or more of the change requests applied.
- If any change was denied; a reason code for that denial is supplied.

FAILED

- The number of attempts has exceeded the retry count maximum.

- PIP0A1, "Notification of Failure," has been executed. (This is a RosettaNet convention.)
- Change requests not applied.

3.6   Partner Role Descriptions

Table 3.1 describes the partner roles in this PIP.

Table 3.1   Partner Role Descriptions

Role Name	Role Description	Role Type
Account User	Any trading partner that requires an account to buy or sell products/services.	Functional
Account Supplier	Any trading partner that buys or sells products/ services from customer and/or vendors.	Organizational

3.7   Business Process Activity Controls

Table 3.2 describes the interaction contract between roles performing business activities in this PIP.

Table 3.2   Business Activity Descriptions

Role Name	Activity Name	Activity Description	Pre-Conditions	Post-Conditions
Account User	Request Account Change	This activity involves systematically reviewing the updated account information for completeness and validity and systemically updating the account information in an account provider's system. The activity then informs an account requester which account information was updated and which was invalid.	The account type to be changed is defined as a Customer or a Vendor.	Success or failure of the account change is received. If any change was denied; a reason code for that denial is supplied.

Table 3.3 details the security, audit and process controls relating to activities performed in the PIP.

Table 3.3 Business Activity Performance Controls

Role Name	Activity Name	Non-Repudiation Required?	Time to Acknowledge	Time to Acknowledge Acceptance	Time to Perform	Retry Count	Is Authorization Required?	Non-Repudiation of Origin and Content?
			Acknowledgment of Receipt					
Buyer	Request Account Change	Y	2 hrs	N/A	24 hrs	3	Y	Y

3.8 PIP Blueprint Data

3.8.1 PIP Business Documents

Business Documents listed in Table 3.4 are exchanged by roles performing activities in this PIP. The Business Documents can be downloaded from the RosettaNet Business Document Repository using the Uniform Resource Locator (URL) specified Section 1.6, "Related Documents."

Table 3.4 PIP Business Documents

Business Document	Description
Account Change Request	Specifies change(s) for a particular account
Account Change Response	Contains the result of the requested change(s). A reason code is provided if a change is denied.

3.8.2 Business Data Entities

The business data entities, fundamental business data entities, and global identifying properties can be found in the RosettaNet Business Dictionary using the URL specified in Section "Related Documents."

Business Data Entity Security

There are no security controls specified for this PIP.

4   Functional Service View

The two major components in the FSV are the network component design and possible network component interactions, listed in sections 4.1 and 4.3.

4.1   Network Component Design

A network component design specifies the network components necessary to execute the PIP and the network component collaboration. A network component design is comprised of Agent components and Business Service components that enable roles to perform business activities in a networked environment. Network components collaborate by exchanging business action messages and business signal messages.

4.1.1   *Network Component Collaboration*

Figure 4.1 specifies the network components and their message exchange.

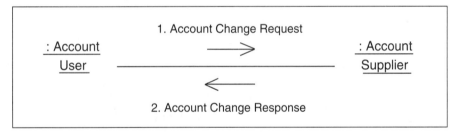

Figure 4-1   Maintain Account

4.1.2   *Network Component Specification*

Each network component maps onto a role in the BOV of the PIP model. Table 4.1 specifies the mapping between roles in the BOV and network components in the FSV.

Table 4.1   Network Component Specification

Network Component in FSV	Classification	Maps to Role in BOV
Account User Service	Business Service	Account User
Account User Agent	Agent	Account User
Account Supplier Service	Business Service	Account Supplier
Account Supplier Agent	Agent	Account Supplier

4.2   Business Action and Business Signal Specification

Each business action maps onto a business document in the BOV of the PIP model. Table 4.2 specifies the mapping between business documents in the BOV and business actions in the FSV.

Table 4.2   Business Action–Business Document Mapping

Business Action in FSV	Maps to Business Document in BOV
Account Change Request Action	Account ChangeRequest
Account Change Response Action	Account Change Response

4.3   Business Transaction Dialog Specification

Each business activity between roles in the BOV is specified as a business transaction dialog between network components. There are two fundamental network components modeled in the Functional Service View.

1. **Service network component.** Implements protocols that include the service layer, transaction and action layer. A service has "network identity" as a business service. The service has an identity URI that can be registered in directories and used for component communication in a distributed computer system.
2. **Agent network component.** Implements protocols that include the action layer and the agent layer. There is no service layer or transaction layer.

The FSV allows the following network component interaction configurations.

1. **Agent-Service interaction configuration.** An agent can request service from a service component and a service can respond to the request. Agents cannot respond to requests for service.
2. **Service-Service interaction configuration.** There can be any number of services between end-point services, but no agents. Services both provide services to agents and other requesting services as well as request services for other services.
3. **Agent-Agent interaction configuration.** One agent can transfer an action to another agent.

From these three interaction configurations it is possible to derive three additional network-component configurations specific to a trading partner agreement.

1. **Service-Agent-Service interaction configuration.** Services interact using two or more agents as a bridge. This configuration is typical in configurations where the two services do not know each other's identity, or when an employee must include additional private information to an action that is sent to another service.
2. **Service-Service-Agent interaction configuration.** The second service acts as a mailbox for the agent.
3. **Agent-Service-Service interaction configuration.** A service-to-service transaction is a sub-transaction of a larger agent-service transaction.

The rest of section 4.3 specifies the network component configurations possible for this PIP. Each figure specifies the message exchange sequence as network components collaborate to execute this PIP. Each table shows the properties for each of the messages exchanged by the interactions in the corresponding figure.

4.3.1 Request Account Change Dialog: Service-Service

The following figure specifies the message exchange sequence as network components collaboration to execute this PIP.

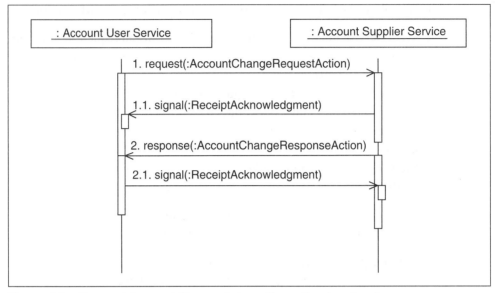

Figure 4.2   Request Account Change Interactions: Service-Service

The following table shows the properties for each of the messages exchanged by the interactions in the above figure.

Table 4.3   Message Exchange Controls—Request Quote

#	Name	Time to Acknowledge Receipt Signal	Time to Acknowledge Acceptance	Time to Respond	Included in Time to Perform	Is Authorization Required?	Is Non-Repudiation Required?	Is Secure Transport Required?
1.	Account Change Request Action	2 hrs	N/A	24 hrs	Y	Y	Y	Y
1.1.	Receipt Acknowledgment	N/A	N/A	N/A	Y	Y	Y	Y
2.	Account Change Response Action	2 hrs	N/A	N/A	Y	Y	Y	Y
2.1.	Receipt Acknowledgment	N/A	N/A	N/A	N	Y	N	Y

4.3.2   *Request Account Change Dialog: Service-Agent-Service*

The following figure specifies the message exchange sequence as network components collaborate to execute this PIP.

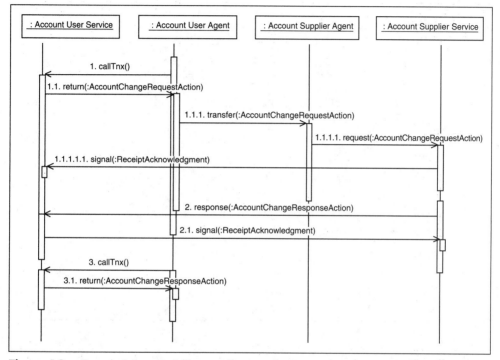

Figure 4.3   Request Account Change Interactions: Service-Agent-Service

The following table shows the properties for each of the messages exchanged by the interactions in the above figure.

Table 4.4   Message Exchange Controls–Request Account Change

#	Name	Time to Acknowledge Receipt Signal	Time to Acknowledge Acceptance	Time to Respond	Included in Time to Perform	Is Authorization Required?	Is Non-Repudiation Required?	Is Secure Transport Required?
1.1.	Account Change Request Action	2 hrs	N/A	24 hrs	Y	Y	Y	Y
1.1.1.	Account Change Request Action	N/A	N/A	N/A	Y	N/A	N/A	Y
1.1.1.1.	Account Change Request Action	N/A	N/A	N/A	Y	N/A	N/A	Y
1.1.1.1.1	Receipt Acknowledgment	N/A	N/A	N/A	Y	Y	Y	Y
2.	Account Change Response Action	2 hrs	N/A	N/A	Y	Y	Y	Y
2.1.	Receipt Acknowledgment	N/A	N/A	N/A	N	Y	N	Y

4.3.3   *Request Account Change Dialog: Agent-Service-Service*

The following figure specifies the message exchange sequence as network components collaborate to execute this PIP.

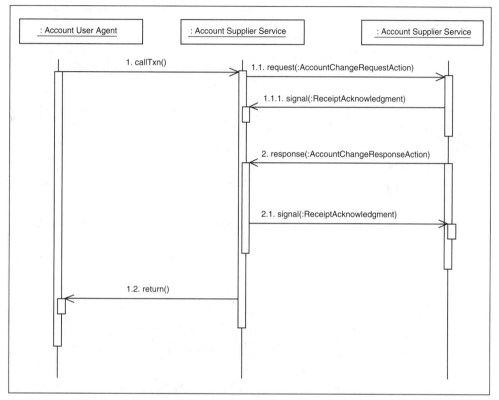

Figure 4.4   Request Account Change Interactions: Agent-Service-Service

The following table shows the properties for each of the messages exchanged by the interactions in the above figure.

Table 4.5   Message Exchange Controls—Request Account Change

#	Name	Time to Acknowledge Receipt Signal	Time to Acknowledge Acceptance Signal	Time to Respond	Included in Time to Perform	Is Authorization Required?	Is Non-Repudiation Required?	Is Secure Transport Required?
1.1.	Account Change Request Action	2 hrs	N/A	24 hrs	Y	Y	Y	Y
1.1.1	Receipt Acknowledgment	N/A	N/A	N/A	Y	Y	Y	Y
2.	Account Change Response Action	2 hrs	N/A	N/A	Y	Y	Y	Y
2.1.	Receipt Acknowledgment	N/A	N/A	N/A	N	Y	N	Y

5   Implementation Framework View

The Implementation Framework View (IFV) of the PIP model specifies the message format and communications requirements between peer-protocols supported by network components in the RosettaNet Implementation Framework.

The following sections specify the business messages and their communications requirements for executing this PIP.

5.1   Request Account Change Dialog: Service-Service

Table 5.1   **Business Message and Communications Specification**

#	Business Message Guideline	Digital Signature Required?	SSL[1] Required?
1.	Account Change Request Guideline	Y	Y
1.1.	Receipt Acknowledgment Guideline	Y	Y
2.	Account Change Response Guideline	Y	Y
2.1.	Receipt Acknowledgment Guideline	Y	Y

5.2   Request Account Change Dialog: Service-Agent Service

Table 5.2   **Business Message and Communications Specification**

#	Business Message Guideline	Digital Signature Required?	SSL[2] Required?
1.1.1.	Account Change Request Guideline	Y	Y
1.1.1.1.1.	Receipt Acknowledgment Guideline	Y	Y
2.	Account Change Response Guideline	Y	Y
2.1.	Receipt Acknowledgment Guideline	Y	Y

[1]Secure Socket Layer

[2]Secure Socket Layer

5.3   Request Account Change Dialog: Agent-Service-Service

Table 5.3   Business Message and Communications Specification

#	Business Message Guideline	Digital Signature Required?	SSL[3] Required?
1.1.1.	Account Change Request Guideline	Y	Y
1.1.1.1.	Receipt Acknowledgment Guideline	Y	Y
2.	Account Change Response Guideline	Y	Y
2.1.	Receipt Acknowledgment Guideline	Y	Y

[3]Secure Socket Layer

APPENDIX B

Where XML Fits with Application Integration

Fundamentally, application integration is about loosely coupling applications and data stores together to solve intraenterprise business problems. Its strength is facilitating the free flow of information from any system to any other system, one-to-one or many-to-many, with each of those systems gaining access to perfect external information in real time.

Application integration typically integrates ERP packages such as SAP, PeopleSoft, and Baan in addition to Customer Relationship Management (CRM) packages, databases, and older mainframe systems. Application integration also allows organizations to externalize existing enterprise application information to interested parties, including real-time B2B information exchanges, and Web-enabled applications.

XML comes into the application integration picture at several levels, including data interchange, schema transformation, metadata management, process integration, and even message persistence. However, the use of XML within the firewall needs some architectural thought, with the objective to leverage the appropriate XML technologies to address the appropriate technical problems. Complicating this is the fact that XML standards are either emerging or changing, and many enterprise architects and CIOs may consider leveraging XML-enabled technologies for application integration to be high risk, at least in the short term. This is not to be confused with the B2B problem domains, where the use of XML is more acceptable.

Understanding the Application Integration Problem

There are three major problems to solve when considering application integration: application semantics, information content, and platform heterogeneity.

We know that *application semantics* are different from application to application. For example, how you define a customer within one application is very different from how you define a customer in another. So, if you're looking to move information between two or more applications you must account for the differences in application semantics by changing the structure or schema of that information, typically on the fly as information moves from application to application.

Accounting for application semantics typically deals with the process of transformation, or changing the structure of a message or a document moving from one application to another. Most application integration-oriented technologies, such as message brokers or Business to Business Integration (B2Bi) servers, have some transformation facilities built in. Lately, as we'll discuss below, application integration technology vendors have been looking at standard transformation mechanisms based on XML, namely XSLT.

Just as we adjust the structure of information so it fits nicely into the data structure of the target application or applications, we need to alter the *information content* in real time as well. Using the same transformation mechanism, information content within the document or message is translated into something the target system or systems will understand. For example, while 01/01/00 might work in Application A, Application B will need that same information represented as January 1, 2000. Other typical problems we need to solve include numeric to alphanumeric, and back; fixed to variable, and back; and even looking up information on the fly for transformation such as finding the current exchange rate from yen to U.S. dollars. Once again, XSLT is proving useful for accounting for differences within both application semantics and information content.

Finally, application integration needs to account for operating system and interface differences, or *platform heterogeneity*. Information is not stored in the same way across platforms, nor are the native interfaces the same. For example, accessing mainframe information may require a gateway-type interface, such as ACCP, where accessing information contained inside a database uses a more traditional database interface, such as JDBC. Moreover, the way information is stored—such as EBCDIC or ASCII—varies from platform to platform. At some point, application integration developers have to figure out the best way to inter-face with source or target systems, and consume information from, as well as publish information to, specific platforms. Typical application integration problem domains consist of mainframe-based applications, ERP packaged applications, CRM applications, transaction processors, and a variety of database flavors.

The platform heterogeneity problem resolves itself in one of two ways. First, some application integration-oriented middleware provides APIs, allowing developers to create custom interfaces between the source and target systems. This typically entails creating a small application between the applications and the integration server (e.g., a message broker). Second, some application integration vendors provide adapters or prebuilt connections for a variety of systems. Adapters are able to interact with specific source and target systems using whatever native point of integration is available, ultimately consuming information into the integration technology, using a common message or document (e.g., XML). Likewise, adapters publish information to target systems using the same mechanisms.

Integration Realities and XML

Adapters are important. In order for applications using XML to be integrated, the applications must externalize the information as XML. Currently, few applications are capable of doing so. In order to be most successful, the existing applications must either change so they produce and consume XML or, better yet, they must leverage XML-enabled middleware technology and adapters.

XML-enabled middleware technology manages the extraction of information from the source system (or systems) as well as the conversion of the information into XML (if required) and the placement of the information in the target system (or systems). All this occurs automatically and is transparent to the end user.

However, XML does not make a good message format for information exchange, either with B2B application integration or enterprise application integration. XML is text based, and thus information that would normally exist in a binary message as "512 KB" could easily map to an XML document 20 times that size.

Although XML provides a good point of integration when communicating with source or target applications within or between enterprises, moving information using native XML demands a huge overhead. As a result, most integration server vendors still use a binary message format, either proprietary or open, to move XML data and metadata from one system to another. These systems consume and produce XML, but use their own internal formats for efficiency. This fact is not well known because most middleware vendors promote their products as using "native" XML, although they merely interact with the XML standard.

XML Meets Middleware

Now that we have established that XML is a simple, text-based standard and, as such, cannot provide everything needed to integrate disparate applications, it quickly becomes clear that in order to provide maximum value to the application integration solution set, XML needs middleware (and, conversely, middleware most likely needs XML).

XML's value to middleware is clear. Middleware simply "carries the load." It moves messages (XML documents) that encapsulate or abstract XML and ensures that those messages are understood by any source or target applications that need that information. Middleware may also manage the interfaces with the source or target applications and move information into and out of the applications through an unobtrusive point of integration such as a database or an API.

Because of XML's value, every middleware vendor, new and old, has declared dominance in the XML space, applying its technology to application integration problem domains. None of us should be surprised that there is a certain degree of "puffery" to these declarations. The truth is that it is not particularly difficult to XML-enable a product. Therefore, vendors were able to react quickly.

XML-enabling a product is simply a matter of embedding a parser within the middleware and teaching the product to read and write XML from and to the canonical message format. In addition, because many of these products already have native connectors to traditional enterprise systems and data stores, such as SAP, PeopleSoft, and DB2, they provide enterprises with the ability to produce and consume XML without impacting the applications.

Integration Solutions

Now that we understand how middleware and XML coexist, we can turn our attention to XML-enabled solutions that include the available technology and approaches. In doing so, let's consider the macro problem domains: B2B application integration and application integration.

Within the domain of application integration, XML plays a lesser role, but its role is becoming more important. This somewhat-convoluted observation is based on the fact that most systems within an enterprise come under central control. As a result, the integration solutions run deeper and may not benefit from converting information to XML for movement to other applications. Typically, standard information-exchange mechanisms, such as XML, take a back seat to native points of integration and binary messages as a simple matter of efficiency when we consider application integration. However, as information becomes less centrally controlled, XML will become more important.

Let us look, for example, at a situation in which an enterprise needs to exchange information between its PeopleSoft packaged application, its older COBOL/ISAM application running on the mainframe, and its new data warehouse. Although there are many ways to approach this problem, most enterprises would use some type of message broker to exchange information between the systems in real time, using whatever native interface the source or target applications provide. Although there is always the opportunity to convert the data moving between the applications into XML, binary messages typically provide better efficiency, as we noted earlier.

Although native interfaces currently dominate application integration solutions, we are rapidly moving to a world where most applications and databases will be XML-aware. Therefore, XML will become a common point of integration rather than the hodgepodge of proprietary and complex native interfaces in use today. Taking this reality into account, we recognize that XML is becoming a more prominent player in application integration. Many packaged applications, including PeopleSoft and SAP, are going to leverage XML as the preferred native interface to their systems. Indeed, PeopleSoft has already defined its Open Integration Framework (OIF) and has outlined how information will move into and out of the PeopleSoft application using XML. SAP is not far behind.

Even as developers build interfaces to new and existing custom applications, XML is becoming the mechanism of choice for producing and consuming information within those systems. Moreover, most database vendors, including Oracle, Sybase, and Informix, are providing mechanisms within their database engines to allow them to read and write XML directly from the database.

XML provides the most value within the domain of B2B application integration. Here we typically integrate applications that are not under centralized control and thus difficult to change. As we have explained, XML provides a reasonably good format for information exchange. Perhaps most important, the majority of businesses can agree upon XML as the way information moves into and out of enterprises. XML standards provide additional value by including common metadata layers that may exist between one or more trading partners and even standard transformation mechanisms such as XSLT.

As we look ahead, the ultimate application integration solution will be some hybrid of enterprise application integration and B2B application integration, providing integration within and between enterprises by using a similar, compatible infrastructure. Getting to this "glorious future" will be accomplished in stages. Enterprises will first learn to integrate their own applications, including understanding everything about the source and target systems that they own, and then will learn to integrate their applications with their trading partners' applications. XML belongs in this mix, but the majority of work in getting to the solution is associated with exploring both problem domains, understanding the requirements, and mapping the correct technology to the solution. In reality, most organizations have just begun the journey down this rather long and expensive road.

XML Standards and Application Integration

The XML bandwagon is filling up, joined by many standards organizations. These entities are looking to standardize the way we integrate applications, using the common infrastructure they define and vendors provide.

The sad reality is that this bandwagon is overfull—there are more XML standards organizations than vendors and end users require. Fallout is bound to occur as one or two standards get traction and others do not. The few that appear to be most relevant in the world of XML and application integration include RosettaNet, BizTalk, and XSLT.

RosettaNet is a consortium of product vendors and end users that defines a framework for data and process interchange with e-Business. Primarily organized for the high-tech industry, RosettaNet outlines standard message data using XML as well as standardized process flows, to react to standard business events. What's significant about RosettaNet for the application integration problem domain is that it brings a nice process integration standard for use between enterprises, as well as within an enterprise (although currently this standard is more B2B oriented).

BizTalk is an industry consortium founded by Microsoft to define a standard XML grammar for XML-based messaging and metadata. Microsoft is providing a BizTalk server to support this standard. Like other similar technology, both the product and the standard seek to solve application integration problems within and between enterprises.

XSLT seeks to provide a standard XML document-transformation mechanism using a stylesheet as a common processing engine. XSLT is important to application integration because schema and information content often must be altered as information flows between applications, as we already alluded to above.

XML and Application Integration

XML and application integration are coupled. Application integration represents the larger problem of moving information between applications and data stores for any business purpose. XML provides a common mechanism for data exchange and integration with a variety of applications supporting a variety of design patterns.

What XML brings to the application integration party is not great technology, but the fact that XML, and some of the derivative standards, are forcing the application integration vendor community into leveraging standard mechanisms including XSLT and RosettaNet, within their now-proprietary products. What's more, the use of XML within the enterprise allows easy migration to a strategic B2B information exchange platform. It's just a matter of pushing the XML documents to B2B integration servers.

Even with all the promise and "presence" of XML, we've also learned that it is not a panacea. Users must understand the limits, as well as the potential, of the technology before leveraging it for their application integration solution. The real power of XML is the notion of the standard information interchange it brings between one or many applications existing within a single organization or within a trading community. It's just going to take some time before we're able to reinvent our existing middleware technology and applications around XML. But that day is coming—and it's going to be here sooner than we think.

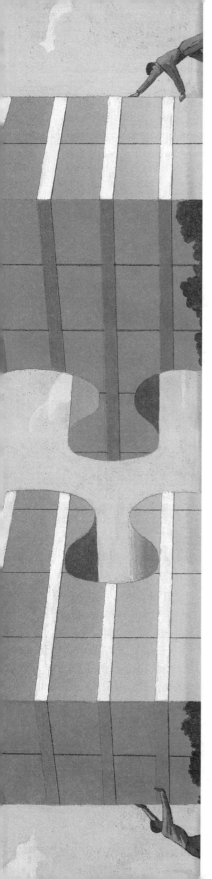

Knowledge-Oriented Middleware

While middleware underlies application integration, the technology itself is still fairly primitive and without true intelligence. Organizations can connect disparate systems and applications, but developers must still customize the application integration technology, or perhaps the applications themselves, to meet specific requirements of businesses, applications, and systems.

Knowledge-Oriented Middleware (KOM) resolves this problem. KOM not only allows developers to link various systems, it also understands the features and the context of the applications it is connecting, thus eliminating programming requirements. Moreover, KOM is created to understand a particular vertical sector; it provides "canned" information defining the connection between the systems and industry-specific interfaces. It also contains industry-specific detail as to how the information moves throughout an enterprise, in an EAI scenario, or between enterprises in a B2B integration scenario. KOM also defines how applications interact with external resources, enabling businesses to leverage their existing resources and to take advantage of new technologies.

The Next Level of Middleware

KOM takes middleware to the next level. IS professionals can now access information and processes on different systems as well as understand the solutions that exist in each of those systems. What is more, KOM provides an intelligent middleware solution that is tailored for a specific vertical market such as telecommunications, health care, manufacturing, or finance; in other words, intelligent middleware that has knowledge of a particular industry, is able to understand how the information should move, and can build a base of knowledge to further determine best practices for a particular enterprise. KOM can integrate packaged, custom-developed, and legacy applications without a significant amount of customization and development, and KOM is able to assist in the movement of that information between or throughout an enterprise based on best practices for a particular industry stored in a knowledge base linked with the middleware.

KOM is able to move information in and out of most enterprise systems, providing adapters to link into most types of systems and enabling technologies, and can automatically translate and route information throughout an enterprise using this best-practice information. The notion of KOM is to create a technology that's able to link many systems together, allowing them to share information without changing the participating applications or data, and do so in such a way as to optimize the flow of information through a particular vertical business sector.

Layers

KOM has four separate layers: messaging, transformation and formatting, business process and workflow, and knowledge-orientation.

1. The messaging level is made up of traditional message-oriented middleware products and provides a transportation mechanism for messages to and from all of the source and target systems.

2. The transformation and formatting layer provides message-brokering capability, providing for the reformatting of information as it's being moved from one system to another.

3. The business process and workflow layer provides a modeling tool and mechanism that defines how information is moved throughout and between enterprises and how the movement of information relates to business events.

4. Finally, the knowledge-orientation layer provides a memory of expert behavior to the middleware, allowing the middleware to retain "experiences" as well as reuse industry-specific experiences built within the knowledge-oriented layer prior to installation (a knowledge base).

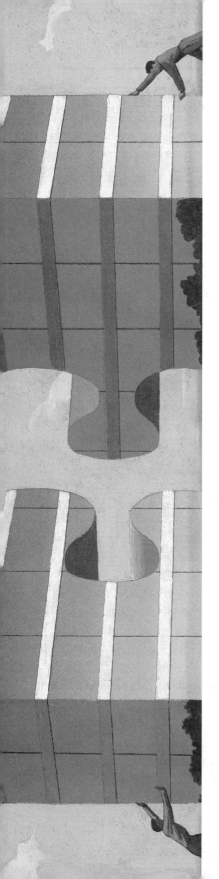

Bibliography

Aberdeen, "Advanced Technologies and a Sense of Process," *Aberdeen Group Report.* 1998.

Akkerman, "What are Ontologies?—An Executive Summary." January 15, 2001.

Berners-Lee, Tim, James Hendler, and Ora Lassila, "The Semantic Web," *Scientific American.* May 2001.

Berson, A., *Client/Server Architecture*, New York: McGraw-Hill, Inc. 1992.

Black, U.D., *Data Communications and Distributed Networks, Second Edition*, Englewood Cliffs, N.J.: Yourdon Press, Prentice-Hall. 1987.

Boar, B.H., *Implementing Client/Server Computing, A Strategic Approach*, New York: McGraw-Hill. 1993.

Booch, G., *Object-Oriented Analysis and Design with Applications, Second Edition*, Reading, Mass.: Addison-Wesley. 1994.

Booch, G., *Unified Method for Object-Oriented Development*, Version 0.8, Rational Software Corporation.

Byous, Jon, *Single Sign-On Simplicity with SAML: An Overview of Single Sign-on Capabilities Based on the Security Assertions Markup Language (SAML) Specification.* 2002.

Chorafas, D.N., *Systems Architecture & Systems Design*, New York: McGraw-Hill. 1989.

Claybrook, B., *OLTP, Online Transaction Processing Systems,* New York: John Wiley & Sons, Inc. 1992.

Coad, P., and E. Yourdon, *Object-Oriented Analysis, Second Edition,* Upper Saddle River, N.J.: Prentice-Hall. 1991.

Cui, Zhan, Dean Jones, and Paul O'Brien. "Issues in Ontology-based Information Integration." 2002.

Date, C.J., *An Introduction to Database Systems, Volume I, Fourth Edition,* Reading, Mass.: Addison-Wesley. 1987.

Date, C.J., *An Introduction to Database Systems, Volume II,* Reading, Mass.: Addison-Wesley. 1985.

Firesmith, D.G., *Object-Oriented Requirements Analysis and Logical Design, A Software Engineering Approach,* New York: John Wiley & Sons, Inc. 1993.

Fonseca, Frederico, Max Egenhover, and Clodoveu David. "Ontology-Driven Information Integration." 1999.

Gartner Group, "Application Integration: "Better Ways to Make Systems Work Together," *Gartner Group Conference Proceedings,* November 18-20, 1998.

Goldberg, A., *Object-Oriented Project Management,* Tutuorial TOOLS, Europe, Paris. 1991.

Goldberg, A., and D. Robson, *Smalltalk-80: The Language and Its Implementation,* Reading, Mass.: Addison-Wesley. 1983.

Goldman, Kenneth J., "Data Abstraction." 1996-97.

Gray, J., and A. Reuter, *Transaction Processing: Concepts and Techniques,* San Mateo, Calif.: Morgan Kaufmann Publishers. 1993.

Green, J.H., *Local Area Networks, A User's Guide for Business Professionals,* Glenview, Ill.: Scott, Foresman and Company. 1985.

Hackathorn, R.D., *Enterprise Database Connectivity,* New York: John Wiley & Sons. 1993.

Hutchison, D., *Local Area Network Architectures,* Reading, Mass.: Addison-Wesley. 1988.

Kerninghan, B.W., and D.M. Ritchie, *The C Programming Language, Second Edition,* Upper Saddle River, N.J.: Prentice-Hall. 1988.

Krol, E., *The Whole Internet User's Guide and Catalog,* Cambridge, Mass.: O'Reilly & Associates, Inc. 1992.

Linthicum, D.S., *Enterprise Application Integration,* Reading, Mass.: Addison-Wesley. 1999.

Linthicum, D.S., *Guide to Client/Server and Intranet Development,* New York: John Wiley & Sons, Inc. 1997.

Linthicum, D.S., "Client/Server Protocols: Choosing the Right Connection," *DBMS Magazine,* January 1994, Vol. 7, No. 1, p. 60.

Linthicum, D.S., "Moving Away from the Network, Using Middleware," *DBMS Magazine*, January 1994, Vol. 7, No. 1, p. 66.

Linthicum, D.S., "Operating Systems for Database Servers," *DBMS Magazine*, February 1994, Vol. 7, No. 2, p. 62.

Linthicum, D.S., "Client/Server Strategy," *DBMS Magazine*, April 1994, Vol. 7, No. 4, p. 46.

Linthicum, D.S., "4GLs: Productivity at What Cost?" *DBMS Magazine*, May 1994, Vol. 7, No. 5, p. 22.

Linthicum, D.S., "A Better PC?" *DBMS Magazine*, July 1994, Vol. 7, No. 7, p. 24.

Linthicum, D.S., "Defending OOP with VisualAge," *DBMS Magazine*, September 1994, Vol. 7, No. 9, p. 22.

Linthicum, D.S., "CASE Does Powerbuilder," *DBMS Magazine*, October 1994, Vol. 7, No. 10, p. 24.

Linthicum, D.S., "Lockhead Succeeds with C/S," *DBMS Magazine*, Vol. 7, No. 13, p. 26.

Linthicum, D.S., "A Multiplatform Power Tool," *DBMS Magazine*, January 1995, Vol. 8, No. 1, p. 20.

Linthicum, D.S., "System Architect 3.0," *DBMS Magazine*, January 1995, Vol. 8, No. 1, p. 62.

Linthicum, D.S., "Reconsidering Message Middleware," *DBMS Magazine*, March 1995, Vol. 8, No. 3, p. 24.

Linthicum, D.S., "EOF – a Next Step for C/S," *DBMS Magazine*, April 1995, Vol. 8, No. 4, p. 26.

Linthicum, D.S., "Rethinking C++," *DBMS Magazine*, May 1995, Vol. 8, No. 5, p. 23.

Linthicum, D.S., "Symantec Enterprise Developer 2.0," *DBMS Magazine*, July 1995, Vol. 8, No. 7, p. 22.

Linthicum, D.S., "Delphi 1.0," *DBMS Magazine*, July 1995, Vol. 8, No. 7, p. 28.

Linthicum, D.S., "Putting TP Monitors in Their Place," *DBMS Magazine*, August 1995, Vol. 8, No. 8, p. 22.

Linthicum, D.S., "Breaking Up is Easy to Do," *DBMS Magazine*, September 1995, Vol. 8, No. 9, p. 22.

Linthicum, D.S., "One-Stop Shopping with Oracle," *DBMS Magazine*, October 1995, Vol. 8, No. 10, p. 28.

Linthicum, D.S., "Travel Like a Native," *DBMS Magazine*, November 1995, Vol. 8, No. 11, p. 24.

Linthicum, D.S., "Keeping an Eye on Your Database Server," *DBMS Magazine*, December 1995, Vol. 8, No. 12, p. 60.

Linthicum, D.S., "Banking on Delphi," *DBMS Magazine,* 1995, Vol. 8, No. 13, p. 26.

Linthicum, D.S., "The Client/Server Internet," *DBMS Magazine,* January 1996, Vol. 9, No. 1, p. 26.

Linthicum, D.S., "Visual Basic 4.0: Ready for the Enterprise?" *DBMS Magazine,* January 1996, Vol. 9, No. 1, p. 11.

Linthicum, D.S., "ProtoGen+ Goes Virtual," *DBMS Magazine,* February 1996, Vol. 9, No. 2, p. 24.

Linthicum, D.S., "Moving Towards Remote Controlled OLE," *DBMS Magazine,* March 1996, Vol. 9, No. 3, p. 28.

Linthicum, D.S., "Cruising the Galaxy," *DBMS Magazine,* April 1996, Vol. 9, No. 4, p. 30.

Linthicum, D.S., "Battle of the Visual Masters," *DBMS Magazine,* April 1996, Vol. 9, No. 4, p. 91.

Linthicum, D.S., "Rise of the Intranet," *DBMS Magazine,* May 1996, Vol. 9, No. 5, p. 24.

Linthicum, D.S., "The Successes and Failures of Application Development Tools," *DBMS Magazine,* May 1996, Vol. 9, No. 5, p. 71.

Linthicum, D.S., "DCE Lightens its Load," *DBMS Magazine,* July 1996, Vol. 9, No. 7, p. 24.

Linthicum, D.S., "Partitioning Power," *DBMS Magazine,* August 1996, Vol. 9, No. 8, p. 28.

Linthicum, D.S., "Selecting a Client/Server Application Development Tool," *DBMS Magazine,* August 1996, Vol. 9, No. 8, p. 41.

Linthicum, D.S., "Selecting a DBMS," *DBMS Magazine,* August 1996, Vol. 9, No. 8, p. 48.

Linthicum, D.S., "Here Comes the Java Tools," *DBMS Magazine,* September 1996, Vol. 9, No. 9, p. 24.

Linthicum, D.S., "C++ Tools for Client/Server Development," *DBMS Magazine,* September 1996, Vol. 9, No. 9, p. 89.

Linthicum, D.S., "The Staying Power of C++," *DBMS Magazine,* October 1996, Vol. 9, No. 10, p. 24.

Linthicum, D.S., "Objects Meet Data," *DBMS Magazine,* October 1996, Vol. 9, No. 10, p. 72.

Linthicum, D.S., "The ABCs of SAP R/3," *DBMS Magazine,* November 1996, Vol. 9, No. 11, p. 28.

Linthicum, D.S., "Tool Time," *DBMS Magazine,* November 1996, Vol. 9, No. 11, p. 15.

Linthicum, D.S., "The JDBC Connection," *DBMS Magazine,* November 1996, Vol. 9, No. 11, p. 21.

Linthicum, D.S., "Distributed Objects Get New Plumbing," *Internet Systems,* January 1997, Vol.10, No. 1, p. 4.

Linthicum, D.S., "OLE-Enabled Middleware," *DBMS Magazine,* January 1997, Vol. 10, No. 1, p. 26.

Linthicum, D.S., "Reevaluting Distributed Objects," *DBMS Magazine,* January 1997, Vol. 10, No. 1, p. 44.

Linthicum, D.S., "The Good, the RAD, and the Ugly," *DBMS Magazine,* February 1997, Vol. 10, No. 2, p. 22.

Linthicum, D.S., "Moving to N-Tier RAD," *DBMS Magazine,* March 1997, Vol. 10, No. 3, p. 24.

Linthicum, D.S., "Complexity Revisited," *Internet Systems,* April 1997, Vol. 10, No. 4, p. 4.

Linthicum, D.S., "The Java APIs," *Internet Systems,* April 1997, Vol. 10, No. 4, p. 16.

Linthicum, D.S., "Driving Development," *DBMS Magazine,* April 1997, Vol. 10, No 4, p. 36.

Linthicum, D.S., "Visual Basic 5.0," *DBMS Magazine,* April 1997, Vol. 10, No. 4, p. 50.

Linthicum, D.S., "Building in Java," *Internet Systems,* May 1997, Vol. 10, No. 5.

Linthicum, D.S., "Another Tool, Another Repository," *DBMS Magazine,* May 1997, Vol. 10, No. 5, p. 26.

Linthicum, D.S., "Microsoft Repository 1.0," *DBMS Magazine,* June 1997, Vol. 10, No. 7, page 27.

Linthicum, D.S., "Performance Anxiety," *DBMS Magazine,* July 1997, Vol. 10, No. 8, p. 26.

Linthicum, D.S., "The Midas Touch," *DBMS Magazine,* August 1997, Vol. 10, No. 9, p. 22.

Linthicum, D.S., "Fun with Partitioning," *DBMS Magazine,* September 1997, Vol. 10, No. 10, p. 24.

Linthicum, D.S., "Next-Generation Middleware," *DBMS Magazine,* September 1997, Vol. 10, No. 10, p. 69.

Linthicum, D.S., "Patterns Demystified," *DBMS Magazine,* October 1997, Vol. 10, No. 11, p. 26.

Linthicum, D.S., "Get the Message," *DMS Magazine,* November 1997, Vol. 10, No. 12, p. 24.

Linthicum, D.S., "Mixing Tuples and Objects," *DBMS Magazine,* December 1997, Vol. 10, No. 13, p. 22.

Linthicum, D.S., "Finding Your Way," *DBMS Magazine,* November 1997, Vol. 10, No. 12, p. 55.

Linthicum, D.S., "The Magical Framework Myth," *DBMS Magazine,* January 1998, Vol. 11, No. 1, p. 22.

Linthicum, D.S., "Crossing the Streams," *DBMS Magazine,* February 1998, Vol. 11, No. 2, p. 24.

Linthicum, D.S., "Getting Along," *DBMS Magazine,* March 1998, Vol. 11, No. 3, p. 26.

Linthicum, D.S., "Integrating Enterprise Applications," *DBMS Magazine,* March 1998, Vol. 11, No. 3, p. 38.

Linthicum, D.S., "Java Realities," *DBMS Magazine,* April 1998, Vol. 11, No. 4, p. 24.

Linthicum, D.S., "Conducting Components," *DBMS Magazine,* May 1998, Vol. 11, No. 5, p. 26.

Linthicum, D.S., "Emerging Solutions," *DBMS Magazine,* June 1998, vol. 11, No. 6, p. 32.

Linthicum, D.S., "Please Move to the Middle," *DBMS Magazine,* July 1998, Vol. 11, No. 7, p. 22.

Linthicum, D.S., "Middleware Performance," *DBMS Magazine,* August 1998.

Linthicum, D.S., "Database-enabled Java Tools," *Software Development,* August 1998.

Linthicum, D.S., "Site Building," *Computer Shopper,* August 1998.

Linthicum, D.S., "Profiting from the Year 2000," *Computer Shopper,* August 1998.

Linthicum, D.S., "Standards Smooth Software Development," *Network World,* August 10, 1998.

Linthicum, D.S., "Message Brokers Rising," *DBMS Magazine,* September 1998.

Linthicum, D.S., "Site Building: Building Web Sites with SMIL," *Computer Shopper,* September 1998.

Linthicum, D.S., "Site Building: Microsoft Provides New Interfaces for IIS," *Computer Shopper,* October 1998.

Linthicum, D.S., "Site Building: Understanding Internet Application Servers," *Computer Shopper,* November 1998.

Linthicum, D.S., "Site Building," *Computer Shopper,* December 1, 1998.

Linthicum, D.S., "Site Building: Understanding Directory Services," *Computer Shopper,* January 1999.

Linthicum, D.S., "Intershop 3 Merchant Edition," *PC Magazine,* January 5, 1999.

Linthicum, D.S., "AbleCommerce Developer 2.6," *PC Magazine,* January 5, 1999.

Linthicum, D.S., "Site Building," *Computer Shopper,* February 1999.

Linthicum, D.S., "Site Building," *Computer Shopper,* March 1999.

Linthicum, D.S., "Enterprise Application Integration from the Ground Up," *Software Development,* April 1, 1999.

Linthicum, D.S., "Site Building," *Computer Shopper,* April 1, 1999.

Linthicum, D.S., "Site Building: Getting Your Site Ready for the 5.0 Browers," *Computer Shopper,* May 1, 1999.

Linthicum, D.S., "Mastering Message Brokers," *Software Development,* June 1, 1999.

Linthicum, D.S., "Site Building: Getting Yourself and Your Site Ready for P3P," *Computer Shopper,* June 1, 1999.

Linthicum, D.S., "Integrating with PeopleSoft," *EAI Journal,* July/August 1999, Vol. 1, No. 2, p. 22.

Linthicum, D.S., "Site Building," *Computer Shopper,* July 1, 1999.

Linthicum, D.S., "Tag Your Site for High Visibility," *Computer Shopper,* August 1, 1999.

Mann, John, "Workflow and Enterprise Application Integration," Messageq. com.

Mercator White Paper. January 2001. "Supply Chain Visibility." www.mercator. com.

Object Management Group, *The Common Object Request Broker: Architecture and Specification,* OMG Document Number 91.12.1, Revision 1.1, 1992.

Object Management Group, *CORBA Services: Common Object Services Specification,* OMG Document Number 95-3-31, 1995.

Orfali, R., and D. Harkey, *Client/Server Programming with OS/2 Extended Edition,* New York: Van Nostrand Reinhold, 1991.

Orfali, R., D. Harkey, J. Edwards, *Essential Client/Server Survival Guide,* New York: Van Nostrand Reinhold. 1994.

Partridge, Chris, "The Role of Ontology in Semantic Integration." 2002.

Quine, W.V., "On What is There." In "Review of Metaphysics," Vol. II, No. 5. 1948. Reprinted in *From a Logical Point of View* (1961).

Renaud, P. E., *Introduction to Client/Server Systems,* New York: John Wiley & Sons. 1993.

Rumbaugh, J., M. Blaha, W. Premerlant, F. Eddy, W., Larensen, *Object-Oriented Modeling and Design,* Upper Saddle River, N.J.: Prentice-Hall. 1991.

Salemi, J., *PC Magazine Guide to Client/Server Databases*, Emeryville, Calif.: Ziff-Davis Press, 1993.

Shlaer, S., and S.J. Mellor, *Object-Oriented Systems Analysis—Modeling the World in Data*, Upper Saddle River, N.J.: Prentice-Hall, 1988.

Smith, J.D., *Reusability & Software Construction: C and C++*, New York: John Wiley & Sons, Inc. 1990.

Smith, P., *Client/Server Computing*, Carmel, Ind.: Sams Publishing (A Division of Prentice-Hall Computer Publishing). 1992.

Tannenbaum, A.S., *Distributed Operating Systems*, Englewood Cliffs, N.J.: Prentice-Hall. 1995.

UCCnet. *Technical Users Guide*, http://knowledgebase.uccnet.org.

W3C XSLT Specification, www.w3c.org.

Web Ontology Language (OWL) Guide Version 1.0, www.w3c.org.

Web Services Security (WS-Security) Specification, http://www-106.ibm.com/developerworks/webservices/library/ws-secure/

Webster's New World *Dictionary, Dictionary of Computer Terms*, Upper Saddle River, N.J.: Prentice-Hall. 1988.

Weerawarana, Sanjiva, *Understanding BPEL4WS, Part 1*. August 2002.

Wirfs-Brock, R., B. Wilkerson, L. Wiener, *Designing Object-Oriented Software*, Upper Saddle River, N.J.: Prentice-Hall. 1990.

www.ebXML.org.

www.hipaa.org

XML Key Management Specification (XKMS), March 2001.

Index

Note: Tables and figures are indicated by *italicized* page locators.